LEADERSHIP EDUCATION I:
Citizenship, Character, and Air Force Tradition

D1319362

Published for the

Air Force Junior Reserve Officer Training Corps

Maxwell Air Force Base, Alabama 36112-6106

V-7101T

Mc Graw Hill **Custom Publishing**

Boston   Burr Ridge, IL   Dubuque, IA   Madison, WI   New York   San Francisco   St. Louis
Bangkok   Bogotá   Caracas   Lisbon   London   Madrid
Mexico City   Milan   New Delhi   Seoul   Singapore   Sydney   Taipei   Toronto

LEADERSHIP EDUCATION I
Citizenship, Character & Air Force Tradition

Government content extracted from the following sources:

Leadership Education I: Introduction to Air Force Junior Reserve Officer Training Corps (AFROTC) by Naomi L. Mitchell. Published in 1998 by the Air Force Junior ROTC, Maxwell AFB AL.

Etiquette content contained in this Air Force book is the property of the U.S. government, courtesy of the U.S. Army Cadet Command, Fort Monroe VA. and can also be found in *Army JROTC Leadership Education and Training (Let 1)* written by Carol Carter, Joyce Bishop, Sarah Lyman Karvits, B. E. Pruitt, Kathy Teer Crumpler, Deborah Prothrow-Stith. Published by Pearson Custom Publishing © 2005.

Copyright © 2005 by The McGraw-Hill Companies, Inc. for content repurposed from the following sources:

Teen Health: Course Three by Mary Bronson Merki, Michael J. Cleary, and Betty M. Hubbard. Copyright © 2003 by Glencoe/McGraw-Hill, a division of The McGraw-Hill Companies, Inc. *Civics Today: Citizenship, Economics, & You* by Richard C. Remy, John J. Patrick, David S. Saffell, and Gary E. Clayton. Copyright © 2003 by The McGraw-Hill Companies, Inc.

Glencoe Health, Ninth Edition by Mary Bronson Merki and Don Merki with contributing authors Michael J. Cleary and Kathleen Middleton. Copyright © 2004 by Glencoe/McGraw-Hill, a division of The McGraw-Hill Companies, Inc.

United States Government: Democracy in Action, Teacher Wraparound Edition by Richard C. Remy and Congressional Quarterly. Copyright © 2003 by The McGraw-Hill Companies, Inc.

4 5 6 7 8 9 0 QPD QPD 0 9 8 7 6

ISBN 0-07-353256-8
Part of Set ISBN 0-07-320152-9

Project Manager: Paula Kefover
McGraw-Hill Editor: Judith A. Wetherington
Department of the Air Force Editors: Roger D. Ledbetter and Linda F. Sackie
Developmental Editing: ToucanEd, Inc.
Production Editor: Carrie Braun
Photography: Jack Opatrany Photo Art Studio, Houston, TX & JK Photography, York, SC
Cover Design: Fairfax Hutter
Book Design: Karen Fleckenstein, Fleck's Communications, Inc., Peosta, IA
Printer/Binder: Quebecor World

UNIT **1** Heritage, Organization, and Tradition   1

Table of Contents

UNIT 2 Individual Self-Control   71

UNIT 3 Wellness and Fitness 145

Chapter 4   Physical Activity and Fitness 183

UNIT 4 Citizenship in the United States 255

→ Preface

Leadership Education I: Citizenship, Character, and Air Force Tradition introduces cadets to the Air Force Junior Reserve Officer Training Corps (AFJROTC) program. It provides information about military traditions, citizenship, the U.S. government, wellness, health, fitness, and how to exercise self-control.

Unit 1 begins with the history, organization, mission, goals, and objectives of AFJROTC. Next follows the military uniform and appearance standards, including the history of the uniform and grooming standards for male and female cadets. The remainder of Unit 1 includes customs and courtesies for AFJROTC; information about attitude, discipline, and respect; and ethics, which is important for leadership and decision-making. You will learn about saluting properly, recognizing rank, and using military titles. Discipline (including drill) and respect are vital parts of the Air Force and AFJROTC.

Unit 2 covers your personal behavior and responsibility. It begins with common courtesies and etiquette in formal and informal situations. Next is a lesson on stress management, including the causes of stress, its emotional and physical effects, and positive ways to manage stress. In the lesson on behaving positively, you will learn about making decisions, setting goals, methods of communicating effectively, and using refusal skills. Unit 2 also includes a lesson on mental and emotional health care. It covers expressing your emotions, common mental disorders, warning signs of clinical depression, and where to get help. Because statistics show that more than 5,000 young people reportedly kill themselves each year, there is information about suicide and its prevention. Unit 2 ends with information about avoiding and preventing violence.

Unit 3 provides information about physical fitness and the benefits of making safe, drug-free decisions. You will learn about health care methods in the United States, the basics of good nutrition, and how to use first aid techniques. Next you will study physical activity for health and fitness and the different types of exercise you can choose. You will also learn about appropriate weight standards and body image issues and get some weight management tips. Making safe, drug-free decisions is part of good health and responsible behavior, so Unit 3 includes information about medicine and drug abuse and misuse, as well as tobacco and alcohol.

Unit 4 provides an in-depth study of citizenship in the United States and introduces you to the different forms of government throughout the world. It includes lessons on the American flag and other important symbols, civics, the U.S. Constitution, the Bill of Rights, the U.S. national government, and comparing systems of government. There are proper ways to handle and display the American flag, which you need to know as cadets. The use of the Star Spangled Banner and Pledge of Allegiance honors the American flag and its heritage. The functions of our democratic government, what it means to be a good citizen, and how people become citizens are important for everyone to know. The Constitution protects our rights and freedom as American citizens and the Bill of Rights—the first 10 amendments to the U.S. Constitution—guarantees certain basic rights to all Americans. All U.S. citizens need to learn about our government, and learning about other governments will help you understand why there can be disagreements among nations.

This book has been prepared especially for cadets—to increase your knowledge and success as American citizens and members of the Air Force JROTC.

➤ Acknowledgments

The subject matter in *Leadership Education I: Citizenship, Character, and Air Force Tradition* was based on suggestions received from Air Force Junior Reserve Officer Training Corps (AFJROTC) instructors from around the world. The Air Force Officer and Accession Training Schools (AFOATS) Curriculum Section (CR) team involved in this production effort was under the direction of Dr. Charles Nath, III, Director of the Curriculum Division, at Maxwell Air Force Base, Alabama. His deputy, Lieutenant Colonel Charles Capps, and the Chief of Junior ROTC Curriculum, Lieutenant Colonel John Kiecana, completed a superb leadership team, resulting in an outstanding product for the AFJROTC program. Special thanks go to the CR team's primary editors, Roger Ledbetter and Linda Sackie. Their persistent efforts to produce the best academic materials possible for our over 800 AFJROTC units is commendable.

AFOATS/CR would like to express its gratitude to the McGraw-Hill Education team for all its hard work in publishing this outstanding new book for AFJROTC. That team consisted of subcontractors at Toucan Ed, Kathleen Middleton, Netha Thacker, Janet Ring, Pamela King, Brett Carey, Karen Fleckenstein of Fleck's Communications, Inc., and numerous McGraw-Hill personnel including Paula Kefover, Judith Wetherington, Carrie Braun and Fairfax Hutter.

AFOATS/CR also wishes to thank Donna Rice and Constance Yelverton of the U.S. Army Cadet Command at Fort Monroe, VA, for granting approval to use some of the material from their Army Junior ROTC book in ours. We also want to thank the following AFJROTC units for their support in allowing McGraw-Hill Education photographers to take photos of their facilities, cadets, staff, and activities for publication in this text: TX-781, Oliver Wendell Holmes High School, San Antonio, TX; SC-932, James F. Byrnes High School, Duncan, SC; SC-041, Gaffney High School, Gaffney, SC; and SC-061, Northwestern High School, Rock Hill, SC. These units' participation allowed us to make this new text more appealing to our high school audience, who are clearly some of the finest young people on Earth.

UNIT
1

Heritage, Organization, and Tradition

Unit Chapter

Chapter 1   Introduction to Air Force Junior Reserve Officer Training Corps

In Your Home and Community

Goal Setting

In the Air Force, thousands of people combine their efforts to carry out a large security mission. Your Air Force Junior ROTC unit also has a mission. How does your unit give back to your community? Look at your unit's history and activities. List at least three ways that you can contribute to your community through your participation in Air Force Junior ROTC.

Introduction to Air Force Junior ROTC

✓

Chapter Outline

- **Lesson 1**   **Organization of the AFJROTC**

- **Lesson 2**   **The Military Uniform and Appearance Standards**

- **Lesson 3**   **Customs and Courtesies for Air Force Junior ROTC**

- **Lesson 4**   **Attitude, Discipline, and Respect**

- **Lesson 5**   **Ethics**

Quick Write

What do you know about Air Force Junior ROTC (AFJROTC)? Write two or three sentences about why you chose to take AFJROTC classes.

Organization of the AFJROTC

LEARN ABOUT...

- the purpose of Air Force Junior ROTC.
- the mission of Air Force Junior ROTC.
- the objectives of the Junior ROTC program.
- the line of responsibility and authority in AFJROTC.
- job descriptions and organizational charts.
- selection of commanders and staff positions.

History

As a cadet in the Air Force Junior Reserve Officer Training Corps (ROTC), you are part of a time-honored and distinguished tradition of preparing young people to be the leaders of tomorrow through a blend of education and military training. The first purely technical and military school in the United States for training students in citizen soldiery was founded almost 200 years ago in Norwich, Vermont. In September 1820, the American Literary, Scientific and Military Academy was founded by Army Captain Alden Partridge. Today this institution is known as Norwich University. Captain Partridge firmly believed that a citizenry educated in the art of war would serve the nation well. The school became known for its excellent academic program embedded in a tough, disciplined military environment.

Another Army officer, Lieutenant Edgar R. Steevers, was the first to organize Junior ROTC programs in 1911. Lieutenant Steevers, who also believed that the teaching of military training could help create better citizens, merged traditional education with military training in a public high school in the city of Cheyenne, Wyoming. He wanted to teach young men the advantages of a strong body and a clean mind, the value of self-control and restraint, civic duties, and responsibilities.

The Army formally adopted Junior ROTC the same year that the National Defense Act of 1916 authorized a junior course for non-college military schools, high schools, and other non-preparatory schools. But it wasn't until 1964 that Junior ROTC made its way into all branches of the military. Public Law 88-647, also known as the Reserve Officer Training Corps Vitalization Act of 1964, directed the secretaries of each branch of the military to establish and maintain Junior ROTC units at public and private secondary schools.

Interested schools must apply and meet eligibility criteria established by each secretary. Schools must also agree to provide a three-year (or more) course of military instruction as outlined by the specific military branch. Another requirement is that an enrollment of at least 100 physically fit students or 10 percent of the study body, whichever is less, must be maintained in the Junior ROTC program. Students must be U.S. citizens and enrolled in the ninth grade or higher. School selection is also based on ensuring a fair and equitable distribution of Junior ROTC programs throughout the nation. The law offers incentives to participating schools to employ retired officers and noncommissioned officers (NCOs) as instructors. In addition, the law authorizes each military branch to provide equipment, uniforms, and a portion of the instructors' pay. In 1973, Public Law 93-165 allowed females to be counted toward enrollment in Junior ROTC units.

VOCABULARY
- group
- squadron
- flight
- Senior Aerospace Science Instructor (SASI)

Air Force Junior Reserve Officer Training Corps (AFJROTC)

With a modest beginning of 20 units in 1966, Air Force Junior ROTC has grown to over 740 units operating throughout the world in 2005, with more than 104,000 cadets enrolled. This growth is projected to continue, increasing the number of Air Force JROTC units to more than 900 by 2006. In the beginning, only young men were allowed as cadets. However, that changed in 1972 when 2,170 young women were admitted, making up nine percent of the corps. Since then the number of young women in AFJROTC has increased to more than 45,300—more than 43 percent of the cadet corps.

The purpose of Air Force Junior ROTC is simple: to help make high school students better citizens, while acquainting them with the Air Force and the field of aerospace science. Its formal mission, goals, and objectives are as follows:

Mission. The mission of AFJROTC is to build better citizens for America.

Goals. "[The] purpose of Junior Reserve Officers' Training Corps [is] to instill in students in United States secondary educational institutions the value of citizenship, service to the United States, personal responsibility, and a sense of accomplishment." (10 USC Section 2031)

Objectives. The objectives of AFJROTC are to educate and train high school cadets in citizenship; promote community service; instill responsibility, character, and self-discipline; and provide instruction in the fundamentals of air and space science.

Cadet Activities

During one's years as a cadet, aerospace science courses will be studied, such as Frontiers of Aviation History, The Science of Flight, The Exploration of Space, Policy and Organization, Survival, and Geography. You will also learn about military traditions and flag etiquette and receive instruction in basic military drill. In addition, you will immerse yourself in topics such as personal behavior, personal responsibility, citizenship, wellness, effective communication skills, individual and group behavior, and management theories. And you will do more than study. Air Force Junior ROTC cadets have opportunities to attend dances and military balls; to engage in fund-raising events; and to participate in athletics, color guards, and drill teams. As you continue in the program, it will become more meaningful and evident that the overall goal of Air Force Junior ROTC is to help develop future leaders for, and better citizens of, our great country.

Chain of Command and Organization

Whenever two or more people combine their efforts to do a job, an organization exists. In the Air Force, thousands of people combine their efforts to carry out a large national security mission. This huge organization is able to do its job because it has been specifically organized for that purpose. A line of responsibility and authority extends from top to bottom, and relationships between and within sections are spelled out.

Every Air Force Junior ROTC unit is organized in a specific way, with the main jobs of the organization normally displayed on a chart. Job descriptions exist for every separate duty in the unit. These charts and job descriptions provide a quick, detailed view of the operation of any section and show how a unit carries out its assignments. The Air Force Junior ROTC models its organizational charts and job descriptions on those found in the U.S. Air Force. Typical Air Force Junior ROTC organization charts and job descriptions are shown in Tables 1–1 through 1–5.

When organizing any operation, it is necessary to do three things:
1. Identify skills needed.
2. Set up a working structure.
3. Assign available resources within the structure to carry out the mission successfully.

Organization of the Cadet Corps

Cadet corps units are organized into the following structures:
- **wings** (two or more groups)
- **groups** (*two or more squadrons*)
- **squadrons** (*two or more flights*)
- **flights** (*two or more elements*)
- **elements** (three or more cadets, including the element leader)

A wing has a corps size of 251 cadets and above. Groups have a corps size of 250 cadets or less. The Air Force Junior ROTC organizational chart, Table 1–1, shows a typical cadet wing's structure. The organization of a typical cadet group is seen in Table 1–2. The charts are based on a cadet corps at a school that has a fully established program.

The **Senior Aerospace Science Instructor (SASI)** is *responsible for the overall function and management of the Air Force Junior ROTC unit.* The SASI selects the cadet wing/group/squadron commander and various staff members. The cadets selected for staff positions help the cadet wing, group, or squadron commander run the

Organizational Charts

Table 1–1. Organizational Chart for a Typical Cadet Wing

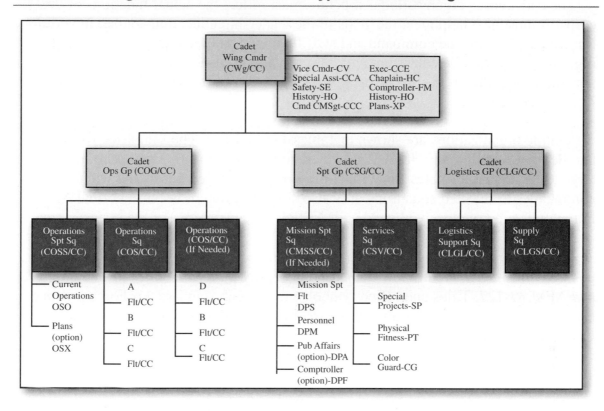

Table 1–2. AFJROTC Organizational Chart for a Typical Cadet Group

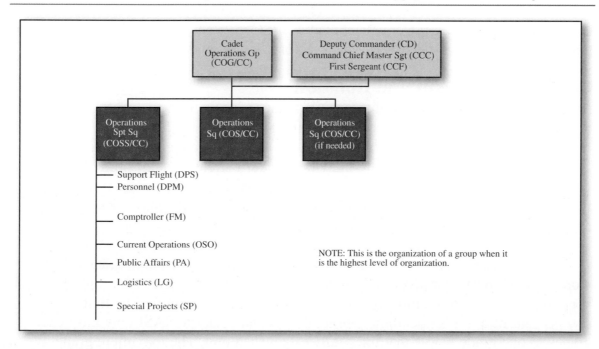

corps. The various staff positions closely mirror those found in Air Force staff structure.

The cadet corps organizational structure must reflect the actual functions of the corps. It must also help meet the goals of the leadership education course. In addition, it must clearly describe command and staff functions and recognize cadet rank. The organization should be consistent with military organizational principles. It should generally meet the provisions of Air Force Instruction (AFI) 38–101, entitled *Air Force Organization.*

Sample organizations are shown in Tables 1–1 and 1–2. The samples closely parallel that found in AFI 38-101. However, to keep wing staffs from becoming too large, this sample delegates some functions normally carried out by the wing commander to selected squadrons. It is also slightly different because normal Air Force units are not closely aligned with AFJROTC cadet wings in the services area.

The SASI may add positions to the organizational structure. However, those positions must have identifiable duties and generally meet guidelines in AFI 38-101 and AFM 37-127. Titles and office symbols must match standard Air Force practice. For example, CC is used for a wing or group Commander position, OG for the Operations Group, PA for Public Affairs, etc. The 3rd AFJROTC Cadet Wing commander, for example, would use the office symbol 3rd Cadet WG/CC, and the same unit's Logistics Group commander would use 3rd Cadet LG/CC.

Regardless of the size or structure of the corps, efficient organization is important to ensure effective leadership education. Units should maintain an organizational chart showing all designated cadet corps positions. This chart should be posted where cadets can see and become familiar with it. In addition, job descriptions should be written for each position shown on the organizational chart. Copies should be maintained in files that are accessible to cadets. See Table 1–3 for sample job descriptions.

Cadet Appointment and Rotation

Based on the requirements of the unit's organizational structure, the SASI selects the cadet corps commander, subordinate commanders, and staff members. The SASI is responsible for maintaining a written policy on an equitable appointment and rotation system. The SASI will consider an individual cadet's strengths and shortcomings when assigning positions. The intent is to ensure that cadets are assigned to positions where they will gain the greatest leadership benefits. The SASI may consider adopting a below-the-zone promotion system that parallels the Air Force system.

Cadet grades should not be confused with United States Air Force grades. The word "cadet" must be a part of any written reference to a specific cadet rank. In keeping with usual promotion systems, cadet rank is limited during the first and second year of a unit's operation. During the second year, the SASI may limit cadet grades to one grade below that for a fully established unit. The maximum grade authorizations are listed in Table 1–4 for a cadet wing and Table 1–5 for a cadet group.

Table 1–3   Sample Job Descriptions

Sample Job Descriptions

The cadet **wing commander (CWg/CC)** is responsible for:

- The appearance, discipline, efficiency, training, and conduct of the wing.
- Planning and coordinating all wing activities, facilities, and resources.
- Ensuring all members of the cadet corps have the opportunity to develop leadership commensurate with their individual abilities.
- Coordinating with the SASI.

The cadet **wing vice commander (CWg/CV)** is responsible for:

- Command of the wing during absence of the wing commander.
- Supervising the wing staff.
- Administration of wing headquarters.

The cadet **special assistant (CWg/CCA)** is responsible for all duties assigned by the SASI. Fill this position with a 3rd-year cadet in a 3-year program or fourth-year cadet in a 4-year program who has been rotated from the position of corps commander.

The **executive officer (CWg/CCE)** is responsible for:

- All tasks assigned by the cadet wing commander.
- Scheduling and coordinating activities of the cadet wing commander.

The cadet **command chief master sergeant (CWg/CCC)** is responsible for:

- Providing recommendations to the CWg/CC based on inputs from lower class cadets and acts as liaison between the corps and wing staff.
- Advising the CWg/CC on problems with the corps and suggesting possible solutions.
- Performing other duties as assigned by the CWg/CC.

The cadet **plans officer (CWg/XP)** is responsible for:

- Developing and posting contingency plans for all operations of the cadet wing.
- Performing other duties as assigned by the CWg/CC.
- Note: The SASI has the option to align this normal wing commander staff function under the COSS/CC. If this option is exercised, then the office symbol is COSS/OSX.

The cadet **safety officer (CWg/SE)** is responsible for:

- Conducting a weekly safety inspection of all cadet facilities.
- Reporting all safety violations or findings to the CWg/CC or the SASI and providing recommendations for correcting safety-related problems.

The cadet **historian (CWg/HO)** is responsible for:

- The recording and recovery of historical information and data pertaining to corps activities.
- The documentation of historical information and data pertaining to corps activities on electronic media.
- Performing other duties as assigned by the CWg/CC.

Table 1–3   Continued

The cadet **chaplain (CWg/HC)** is responsible for:

- The morale and welfare of members of the cadet corps and recommending solutions to problems concerning morale and welfare issues to the CWg/CC.
- Delivering inspirational services as required for Dining-ins or outs, and other corps activities.
- Performing other duties as assigned by the CWg/CC.

The cadet **comptroller (CWg/FM)** is responsible for:

- Ensuring adequate controls are established for proper accounting of all corps money.
- Controlling all cadet financial transactions.
- Maintaining accurate, descriptive, and up-to-date records of all financial transactions.
- Ensuring all checks are issued in accordance with policies established by the CWg/CC.
- Maintaining ledgers and account transactions in accordance with generally accepted accounting standards.
- Presenting a weekly audit report to the cadet staff + JROTC staff.
- Signing and initialing all checks payable from wing funds.
- Preparing budget projections for successive weeks and terms.
- Performing other duties as assigned by the CWg/CC.
- Note: The SASI has the option to align this normal wing commander staff function under the CMSS/CC. If this option is exercised, then the office symbol is CMSS/DPF.

The cadet **public affairs officer (CWg/PA)** is responsible:

- For establishing an active public affairs program.
- For preparing, publishing, and distributing a wing yearbook.
- For submitting news articles to school and local newspapers concerning cadet activities.
- For providing all wing photographic service.
- Assisting briefers in graphic support.
- Performing other duties as assigned by the CWg/CC.
- Cadet public affairs officer continued:
- Note: The SASI has the option to align this normal wing commander staff function under the CMSS/CC. If this option is exercised, then the office symbol is CMSS/DPA.

The cadet **operations group commander (COG/CC)** is responsible for:

- The appearance, discipline, effectiveness, training, and conduct of the cadet operations group.
- Attending Wing staff meetings.
- Performing other duties as assigned by the CWg/CC.

The cadet **operations group deputy commander (COG/CD)** is responsible for:

- Standardization evaluation (StanEval) for the cadet operations group.
- Ensuring all cadet operations group activities are conducted in accordance with current Air Force AETC, AFROTC, and corps instructions, directive policies, and procedures.
- Performing other duties as assigned by the COG/CC.

The cadet **operations support squadron commander (COSS/CC)** is responsible for:

- Overseeing training, standardization, and drill and ceremonies are conducted properly.
- Preparing the cadet wing master operations plan.
- Preparing weekly operations orders.
- Ensuring training goals are met by each cadet.
- Performing other duties as assigned by the COG/CC.

Table 1-3   Continued

The cadet **current operations officer (COSS/OSO)** is responsible for:

- Planning and coordinating extracurricular and cocurricular activities with other school organizations.
- Assisting the SASI in scheduling cadets for base visits and similar activities.

The cadet **operations squadron commander (COS/CC)** is responsible for:

- Overseeing the flight commanders.
- Relaying information from the cadet operations group commander to the flight commanders.
- Acting as a liaison between flights and command staff.
- Performing other duties assigned by the COG/CC.

The cadet **flight commander (Flt/CC)** is responsible for:

- Maintaining the appearance, discipline, efficiency, training, and conduct of the flight.
- Planning and coordinating activities within the flight.
- Recommending the top cadets within the flight for awards and recognition to the COS/CC.
- Performiing other duties as assigned by the COS/CC.

The cadet **support group commander (CSG/CC)** is responsible for:

- The appearance, discipline, effectiveness, training, and conduct of the cadet support group.
- Attending wing staff meetings.
- Performing other duties as assigned by the CWg/CC.

The cadet **support group deputy commander (CSG/CD)** is responsible for:

- Standardization evaluation (StanEval) for the cadet mission support group.
- Ensuring all cadet mission support group activities are conducted in accordance with current regulations, directives, policies, and procedures.
- Performing other duties as assigned by the CSG/CC.

The cadet **mission support squadron commander (CMSS/CC)** is responsible for:

- Ensuring proper maintenance of administrative and personnel files.
- Learning the responsibilities and procedures of each functional area of mission support.
- Performing other duties as assigned by the CSG/CC.

The cadet **mission support flight officer (CMSS/DPS)** is responsible for:

- Writing and posting weekly staff meeting minutes.
- Maintaining the wing administrative files in accordance with policies and procedures established by the CMSS/CC.
- Maintaining the bulletin boards, and posting current and correct wing correspondence, leadership training, and special function notices.
- Maintaining the wing continuity files.
- Maintaining and updating all cadet regulations.
- Performing other duties as assigned by the CMSS/CC.

The cadet **personnel flight officer (CMSS/DPM)** is responsible for:

- Maintaining cadet personnel records following guidelines established by the CMSS/CC.
- Maintaining the wing organizational chart and unit manning document (UMD).
- Publishing a cadet directory.
- Filing all documentation in cadet records or other internal information media.
- Performing other duties as assigned by the CMSS/CC.

Table 1–3 Continued

The cadet **services squadron commander (CSV/CC)** is responsible for:

- Ensuring a high level of morale and esprit de corps is maintained within the wing.
- Promoting high levels of physical fitness within the wing.
- Learning the responsibilities and procedures of each functional area of the services squadron.
- Performing other duties as assigned by the CSG/CC.

The cadet **special projects officer (CSV/SP)** is responsible for:

- The planning, coordinating, and execution of all wing special activities.
- Submitting after-action reports on all special projects.
- Performing other duties as assigned by the CSV/CC.

The cadet **athletics officer (CSV/PT)** is responsible for:

- Operating a voluntary cadet physical fitness program, including supervising stretching exercises prior to any physical fitness activity.
- Posting current health awareness information on the athletic bulletin board.
- Performing other duties as assigned by the CSV/CC.

The cadet **color guard commander (drill team) (SV/CG)** is responsible for:

- Commanding the color guard and drill team.
- Assisting in the planning and coordination for all parades and ceremonies.
- Providing instruction and supervision for all retreat and flag-raising ceremonies.
- Performing other duties as assigned by the CSV/CC.

The cadet **logistics group commander (CLG/CC)** is responsible for:

- The appearance, discipline, effectiveness, training, and conduct of the cadet logistics group.
- Attending wing staff meetings.
- Performing other duties as assigned by the CWg/CC.

The cadet **logistics group deputy commander (CLG/CD)** is responsible for:

- Standardization evaluation (StanEval) for the cadet logistic group.
- Ensuring all cadet logistics group activities are conducted in accordance with current regulations, directives, policies, and procedures.
- Performing other duties as assigned by the CLG/CC.

The cadet **logistics support commander (CLGL/CC)** is responsible for:

- Coordinating logistical support.
- Performing other duties as assigned by the CLG/CC.

The cadet **supply squadron commander (CLGS/CC)** is responsible for:

- Maintaining an inventory of on-hand supplies for the wing.
- Coordinating, in writing, the requirements of the wing with the JROTC unit supply representative.
- Distributing supplies to functional areas in the wing.
- Performing other duties as assigned by the CLG/CC.

Table 1–4 Sample Unit Manning Document for a Cadet Wing

Function	Position Title	Maximum Grade	Authorized
Commander (CC)	Wing Commander	Cadet Col	1
	Vice Commander	Cadet Lt Col	1
	Command Chief Master Sgt	Cadet CMSgt	1
Operations Group	Operations Group Commander	Cadet Lt Col	1
	Drill Team Commander	Cadet Capt	1
	NCOIC	Cadet SMSgt	1
Support Group	Support Group Commander	Cadet Lt Col	1
	NCOIC	Cadet SMSgt	1
Logistics Group	Logistics Group Commander	Cadet Lt Col	1
	NCOIC	Cadet SMSgt	1
Squadron	Commander	Cadet Maj	1
	Superintendent	Cadet SMSgt	1
	First Sergeant	Cadet MSgt	1
	Guidon Bearer	Cadet TSgt	1
Flight	Commander	Cadet Capt	1
	Flight Sergeant	Cadet MSgt	1
	Guide	Cadet SSgt	1
Element	Element Leader	Cadet SSgt	1
	Assistant Element Leader	Cadet SrA	1

Table 1–5   Sample Unit Manning Document for a Cadet Group

Function	Position Title	Maximum Grade	Authorized
Commander (CC)	Operations Group Commander	Cadet Col	1
	Deputy Commander	Cadet Lt Col	1
	Command Chief Master Sgt	Cadet CMSgt	1
	First Sergeant	Cadet MSgt	1
Squadron	Commander	Cadet Lt Col	1
	Superintendent	Cadet SMSgt	1
	First Sergeant	Cadet MSgt	1
	Guidon Bearer	Cadet TSgt	1
Flight	Flight Commander	Cadet Maj	1
	Flight Sergeant	Cadet MSgt	1
	Flight Guide	Cadet SSgt	1
Element	Element Leader	Cadet SSgt	1
	Assistant Element Leader	Cadet SrA	1

Cadets receive permanent grades based on the number of years they have satisfactorily completed AFJROTC. Cadets receive this permanent grade the second semester of each year, providing they have made satisfactory progress that year. Satisfactory performance and behavior—as determined by the SASI—are the keys to retaining permanent grades in any cadet corps. Once a cadet holds the status of officer for two or more grading periods, he or she will remain an officer for the rest of the program. The SASI may make exceptions.

Sometimes cadets are assigned to a position with a higher grade. As a result, the cadet may receive a temporary grade. Once the cadet has completed the duties assigned to that position, the cadet's grade may revert to his or her permanent grade. However, if the cadet is a graduating senior or third-year cadet in a three-year program, the cadet may retain the higher grade. Temporary permanent grades are an administrative option to rotate responsibility and to avoid gross imbalances in grade structure.

The permanent grade for the first year of AFJROTC is cadet airman; for the second year, cadet airman first class; for the third year, cadet senior airman; and for the fourth year (if offered), cadet staff sergeant. At the SASI's discretion, graduating seniors may retain the highest rank they held, regardless of course level. Similarly, third-year cadets in three-year programs may also retain the highest rank they held during their final year.

The rank structure is kept low enough that there is room for later promotions. For example, when a cadet is initially assigned to a command or staff position, the cadet does not receive the highest rank possible within those positions. This allows the cadet to assume greater responsibility and grow within that position and to be promoted based on his or her actual performance.

FIGURE 1-1.
ASI providing direction to cadet after class.

The SASI may authorize top NCO positions to outstanding second-year cadets in three- to four-year programs. Upper class cadets in four-year programs normally outrank lower class cadets. With the exception of temporary grade assignments, cadets only hold a grade that corresponds to their current position.

The SASI may award flight commanders with one higher grade as a motivational device to promote highly qualified and deserving cadets. The highest authorized grade is cadet major.

A flight commander should never outrank a squadron commander (time-in-grade or promotion line numbers should be used as a management tool when equal grades are involved). Ordinarily, a cadet serving in a staff position will be a senior NCO or officer. Promotions from cadet second lieutenant to higher grades should recognize and reward ability and effort.

Lesson 1 Review

Using complete sentences, answer the following questions on a sheet of paper.

1. What does SASI stand for?
2. Who is responsible for the overall function and management of the Air Force Junior ROTC unit?
3. What is a flight?
4. What is a squadron?
5. What is a group?
6. Who was Lieutenant Edgar R. Steevers?
7. What did the National Defense Act of 1916 authorize?
8. What is Public Law 88-647?
9. What change did Public Law 93-165 formally bring to Junior ROTC?
10. What is the purpose of Air Force Junior ROTC?
11. What is the mission of Air Force Junior ROTC?
12. What are the objectives of the Junior ROTC program?

Applying Leadership Skills

13. Develop a poster that describes the purpose and mission of Air Force Junior ROTC. With your SASI's approval, post your poster in the classroom or elsewhere in the school to increase your fellow students' understanding of AFJROTC.

FIGURE 1–2.
A cadet being interviewed for award of Cadet of the Month.

The Military Uniform and Appearance Standards

Uniform Wear and History

What is the first image that flashes into your mind when you think of someone in the military? Like most people, you probably pictured a person in uniform. The military uniform is more than just clothes. It is the public symbol of the nation's defense forces. It represents a long and honorable tradition of devotion to duty in the service of one's country. Therefore, the uniform should be worn proudly and—equally important—it should be worn properly.

The manner in which you wear the uniform reflects upon the U.S. Air Force. Since you will often be in the public eye, you and your fellow cadets must maintain a high standard of dress and personal appearance while wearing the Air Force uniform. The key elements are neatness, cleanliness, safety, and military image.

History of the Uniform

The English word *uniform* comes from a combination of two Latin words, *unus* and *forma,* which means "one form." The word **uniform** means *a distinctive mode of dress.* In ancient times, the Roman togas provided a unique dress. The toga, a loose outer garment worn by citizens appearing in public, came in several styles. The *toga candida* was a white garment worn only by candidates for public office. The *toga palmata* was a fancy toga worn to ceremonial affairs. The *toga praetexta,* a white toga with a purple border, was worn only by emperors. The *toga sordida* was worn by the lower classes, mourners, and people accused of crimes.

Military dress in ancient times acquired a certain degree of sameness, but in a much different sense from modern military uniforms. The Athenian and Spartan soldiers dressed according to

Quick Write

List the first three things you think of when you see a person in uniform.

LEARN ABOUT...

- history of the military uniform.
- do's and don'ts for wearing the Air Force uniform.
- appearance and grooming standards.
- grade insignia for Air Force and AF Junior ROTC.

VOCABULARY

- uniform
- bulk
- insignia

their position in military formations during the Peloponnesian War in the fifth century B.C. The Greek heavy infantryman wore a helmet, breastplate, and armor covering his legs below the knee. He also carried a shield and sword. The light-foot soldier wore no armor and carried a lighter shield and a spear. These were military uniforms in the sense that all soldiers looked alike. To this extent, therefore, we assign the origin of the military uniform to an early date in Western civilization.

During the Great Rebellion (1642–1646) in England, the English Parliament decided to raise and support an army. Thus, national armies, with standardized uniforms, came into being. The English uniform was red, with different colored facings for different regiments. These regiments were named by their facing's colors: blue, red, orange, etc. The uniform styles were really just a version of civilian dress. The uniform had an ample coat, waistcoat, breeches, stockings, and shoes or, in the case of cavalry, boots.

During the late 1600s, the armies of serfs and freemen had no distinctive dress and no standardized weapons of warfare. Colors and standards were used to identify units. Wealthy leaders dressed the troops who served under them in distinctive and colorful uniforms.

From this start, the military uniform evolved. During this slow process, the uniform ranged from very ornamented to very drab. Some claim that the more colorful the uniform, the more uncomfortable the soldier. High, tight collars, tight breeches, and boots that restricted knee action looked fancy, but they weren't good in action.

Uniform Wear and Restrictions

Air Force Junior ROTC cadets generally wear the same uniform—the standard Air Force service uniform—as that worn by active duty personnel in the Air Force. Cadets are expected to honor the uniform—to wear it properly and with pride. The uniform is an important aspect of Air Force Junior ROTC. Whenever you wear the uniform—during indoor and outdoor training periods, at cadet social functions, and during base visits—you represent the corps. How you wear the uniform exposes you and the Air Force to praise or fault from fellow cadets, fellow students, and society at large.

Certain restrictions apply to wearing the military uniform. For example, cadets may not wear the uniform while hitchhiking, in student demonstrations, for crowd control, political events, or for any other inappropriate activity. (However, AFJROTC cadets may wear the uniform while acting as ushers, parking lot attendants, runners, etc., at the discretion of the Senior Aerospace Science Instructor [SASI].)

Parts of the Hatch Act bar military personnel from engaging in any form of public political activity—such as attending rallies and political speeches or passing out political flyers—while in uniform. In addition, military personnel are prohibited from publicly supporting a particular candidate, party, or political issue when it is clear to others that they are members of the U.S. military. The intent of the law is to avoid the perception that any military official supports one political cause, candidate, or party over another.

The role of the military requires absolute obedience to direction from elected civilian leaders, so public perception regarding the allegiance of military members is critical.

However, members of the military are actively encouraged to vote. They are also allowed to place political bumper stickers on their own vehicles and/or signs on their private property. They can participate in political events as long as they are not in uniform and do not identify themselves as military members. Since AFJROTC cadets wear a form of the U.S. Air Force uniform, they should also follow the Hatch Act terms while in uniform.

Air Force Instruction (AFI) 36-2903, *Dress and Personal Appearance of Air Force Personnel,* also forbids those in military uniform to participate in public speeches, rallies, interviews, picket lines, marches, or any other public demonstration where it might be implied that the Air Force supports a particular cause. Engaging in an activity that might imply Air Force endorsement of a commercial interest or engaging in private employment while in uniform is also banned.

FIGURE 1–3.
A male cadet in the standard service dress uniform.

In addition, no item of the U.S. Air Force uniform may be worn by members of groups that sponsor the AFJROTC. Cadet auxiliary societies, for example, may not create a special uniform that includes any item of the U.S. Air Force uniform. This includes school faculty and sponsors other than the SASI or the Aerospace Science Instructor (ASI).

AFJROTC Uniform Standards

Most Air Force Junior ROTC units have published information on the cadet uniform and how to wear it. They base these directives, handbooks, or regulations on AFI 36-2903, *Dress and Personal Appearance of Air Force Personnel;* Air Force Junior ROTC Instruction (AFJROTCI) 36-2001, *Air Force Junior ROTC Operations;* and the *AFJROTC Uniform and Awards Guide.* These three publications provide complete details on fitting standards and wearing instructions for the uniform and personal grooming requirements for AFJROTC cadets. The *AFJROTC Uniforms and Awards Guide* and AFJROTCI 36-2001 include diagrams of uniforms for both female and male cadets. You can find all three of these publications online at the AFJROTC Cyber-Campus Web site. You can download or copy them for unit use.

It is your responsibility to maintain all uniform items in a clean and orderly condition during the school year and when you turn your uniform in. Just as the person on active duty, you are also obligated to wear the uniform properly and proudly. In doing so, you uphold the dignity of the Air Force, your unit, your fellow cadets, and yourself.

With practice and attention to detail, all the dos and don'ts about the proper wear and care of the uniform and personal appearance will become almost automatic. You should be proud of the uniform and the way it looks. A smart appearance is important, not only in drill practice, but also in performing various other duties and attending military functions.

Standard Cadet Uniform

The male service dress uniform consists of the dark blue service coat and trousers, light blue long sleeve shirt, and dark blue tie. The female service dress uniform consists of the dark blue service coat with slacks or skirt, light blue blouse, and tie tab. In both cases, the coat will be form fitted, meaning that it must not be tight in the shoulders, chest, and underarms. The sleeve length should extend to one-quarter inch from the heel of the thumb when the arms are hanging naturally at the sides. The bottom of the coat should extend 3 to 3.5 inches below the top of the thigh.

The trousers for males must be trim-fitted with no bunching at the waist or bagging at the seat. Slacks for female cadets should fit naturally over the hips, with no bunching or bagging at the seat. The trousers or slacks should rest on the top of the shoe with a slight break in the crease. The backs of the trousers or slacks should be seven-eighths inch longer than the front. The proper length of the trousers or slacks can be determined while standing at attention.

Uniform Do's and Don'ts

Here are a few general do's and don'ts about wearing the AFJROTC uniform.

Do's

- Wear the standard Air Force service uniform, as prescribed in AFI 36-2903, properly and with pride.
- Wear the uniform on the day established by the SASI (usually at least one day each week).
- Wear the uniform at other times specified by the SASI.
- Wear the uniform when you fly on military aircraft.

FIGURE 1–4.

A female cadet in the standard service dress uniform.

- Wear the uniform when you participate in a color guard or on a drill team.
- Keep your shoes polished and shined, including the heels and edges of soles.
- Make sure your shoes are appropriate for the activity. For example, wear athletic shoes if you're playing sports or boots if walking through heavy foliage. Safety is the major concern.
- Ensure that badges, insignia, belt buckles, and other metallic devices are clean and free of scratches and corrosion.
- Keep ribbons clean and replace them when they become worn, frayed, or faded.
- If your unit is at a military high school, wear the distinctive uniform required by the institution for special occasions or ceremonies.

Don'ts

- Do not wear the Air Force commissioned officer sleeve braid or the officer silver thread on flight caps.
- Do not wear the uniform with other clothing.
- Do not lend your uniform to anyone who is not a member of the Air Force Junior ROTC program.
- Do not allow articles such as wallets, pencils, pens, watch chains, checkbooks, handkerchiefs, and combs to be visible. (You may allow parts of pens and pencils to be exposed when you carry them in the left shirt pocket of the battle dress uniform [BDU].)
- Do not wear earphones or headphones while in uniform, unless required for duty.
- Do not carry pagers or cell phones, unless required for duty. (When required for duty, they must be clipped to the waistband or purse or be carried in the left hand when not in use.)

Special Team Uniforms

With the approval of AFOATS/JROS, color guards, honor guards, sabre teams, and drill teams may wear additional uniform items or wear a distinctive, yet conservative, uniform of military style. Greater latitude will be permitted in the design of open competition drill team uniforms where the intent is to allow maximum flexibility and freedom of movement in executing complex drill routines. Units using this style of uniform would normally be expected to have their regulation uniform or a second, more conservative military style uniform for the inspection and regulation drill requirements found in most drill meets. Ascots are authorized for wear at the discretion of the SASI.

Except for shoulder cords, these items or uniforms are worn only when performing duty as a member of a specialized group. Only items listed in Allowance Standard 016, in accordance with AFOATSI 23-101, are provided by AFJROTC. This instruction is also posted on Cyber-Campus.

Note: If your uniform does not fit properly, see the SASI or Aerospace Science Instructor (ASI). Do not wait until someone else calls attention to it. Check appearance in a mirror. Remember that how you look influences others.

Cadet Appearance and Grooming Guidelines

When you wear the uniform, you are responsible for presenting a neat, clean, and professional military image. Appearance and grooming standards help cadets present the image of disciplined cadets who can be relied upon to do the job they are called on to do. A professional military image has no room for the extreme, the unusual, or the faddish. The standards for wearing the uniform consist of four elements: neatness, cleanliness, safety, and military image. The first three are absolute, objective criteria for the efficiency, health, and well-being of the force. The fourth standard, military image, is also a very important aspect of military appearance. People, both military and civilian, draw conclusions as to the military effectiveness of the Air Force by how they perceive those in uniform.

The uniform standards in AFI 36-2903 are influenced to some extent by military tradition, and they reflect the image the Air Force desires to project to the civilian community. The basic concept of the Air Force uniform is that it is plain but distinctive dress, with an absolute minimum number of badges, insignia, and devices authorized for wear on it.

Special Uniform and Appearance Rules

Here are some additional guidelines about uniform and appearance. Complete details on uniform and personal grooming requirements for AFJROTC cadets can be found in the AFJROTC *Uniform and Awards Guide,* in AFJROTCI 36-2001, and in AFI 36-2903.

Jewelry

While in uniform, you may wear a wristwatch and rings, but no more than three rings at any one time. You may wear one bracelet if it is neat and conservative. However, the bracelet must not detract from military image, must not be wider than one inch, and must not subject anyone to potential injury. You may not wear ornaments on your head or around your neck.

Female cadets in uniform may wear earrings if the earrings are conservative and kept within sensible limits. For example, you may wear one small spherical (diamond, gold, white pearl, or silver) pierced or clip earring on each earlobe. The earring worn in each earlobe must match. Earrings should fit tightly without extending below the earlobes, unless they are clip earrings.

Male cadets in uniform may not wear earrings.

Eyeglasses or Sunglasses

If you wear glasses, they must not have any ornaments on the frames or lenses. Eyeglass lenses that are conservative, clear, slightly tinted, or have photosensitive lenses may be worn in uniform while indoors or while in military formation. When outdoors and in uniform, sunglasses and eyeglasses must have lenses and frames that are conservative; faddish or mirrored lenses are prohibited. Sunglasses are not allowed while in a military formation. Neither eyeglasses nor sunglasses can be worn around the neck while in uniform.

Tattoos or Brands

Whether you are in or out of uniform, tattoos or brands anywhere on the body are not allowed if they are obscene or if they advocate sexual, racial, ethnic, or religious discrimination. Tattoos or brands that might harm good order and discipline or bring discredit upon the Air Force are also barred, whether you are in or out of uniform.

Excessive tattoos or brands, even though they do not violate the prohibitions in the above paragraph, will not be exposed or visible (including visible through the uniform) while in uniform. Excessive is defined as any tattoo or brands that exceed one-quarter of the exposed body part, and those above the collarbone and readily visible when wearing an open collar uniform.

Body Piercing and Other Attachments to Body Parts

Cadets in uniform are not allowed to attach or display objects, articles, jewelry, or ornamentation to or through the ear, nose, tongue, or any exposed body part (including anything that might be visible through the uniform). Female cadets in uniform, however, are allowed to wear conservative earrings, pierced or clip style, in their earlobes.

Specific Female Cadet Guidelines

Here are some specific guidelines for female cadets.

Hair

Your hair should be no longer than the bottom of the collar edge at the back of the neck. Your hairstyle must be conservative—no extreme or faddish styles are allowed. It should also look professional and allow you to wear uniform headgear in the proper manner, so your hair must not be too full or too high on the head. In addition, your hairstyle shouldn't need many grooming aids. If you use pins, combs, barrettes, or similar items, they must be plain, similar in color to your hair, and modest in size. Wigs or hairpieces must also conform to these guidelines.

Skirts

The length of your skirt may not vary beyond the top and bottom of the kneecap. Your skirt should fit smoothly, should hang naturally, and must not be excessively tight. You must wear hosiery with the skirt. Choose a sheer nylon in a neutral dark brown, black, off-black, or dark blue shade that complements the uniform and your skin tone.

FIGURE 1–5.
An example of a proper hair style for a female cadet in uniform.

Specific Male Cadet Guidelines

Here are some specific guidelines for male cadets.

Hair

Keep your hair clean, neat, and trimmed. It must not contain large amounts of grooming aids such as greasy creams, oils, and sprays that remain visible in the hair. When your hair is groomed, it should not touch your ears or eyebrows, and only the closely cut or shaved hair on the back of your neck should touch the collar.

Your hair should not exceed 1¼ inch in bulk regardless of the length. **Bulk** is *the distance that the hair projects from the scalp when groomed* (as opposed to length of the hair). The bulk and length of your hair must not interfere with wearing any Air Force headgear properly, and it must not protrude below the front band of the headgear. Your hair must have a tapered appearance on both sides and back, both with and without headgear. A tapered appearance means that, when viewed from any angle, the outline of the hair on the side and back will generally match the shape of the skull, curving inward to the end point.

Your hair may not contain or have attached to it any visible foreign items. If you dye your hair, it should look natural. You may not dye your hair an unusual color or one that contrasts with your natural coloring. You may have sideburns if they are neatly trimmed and tapered in the same manner as your haircut. Sideburns must be straight and of even width (not flared) and end in a clean-shaven horizontal line. They may not extend below the lowest part of the outer ear opening. No extreme or faddish hair styles are allowed.

FIGURE 1–6.
A close-up of accoutrements placed on a male cadet uniform.

Insignia of Grade

Members of the Air Force perform duties that reflect their skill and grade. This also applies to Air Force Junior ROTC. The higher the rank or grade, the more responsibility cadets are given. In turn, cadets are expected to perform their duties in accordance with this increased responsibility.

Active Duty Insignia of Grade

An **insignia** is *a badge or mark of office or honor.* Grade insignia identify the rank of each member of the Armed Forces. The Air Force grade insignia system is broken down into two categories: officer grades and enlisted grades. First we will review active duty grade insignia and follow with the Air Force JROTC grade insignia. (See Figure 1–7 for active duty officer and enlisted grade insignia.)

Officers

Table 1–6 describes the grade insignia and provides the abbreviation and pay grade for each commissioned officer title. The "O" in the table indicates officer status. The subdued insignia worn on the BDU is made of cloth. Gold appears as brown and silver appears as dark blue.

Proper methods of address when speaking to officers are

- "Lieutenant" for a Second Lieutenant and a First Lieutenant.
- "Colonel" for either a Lieutenant Colonel or a Colonel.
- "General" for all generals.

Use full titles for official correspondence.

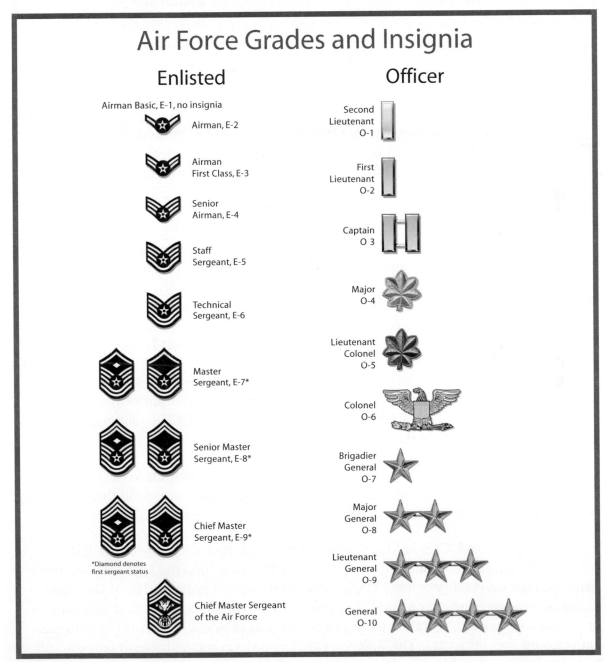

FIGURE 1–7.

Active Duty Grades and Insignia.

Table 1–6   Officer Grade Insignia

Title	Pay Grade	Grade Insignia
Second Lieutenant (2d Lt)	0–1	a gold bar
First Lieutenant (1st Lt)	0–2	a silver bar
Captain (Capt)	0–3	two connected silver bars
Major (Maj)	0–4	a gold leaf
Lieutenant Colonel (Lt Col)	0–5	a silver leaf
Colonel (Col)	0–6	a silver eagle
Brigadier General (Brig Gen)	0–7	a silver star
Major General (Maj Gen)	0–8	two silver stars in a line
Lieutenant General (Lt Gen)	0–9	three silver stars in a line
General (Gen)	0–10	four silver stars in a line

Noncommissioned Officers

Enlisted grades are subdivided into two categories: Noncommissioned Officer (NCO) and airman grades. NCOs are airmen serving in the grades of staff sergeant through chief master sergeant. NCOs play such an important role in troop leadership that there are five distinct grade insignia to identify them. The "E" in the table indicates enlisted status. (See Table 1–7.)

The NCO chevron has changed a great deal since the Continental Army, when a brightly colored ribbon tied around the arm identified NCOs. Through the years, the American NCO's chevron has varied in design and has been worn in different locations. It has been worn not only above the elbow, as it is today, but also below the elbow. The inverted and curved chevron of today's Air Force is distinct from that of the NCOs and petty officers of other branches of the U.S. Armed Forces.

The background of the chevrons for NCOs is blue, and the stripes are silver with a silver star in the center. The subdued insignia worn on the BDU uniform consists of dark blue stripes on a green background with a dark blue star. (The pay grade is always one number higher than the number of stripes worn.)

First sergeants wear a diamond device above the star on their chevrons. The diamond device stands for a job position only. First sergeants may hold the rank of Master Sergeant, Senior Master Sergeant, or Chief Master Sergeant.

These top senior NCOs hold a position of trust and responsibility as the link between the commander and unit personnel. As this vital link, the first sergeant must make sure all enlisted personnel know their commander's policies. He or she also represents the interests of enlisted personnel to the commander. The first sergeant promotes the welfare, morale, and health of enlisted personnel by working with base agencies on special issues. The first sergeant helps the commander maintain discipline and standards of conduct. He or she also provides professional guidance on matters of leadership, military justice, and customs and courtesies.

Table 1–7   Noncommissioned Officer Grade Insignia

Title	Pay Grade	Grade Insignia
Staff Sergeant (SSgt)	E-5	Chevron of 4 stripes
Technical Sergeant (TSgt)	E-6	Chevron of 5 stripes
Master Sergeant (MSgt)	E-7	Chevron of 6 stripes with one stripe in inverted position above the star
Senior Master Sergeant (SMSgt)	E-8	Chevron of 7 stripes with two stripes in inverted position above the star
Chief Master Sergeant (CMSgt)	E-9	Chevron of 8 stripes with three stripes in inverted position above the star

A Chief Master Sergeant is addressed as "Chief." All other sergeants are addressed as "Sergeant." Full titles are used in official correspondence.

The highest position held by any enlisted personnel is Chief Master Sergeant of the Air Force (CMSAF). The CMSAF acts as personal advisor to the Air Force Chief of Staff and Secretary of the Air Force, providing information about the welfare, effective use, and progress of the enlisted force. The grade insignia is a chevron of eight stripes with a wreath around the bottom and sides of the star and the Great Seal of the United States of America with two stars in the upper blue field (see Figure 1–7).

The CMSAF position was created to add prestige to the NCO Corps. Air Force Chief of Staff General John P. McConnell announced the creation of this position on October 24, 1966. The first CMSAF was Chief Paul W. Airey. He was awarded the unique insignia with the wreath around the star in April 1967. Over the next decade, support for the office grew among both the senior Air Force leadership and the enlisted force. The creation of this office, as well as the appointment of command chief master sergeants and the granting of more responsibility to all senior NCOs, represented the Air Force's concrete recognition of the professionalism of its enlisted force, especially its NCOs.

Airmen

There are four airman grades:

1. Airman Basic (AB)
2. Airman (Amn)
3. Airman First Class (A1C)
4. Senior Airman (SrA)

FIGURE 1–8.
Chief Master Sergeant in standard blue uniform.

An Airman Basic (AB) doesn't wear any grade insignia (see Figure 1–7). An Airman's grade insignia is a chevron of one silver stripe with a silver star in the middle. An AIC insignia is a chevron of two silver stripes with a silver star in the middle. The Senior Airman grade insignia is a chevron of three silver stripes with a silver star in the middle. Pay grades for airmen are: AB (E-1), Amn (E-2), AIC (E-3), and SrA (E-4). (See Table 1–8 for Airmen Grade Insignia.)

Air Force Junior ROTC Insignia of Grade

Figure 1-9 shows Air Force Junior ROTC cadet grade insignia.

Officers

Table 1–9 describes the grade insignia for each cadet officer title. Grade insignia for active duty officers are very different from grade insignia for cadet officers.

Enlisted

A comparison of active duty insignia (Figure 1–7) and Junior ROTC cadet grade insignia (Figure 1–9) shows only slight differences between enlisted grades. The star inside the chevron for active duty personnel is replaced with a torch for cadets, and

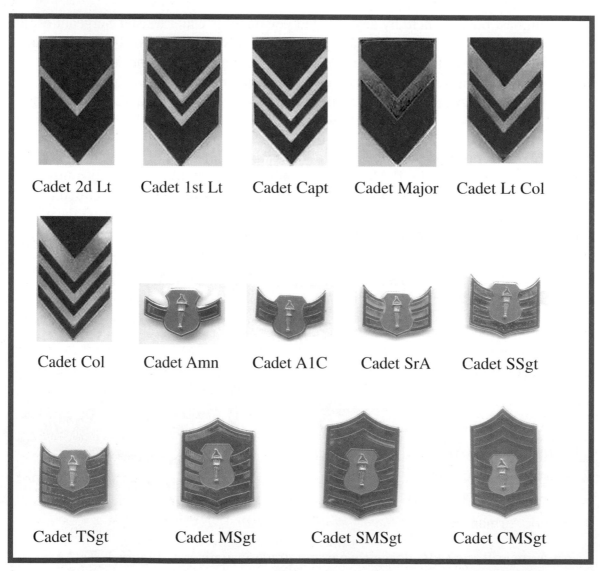

| Cadet 2d Lt | Cadet 1st Lt | Cadet Capt | Cadet Major | Cadet Lt Col |

| Cadet Col | Cadet Amn | Cadet A1C | Cadet SrA | Cadet SSgt |

| Cadet TSgt | Cadet MSgt | Cadet SMSgt | Cadet CMSgt |

FIGURE 1–9.

AFJROTC Cadet Grade Insignia

the chevron is pointed at the bottom. Cadets, like active duty personnel, may wear other insignia. Figure 1–10 shows other insignia (badges) for Air Force Junior ROTC cadets and Figure 1–12 shows other insignia (badges) for active duty personnel, and Figure 1–13 displays the ribbons authorized for wear on the Air Force Junior ROTC uniform, as ribbons are awarded.

Figure 1–13 shows the Air Force Junior ROTC ribbons.

Table 1–8 Airmen Grade Insignia

Title	Pay Grade	Grade Insignia
Airman Basic (AB)	E-1	none
Airman (Amn)	E-2	Chevron of 1 stripe
Airman First Class (A1C)	E-3	Chevron of 2 stripes
Senior Airman (SrA)	E-4	Chevron of 3 stripes

Table 1–9 Cadet Officer Grade Insignia

Title	Grade Insignia
Cadet Second Lieutenant (2d Lt)	Chevron of 1 inverted stripe
Cadet First Lieutenant (1st Lt)	Chevron of 2 inverted stripes
Cadet Captain (Capt)	Chevron of 3 inverted stripes
Cadet Major (Maj)	Chevron of 1 double-wide inverted stripe
Cadet Lieutenant Colonel (Lt Col)	Chevron of 2 inverted stripes; 1 double-wide, 1 regular
Cadet Colonel (Col)	Chevron of 3 inverted stripes; 1 double-wide, 2 regular

Table 1–10 Cadet Enlisted Grade Insignia

Title	Grade Insignia
Cadet Airman (Amn)	Pointed Chevron of 1 stripe, with torch in the middle
Cadet Airman First Class (A1C)	Pointed Chevron of 2 stripes, with torch in the middle
Cadet Senior Airman (SrA)	Pointed Chevron of 3 stripes, with torch in the middle
Cadet Staff Sergeant (SSgt)	Pointed Chevron of 4 stripes, with torch in the middle
Cadet Technical Sergeant (TSgt)	Pointed Chevron of 5 stripes, with torch in the middle
Cadet Master Sergeant (MSgt)	Pointed Chevron of 6 stripes, with one stripe inverted above the torch in the middle
Cadet Senior Master Sergeant (SMSgt)	Pointed Chevron of 7 stripes, with two stripes inverted above the torch in the middle
Cadet Chief Master Sergeant (CMSgt)	Pointed Chevron of 8 stripes, with three stripes inverted above the torch in the middle

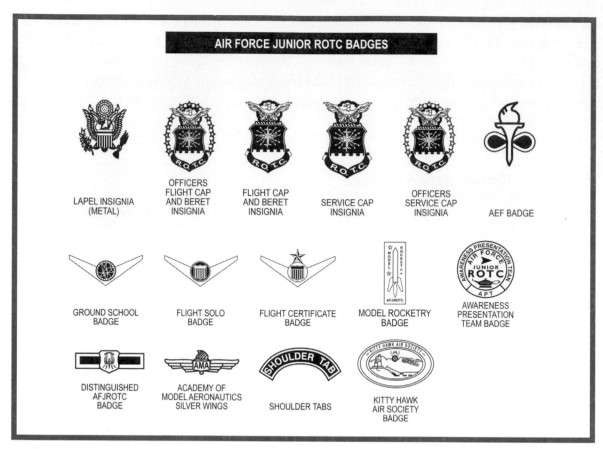

AIR FORCE JUNIOR ROTC BADGES

LAPEL INSIGNIA (METAL)

OFFICERS FLIGHT CAP AND BERET INSIGNIA

FLIGHT CAP AND BERET INSIGNIA

SERVICE CAP INSIGNIA

OFFICERS SERVICE CAP INSIGNIA

AEF BADGE

GROUND SCHOOL BADGE

FLIGHT SOLO BADGE

FLIGHT CERTIFICATE BADGE

MODEL ROCKETRY BADGE

AWARENESS PRESENTATION TEAM BADGE

DISTINGUISHED AFJROTC BADGE

ACADEMY OF MODEL AERONAUTICS SILVER WINGS

SHOULDER TABS

KITTY HAWK AIR SOCIETY BADGE

FIGURE 1–10.
Air Force Junior ROTC Badges.

FIGURE 1–11.
A close-up of accoutrements placed on a female
cadet uniform.

Air Force Badges

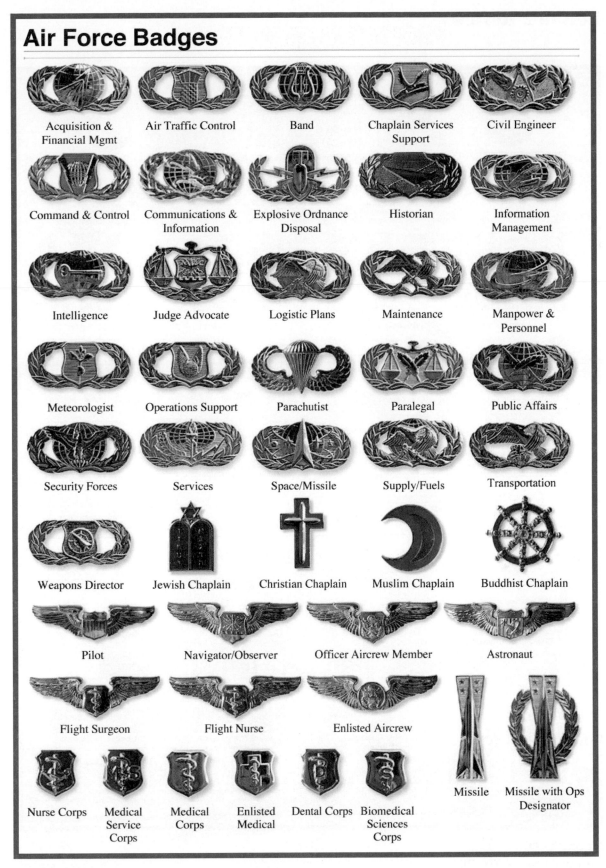

Acquisition & Financial Mgmt

Air Traffic Control

Band

Chaplain Services Support

Civil Engineer

Command & Control

Communications & Information

Explosive Ordnance Disposal

Historian

Information Management

Intelligence

Judge Advocate

Logistic Plans

Maintenance

Manpower & Personnel

Meteorologist

Operations Support

Parachutist

Paralegal

Public Affairs

Security Forces

Services

Space/Missile

Supply/Fuels

Transportation

Weapons Director

Jewish Chaplain

Christian Chaplain

Muslim Chaplain

Buddhist Chaplain

Pilot

Navigator/Observer

Officer Aircrew Member

Astronaut

Flight Surgeon

Flight Nurse

Enlisted Aircrew

Nurse Corps

Medical Service Corps

Medical Corps

Enlisted Medical

Dental Corps

Biomedical Sciences Corps

Missile

Missile with Ops Designator

FIGURE 1–12.
Air Force Active Duty Badges.

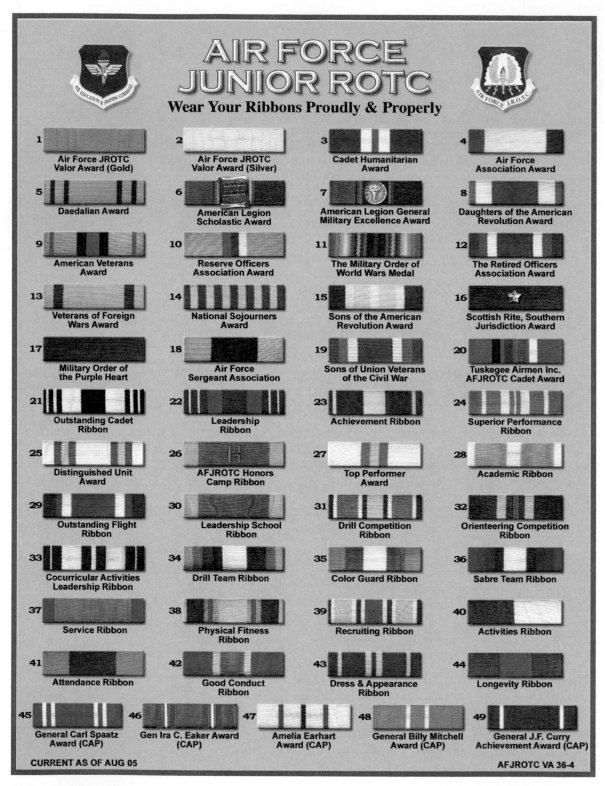

FIGURE 1–13.
Air Force Junior ROTC Ribbons.

CHECKPOINTS

Using complete sentences, answer the following questions on a sheet of paper.

1. What is bulk?

2. What is grade insignia?

3. What are the two categories of the Air Force insignia system?

4. What do the grade insignia look like for the following Air Force ranks?
   - Major
   - Brigadier General
   - Major General
   - Captain
   - General
   - Staff Sergeant
   - Master Sergeant
   - Chief Master Sergeant
   - Airman Basic
   - Senior Airman

5. What device is worn by first sergeants on their chevrons to distinguish them?

6. What are some of the duties of a first sergeant?

7. What is the highest position held by any enlisted personnel?

8. Why was the position of CMSAF created?

9. What do the grade insignia look like for the following Air Force Junior ROTC ranks?
   - Second Lieutenant
   - Captain
   - Major
   - Colonel
   - Senior Airman

Applying Leadership Skills

10. Look at the appearance and grooming standards for cadets. How well do you meet these standards? Are there any improvements you would like to make? Write your goals for meeting the standards.

Customs and Courtesies for Air Force Junior ROTC

Quick Write

Jot down three everyday customs you think are important. Why are they important?

LEARN ABOUT...

- the difference between a custom and a courtesy.
- the position of honor.
- how, when, and whom to salute.
- how to recognize an officer.
- how to report to an officer.
- the importance of military titles.
- how to plan a Military Ball.

What Are Customs and Courtesies?

Webster's *II New Riverside University Dictionary* defines **custom** as *a common tradition or usage so long established that it has the force or validity of law; a practice followed as a matter of course among a people; or the habit or practice of an individual.* Although we often use the term, we rarely think about how customs affect our lives.

Consider clothing. By custom, certain types of clothing are okay for some occasions but not for others. While shorts or jeans might be just right for a backyard cookout, they would be considered highly unsuitable for a formal dinner. Although there's no logical connection between what someone wears and what or where that person eats, custom dictates that some functions require dressier attire than others. People who mock an established custom—by wearing shorts to a formal dinner, for example—show an indifference to or lack of consideration for the standards and feelings of other members of society.

Every group involved in a common undertaking observes customs. Customs vary from family to family, from region to region, and from country to country. For example, families celebrate major holidays differently; lacrosse is a common school sport in some regions of this country and not in others; and many people in other countries bow, rather than shake hands, when they meet a friend.

Even professions have customs. Doctors and lawyers, for example, respect the confidence of their patients or clients. If doctors gossip about their patients, they will lose them. If a lawyer violates the confidence of a client, the lawyer's reputation and practice will suffer. In addition, professionals who betray their patients' or clients' confidentiality may be sued or subject to professional sanctions.

VOCABULARY

- custom
- esprit de corps
- allegiance
- RHIP
- taboo
- court martial
- dining-in
- dining-out
- protocol
- comradeship

Custom, then, is an unwritten law. People obey customs because they help us get along with others. People cannot create their own customs and expect others to follow them. As a member of the Air Force Junior ROTC, you will inherit many customs. Some customs began with the Army; others developed in the Air Force. All of these customs serve as a key to Air Force living. Paying attention to these customs will help you adjust to your Air Force Junior ROTC unit.

Military customs and courtesies go beyond basic politeness. They help build morale, discipline, and **esprit de corps**, which is *a common spirit of enthusiasm and devotion to a cause among the members of a group.* By teaching respect for the flag, military customs remind us of our **allegiance**, which is *loyalty or the obligation of loyalty, as to a person, nation, sovereign, or cause.* They also remind us of the sacrifice required of all military personnel.

Military customs and courtesies also contribute to a mission's effectiveness. Customs and courtesies ensure proper respect for the chain of command, and they build the base for the self-discipline we need in times of crisis. Traditional ceremonies allow us to properly honor those who have served well and faithfully, and the customs and courtesies surrounding mass formation help develop units that act together in their efforts to reach a common goal.

Historic Customs and Courtesies

Many customs and courtesies have a long history as part of people's behavior.

Position of Honor

We learn, as part of military courtesy, to walk or sit to the left of seniors. This custom began centuries ago when men still fought with swords. Because most men were right handed, the heaviest fighting occurred on the right. The shield was carried on the left arm, and the left side became defensive. Men and units were proud of their fighting ability; they considered the right of a battle line to be a post of honor. When an officer walks on your right, he or she is symbolically filling the position of honor.

Hand Salute

The hand salute is another example of a military custom that began long ago. In fact, it is so old that its origin is uncertain. Some say it began in later Roman times (1 A.D. to 500 A.D.), when assassinations were common. Others trace the beginnings of the hand salute to the Middle Ages. Knights wore suits of armor, which included a helmet and a visor. When two knights on horseback met, they would raise their visors to expose their faces. If the knights recognized one another as allies, they would leave their visors up and drop their hands. This was always done with the right hand, since the left hand held the horse's reins.

The salute changed when European free men who served as soldiers began carrying their own weapons. When these soldiers met, they would raise their right hands to show that they held no weapons and that the meeting was friendly. This practice gradually became a way of showing respect. In early American history, the custom sometimes involved removing the hat. By 1820, this was modified to touching the hat. Since then, the hand salute has become the one used today.

All military personnel—regardless of differences in military grade—greet one another with a hand salute. Though it varies in form across the globe, the hand salute says, "I greet you." It is also customary to greet another member of the military with words when you meet face-to-face. When you salute an officer, say, "Good morning, sir/ma'am," "Good afternoon, sir/ma'am," or "Good evening, sir/ma'am," depending on the time of day. By returning the salute you say, "I return your greeting." Salute your fellow cadets and officers with pride in a friendly, cheerful, and willing manner. The salute signals that you recognize and respect your comrades in the honorable profession of arms. When you honor the Colors with a hand salute, you show respect for your country.

How you salute tells a lot about your attitude as a cadet. If you salute proudly and smartly, it shows your personal pride and your pride in the unit. It shows that you have confidence in your abilities as a cadet. A sloppy salute, on the other hand, shows a lack of confidence. People may think that you do not understand the meaning of the salute or that you are not proud of the unit.

How to Salute

To execute the hand salute (Figure 1–14), raise your right hand smartly so the tip of your forefinger touches the lower part of your headgear just to the right of your right eye. When you are not wearing headgear, your forefinger should just touch your right eyebrow. Your arm, shoulder to elbow, should be parallel to the ground at a natural angle (about 115 degrees forward) from your body. Your thumb and fingers should be extended and joined,

FIGURE 1–14.
A hand salute.

with a straight line between the tip of your middle finger and your elbow. Your posture should be erect and alert; head and eyes should be turned toward the person being saluted. Be careful not to tilt your head toward your hand; bring your hand all the way up. Drop the salute smartly. Move your hand smoothly to your side in one motion without slapping your side. Never have anything in your mouth or your right hand when saluting.

Individuals must be in one of the following positions before rendering the salute: standing at attention or marching at attention. The junior member should begin the salute in time for the senior to return it before passing the junior. When rendering a salute to an officer or to the Colors, or when returning a salute, turn your head and eyes toward the officer or the Colors, and salute. While you are saluting an officer, extend a verbal greeting. Verbal greetings should always be rendered when officers or enlisted members meet face to face.

Whom to Salute
Salute the President of the United States, all commissioned and warrant officers of the United States Armed Forces, and officers of friendly foreign nations. Usually, you should also salute the Secretary of Defense and the Secretary of the Air Force.

Officer Recognition
Even though you may not be able to distinguish the specific rank, you can recognize an officer by:

- service hat visor or band
- the hat/beret insignias
- flight cap

In addition, marked government vehicles and staff cars also indicate that an officer is on board.

When to Salute
Members of the Armed Forces, which are a nation's military forces, exchange salutes in many situations when in uniform. The person who is saluted always returns the salute, unless he or she is unable to do so because of physical incapacity or when the right hand cannot be freed, as in carrying packages. A superior whose hands are full with packages, etc., need not return the salute. However, the junior member must salute and the senior member should nod in return or verbally acknowledge the salute. An exchange of verbal greetings is also appropriate if the junior member is carrying articles in both hands.

Tradition has it that if you are of junior rank, you salute first. The only exception to this occurs when a unit commander gives an official report to an adjutant who might be junior. Military officers are to be saluted while in civilian clothes, if recognized by the junior military member. Always return salutes by those of lower rank.

The basic rule is that, upon recognition, the military hand salute is rendered to all officers outdoors with some exceptions. The military hand salute is not rendered indoors, except when performing a formal report to an officer or when receiving a formal award from an officer.

Salutes are also exchanged at the conclusion of a conversation. Distance and uniform should not be criteria for saluting. When outdoors, salute your seniors whether they are in uniform or civilian clothing. Salute them regardless of location. There often seems to be some misunderstanding about exactly when to salute. The following information should answer some common questions about when to salute.

Outdoors

Outdoor salutes are exchanged upon recognition between officers and warrant officers, and between officers or warrant officers and cadets or enlisted members of the Armed Forces. The term *outdoors* means being outside a building, including areas such as open porches, covered sidewalks, bus stops, covered or open entryways, and reviewing stands. Salutes will be exchanged outdoors any time officers and warrant officers and cadets or enlisted members of the Armed Forces cross paths. The salute will be exchanged with a person on the sidewalk or with a person approaching or in the same structure. This applies both on and off military installations. Even when two out-of-uniform members of the military are outdoors and recognize one another, they usually exchange salutes (if the exchange of salutes is otherwise appropriate).

Exceptions

Here are some special circumstances when salutes may not be exchanged.

Marked Government Vehicles/Staff Cars: Military pedestrians (including gate sentries) and officers in moving military vehicles do not have to exchange salutes. However, when the passengers in a vehicle are easily seen to be officers (for example, officers in appropriately marked vehicles), they must be saluted.

Standing in a Group: If you are part of a small group that is not in formation, the first person to see the officer calls the group to attention, and everyone should face the officer and salute. If an officer addresses the group or an individual in the group, everyone should remain at attention until the end of the conversation, unless otherwise ordered. At the end of the conversation, everyone should salute the officer.

In Formation: If you are in formation and an officer approaches, the person in charge of the group calls the members to attention and salutes for the group.

Work Details: If you are in charge of a work detail, salute for the entire group when you meet an officer.

Civilian Clothes: Saluting is not required if a person is wearing civilian clothes, but it is not prohibited.

Rank, Recognition, and Respect

Common acts of courtesy among all Air Force personnel help maintain discipline and promote the smooth conduct of military affairs. When courtesy is not maintained within a unit, discipline also decreases and the success of the mission can be put in danger. Although many Air Force courtesies involve the salute, other courtesies are also important.

Reporting to an Officer

When you have officially asked for and received permission to speak to an officer—or if you have been notified that an officer wishes to speak to you—you are required to report to the officer. The manner in which you report to an officer will create a good or bad impression. Remember that your advancement in Air Force Junior ROTC depends partly on the impression you make on the SASI and ASI. You will make a good impression if you report to an officer properly and demonstrate good military bearing. The reporting procedure is broken down into three separate steps: entrance, reporting, and departure.

Entrance

Before entering the room or office, knock once firmly and loudly enough to be heard in an average-sized room. If you don't get an answer in a reasonable amount of time, knock again. When told to enter, march in at the position of attention. Take the most direct route to the officer. Halt approximately two paces from the officer or from the desk if the officer is seated. Always halt in a way that places you squarely facing the officer.

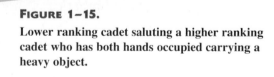

FIGURE 1–15.
Lower ranking cadet saluting a higher ranking cadet who has both hands occupied carrying a heavy object.

Reporting

Reporting is the most critical step. Report in a military manner with snap and precision, but do not exaggerate the movements. The first thing to do is to salute properly. Begin your reporting statement at the time your hand reaches the saluting position. Speak in a clear, conversational tone of voice. If you were told to report, say "Sir/Ma'am, Cadet (your last name) reports as ordered." If you are reporting on your own, say "Sir/Ma'am, Cadet (your last name) reports." Hold the salute until you have completed the reporting statement and the officer has returned your salute. Stand at attention unless ordered otherwise. When the conversation is finished—or the officer has dismissed you—come to attention and properly salute. Hold the salute until the officer returns it, then drop the salute.

Departure

As soon as you drop the salute, complete the appropriate facing movement (about face, left face, right face, or a face in marching) and march or walk at the position of attention. Take the most direct route. Maintain proper military bearing at all times.

Personal Courtesies

When you are involved with officers—whether they are Air Force Junior ROTC cadet officers or commissioned officers in any branch of the military—always take care to observe personal courtesies. These courtesies are usually simple acts of politeness anyone would follow. Only a few courtesies are unique to the military or the Air Force. As mentioned earlier, walk, ride, or sit to the left of a senior person. That means to always give the senior person, whether an officer or enlisted personnel, the place of honor. If you are seated when a senior officer speaks to you, stand. If you are in a parked vehicle, always get out before speaking to or replying to a senior who is not in the vehicle.

When military personnel enter an automobile, the senior officer enters last. Juniors enter a vehicle first and take the seat that will be to the senior's left. Since the senior gets in last, he or she will be the first one out. This allows the senior officer to be the first one greeted by any waiting parties.

One military rule states: "The senior will never think of the difference in grade; the junior will never forget it." Whether you are the junior or the senior in any type of relationship, this is an excellent rule to remember. In some official situations, the senior officer may prefer to call the junior by the cadet's first name. Assignments requiring close and frequent contact between seniors and juniors usually tend to create an air of informality. In such instances, the junior cadet must remember to display proper respect to the senior, so the relationship stays between junior and senior, not between peers.

Officers should practice common courtesy and good human relations with enlisted personnel. They must realize that NCOs are valuable members of the Air Force team and must be treated as such. Officers should also provide NCOs with the proper amount of status, authority, and practical support to carry out their responsibilities.

Figure 1–16.
A cadet gives a senior cadet the place of honor.

The letters **RHIP** stand for *"rank has its privileges."* Why does rank have privilege, in addition to higher pay and prestige? Because privilege and responsibility go hand-in-hand. The two are inseparable in the Air Force, just as they are in civilian life. A person who assumes more responsibility should enjoy a few special privileges and courtesies. The President of the United States, as head of our government's executive branch, for example, enjoys privileges such as living in the White House and having government transportation and personal protection.

Depending upon their rank and position, members of the Air Force also enjoy certain privileges. For example, NCOs are exempt from manual labor while supervising work details. And senior ranking officials often receive reserved parking spaces. However, one precaution must be heeded in the area of RHIP. Positions must never be abused. NCOs who use airmen to run personal errands are misusing their positions and their privileges.

Always remember that the mission, along with the unit's morale, must come first. Whenever you are awarding or receiving privileges ask: How will this affect the mission and the unit? Problems may arise if members of the unit feel that a privilege has been undeserved or is unfair. As a result, morale might decrease, and disciplinary problems could affect the mission. The privileges of rank and position are indeed worth working for and attaining. But the best privileges are those you earn, not those you take and have not earned.

Use of Military Titles

Using correct titles is another important act of military courtesy. It shows respect for the individual's grade. You might wonder why the Air Force places so much emphasis on titles, but consider for a moment what a title is. It is a formal name given to a person because of office, grade, hereditary privilege, or as a mark of respect. In the Air Force, individuals hold a title that matches a particular grade. As members move from one grade to the next, they also earn the title associated with each grade. You will find that Air Force personnel are proud of their titles because they signify hard work and success. When you address personnel by their titles, you are showing proper courtesy and respect to them as individuals as well as to their grade. In addition, you are demonstrating your professionalism and discipline as a military member.

Even though the Air Force encourages the use of official military titles, seniors may address those under them by their first names. However, juniors must not communicate with seniors in such an informal manner.

The correct use of military titles depends on whether communication is informal or formal. Use the title *Lieutenant* for a second or first lieutenant in informal communication. Use the full title in the address element and the salutation of official written correspondence. When you address officers orally, use their correct military titles, such as Captain or Major. You many also use Sir or Ma'am, depending upon the officer's grade. Address a Chief Master Sergeant as Chief Master Sergeant or Chief. Address NCOs below the grade of Chief Master Sergeant by their full title or Sergeant. Address airmen by their full title or Airman. Address civilians as Mr., Mrs.,

Miss, or Ms. In addition, you may address medical and dental officers, as well as veterinarians, as Doctor. A chaplain in the Air Force is officially designated Chaplain, regardless of grade. A chaplain may also be addressed by more traditional titles such as Father, Reverend, or Rabbi. Address Air Force senior and junior ROTC cadets as Mister/Miss, Cadet, or by cadet rank followed by the last name.

Retirees are an integral part of the Air Force. Treat them with the same respect and courtesies you show active duty members. By public law, they have earned and are entitled to enjoy certain benefits, rights, and privileges from the U.S. government. One of these rights is that retired military members are entitled to be addressed, both in written and verbal communication, by their retired rank. "Once an Air Force member, always an Air Force member."

Additional Courtesies

Calling a Room to Attention
When an officer enters a room, stand at attention. If more than one person is present, the first person to see the officer calls the group to attention. However, if an officer of equal or higher rank is already in the room, do not call the room to attention. Call the room to attention again as the officer departs. If you are by yourself, do not call the room to attention; however, you must stand at attention.

Showing Respect
Show respect to the person in authority at all times by recognizing the person's presence and by being courteous and respectful in bearing, behavior, and speech. An example of this is standing up and extending a verbal greeting when someone of senior rank enters the room or approaches, whether it's in an office area, classroom, or elsewhere. Courtesy is contagious.

Don't Keep People Waiting
One of the most valuable habits you can develop is to always be on time. Nothing is more irritating than being asked to be somewhere at a specific time and then having to wait after you arrive. At times, you may not be able to avoid being late. If this happens, call ahead to inform those who are waiting for you that you are going to be late or to reschedule the appointment.

Taboos

Avoiding taboos goes hand in hand with observing customs and courtesies. A **taboo** is *a prohibition excluding something from use, approach, or mention.* Taboos may be the result of long tradition or the requirements of good taste. We may feel inclined to scoff at taboos when they strike us as absurd. But taboos, like customs and courtesies, are part of our traditions.

The Senior's Desk
It is disrespectful to lean or flop against the SASI's or ASI's desk. Always maintain the proper military bearing when in the presence of a senior.

Showing Disrespect to the Uniform

Bad conduct in uniform is a longstanding taboo. Aside from the disrespect a person reaps as a result of bad conduct, it is a disgrace to the uniform and the branch of service represented. The good impression created by a large number of cadets who have dressed and behaved properly in public can be destroyed by just one person who presents a poor appearance or acts poorly.

You can be court-martialed for disgracing the uniform through bad conduct or by violating the regulations that govern wearing of the uniform again and again. A **court martial** is *a military or naval court of officers and, occasionally, enlisted personnel appointed by a commander to try offenders under military law.* Part of the Air Force mission is to keep people of the United States interested in airpower. As a result, anything that detracts from a favorable impression also detracts from the success of the Air Force mission.

Courting Favor

If you court favor with a superior, you will earn the dislike of your peers. Such practice is beneath the conduct expected of officers and enlisted personnel. "Bootlicking" marks individuals as incapable of making their own way on personal ability. It is regarded as a display of weakness.

The Old Man or Old Lady

The commander is often referred to as the Old Man or Old Lady. The term is one of admiration; it refers to position, not age. However, never use the term in the commander's presence. Using the term in the commander's presence would show disrespect.

Gossip

Gossip, because it often causes quarrels and disputes, is considered taboo. A unit's morale may be damaged by feuds that arise from gossip.

Vulgar Conduct and Language

Vulgar conduct and language are definitely taboo. Neither cadets nor officers should lose their temper to the point of using profanity, particularly in addressing a junior. Officers and cadets who use abusive and profane language to make a point show lack of self-control, as well as a very limited vocabulary. Cadets and officers risk receiving an official reprimand if their conduct is poor. Worse, they undermine their effectiveness as leaders.

Dining-In and Dining-Out

You should be familiar with the terms *dining-in* and *dining-out,* which refer to formal military dinners. **Dining-in** is *a formal dinner for members of the military only.* **Dining-out** is *a formal dinner to which non-military guests are invited.* The protocol for these affairs often reflect long-standing traditions within a unit of the armed forces. **Protocol** is *a code of precedence in rank and status and of correct procedure in ceremonies; a form of etiquette observed in ceremonies; a combination of good* *manners and common sense that facilitates effective communication.* The intent is to promote cordiality, **comradeship**, which is *companionship,* and esprit de corps.

Some believe that dining-in extends back to the Roman practice of holding great banquets to celebrate victory and parade the spoils of war. However, most believe that dining-in began as a custom in English monasteries. It was then adopted by the early universities. Later, it spread to military units when the officers' mess began. The customs and traditions of our modern dining-in come from those of the British Army Regimental Mess. The British mess was an occasion to observe the unit's long-standing customs and traditions. It also provided a time for satire, solemn formality, horseplay, and an excuse for living beyond one's means.

The first recorded American dining-in occurred in September 1716 when Governor Spotswood of Virginia, along with a company of Rangers, celebrated after crossing the mountains and descending into the Shenandoah Valley. Air Force dining-in began in the Air Corps when the late General Henry H. (Hap) Arnold held his famous "wing-dings." The custom also grew in popularity during World War II, when the U.S. Army Air Corps participated in British dinings-in. The dining-in is now recognized as an occasion where ceremony and tradition combine with good fellowship as an important element in Air Force life.

The primary elements are a formal setting, posting of the Colors, invocation, traditional toasts (may be at the conclusion of dinner), a fine dinner, comradeship of cadets, benediction, and retirement of the Colors.

The dining-in and dining-out provide an opportunity to recognize individual, flight, and unit achievements for the school year. They also give cadets an opportunity to honor teachers, principals, and other school personnel. The dining-in can also be used to present individual and/or unit awards. As such, the dining-in helps build esprit de corps within Air Force Junior ROTC; it also provides an enjoyable time for cadets. In addition, a dining-out may include entertainment after the formal portions, such as a concert band or dancing.

Toasting at a Dining-In

Toasting is a universal custom. It is a simple courtesy to the person being honored. It is improper to drain the glass after each toast; it is also improper to raise an empty glass to make a toast. You need to know how many toasts are being given so you can gauge how much to drink with each toast.

Toasts are made standing up. One person will present the toast by saying, "Ladies and Gentlemen, the President of the United States" or "Ladies and Gentlemen, I propose a toast to the President of the United States." All will then raise their glasses and say "The President" or "To the President," respectively.

On the presentation and retirement of the Colors, face toward the Colors at attention until the ceremony is completed. Remain standing for the toasts and the invocation at the beginning of the program. You are expected to rise again for the benediction at the end of the program

The Military Ball

Another widespread custom in Air Force Junior ROTC is the Military Ball. This formal event requires cadets and their guest to wear semiformal dress. The military ball presents certain rules, procedures, and protocol to be observed. For example, you must wear the uniform the SASI prescribes, and your date should also be dressed in appropriate attire.

An important element of a military ball is the receiving line, which is made up of the official hosts and hostesses. We'll learn more about proper etiquette for the receiving line in Unit 2.

FIGURE 1–17.
Cadets at a Military Ball.

Planning a Military Ball

Careful planning is needed to ensure that the Military Ball—or any social occasion—is successful. The first step is for the SASI to appoint a planning chairperson. This person should be given the authority to make many of the planning decisions, although some decisions may be subject to the SASI's approval.

One of the chairperson's first duties should be to review the file reports on previous cadet balls. These reports will provide the chairperson with details on what must be done to ensure a successful ball. These activities include:

- Establishing committees, appointing committee leaders, and providing them with the necessary people and other resources. The chairperson also is responsible for supervising these committees. At a minimum, the chairperson will need to create the following committees:
  - advertising
  - decorating
  - entertainment
  - food
  - fund-raising
  - invitations, including the special guests
  - program and seating arrangements
- Establishing short-term and long-term goals, identifying the tasks necessary for the achievement of these goals, and delegating the tasks to committees for execution.
- Identifying problem areas and lessons learned from previous cadet balls, and preventing them from reoccurring.

The chairperson and all committee leaders should think through the details and develop a plan to get everything done. The chairperson should be sure to establish alternative (or back-up) plans where necessary. This will help avoid last-minute embarrassment.

Invitations should be sent out as early as possible. If some guests do not accept, this allows time to invite others without offending them with a last-minute invitation. The invitation must clearly state the location, time, and dress requirements. Guests should know exactly what is being planned and what is expected of them.

Helpful Planning Tips

Helpful planning tips include:

- Be sure that all arrangements are carefully made for the special guests.
- Select a band that plays a variety of music, as well as music that does not offend anyone. Another option is a disc jockey (DJ). DJs can provide quality music at a reduced cost. If the ball is to be held during a holiday season, contact the band or booking agency at least six months in advance and provide them with a list of tentative dates.
- Arrange to have a photographer.
- Arrange to have several door prizes if you can find sponsors to donate them.
- Give credit in the program to all sponsors, as well as to individuals and organizations that helped put the ball together.
- Rehearse the Color Guard, the sequence of events, and any special activities at the actual location at least one day prior to the actual event.
- Be sure that the staff at the site will prepare the correct number of meals and provide the correct number of chairs and tables, and check that the seating arrangements match the seating chart.

Other pointers include:

- Sign a contract that specifies the date, fees, and total hours the hall or ballroom will be available. The hours need to include time before the ball for decorating, as well as time after the ball for cleaning up. The band or DJ contract should specify the hours the band will play.
- Reserve the site and the band early, so you can be sure they are available on the desired date. A National Guard armory, officer or NCO club, American Legion hall, or high school gym are some of the appropriate places for a cadet ball. The location you choose should include a kitchen.
- Set a working budget. Expenses include band or music fees, rent for the dance hall, security guard(s), decorations, tickets, food, flowers, invitations, and postage.
- Appoint a ticket chairperson if cadets are going to be charged in order to pay for the ball. Ticket sales should start early, and then be cut off at least one week before the ball. Ending sales a week before the ball gives you an accurate count of the number of people who will attend. Even if your unit has plenty of money, cadets should be charged a minimum amount for the ball, so they will value the event.
- Appoint a publicity chairperson to write up a series of news stories before and after the ball. Photos should be taken to go with the stories.

- The decorations chairperson should look over the site and start planning decorations. Supplies should be ordered or purchased at least one month in advance to ensure they are available. Major portions of the decorations should be completed no later than the day before the ball.
- Mail handwritten or engraved invitations to faculty members and special guests at least three weeks before the event. Keep a list of responses, and provide nametags for all expected guests.
- The food and refreshments chairperson must know how much money has been budgeted for food and refreshments. If catering is too expensive or inappropriate, cadets can contribute food items in lieu of paying for tickets.
- Formal dances often provide a commercial photographer to take pictures of cadets and their dates. If a photographer is hired for this purpose, be sure that everyone knows how much the pictures will cost before they are taken.
- If awards are to be presented, they should be ordered, engraved, picked up, and presentation scripts written.

CHECKPOINTS

Lesson 3 Review

Using complete sentences, answer the following questions on a sheet of paper.

1. What is a custom?
2. What is esprit de corps?
3. How do you define allegiance?
4. Which civilians may be saluted by persons in uniform?
5. What clues would you look for to recognize an officer when you can't distinguish a specific rank?
6. If you are the first person to see an officer and you're part of a small group that is not in formation, what would you do?
7. What would you do if you were seated and a senior officer spoke to you?
8. In which order of rank do military personnel enter an automobile?
9. What should a cadet do when a senior official enters a room?
10. What is a taboo?
11. What is a court martial?
12. What are the differences between dining-in and dining-out?
13. What is a protocol?

Applying Leadership Skills

14. Think about the esprit de corps of your AFJROTC unit. List three specific things you can do as an individual to contribute to your unit's esprit de corps.

Attitude, Discipline, and Respect

Quick Write

List five words that describe your attitude about AFJROTC.

LEARN ABOUT...

- the importance of a positive attitude.
- the importance of discipline.
- how drill helps instill discipline.

VOCABULARY

- attitude
- discipline
- integrity

Attitude

Have you ever heard someone comment on another person's attitude? After a basketball game, for example, a coach might say, "Jim has a fine attitude. He's a real asset to the team." Or maybe you've heard someone say, "Bill won't succeed because he has a negative attitude." Did you ever wonder exactly what this means? Why is a good attitude considered important for success in almost every activity?

Attitude is *a state of mind.* It may be positive or it may be negative. Your attitude affects the success or failure of most of your activities. Your attitude reflects your personal philosophy of life as it is shown by your actions. Your attitude is the frame of mind in which you view yourself, your work, and others.

Attitude, whether positive or negative, is catching. One player with a positive attitude, for example, can increase the winning spirit of an entire basketball team. Regardless of how far the team is behind, that person's hustle and drive—signs of positive attitude—can energize the team's effort. On the other hand, a player who goes out onto the court and holds back because he or she feels it's not worth the effort—a sign of a negative attitude— can slow down all of the players. A negative attitude is just as contagious as a positive one.

Attitude and the Air Force

It is especially important to have a positive attitude whenever you assume a leadership role. When you're in a position of leadership, those under you will reflect your attitude. The following story illustrates how the attitude of a leader can affect the entire group.

Two airmen, both well-trained mechanics fresh out of maintenance school, had just joined an aircraft maintenance unit.

One day while working on a jet, they overheard the assistant crew chief, a technical sergeant, loudly complain to the line chief, a master sergeant. "The sooner I get transferred out of this sorry outfit, the better! How come our squadron has to work again this Saturday? Every other maintenance outfit gets the whole weekend off," the assistant crew chief carped.

"The reason is our commander—he's the worst on the base," the line chief replied. "He doesn't buck anybody. Even the supply officer tells him off!"

The two airmen soon agreed that, from what they had heard, they had joined a poor outfit. This single incident had affected their performance. They goofed off the remainder of the day. Later, they completely ignored the technical sergeant's request to make better use of their time because of new job commitments. Over time, they picked up the same negative attitudes their supervisors had.

This story should make the point clear: In any type of supervisory role, be especially careful to express only a positive attitude. Otherwise, group efficiency will fall to the level of the attitude displayed, and all initiative, sound judgment, and good work will be stifled.

Attitude and AFJROTC

Within a week of the beginning of the first class in the Air Force Junior ROTC program, the SASI can determine what your attitude is. How? By the expression on your face, your posture, your tone of voice, the way you salute, the way you tie your tie, or the amount of effort you put into meeting grooming standards. The SASI can also tell what your attitude is by the way you prepare for class, your quiz scores, or the manner in which you address the SASI. In short, the SASI or anyone else can get a pretty good idea of how you feel about what you are doing by observing you.

The Air Force Junior ROTC program is built around the individual. Every person in the program is a key to the success of his or her unit, and, therefore, is a key to the success of the entire unit. If you have a good attitude (that is, you will work to your potential while actively participating in the program), you will be doing your share in the cooperative operation of Air Force Junior ROTC.

FIGURE 1–18.
A SASI inspects cadets.

But if you have a poor attitude and fail to meet specified Air Force Junior ROTC goals, you can easily put the whole operation in jeopardy. You play an important role in your unit's success. Strive for a positive attitude in every aspect of Air Force Junior ROTC.

FIGURE 1–19.

Saluting, keeping a good appearance, and executing drill are important to developing a positive attitude.

How can you develop a proper attitude toward Air Force Junior ROTC, its requirements, and procedures? The key to a good attitude lies in understanding. You must try to understand the reason behind Air Force Junior ROTC activities and requirements.

For example, a cadet who thinks saluting, keeping a good appearance, and executing drill are just hassles to annoy cadets is unlikely to develop a good attitude toward the program. If, however, you understand that these are needed steps in military training that have been thought out and tested through the years, you will be well on the way toward forming a positive attitude in Air Force Junior ROTC. A positive attitude will greatly increase your chances of success in the Air Force Junior ROTC Program.

Discipline and the Air Force

Most people do not understand the real meaning of the term *discipline.* They associate it with harshness, political power, undue severity, and restrictions. In fact, the popular conception of discipline is that it is something found only in the military service and that it is arbitrary, unpleasant, and sometimes downright unreasonable.

But the following story illustrates the importance of strict discipline. One night a captain saw four soldiers warming their hands around a fire. An enemy shell burst many yards out in front of the fire, but he knew from experience that the next round would be more accurate. He shouted to the men to take cover. They looked at him but did not move. He was not one of their officers, so they ignored him. Only seconds later an enemy shell smacked into the fire. If the soldiers had obeyed the command the moment it was given, they would have survived. In such a case, automatic obedience could only have been achieved through discipline.

Webster's New International Dictionary states that the word *discipline* comes from the Latin *discipulus,* meaning pupil, and one of its alterations, *disciplina,* meaning teaching or training. Over the centuries, however, this meaning has been lost, particularly in the military service. The word discipline now refers to instruction aimed at guiding the pupil toward proper conduct or action, or to the orderly conduct and action that results from such training. In much simpler terms, military **discipline** is *that mental attitude and state of training that renders innate obedience and proper conduct under all conditions.*

The basic function of the military is to protect the country. This is serious business. The Air Force, for example, must be organized, trained, and equipped for prompt and sustained combat operations. This broad responsibility means that members of the Air Force must be trained to carry out that mission unhesitatingly and efficiently. They must have discipline.

Air Force discipline is an extension and adaptation of the discipline you have experienced throughout your life. Just as in civilian life, the Air Force exists on disciplined behavior. Disciplined actions bring rewards; undisciplined actions bring punishment.

Discipline and Air Force Junior ROTC

What about discipline in Air Force Junior ROTC? What is the purpose behind this discipline? What is the reason for shined shoes and drill, saluting and drill, inspections and drill? Why all the drill?

At one time, drill was absolutely necessary as training for war. When armies marched and maneuvered en masse and the first muskets came into use, close order drill was an essential combat requirement. Obviously, close order drill is no longer needed as a military strategy. Today, close order drill is seldom used for mass movement of men except in basic training or in ceremonies. However, close order drill still has its place in the military service. It is used to teach the basic principles of discipline, leadership, and teamwork.

Drill, along with uniform dress, respect for seniors, pride in appearance, and the other requirements of Air Force Junior ROTC, gives you basic military training in several ways. First, drill and specific standards of performance teach cadets to act in unison. By dressing alike and marching in flight or squadron formation, cadets really begin to feel a part of something larger than the individual. Each cadet begins to feel like a member of a team. The effects of a mistake by a single member of the team are nowhere more apparent than on the drill field, when one individual takes a wrong turn and marches off at an acute angle to the others. As we have pointed out, learning that the individual is a vital member of the Air Force team is indeed basic to aerospace training.

Second, drill teaches individual cadets to respond instantly and subconsciously to a word or command. Close order drill teaches cadets to react like disciplined military members. If a cadet is marching in an Air Force Junior ROTC flight and executes a right flanking movement when the command called for a left flank, it will mean little more than embarrassment and perhaps a stubbed toe. But consider the consequences if someone were flying on the left wing in a flight of F-16s and banked right when the commander quickly ordered to bank left; it would mean a great deal more than embarrassment. It is for situations such as this that cadets train and acquire discipline.

Third, the Air Force Junior ROTC uniform, the drill, and the common responsibilities shared by all cadets give each cadet a feeling of belonging, a feeling of fellowship, which we call esprit de corps. Realizing that the ability of the group depends on the performance of each cadet, and that each cadet is judged by the group, will help you feel that you are part of a team that is working toward common goals. Thus, esprit de corps raises individual morale and fosters teamwork within the unit.

Fourth, discipline in Air Force Junior ROTC should be viewed as self-discipline, not imposed discipline; the discipline should come from within.

If drill ever gets to be boring, if the uniform gets hot on a nice spring day, or if you are torn between shining your shoes or watching TV, remember why these things are necessary. View these activities as essential elements of basic military training, not as punishment or endless routine. The Air Force knows from the past that discipline will determine how well a unit will perform and survive in combat. In other words, the Air Force is training you so that if you are ever warming your hands around a campfire and a captain orders you to take cover, you will be around to tell the story.

Attitude and discipline go hand-in-hand to ensure a smooth running, competent Air Force. Air Force Junior ROTC is the place where cadets form initial attitudes toward the Air Force and where they will develop basic concepts of Air Force discipline. We hope you will come out of the program well disciplined and with a positive attitude toward military service and any other occupation. We firmly believe that if you have a positive attitude, you will have a head start on success in whatever you attempt.

Respect

Respect for authority and discipline also reinforce one another. But you must first acquire discipline. Self-discipline involves full and voluntary acceptance of authority. Understanding that some things—both pleasant and unpleasant—simply must be done and that there must also be people to ensure that those things get done will help you to respect authority.

Integrity

The term *ethics* suggests to some people a very personal, individual standard or philosophy. However, the basic principles of integrity and conduct are guided by a sense of right and wrong. A cadet's sense of right and wrong must be so strong that his or her behavior and motives are above suspicion. The Air Force believes that integrity is important.

The military could not function without integrity, because others have to be trusted to do their jobs. The security of our nation depends upon people in the military who are willing to lay down their lives in its defense. We have to be able to trust each other to make this sacrifice. **Integrity** is *a firm adherence to a code of especially moral or artistic values.* In other words, integrity is honesty.

Integrity is not something you learn overnight. Most people have already incorporated integrity into their set of values. Your parents or guardians and schoolteachers, for example, have helped you understand the difference between right and wrong. But the military holds a higher standard of honesty than society demands, so you must begin to build upon the foundation you have already established.

In the Air Force, everyone else relies on you to do your part. The only way anyone knows what has been done is by word. Integrity makes your word sound. Other people know when you say you did your job that they can bet their lives on it—and in the Air Force, sometimes their lives *do* depend upon that trust. Integrity and self-discipline are cornerstones of the Air Force. Integrity starts with the individual, and it starts with you right now.

CHECKPOINTS

Lesson 4 Review

Using complete sentences, answer the following questions on a sheet of paper.

1. What is attitude?
2. Why is a positive attitude important, especially in positions of leadership?
3. What are three ways your SASI can tell what your attitude toward AFJROTC is?
4. What is the definition of discipline?
5. What are three ways in which drill promotes discipline?
6. What is integrity?

Applying Leadership Skills

7. Attitude, responsibility, integrity, discipline: Choose one of these words and create a slogan that demonstrates the importance of that concept. With the SASI's approval, post your slogans around the classroom.

Lesson 5

Ethics

Quick Write

Jot down three personal guidelines you would use to decide whether it would be right or wrong to take a specific action.

LEARN ABOUT...

- four basic rules of ethics.
- core values of the U.S. Air Force.
- four types of values.
- making ethical decisions.
- the Universal Declaration of Human Rights.
- ethical traits.
- qualities of effective leadership.

VOCABULARY

- ethics
- value system
- universal norms
- conscience

Personal Standards

What comes to mind when you hear the word *ethics?* Do you think of bank robbers and murderers? Or do you think of saving the whales and cleaning the air? How about letting someone copy your homework or telling your best friend the latest gossip? All of these involve decisions based on ethics.

Adults make complex ethical decisions every day. We also know from psychology, which is the study of the mind and of behavior, that children at about the age of three begin to develop a conscience, a sense of right and wrong. So what is ethics and what effect does it have on us?

Ethics is a branch of philosophy, the study of people's most fundamental and basic beliefs and how these beliefs are justified. Not all philosophers agree on one definition of ethics. For our purposes, we define **ethics** as *the rules of conduct that people should follow.* Ethics deal with the struggle between good and evil—judging whether something we do, say, choose, or think is right or wrong. These rules of conduct may change through the years to keep pace with changes in society.

Since *conduct* is a key word, events over which we have no control are not part of a discussion on ethics. Earthquakes are an example. We cannot make a judgment about whether earthquakes are good or bad, right or wrong. Earthquakes happen. They are part of the world studied by science. Whether we lend our help to earthquake victims is a value or moral issue. We are then making an ethical decision. We are deciding to do something or do nothing regarding human life and well-being. Science deals with facts; ethics deals with beliefs, values, and morals.

From the writings of renowned philosophers such as Kant and Aquinas, four basic rules of ethics have endured:

1. Do good; avoid evil.
2. Be fair and equitable.

3. Respect the dignity of all people.

4. Be autonomous (self-governing).

The following list, derived from the four basic rules of ethics, contains a set of guidelines for human decency and well-being. Of course, this list does not contain every possible guideline. Also, a rule can be overridden if it is in conflict with another rule.

1. Be honest.

2. Keep promises.

3. Obey and be loyal to proper authorities.

4. Be courageous.

5. Grow in knowledge.

6. Be willing to work.

7. Be moderate (don't do anything to excess).

8. Maintain and enhance your health.

9. Don't harm people.

FIGURE 1–20.
Willingness to work is just one of the guidelines for human decency.

Most of our moral beliefs are actually habits we learned as children. Doing the right thing brought praise, or at least no negative response. For example, when we walked on the rug with muddy shoes, our parents scolded us. With repetition, we learned to take off our shoes—or at least wipe them off before entering the house. Then we weren't scolded.

For adults, the penalties and rewards of their habits are not so obvious—but they are just as real. Over the course of a lifetime, adults develop habits (good or bad) that can affect their reputations, social status, finances, or overall sense of well-being. Even though habits are learned in social settings and reinforced by rewards and punishments, not all habits are right. Habits are right when they are ways of helping ourselves and others. That is, they help us to develop our best potential and to respect people's basic rights.

We use terms such as *right, good, should,* and *ought* in everyday conversations, but what do these terms mean? How do these words function in moral language? If we say an act is right, does that mean we approve of it? When we say we should not do something, is it because society disapproves of it? These are difficult questions. Both consequences and motives seem to be important in deciding what makes an act right or good. Philosophers continue to wrestle with these concepts. Meanwhile, each of us has an idea of what we believe to be right. Our beliefs may be based on what society or our parents believe or what our experiences have taught us. A combination of factors probably shapes many of our concepts. In any case, we need to be tolerant of other people's concepts, beliefs, and feelings.

As we said, not all decisions involve ethics. But many decisions that seem unrelated to ethics may actually have an ethical aspect. Consider the scientist who mixes together several harmless chemicals and then applies heat or pressure. The resulting product—say, disposable plastic containers—is helpful to restaurants for take-out service. The effect on the environment, however, can be very harmful. Plastic does not break down easily, and animals are harmed when they eat it. So we must ask ourselves which we value more—the convenience of the disposable containers or the environment. These are not easy decisions to make. Technology continues to bring us new and better products; with these products come new and tougher decisions.

Our code of ethics is based upon our value systems, that is, our beliefs about what is and is not important. Freedom, happiness, equality, peace, and love are some of the basic American values.

Values

Every day, students add to their value systems. A **value system** consists of *our set of ideals, beliefs, interests, likes, and dislikes that we use every day to make decisions.* Activities like dating, skipping class, and even what we wear reflect our value systems. Deciding to date someone exclusively probably means we value that man or woman's company. Skipping a class may mean that we do not highly value the opportunity to get an education.

Values do not involve involuntary behavior, such as blinking the eyes. Ethical conduct involves freely chosen behavior (chosen by a person or group of people) based on beliefs that are thought to be very important.

Some people believe in doing whatever they want to do. Others believe in doing what helps other people, whether they really want to or not. Our beliefs are very personal to each of us.

How do we know what values we have? One way is through voicing our likes and dislikes, and we do this fairly often. Another way is through positive or negative feedback on our behavior. Receiving an *A* on a test tells us we did well and may reflect the value we put on our studies. One way to determine what we value as a society is through compiling statistics on what we do and don't buy.

Our military has its own set of values as an organization. The men and women who serve in the military also have a set of values—for the most part, these values are consistent with those of the organization.

United States Air Force Core Values

Integrity first, Service before self, and *Excellence in all we do.* These are the Air Force Core Values. These values exist for all members of the Air Force family—officer, enlisted, and civilian; active reserve, and retired; senior, junior, and middle management; civil servants; uniformed personnel; and contractors.

Definitions

Integrity First. Integrity is a character trait. It is the willingness to do what is right even when no one is looking. It is the moral compass—the inner voice, the voice of self-control, the basis for the trust needed in today's military. Integrity is the ability to hold together and properly regulate all elements of one's personality. People of integrity, for example, are capable of acting on conviction, or their strong beliefs. They can control their impulses and appetites.

Service before Self. This statement tells us that professional duties take precedence over personal desires.

Excellence in All We Do. This expression directs us to develop a passion for continuous improvement and innovation that will propel the Air Force into a long-term, upward spiral of accomplishment and performance.

Types of Values

We can identify four different types of values: personal, prudent, conventional, and moral.

Personal Values

Our personal values guide our conduct. We get our personal values in many different ways. Parents, friends, family, church, and schools often affect our personal values. As we already mentioned, freedom, happiness, equality, peace, and love are some of the values that Americans hold. A profession often establishes methods of transmitting its values to those who become members of the profession. Personal values may develop over time due to a number of different factors.

FIGURE 1-21.

Our values are based on beliefs that are very important to us.

Prudent Values

Values of prudence are those that will serve our best interests when we use them to guide our behavior. For example, it is prudent to stay out of trouble with the law, to maintain your physical and mental health, and to establish a savings account. Sometimes people do not think ahead and therefore are not prudent. Sometimes they let values other than prudence guide their conduct. Although these values are important, other types of values may be more important.

Conventional Values

Conventional values are generally accepted and enforced within a given social order. They are binding upon the members of that social order. A social order might be as inclusive as a whole country or as specific as a sub-society within a larger group—such as members of a church, a high school or college community, or the United States Air Force. At one time, for example, protecting women was an accepted Air Force value. As a result, women were not permitted to fly fighter aircraft.

Moral Values

Moral values are rooted in a comprehensive view of human life, social living, and views of the ultimate purpose and meaning of life. People, even those who spend their lives devoted to the study of moral values, do not always agree completely about the nature of moral values. Sooner or later, many people ground their moral values in a religious concept that makes an appeal to God. Others find secular, or non-religious, ideas about the ultimate purpose and meaning of life more appealing.

People with strong moral values believe they are the most important values to guide their lives. Moral values provide a point of view that people use to argue for social and personal change to an ideal set of values.

Morals and Ethics

Ethics are the accepted rules of conduct in a society. They have to do with the struggle between good and evil. The ethics of a society are written or stated to help us understand how we should act. In general, the term *morals* refers to our behavior, but often it is simply a substitute for the word *ethics*. The moral code of Western society is based on Greek and Roman philosophy and the Judeo-Christian ethic. The Ten Commandments and the Golden Rule are Judeo-Christian contributions. So the rules we live by today have evolved through thousands of years. Some of our rules take the form of laws, such as laws against murder and arson. Others are customs, such as standing when the National Anthem is played. Still others are moral standards, such as rules against breaking promises or gossiping about someone.

FIGURE 1–22.

It is a custom to stand during the playing of the National Anthem.

Just as our living conditions change, our rules may change. For instance, we treat people with mental illness, people with disabilities, and people who struggle with alcoholism differently today than we did only 25 years ago. Now we better understand the causes of their disorders and what they need. In spite of changing conditions, however, we can agree on some common principles and rules of ethics. For example, in our society, we agree it is immoral for one of us to steal the worldly goods of another.

Some people say a moral code is meaningless because people always do what they believe is in their own best interest. They go on to say that we may claim we are interested in the welfare of others, but we always put ourselves first. For example, we tend not to conserve, preserve, or recycle unless laws force us to do so or we see a financial benefit in doing so. Some people won't conserve water unless the water rates are raised. Endangered species may have to be protected by law. Yet, we should be conserving, preserving, and recycling without these incentives, so future generations derive the same benefits we do from the environment. As a society, we need to find better solutions, ones that will meet everyone's needs. We need to internalize our moral and ethical values so completely that we *do unto others* automatically, without having to be urged or forced to do what is right.

At times we act selfishly on a personal level, too, despite what we may say or think we believe. When we drive our cars faster than the speed limit allows, we are breaking a rule set by society for the well-being of all people on the highway. All of us are sometimes tempted to do what is in our own interest. If we are going to live together and develop into caring people, however, we must use good judgment in making moral decisions. This requires foresight, emotional control, and empathy, the ability to identify with another person's feelings and thoughts.

Cultural Rules

We all have certain habits of work, play, cleanliness, and eating. In each culture, people know what is good and what is bad, what success is, and what failure is. They have definite ideas about morality. They hold sacred certain institutions that meet their needs. While customs, habits, and institutions vary a great deal from one culture to another, cultural groups are alike in that they all have morals, values, and a concept of basic human rights.

All people have the same physical needs. We all need a reliable food supply, basic shelter from weather, and security. Some governments do a better job than others in meeting the basic needs of their people, and most governments try to satisfy the needs of the people. If not, they are in danger of being replaced by a government that does try. So, we share a set of basic needs with the rest of the world.

As we said, customs and values depend upon the culture in which we live. What is considered to be right in one culture may be considered wrong in another culture. Women in many southwest Asian countries, for example, are required to cover their arms, legs, and faces in public. Most Americans have a different view of what women are allowed to wear in public. However, we need to respect each other's right to be different. We should understand that a culture's value systems are as right for the people who live within that culture as ours are for us. We usually embrace our society's values as our own because we have been taught to see them as right. The same is true of all people in different cultures the world over.

In addition to the broad set of values recognized by our society, the groups to which we belong—such as family, school, and JROTC—set moral codes. It is important that we know and respect the guidance each of these groups offers.

Making Ethical Decisions

Morality presents many tough questions. For instance, is someone who does what is right simply out of fear of getting caught a moral person? Another such question is Does the end justify the means? Did the good of ending World War II quickly, for example, justify dropping the atomic bomb? We all must decide on the answers to such questions for ourselves. But how do we find answers to questions that may pose a moral dilemma? Here is a systematic process to help you make tough decisions.

1. Consider all the facts.

2. Determine the moral values or obligations at stake.

3. Act or make decisions in light of your knowledge of the values and facts in a way that is respectful of the life and well-being of all people.

4. Choose the lesser of two evils (or the least of many) when no better solution can be found.

Students are faced with complex ethical decisions in their daily lives. Rules, principles, values, and situations influence what we determine to be right. Exactly how do these affect our decisions?

Rules and Principles

Rules and principles have the greatest influence on our ethical decisions. We often ask ourselves, "What should I do?" Society has standards for knowing what is required or what is right. The primary ethical pressures in our culture, though, are telling the truth, keeping promises, and respecting people and property. Cadets, more than most students, also live with clear standards of order, obedience, and discipline.

FIGURE 1–23.
Cadets, more than most students, live with higher standards of order, obedience, and discipline.

Universal norms are *the normal beliefs of people in most cultures.* Anthropologists have found that lying, stealing, violating a group's sex codes, and committing murder are almost always condemned by people everywhere. However, this fact doesn't mean that all cultures look at these actions in the same way. For example, in some cultures, lying to outsiders is considered acceptable. If we were to view such behavior, we might conclude that the culture did not value honesty as we do. However, those same cultures consider lying to members of one's group as highly unethical. In fact, every society believes that lying under some circumstances is wrong and exacts some penalty to punish people who lie repeatedly.

The same is true with theft. For example, an American Indian who stole a horse from a fellow tribesman was severely punished. However, if he took a horse from an enemy tribesman, he was not punished. If he took a horse from a European, he was celebrated. The behavior was considered stealing only if he took the horse from his own people. The settlers, who thought of the Indians as thieves, would have been surprised to learn that the Indians did not think of themselves in the same way.

The same holds true for killing people. Every single society regards murder as wrong. However, killing people and murdering people may be quite different acts in the eyes of the group defining the action. Many people, for example, do not consider killing people in war to be murder. And just as our society once put people to death on the suspicion that they were witches or sorcerers, some cultures continue to do so. So, even though there may be universal norms, or values shared by all people, the behaviors resulting from cultural definitions and interpretations of those values may vary widely around the world.

Without rules or norms, institutions would crumble. Keeping promises is a good example. We're all expected to do what we have said we will do. Most people keep their promises; if they didn't, society would fall into disorder. As citizens, we have an obligation to honor constitutional justice, civil law, and the moral norms of our communities.

In 1948 the United Nations adopted the Universal Declaration of Human Rights. This landmark document asserts that *every* citizen of *every* nation has the right to life, liberty, and freedom from personal attack; freedom from slavery; recognition before the law and the presumption of innocence until proven guilty; freedom from torture; freedom of conscience and religion; freedom of expression; the right to privacy, family, and correspondence; freedom to participate freely in community life; the right to education; and the right to a standard of living adequate for maintaining health and well-being. True, not all nations consistently respect these rights in the actual way they treat their citizens. But failure to live up to the Universal Declaration of Human Rights in no way denies the universal soundness of the moral values underlying the document.

Non-universal Norms

Non-universal norms, by contrast, do not carry a universal moral obligation. These include values such as duties specific to one's religion—for example, worshipping, fasting, observing holy days—toward which some people may feel a serious personal obligation. But they should not impose their personal obligations on others.

Rules and Values

We also use values, in addition to rules, to help us make ethical decisions. In discussing rules, we asked, "What should I do?" The questions here are "What is good? What value or ideal should I hold?" But values can sometimes be at odds with each other, too. The people who represent us in Congress must keep this philosophy in mind every time a bill comes up for a vote. Do we spend more of our tax dollars on defense and less on social programs? Do we need more aircraft carriers to keep sea lanes open, or do we need more research on diseases such as cancer and acquired immune deficiency syndrome (AIDS)? We have only a limited supply of tax money, so we should consider putting the money where it will do the most good for everyone affected by the decision. That means everyone, not just Americans.

For the military professional, the greatest value is the public good. The aim of our defense forces is to assure the security of the United States, and that may mean taking a new assignment every few years. On the personal side, individuals in the military want job satisfaction, a happy home, and an overall sense of fulfillment in life. Sometimes these personal and family values conflict with the values of the profession. The topic of professional ethics is covered in more detail later on in this chapter.

So, our values are sometimes at odds with each other. We also experience conflict between rules and values. Take football as an example. The main goal (value) is to score enough points to win the game. In doing so, the players and coaches choose among short-yardage plays, long-yardage plays, running, passing, kicking, and other plays to score a touchdown. All of these actions are governed by rules. If the ball is advanced but the rules are broken, the team can be penalized valuable yards. Thus, if we break the rules, we may not achieve our goals.

Sometimes the quarterback has to change the call made in the huddle. He must adjust to a changing situation. That type of call introduces us to a third element in ethical judgments—one based on the situation.

Situational Ethics

When we make ethical decisions based on the situation, we ask the questions: What is appropriate for this situation? What is fitting in this case? In this approach to ethics, the circumstances (surrounding facts) of a situation help form the basis for deciding what is right or wrong. The goals and rules we have adopted also come into play. Each new situation is similar to, but different from, other situations. There is no hard and fast game plan to follow. We have to use rules, values, and past experiences to make a decision for each particular situation. When shot down behind enemy lines, we know we may have to lie or steal to survive and return to friendly forces. This does not mean, however, that we view lying and stealing as ethical. In that situation—and in that situation only—we may be forced to choose a course of action that violates our code of ethics, our sense of values.

Ethical Traits

These comments about rules and values and their application in specific situations are meant to guide us and to help us think clearly about our decisions and actions. Many traits describe a person with a refined sense of ethics. One such trait is being considerate of other people's feelings and needs. Other traits include integrity and honor.

Concern for Others

We have already studied the importance of basic needs. Physical needs, such as food, air, and shelter, must be satisfied first. Once those needs are met, we move on to higher-level needs. We should be considerate of other people's opinions and feelings. People crave recognition for a job or task well done. A pat on the back, promotion to the next grade, lettering in sports, or a music recital are all examples of praise. People need encouragement, too. Teachers encourage students to excel in academics. Coaches encourage their students to excel in drama, sports, music, or dance. Parents encourage their children to be the best they can be. Our friends cheer us on to make a touchdown or do well on college entrance exams. We all need a boost now and then. We need to know other people care about us, and they need to know we care about them.

Integrity

Integrity means being honest and sincere with ourselves and with others, closely following a consistent code of ethics. Notice the word consistent—not acting by one set of standards on Saturday and another on Sunday night. It means not picking or choosing what rules one wants to believe in. It means doing what is right whether someone is watching or not. It also means having a set of goals and a balanced approach to life. Being honest is sometimes painful. No one likes to admit to being wrong, making a mistake, or failing to do something. The strength of our character is tested here. A true story portrays this point about personal integrity.

FIGURE 1–24.
People crave recognition for a job well done.

Babe Didrikson-Zaharias was a great athlete in the 1932 Olympics. She later became a professional golfer. While playing in a tournament on the golf tour, she noticed she had somehow played the wrong ball. When the round was over, she penalized herself two strokes. This cost her first place in the tournament. Later, in a quiet conversation, one of her friends asked her, "Babe, why did you do that? No one would have known that you used the wrong ball."

"I would have known," Babe answered.

We need to practice this kind of integrity every day. This involves our conscience, a topic that will also be covered later in this chapter.

On the other hand, there are people who would lie for their organization, but who, like Babe, would never lie for personal gain. Yet, integrity is just as important here as in personal affairs. Making false reports to help the institution look good is an example. A lack of integrity in an organization damages the trust of the organization, our own trust, and mutual respect.

Honor

Closely related to the issue of integrity is the problem of placing career before honor. Everyone is concerned about status and about getting ahead. Achievement ranks high in the cadet's code of values. A fine line, however, exists between a true concern for success in one's career or in school and advancing at whatever the cost. We see examples of this kind of blind ambition in our nation's capital and in the financial world. Blind ambition can cloud our judgment. It can lead us to cover up for the person in charge. It can lead us to cover up for ourselves in an effort to look good at all costs. It takes a great deal of personal courage to say "I screwed up" and take the blame. General George C. Marshall once remarked that decisions that require moral courage are much harder to make than decisions that require physical courage.

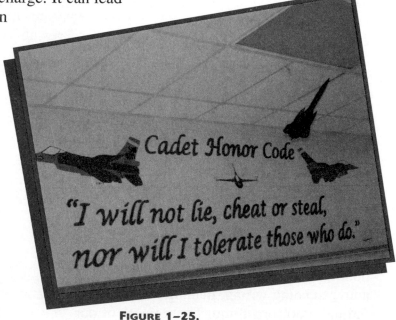

FIGURE 1–25.
Cadet honor code.

Ethics of Leaders

We just finished a discussion of personal codes of ethics and moral standards. Now, let's look at professional ethics—the ethics of leaders.

Leaders are admired for their ability to influence others to achieve goals. Their ability to motivate people goes along with their knowledge in their field. Their technical and professional skills are finely tuned. They are able to evaluate complex situations and to determine the risks involved. They are willing to act on the judgments they make and to assume responsibility for the outcome. Continued success as a leader requires a great deal of self-discipline and personal stability. These qualities, to a large degree, are derived from the moral values and principles that influence their behavior.

Leadership decisions are based on many factors. These factors include all the considerations required by the situation and the abilities of followers. Most decisions require judgment that is influenced by the leader's own values, character, and background. In many cases, it is difficult to choose between the possible courses of action. Occasionally, there is no good alternative, and the leader is faced with having to choose between that which is bad and that which is worse. All leadership decisions that affect the lives and well-being of people have ethical aspects and require moral judgment.

Each profession has a set of standards (moral and otherwise) that is not up for grabs. When we choose to enter a profession (for instance, teaching), we agree to abide by its prescribed set of professional ethical standards. Of course, we may disagree with them, but we must abide by the standards until we can work within the profession to change them. When we can no longer accept the standards and behave accordingly, we are obligated to leave the profession—or we may be kicked out. So, professional ethics are prescribed by the profession or by the larger society the profession serves. Serious action requires serious thought. Every major action should be weighed against the effect it is likely to have on the mission, others around us, our self-respect, and the respect others have for us.

Mission

All of our actions are fruitless if they fail to help accomplish the goals of the organization. Every leadership action should cause resources to be applied to the mission. The ability to use and manage material resources and to influence followers will determine the success of the organization.

Right Choices

Right actions build confidence and self-respect. When we have taken proper action, we generally feel good about it. We regard ourselves as being worthwhile and capable. We have also earned the respect of those affected by our actions.

The ability to choose good behavior over bad behavior distinguishes effective leaders from average or poor leaders. Right choices are often difficult to make. The easy solution is frequently more attractive than the difficult, effective, and sound solution. Every day, we face situations that require action. Our choices in some situations may even call for inaction.

Here are twelve questions that may help you to make right choices.

1. If I do what I'm thinking of doing, would I be willing to have my action enacted into law and required of everyone?

2. If I am considering using someone else for my own personal gain, would I allow myself to be used in the same way?

3. Would I be willing to explain to a jury why I chose this action?

4. Would I do this if I knew it would be on television news tonight?

5. What would I think of this action if it were done by my worst enemy?

6. If my reason for acting this way is that everyone else does it, would I do it if no one else did it?

7. Would I do this if I knew I would have to explain my reasons to my family?

8. Would I be content with this action if it were taken by my boss or a member of my family?

9. Would I be content to have each of my followers behave exactly as I intend to in this situation?

10. My team could win the game by violating a rule. Before I call this play, would I be upset if the losing team took the same action?

11. If what I do hurts no one very much, would I be willing to let everyone do the same thing?

12. If there is very little harm in what I want to do, what kind of person will I become if it gets to be a habit?

Leaders who always try to make right choices show a great amount of moral courage and maturity.

Moral Courage and Maturity

One outstanding military leader, Vice Admiral William P. Lawrence, defined moral courage this way: To know right from wrong, to possess a firm set of values, and the strength to live by those values and do what is right regardless of the consequences. Such courage is gained through knowledge and experience. The key to successful development of moral courage and maturity is the ability to set appropriate goals and achieve them. Cadets already possess:

- a conscience
- a sense of justice
- a personal code of conduct

The goals now are to refine our conscience, improve our sense of justice, and maintain a code of conduct sensitive to the right sort of values.

Conscience

Conscience is *the awareness of a desire to act properly and the awareness of guilt when improper acts are committed or intended.* Our conscience is not an automatic feeling or emotion. It is a product of knowledge and intelligence that allows us to judge right from wrong. The emotion of guilt is triggered by our conscience when we act in a manner contrary to what we know to be right. Our conscience is strengthened as our knowledge increases and we become more sensitive to important human values. New facts learned through experience and study add to our ability to make right choices. Our moral courage is strengthened by our successes in attempting to act out our values. As our conscience continues to develop in the right ways and to mature, we become more realistic in judging the actions of others and more sensitive to their needs and motives.

A properly informed conscience will allow us to be confident without being rigid and overbearing. It will give us strength and purpose that builds character.

Sense of Justice

A true sense of justice is absolutely essential for leadership because it assumes a sense of fair play. As a leader, our sense of justice must prompt us to protect the rights of every follower. It must cause us to be aware of the need for fair distribution of benefits and burdens to all within the organization.

A sense of justice is developed from learning experiences over time. Just as our conscience goes through changes, our sense of justice must be allowed to mature. An effective beginning for developing an informed conscience and a true sense of justice is to be concerned with doing the right thing. It is also important to talk with other people about why our actions should be just and moral.

Personal Code of Conduct

Our code of conduct need not be complicated or overly restrictive. It should not be a list of things we believe. Rather, it should be a list of reminders that cause us to practice right behavior. We should state rules positively, as if they were goals that mean a great deal to us. The list should contain "I will" items. They can be as simple as, "I will do my best to be punctual and cause no one to wait for me," or "I will keep my room neat and orderly." Then we should put these rules or goals into daily practice.

FIGURE 1–26.
The ability to set appropriate goals and achieve them is the key to developing moral courage and maturity.

Living right, that is, by a code of good conduct, has its own rewards. Among those rewards are developing good habits, fewer occasions for having to apologize, greater self-esteem, and the respect of others. Many opportunities that had been withheld will open to us. Our moral courage will increase and the frustration we experience when making choices will lessen in time. In short, we will be living a more fully human life.

Developing permanent good habits is very important. William James, a great American psychologist, said that all of our behavior, our virtues and our vices, is really habit. As we repeat certain behaviors and thoughts, our nervous system "grows" in the ways we have used it, until we have a ready-made response to each sort of impression. We are bundles of habits. James also said that if only young people could realize how soon they would become mere walking bundles of habits, they would pay more attention to how they were acting as their habits were being formed. Since children have no way of knowing these things, their teachers (and parents) must help them develop good habits. As we keep working to build our characters in the right way, we get better and better at whatever we try.

James offered these three practical steps to get rid of bad habits and to form good ones:

1. To form a new habit or to get rid of an old one, begin the change in behavior as strongly as possible. James even recommended taking a public pledge, if possible. He told the story of a man who advertised in his local newspaper a large reward to anyone who, after that date, should see him in the wine shop. The man posted the ad to help him keep a promise made to his wife. No doubt, the thought of having to pay the reward was a strong reason for him to stay away from the wine shop.

2. Never break a new habit before it is firmly fixed in your life. Continuing to do the new behavior over and over helps make it a habit for life.

3. Take every chance you get to act on the change. James said that the effects of practicing a new behavior communicate the new set of actions to the brain. Action, not simply the decision to change, builds the tendency to act in the new way you wish to behave.

Ethical behavior has been a subject of concern throughout history. Every culture has agreed that certain actions are intolerable and others are honorable. We can get a great deal of help and encouragement by considering the sources of guidance that are available to us. These can be found in the great literary and religious works of the world.

Lesson 5 Review

Using complete sentences, answer the following questions on a sheet of paper.

1. What are universal norms?
2. How do non-universal norms differ from universal norms?
3. What is the definition of ethics?
4. How did Vice Admiral William P. Lawrence define moral courage?
5. What do we mean when we say someone has conviction?
6. What does our conscience tell us?
7. What characteristics does a person with empathy display?
8. What is a value system?
9. How do professional ethics govern a professional's behavior?
10. What are moral values?
11. What two things have the greatest impact on our ethical decisions?
12. What distinguishes effective leaders from average or poor leaders?
13. What are the U.S. Air Force core values?
14. What are the four categories of values?
15. What are several ways in which people acquire their personal values?
16. What is the Universal Declaration of Human Rights?
17. What are the four basic rules of ethics according to philosophers Kant and Aquinas?

Applying Leadership Skills

18. Think of one personal habit you would like to change. How would you use the three steps William James suggests to change this habit? Write a plan to help you change the habit.

UNIT
2

Individual Self-Control

Unit Chapter

Chapter 2   Personal Behavior

In Your Home and Community

Advocacy

With your classmates, write a manual or handbook to promote good character in your school. The handbook should promote the character traits of trustworthiness, respect, responsibility, fairness, caring, and citizenship.

Personal Behavior

Chapter Outline

- Lesson 1   **Common Courtesies and Etiquette**
- Lesson 2   **Managing Stress**
- Lesson 3   **Behaving Positively**
- Lesson 4   **Mental and Emotional Health Care**
- Lesson 5   **Avoiding and Preventing Violence**

Quick Write

Think about relationships you admire. They might be between your friends, family members, or neighbors. Explain what you admire about the relationships. What seems to make them work so well?

1

Common Courtesies and Etiquette

Quick Write

What do you think are good rules and practices for courtesy and etiquette? Make a list of at least six things that you do to maintain courtesy and etiquette in your everyday life.

Learn About...

- making introductions.
- dining etiquette.
- handling social invitations.
- formal, informal, and casual wear.
- writing thank-you notes.
- public courtesies.
- hygiene and grooming.

Etiquette versus Manners

During your high school years, JROTC experience, and life after graduation, you will often interact with people. When you know the rules of proper etiquette for a variety of social occasions, you will feel more relaxed and confident in these situations. You will also have the chance make a good impression on others.

Proper social conduct and behavior are important elements in your character development. Although this lesson concentrates on the etiquette and manners required at the cadet Military Ball, the information here will carry over into other aspects of your life.

Etiquette is *a code of behavior or courtesy based on rules of a polite society.* **Manners** are *socially correct ways of acting as shown in widespread customs.* Manners are based on kindness, respect, thoughtfulness, and consideration. The rules of etiquette may vary with the changing times, but good manners are timeless.

As you read about the rules of proper etiquette and the practice of good manners, remember that social etiquette and good manners are nothing more than common courtesy, sincerity, and consideration for others. It is important to treat others in the same way we want others to treat us. This is the very foundation on which a polite society is built.

Social Introductions

Introductions should be simple, direct, and dignified, and the act of making them should be a formal occasion. They should be made whenever people gather socially, even for a short period of time. Introductions should be made automatically and immediately when discovering that two people do not know each other. You may make these introductions or have someone else do it—if custom demands, as in a formal military reception receiving line—but you cannot neglect an introduction without running the risk of being rude or negligent. There is nothing mysterious about making introductions, unless you do not know what to do.

Introductions in a Formal Setting

Introductions at a formal reception, such as at a cadet Military Ball, may often include a receiving line. A **receiving line** is *a group of people, including the host and honored guests, who stand in line and individually welcome guests attending a function.* It is customary, and often mandatory, that all cadets and their guests go through the receiving line upon arrival. The people who would be in the receiving line include:

VOCABULARY
- etiquette
- manners
- receiving line
- dignitary
- place card
- monopolize
- R.S.V.P.
- stilted

- The host (Senior Aerospace Science Instructor (SASI) or commander of the unit holding the reception)
- The spouse or guest of the host
- The ranking honored guest, with his or her spouse or guest
- Other dignitaries with their guests

At a reception, such as at the Military Ball, which people attend as couples, the lady precedes the gentleman through the receiving line. The gentleman, whether or not he is the Junior ROTC cadet, introduces the lady first to the Cadet Corps Adjutant or other corps representative, who often announces the names of all attendees to the host. A lady or gentleman attending without a partner should introduce himself or herself to the adjutant. Even though the adjutant may be a friend of yours, do not shake his or her hand. The adjutant will announce your name to the host as you step in front of him or her. A simple, pleasant greeting and a cordial handshake are all that is necessary when moving through a receiving line. Save lengthy conversation for later. Should your name get lost in the line, repeat it for the benefit of the person doing the greeting.

In the absence of an adjutant, the woman still precedes the man through the receiving line. The man introduces her first, and then introduces himself directly to the host. After you have gone through the receiving line, you may proceed to the serving of refreshments or conversation with other guests and await the signal for the next event. If the receiving and dining rooms are separate, do not enter the dining room until the signal to do so is given.

For the remainder of the event, you will be responsible for making introductions as you move around the room and during dinner. The following guidelines explain what you need to do.

Making Personal Introductions

When making a personal introduction, avoid using elaborate phrases. Remember that introductions should be simple and direct. The most generally accepted introductions are "Colonel Smith, may I introduce Mrs. Foster?" or "Colonel Smith, I would like you to meet Mrs. Foster."

The general rule is that you introduce juniors to seniors (this applies to age and military rank), gentlemen to ladies, and so on. However, the degree of formality used when making the introduction depends on the position of the persons involved or the solemnity of the occasion. To introduce two people who are not near each other, you would typically take the junior to the senior, the young lady to the older person, the gentleman to the lady, and so on.

When introducing someone to a **dignitary**, *a person of importance or someone who holds a high office,* mention the dignitary first to show respect for the office he or she holds. Be sure that you use the correct formal title for the dignitary when making the introduction. A few more common titles include:

- Introduce doctors, judges, or bishops by their titles.
- Introduce members of Congress by Senator or The Honorable.
- Introduce a Catholic priest by Father and an archbishop by Your Grace. Some Protestant clergy use titles such as The Reverend, Pastor, or Doctor; however, others prefer to be addressed as Mr., Mrs., Miss, or Ms. Ask the individual how he or she prefers to be introduced before making the introduction.
- Introduce military personnel by their rank. For example, when introducing your guest to one of your JROTC instructors, you might say "Sergeant Allen, I would like you to meet Miss Jones."

If the situation arose where you had to introduce a teacher to a parent, you would use the teacher's name first. For example, "Major Cooper, I would like you to meet my mother, Mrs. Eastern." If both of your parents were there, you would introduce the woman first and then the man, such as "Major Cooper, I would like you to meet my parents, Mrs. Eastern and Mr. Eastern."

If seated, you should rise to acknowledge an introduction and remain standing while other members of the party are being introduced to one another. When being introduced to ladies or gentlemen who are seated, you need not rise if rising may inconvenience others at the table.

Introductions in Informal Situations

When introducing two people whom you know very well and who have heard you speak about the other, you may be more casual. For example, to introduce a cadet buddy to your sister, you might simply say, "Susie, this is Pete." In this example, it is perfectly acceptable to make the introduction using the first names of both people. However, do not use the first name of an adult, a senior, or another important person when introducing that person.

Methods of Making Introductions

When making an introduction, speak each name slowly and clearly to be sure the names will be understood. When you are being introduced to someone, make a point of listening to the other person's name. Not remembering a name is a common failing, which is easy to forgive. However, forgetting a name is not an excuse for not making an introduction. If you forget the name, or did not hear it, ask—with an apology—the person to restate his or her name. Then use the name several times in conversation to help you remember it. If necessary, ask for the person's name—with appropriate apologies—before starting an introduction to another person. For example, "I beg your pardon, sir (or ma'am), but I have forgotten your name. Thank you, sir (ma'am). Colonel Smith, I would like you to meet Miss Jones."

When you are introduced to others, it is proper to return a courtesy such as "Nice to meet you," "Hello," "I am really glad to meet you," or "How do you do?" When you introduce others, don't walk off and leave the two people staring at each other. As the person who made the introduction, you should either say something about each person to get a conversation started or excuse yourself so that you and your guest can continue to move about the room or participate in some other event.

To start a conversation, mention something of common interest to both parties. For example, "Major Davis, I would like you to meet Michael Knight. Major Davis is my Senior Aerospace Science Instructor, Michael. Sir, Michael hopes to enroll in JROTC next year." Before moving from the person whom you just introduced, your guest should respond with "Good-bye, I am very glad to have met you," or something to that effect.

When leaving a group, it makes no difference if you were introduced or just included in their conversation; you politely and quietly say good-bye to anyone who happens to be looking at you, without attracting the attention of those who are unaware that you are leaving.

When in doubt whether two people have met, it is perfectly fine to ask. Be sure to address the senior first, using a courtesy such as "Colonel Smith, have you met Miss Jones?" If they have not met, make the introduction. Usually, most people will consider your question as equal to an introduction, and will proceed with "how-do-you-do?" The important thing is to not assume that people know each other. There is no harm in introducing people who have already met, but it is inconsiderate to have strangers together without introducing them.

FIGURE 2–1.
Remember to introduce your friends if you aren't sure they have met before.

Cadets sometimes assume, in error, that every cadet knows every other cadet. Do not hesitate to introduce cadets if you are not sure they know each other.

In certain situations, you may find it necessary to introduce yourself to another person. If you are next to someone you do not know and no one is around to make an introduction, it is perfectly fine to introduce yourself. Use a greeting such as "Hello, I am Tom Frazier," while shaking that person's hand. Do not say, "What's your name?" A good reply to you would be "Ted Wentworth, nice to meet you." It is then up to both people to start their own conversation.

When and How to Shake Hands

When gentlemen are introduced to each other, they typically shake hands. Ladies who are JROTC cadets also shake hands during introductions. However, as a more general rule, whenever a lady or gentleman extends her or his hand as a form of greeting, the receiving party should extend her or his in return. Nothing could be ruder than to ignore a friendly gesture. At the end of the introduction or conversation, those who were drawn into it do not usually shake hands when parting.

A proper handshake is brief, but the clasp should feel firm and warm. Maintain eye contact with the person whose hand you are shaking, as shown in Figure 2–2. Do not shake a hand violently, grasp the hand like a vise, keep the handshake going for a long period of time, or offer only your fingertips.

When being introduced to a lady out-of-doors, a gentleman in civilian clothes may remove his hat. In addition, a gentleman will ordinarily remove his glove to shake hands unless he

FIGURE 2–2.
A JROTC cadet shakes hands at a Military Ball.

is a member of a color or honor guard. If a gentleman is confronted with a sudden introduction when he has gloves on and it is awkward to remove a glove while the other person has her or his hand outstretched, it is better to shake hands with the glove on with no apology. You would also use these rules as part of general public behavior, even in casual situations.

Dining Etiquette

Table manners are an important part of social conduct. Proper manners around the table are not just reserved for special occasions; you should use them whenever you dine. Relaxed politeness is the key to any dining situation. When you know what to do, you can relax and enjoy yourself. This section will help you learn the rules of the table.

Manners and Courtesies before Eating

A gentleman does not sit down until all the ladies at his table are seated. He can help with the seating by holding the chair—first for his guest, then for other ladies near him if the ladies outnumber the men. He does this by pulling out the lady's chair from the table far enough for her to move easily in front of it. Then, as the lady sits down, he gently pushes the chair under her until she is seated. When all ladies at the table are seated, he may then take his seat by going around the left side of his chair. Posture at the table should be straight, but not stiff.

If a lady leaves the table at any time, the gentleman who seated her rises. When the lady returns to the table, her escort or the gentleman who seated her rises and repeats the courtesies mentioned in the previous paragraph.

The polite dinner guest will not touch anything on the table, not even the napkin, until after the blessing (or invocation) has been said or until it is obvious that there will be no blessing. Then you may pick up your napkin and partially unfold it on your lap. Do this unnoticeably—do not unfold a dinner napkin completely or above the table.

A Formal Dining Table Setting

At a large dinner, there may be a vast array of silverware at the place setting, including one or two knives, two or three forks, and two or three spoons. A formal table setting is shown in Figure 2–3. If you have any doubt about the correct piece of silverware to use for a particular course, you generally start with the outside piece of silverware and work inward. If you end up without a spoon or a fork, it is fine to ask for a replacement.

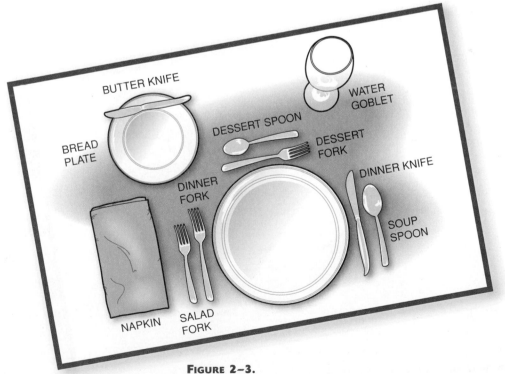

Figure 2–3.
A place setting can be confusing if you're not familiar with it.

Specialized pieces of silverware include: the butter knife, soup spoon, dessert fork and spoon, iced tea spoon, oyster fork, and fish knife and fork. The number of pieces of silverware indicates the number of courses to expect. For example, a six-course meal might include soup, fish, sorbet (a fruit-flavored ice served to cleanse the palate, or clear your taste buds), salad, an entree, and dessert. The placement of the silverware indicates the order of these courses.

Styles of Eating

There are different methods, manners, and courtesies of eating, depending on the situation. You should be familiar with the proper use of silverware, how to eat with your fingers as well as with a soup spoon, the differences between American and European styles of dining, and more.

American vs. European Styles of Eating

In the American style of eating, food is cut as shown in Figure 2–4. Hold the fork in your left hand, tines down, with your index finger on the back of the fork. Secure the food being cut with the knife, which is held in your right hand. Cut in front of the fork, not behind it. After cutting no more than two or three bites of food, place the knife on the plate and transfer the fork to your right hand. This is called the "zigzag" method.

When not using your knife and fork, place them together across the top of your plate as shown in Figure 2–5. This is the resting position. When you have finished the main course, place the knife and fork beside each other on the dinner plate diagonally from the upper left to lower right, or from the 10:00 to the 4:00 position. This is the "finished" position and indicates that your plate may be removed.

FIGURE 2–4.
American style of eating.

In the Continental or European style, hold the fork in your left hand and the knife in your right hand. Cut and eat with your fork, tines down, while still holding it in your left hand. The knife can remain in your right hand throughout the meal to cut food or to help push bits of food onto the fork. Only one bite of food is cut and eaten at a time.

When not using your fork, rest it diagonally on the left side of the plate with the tines down and close to the center of the plate. Rest the knife diagonally on the right side of the plate with its point toward the center of the plate. When finished, place them as described in the American style with the fork tines down.

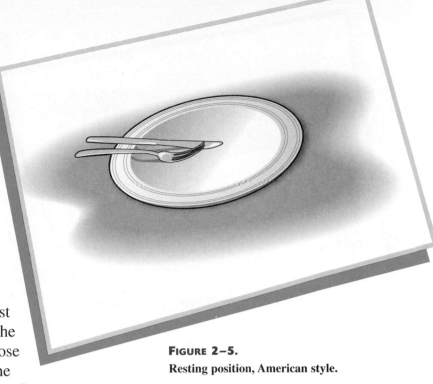

FIGURE 2–5.
Resting position, American style.

Proper Use of Silverware

Various rules govern how to use silverware properly. These rules include:

- After you use a piece of silverware, do not place it back on the table.
- Do not leave a used spoon in a cup; place it on the saucer.
- Do not leave a soupspoon in a soup bowl. You may leave it on a soup plate if one is provided; otherwise, place it on the dinner plate when not in use.
- Do not lay a knife with the handle on the table and the tip of the blade on the edge of the plate. This also applies to the fork.
- Leave unused silverware on the table in its proper position.

How to Eat Finger Foods and Soup

When eating soup, the motion of the spoon should be away from you while filling it. Sip from the side of the spoon; do not slurp. If it is necessary to tip your soup bowl, tip it away from you. If your soup is too hot to eat, let it sit until it cools; do not blow on it.

Bread, rolls, biscuits, nuts, fresh fruit, olives, celery, radishes, raw carrots, cookies, and small cakes may be eaten with your fingers. Place finger foods on the bread plate if there is one. If there is no bread plate, use the salad or dinner plate.

As seen in Figure 2–6, break your individual servings of bread, rolls, and large biscuits into small pieces before buttering and eating them, one piece at a time. Do not cut these items. Buttering and eating a whole roll or whole slice of bread is also not appropriate.

Proper Use of Napkins

You should not tuck the napkin under your belt or wear it like a bib. Napkins are for dabbing lips, catching spills, and covering sneezes. Do not use a napkin to blow your nose. Never lick your fingers; always use your napkin.

Before taking a drink of water or any other beverage, wipe your lips with your napkin to avoid leaving smears on the glassware. One quick, light pass with the napkin should be enough.

FIGURE 2–6.
Break bread, rolls, and biscuits with your fingers before you butter them.

If you must leave the table during dinner, say, "Excuse me, please," with no explanation, and place your napkin on your chair. When leaving the table after dinner, place the napkin on the table in loose folds to the right of your plate. Do not refold, crumple, or twist it. Always push your chair to the table when you leave it.

Basic Table Manners

The following list includes hints about table manners. Follow each one in any dining situation.

- If place cards are used, do not move or remove them. A **place card** is *a name card for a formal dinner.* In addition to showing the specific seating arrangement, place cards are used to make guests feel welcome and to help people get to know one another in large social settings.
- Take small bites. Large mouthfuls of food are unsightly. Do not chew with your mouth open or make loud noises when you eat. It is not polite to talk with food in your mouth.
- If you burp, say, "Excuse me" (to no one in particular) and continue eating. Do not make a big deal out of it.
- Hats, gloves, cameras, purses, sunglasses, and so on do not belong on the table. If it is not a part of the meal, do not put it on the table. Hats and gloves belong in the cloakroom. You may place cameras and purses under your chair.
- Your hands should go no farther over the table than is necessary to eat and to pass things. Between courses, place your hands in your lap or at your side. Do not place your elbows on the table.
- If you cannot easily reach something on the table, ask for it to be passed to you. Say "please" and "thank you." If you are the one passing something, place the items on the table for the person to pick up. When passing salt and pepper, pass them together.

- If food spills off your plate, you may pick it up with a piece of your silverware and place it on the edge of your plate.
- If you drop something, leave it on the floor until the meal is over; then pick it up. If a piece of your silverware falls onto the floor, pick it up if you can reach it and let the server know you need a clean one. If you cannot reach it, tell the server you dropped a piece of your silverware and ask for a clean one.
- Do not season your food before you taste it.
- Hold a long-stemmed glass with the thumb and first two fingers of your right hand at the base of the bowl or on the stem.
- It is not appropriate to ask for a "doggy bag" during a formal occasion.
- Do not scold or correct a server. Make any complaints to the person (cadet) in charge of the ballroom arrangements.
- If food gets caught between your teeth and you cannot remove it with your tongue without being too noticeable, leave the table and go to the restroom where you can remove the food in private.
- At the end of dinner, after the host and honored guests have departed, make sure that you say good-bye to everyone at your table before departing.

Conversation During Meals

Conversation is an important part of social interaction around the table. It is perfect for the enjoyment of good companionship and a pleasant meal. A few important tips include:

- Try not to talk too quickly or too slowly.
- Keep the conversation light. Small talk includes casual, unofficial, interesting things in everyday life, such as the weather, music, upcoming events, movies, or sports. Keep topics of conversation safe and non-controversial. Avoid discussions about religion, race or politics, or any controversial issue. Avoid health issues, off-color jokes, and gossip.
- Answer respectfully when addressed.
- Be mindful of engaging in conversation with a person who has just taken a bite of food. Remember, do not talk with food in your mouth.
- Loud voices or laughter can be disturbing to others. Do not yell; use a pleasant tone of voice that can be heard only at your table. Do not use profane, abusive, or vulgar language.
- Be a good listener. Give others a chance to talk. Do not monopolize a conversation. To **monopolize** means *to take exclusive ownership or control.* Pay attention to the person speaking by making eye contact; do not look at other people when someone is talking to you.
- Do not interrupt. Allow the other person to finish what he or she is saying before speaking. If you and another person start talking at the same time, give way quickly in a friendly manner with a simple "Go ahead, please."
- Do not ridicule or laugh at an unfortunate remark or someone's mistake. Although a person who makes good conversation does not contradict someone in a social setting, it is okay to disagree. In those instances, start by saying, "I disagree with you because," and state your reason.

Handling Formal Social Invitations

When you are invited to attend a social event, which could be a short afternoon visit, a dinner party, or a Military Ball, you have certain obligations that you must observe as a guest.

You must understand the invitation: what you are invited for, where it will be held, when you should be there, and what you should wear. A written invitation will usually spell out most of these things quite clearly. Certain things are implicit in an invitation, as you shall see.

R.S.V.P

R.S.V.P. comes from the French expression "Repondez s'il vous plait," which means "please reply." **R.S.V.P.** means that *you must reply to the hosts to let them know if you can or cannot attend the function to which you've been invited.* On many invitations, you will see R.S.V.P. followed by a telephone number. In this case, the courtesy of a prompt reply by telephone is required to permit the host, hostess, or planning committee to properly plan the event. Call within two or three days to accept or decline the invitation, and make your call between 9:00 A.M. and 6:00 P.M. Do not invite someone else unless the invitation clearly indicates the number and names of those invited.

Several variations on R.S.V.P. are coming into widespread use, especially on informal invitations. One variation is "R.S.V.P. Regrets Only." This notation means that the host or hostess is expecting you unless you notify him or her that you cannot come. If you can accept, you need not reply. Make sure to be there on time.

FIGURE 2–7.
Cadets and guests seated at a Military Ball.

If your plans for that day are unsettled, do not pass this problem on to the host or hostess. It would be much better to decline the invitation than to give a complicated account of your social schedule. Even if the other arrangement or engagement is uncertain, it is best to decline the invitation. After you have declined, do not call back if your plans change.

When declining, it is enough to say to the host or hostess that a conflicting duty or social engagement prevents you from accepting. You can turn down an invitation because you do not want to go. However, use good judgment for the invitations you refuse.

Most written invitations will indicate exactly where the function is being held. Some invitations may include a small map for your convenience.

If the invitation is telephoned to you, repeat back all of the important information to be sure there is no misunderstanding when you accept the invitation. If you must first check your calendar before answering, get all the details and explain that you will call back as soon as you have looked at your schedule. Thank the caller for the invitation, make sure you have the phone number, and promise to call right back. Make sure you call back as you promised.

After you accept an invitation, if an illness or an absolute emergency prevents you from attending, call the host or hostess immediately with regrets and apologies.

Invitations to dinners, receptions, and weddings will usually give a time. For dinners and receptions, this is the time at which you should arrive; do not arrive earlier or later. Plan your timing so you can be punctual. The time on a wedding invitation is the time the ceremony begins; allow enough time to be seated before the ceremony begins.

If you are invited to an open house from 3:00 P.M. to 6:00 P.M., you may arrive any time after 3:00 P.M. and depart before 6:00 P.M. You are not expected to stay the entire three hours. After a dinner party, you should stay at least an hour. If you do not, it hints of "eat-and-run" rudeness.

Formal, Informal, or Casual Wear?

The invitation may specify what you should wear. For example, an Air Force Junior ROTC cadet would most likely wear a semi-formal dress uniform to the cadet Military Ball. In this situation, male guests should wear a suit, while female guests should wear either short or long evening attire.

Some invitations may simply indicate that the dress is formal, informal, or casual. Be sure that you understand what these terms mean. If you are in doubt, ask the host or hostess what to wear when you call to R.S.V.P. As a general rule, use the following guidelines:

- **Formal:** For gentlemen, a suit may be acceptable, although a tuxedo or uniform equivalent is preferred; for ladies, a short or long evening gown may be appropriate.

- **Informal:** For gentlemen, a sport coat and tie is appropriate; for ladies, a dress appropriate for daytime wear or a nice pants suit is acceptable.
- **Casual:** For gentlemen, nice slacks and a sport shirt is appropriate; for ladies, a sundress or nice pants and blouse is appropriate. In some situations, jeans or shorts and a nice shirt or blouse may be acceptable.

Responsibilities to the Host

When attending an open house or a small dinner party, seek out and greet your host or hostess immediately upon arrival. A crowded room should not keep you from properly greeting your host and hostess. You should also delay getting any refreshments until after you have properly greeted the host and hostess.

FIGURE 2–8.

A cadet in semi-formal dress uniform receives an award at a Military Ball.

Because the host and hostess are in charge, let them run things. As a polite, unassuming guest, you can help by making conversation and joining wholeheartedly in whatever activities are planned. You should not sit when other guests are standing in your presence.

Before leaving, you must thank your host and hostess for a wonderful time. Even if there are still dozens of people present, you must seek out the host and hostess to say thank you and good-bye.

Thank-you Notes

Be sure to write a thank-you note within two or three days, but no more than a week after you have been a guest at someone's home. A thank-you note should be handwritten in ink on nice writing paper. It is best to use stationery sets that provide matching paper and envelopes. Be conservative in the choice of color and design. Plain white is always acceptable. The requirements for a thank-you note include:

- Spell out the month—the 3/9/06 format is not used socially. This date would be written as March 9, 2006. Place the date in the upper-right corner, just below the fold line on the informal notepaper.
- Make sure the margins are large enough—leave about 1.25 inches on the left side and about .75 inches on the right, depending on the size of the paper.
- Place the salutation, such as "Dear Mrs. Elliott," at the left margin.

- Indent only the first line of each paragraph. Align the rest of the paragraph with the left margin.
- Place the closing about as far to the right as the date at the top of the page. "Sincerely," or "Sincerely yours," with your first and last names, are acceptable closings. Do not use "Yours truly," and use "Love" only for a family member or close friend, followed by your first name only.
- Do not use "Cadet" or your cadet rank in your signature.
- Place your return address on the envelope, not under your signature.

The thank-you note should be at least three paragraphs long. The first paragraph expresses your thanks specifically and in detail for the occasion. The last paragraph briefly summarizes your thanks. One or more paragraphs in the middle can be on any topic you choose about the occasion you attended. Be careful not to invite yourself back in your thank-you note!

How to Express Yourself

When expressing yourself, be yourself! If you do not normally speak a stilted or flowery language, do not sound that way in your note. **Stilted** means *stiffly or artificially dignified or formal, pompous, or lofty.* Sincerity is far more important than eloquence. For example, "I was overwhelmed by the sumptuousness of the repast in your exquisite domicile" is pretty silly from most people. "I enjoyed the dinner in your attractive home" sounds much more natural. If you particularly enjoyed the soup or if the chocolate cream pie was out of this world, by all means say so in your note.

Sincerity is the first rule in social correspondence. Simplicity is the second rule. You can hardly go wrong with a few simple and direct statements about the things that pleased or amused you. Write just as you would say it to someone you know very well. Also, use correct grammar and spelling, and keep it neat.

The thank-you note is an individual responsibility. If more than one of you enjoyed a dinner party at someone's home, it is not proper to send one thank-you note. Each of you should write your own note.

If you are on the planning committee for a Military Ball, you should also send thank-you notes to the special guests, the organizations that sponsored the event, and the organizations that provided services and entertainment.

Addressing Thank-you Notes

Make sure that you use a block style when addressing the envelope. Include the proper title with the name (such as Mr., Mrs., Miss, Dr., Colonel, MSgt, and so on). Place the city, two-letter state abbreviation, and zip code on the same line.

Place your return address on the front top left corner of the envelope. You may use an address label. You may also include "Cadet" in your title, but not your cadet rank. For example, Cadet John C. Scott is acceptable, but Cadet Captain John C. Scott is not correct.

Public Courtesies

Life is full of ways to show courteous behavior toward others. This section describes just a few ways you can act in a thoughtful and civilized manner.

Telephone Courtesy

The telephone is a valuable time-saver and an effective means of communication. Here are some tips for proper telephone usage.

Avoid calling others during meal hours. If you are in doubt, ask the person you are calling if this is a convenient time, and offer to call back later if necessary. Let the phone ring at least six times to allow the person to reach the phone.

Identify yourself when placing a call. Unlike talking to someone face-to-face, the person on the other end of the phone may not recognize your voice until you identify yourself. While talking on the phone:

- Be polite. This applies to any conversation.
- Speak slowly and clearly. Do not eat, drink, or chew gum.
- Do not sneeze or cough into the receiver. Turn your head or excuse yourself.
- Do not carry on a conversation with someone in the room while talking on the phone.
- Call back immediately if you get disconnected and you placed the call.
- When answering a call for someone else, say, "May I ask who is calling?" This sounds better than "Who is this?"

FIGURE 2–9.
Cadet using a cell phone.

No matter how careful you are you may still dial a wrong number. When that happens, apologize to the person who answers. That person is not interested in hearing a story about how you misdialed, just tell him or her "I'm very sorry to have disturbed you," and hang up. Then make sure you have the correct number, and try again. It is rude to hang up without an apology.

When leaving a message on an answering machine, clearly state your name, the date and time of your call, and a brief message. Leave a phone number only if you need to be called back.

Special Cell Phone Courtesies

Because cell phones can be used virtually anywhere, cell phone users need to remember common-sense courtesy. Results from a nationwide survey show that wireless users need to improve their phone etiquette and put people before phone calls. A few tips to follow:

- Use of wireless phones is prohibited in most schools and at school functions.
- Use of wireless phones during social gatherings or appointments is not appropriate.
- Do not place a cell phone on the table during a meal. It is considered impolite to make or receive cell phone calls during a meal.
- Do not drive and use a cell phone. If you need to have a conversation while driving, be sure to pull off the road while talking.
- Do not use a wireless phone when it will inconvenience or disturb others.
- When in public places or at gatherings, limit your cell phone use.

Assisting the Elderly and Disabled

If an older woman or gentleman wants some support, it is appropriate for you to offer your arm. The cadet does not offer his or her hand. Hand holding in public is not appropriate and is considered a public display of affection, which is improper when in uniform. A cadet may offer his or her hand only when it is not practical to offer the arm, for example, to help an elderly lady or gentleman out of a car. Offer your hand palm up, and do not force it upon the person to whom you are offering it. Withdraw your hand as soon as it is no longer needed.

When walking with a lady, a gentleman may walk on the curbside, or on her left if there is no curb.

Opening Doors for Others

If a gentleman arrives at a door first, he should open it and allow others to pass through. If a lady arrives at the door first and opens it, the gentleman may hold the door for her to continue.

If you are driving or riding to a social event in a privately owned vehicle, open the car door for your passenger to enter first on the right side of the car. Then go around it and take your seat, either behind the wheel or in the back seat beside your guest. When you reach your destination, walk around the car and open the door for your guest if he or she has not already exited the vehicle.

Being Responsible for Your Guest

Depending upon the nature of the social occasion, cadets should inform their guests about the traditions and courtesies of the occasion before arriving. For example, for the Military Ball, cadets should inform their guests about appropriate dress, conduct, the receiving line, traditions, and so on. Remember, if you invite a guest, you are responsible for your guest's behavior. If you have duties to perform after you arrive at the social, arrange for someone else to act as an escort for your guest until you are free. Introduce your friends and ensure that your guest is cared for.

Respect for Authorities and Senior Citizens

By this time in JROTC, you should not have any difficulty showing respect to military seniors; in fact, it should be automatic. You should also show respect for elders, as well as parents, teachers, and others in a position of authority. In short, you should treat all persons with the utmost respect.

Because it is unacceptable to use slang or poor grammar, such as "yeah," "nope," or "uh-huh" to a JROTC instructor, it is also socially rude to say these things to others.

You may also encounter situations when seniors address you by your first name. Although this may be flattering, you should never address a senior by his or her first name, unless that person specifically asks you to do so.

Chewing Gum

You may chew gum in public as long as you do it in a non-offensive way—quietly and inconspicuously. Do not chew gum in formal situations, at work, if you are a host or hostess, or if you are around food.

Waiting in Line

In public places, do not make a lot of noise with friends that might upset other people.

Do not push ahead of anyone. Wait your turn in line to go though a door, into an elevator, or onto an escalator.

Politeness

Use "Please," "Thank you," "You're welcome," "Excuse me," and "I'm sorry" naturally and sincerely in conversations. Say "Excuse me" if you accidentally brush against someone. You can also say "I beg your pardon," but do not use the phrase "Pardon me."

Hygiene and Grooming

Careful attention to all aspects of personal hygiene will help you be welcome in social situations. Be certain that you are well groomed every time you make a social appearance. One dirty or untrimmed fingernail may seem like a small thing to you, but it may be the basis for a negative impression. You never have a second chance to make a first impression. The following are just a few of the basics you should already be doing to make sure your appearance is up to standards.

- Make sure your hair is clean, neatly trimmed or styled, and combed at all times.
- Shower daily and use deodorant as part of your daily routine.
- Brush your teeth and floss daily. Try to brush after meals.
- For young men who already have to shave: if it is necessary for you to do so once or twice a day to be presentable, then do so.

FIGURE 2–10.
Cadets clean uniforms before color guard duty.

Good grooming is an individual responsibility. It should not be necessary for an instructor or a senior cadet to tell you to maintain proper personal hygiene. Additionally, cadets must make sure that their uniforms are clean, pressed, and presentable.

CHECKPOINTS

Lesson 1 Review

Using complete sentences, answer the following questions on a sheet of paper.

1. What is the difference between etiquette and manners?
2. Explain why it is important to present a good appearance at all times.
3. Compare American-style dining with European-style dining.
4. Give three examples of proper dinner conversation topics.
5. Give three examples of improper dinner conversation topics.

Applying Social Skills

6. Pretend you are taking a date to your Military Ball. Write a role-play showing how you would introduce your date to your SASI.

Managing Stress

Quick Write

Jot down the types of situations that are most likely to cause you to feel stress.

LEARN ABOUT...

- the causes of stress.
- how your body responds to stress.
- positive ways to manage the stress in your life.
- ways to manage your time.
- good study habits.

VOCABULARY

- stress
- eustress
- distress
- stressor
- fight-or-flight response
- adrenaline
- fatigue
- stress management skills
- endorphin
- time management

What Is Stress?

The teen years are a time of many changes. Your body is changing, you are gaining new responsibilities, and you are forming new kinds of relationships. **Stress** is *your body's response to change* and a normal part of life.

Stress is not necessarily bad. *Positive stress,* called **eustress,** can make your life more pleasurable. It can help you reach your goals and motivate you to do your best. Eustress is an exciting feeling. It might help you find the energy to score the winning goal in a soccer match or do exceptionally well on a school project.

Some stress can have unhealthy effects, however. This type of *negative stress* is called **distress.** You might react to distress by having an upset stomach before giving a report, or by losing sleep after you argue with a friend. You can't always avoid negative stress, but you can learn to manage it.

Emotional stress distorts the way you view yourself, others, and the world in general. Your self-esteem may decrease, creating feelings of incompetence, being unloved, and worthlessness. Relating to people becomes harder. Prolonged stress will make you feel listless, unable to enjoy life to its fullest, and may even cause illness.

What Causes Stress?

To handle stress, you need to know what causes it. *Anything that causes stress* is called a **stressor.** Stressors range from everyday annoyances to serious personal problems. They also affect different people in different ways. Whereas you might feel nervous about auditioning for the choir, your friend might find the same situation exciting. Figure 2–11 shows some of the things that cause stress for teens.

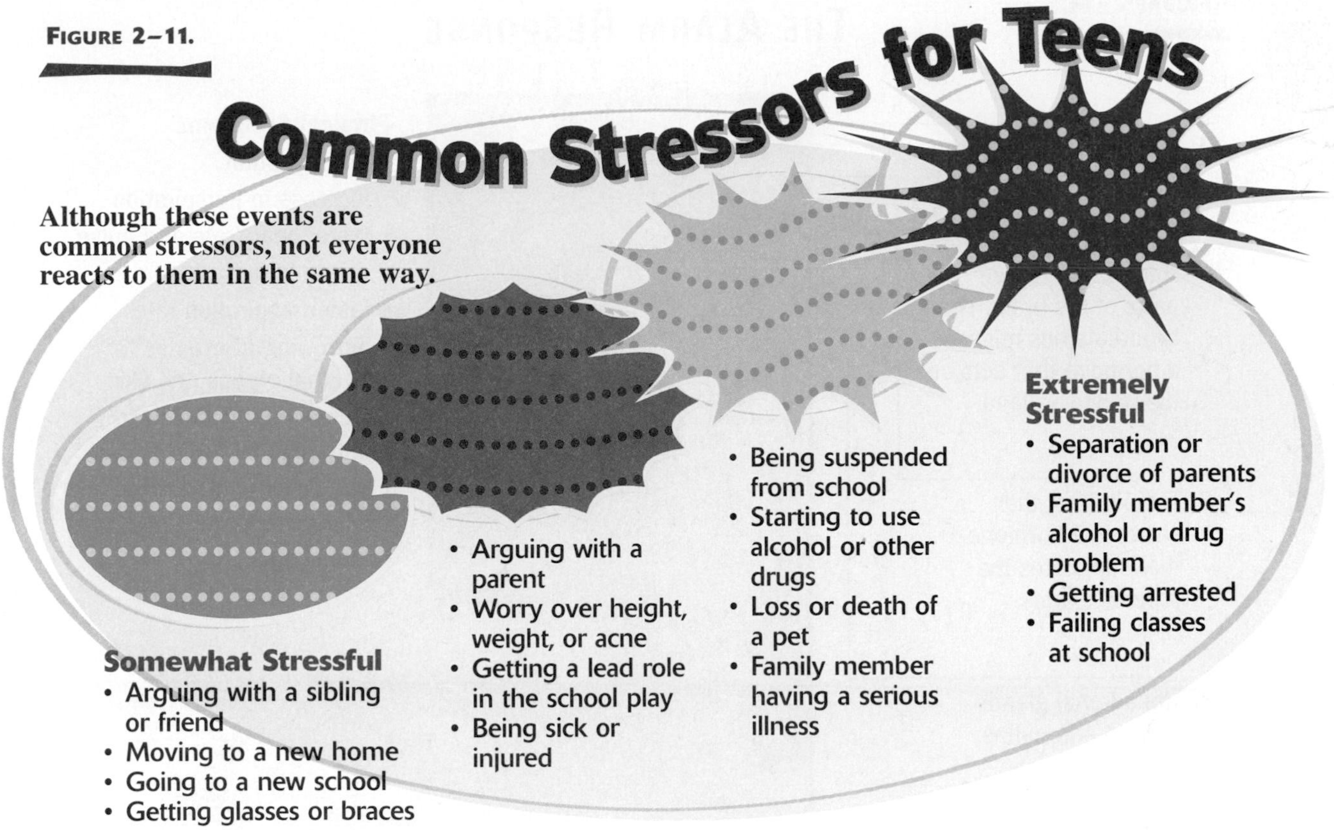

FIGURE 2–11.

Common Stressors for Teens

Although these events are common stressors, not everyone reacts to them in the same way.

Somewhat Stressful
- Arguing with a sibling or friend
- Moving to a new home
- Going to a new school
- Getting glasses or braces

- Arguing with a parent
- Worry over height, weight, or acne
- Getting a lead role in the school play
- Being sick or injured

- Being suspended from school
- Starting to use alcohol or other drugs
- Loss or death of a pet
- Family member having a serious illness

Extremely Stressful
- Separation or divorce of parents
- Family member's alcohol or drug problem
- Getting arrested
- Failing classes at school

How Your Body Responds to Stress

When you perceive a situation or event to be a threat, your body begins a stress response. For example, if a car alarm suddenly goes off as you walk by, you may jump at the sound or feel your heart start to race. The sudden, loud noise is a stressor that makes you respond instantly, without even thinking about it.

Two major body systems, the nervous system and the endocrine system, are active during the body's response to stressors. This response is largely involuntary, or automatic. It happens in three stages and can occur regardless of the type of stressor.

Alarm

Alarm is the first stage in the stress response. This is when the body and mind go on high alert. This reaction, illustrated and explained in Figure 2–12, is sometimes referred to as the **"fight-or-flight response"** because it *prepares the body to either defend itself or flee from a threat.*

FIGURE 2–12.

THE ALARM RESPONSE

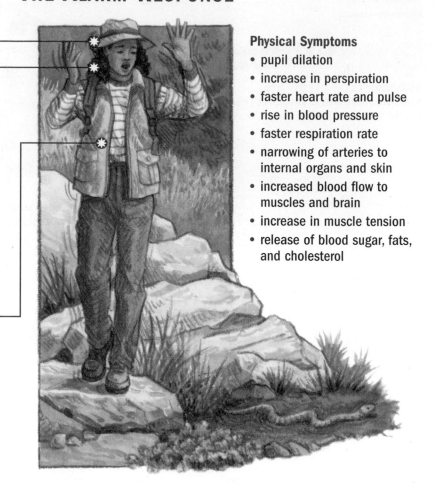

1. Alarm begins when the hypothalamus, a small area at the base of the brain, receives danger signals from other parts of the brain. The hypothalamus releases a hormone that acts on the pituitary gland.

2. The pituitary then secretes a hormone that stimulates the adrenal glands.

3. The adrenal glands secrete adrenaline. Adrenaline is the "emergency hormone" that prepares the body to respond to a stressor.

Physical Symptoms
- pupil dilation
- increase in perspiration
- faster heart rate and pulse
- rise in blood pressure
- faster respiration rate
- narrowing of arteries to internal organs and skin
- increased blood flow to muscles and brain
- increase in muscle tension
- release of blood sugar, fats, and cholesterol

Resistance

If exposure to a stressor continues, the next stage of the stress response is resistance. During this stage, your body adapts to the rush created by alarm and reacts to the stressor. This is the stage in which you "fight" or take "flight." Your body is briefly able to perform at a higher level of endurance. In the case of "fight," your ability to resist a physical challenge or attack may be enhanced. In the case of "flight," you may be able to run faster and farther than you normally could to escape from danger. The resistance stage is why people in extremely high-stress situations have been known to accomplish incredible feats, such as lifting an automobile to save a child trapped underneath.

Fatigue

When exposure to stress is prolonged, the body loses its ability to adapt to the situation and **fatigue** may set in. During fatigue, the third stage of the stress response, a tired feeling takes over that lowers your level of activity. In this stage, your ability to manage other stressors effectively is very low. Both the mind and body have become exhausted. Fatigue can affect the body in several ways.

- Physical fatigue results when the muscles work vigorously for long periods, often leading to soreness and pain. Reaction time becomes impaired, and muscles tire very quickly.

- Psychological fatigue can result from constant worry, overwork, depression, boredom, isolation, or feeling overwhelmed by too many responsibilities.
- Pathological fatigue is tiredness brought on by overworking the body's defenses in fighting disease. Anemia, the flu, being overweight, and poor nutrition can all bring on pathological fatigue. Use of drugs such as alcohol can intensify the feeling of fatigue.

Prolonged or repeated stress can lead to stress-related illnesses caused by the changes that take place in your body during these three stages. Although a stress-related illness can be minor, such as sleeplessness or upset stomach, it can also be life threatening, such as high blood pressure, heart disease, or stroke. Even the effects of stressors that are often ignored, such as the bothersome hassles in a daily routine, can build up over time and cause problems.

Symptoms of stress in teens include:

- Lack of energy
- Tantrums
- Apathy
- Whining
- Lying
- Stealing
- Violence
- Withdrawal
- Nightmares
- Bed-wetting
- Drug or alcohol use
- Confusion
- Nail-biting
- Changes in sleeping/eating habits
- Headaches
- Suicidal thoughts or attempts
- Lack of concentration
- Crying
- Moodiness
- Stuttering
- Cold hands and feet
- Ulcers
- Fatigue
- Anxiety
- Grinding teeth
- Muscle Tension
- Depression

Stress and Your Health

Stress is an unavoidable part of life. Sometimes stress can make life fun, exciting, enjoyable, and challenging. Excessive or prolonged stress, however, can negatively impact all aspects of your health.

Physical Effects

Sometimes stress can lead to a psychosomatic response. This is a physical reaction that results from stress rather than from an injury or illness. Psycho means "of the mind," and somatic means "of the body." Psychosomatic responses may include sleep disorders, skin disorders, and stomach and digestive problems. Other health problems that may sometimes be stress-related include:

- **Headache.** Headache caused by stress is the most common type of headache. It is estimated that, in any given year, about 70 percent of all people worldwide will have at least one stress headache. Many headaches are related to tension. When stressed, the muscles in the head and neck contract. Migraine headaches, which affect about one in ten people, may also be triggered by stress. During a migraine attack, inflamed blood vessels and nerves around the brain cause severe throbbing, which is often accompanied by nausea and vomiting.

- **Asthma.** For some people, stress can trigger an asthma attack. During an asthma attack, breathing becomes difficult as the bronchioles, or air-carrying tubes of the lungs, constrict. The person may cough, wheeze, or fight to get air. If untreated, some cases of asthma can be life threatening. If you have asthma, it is important to discover what sets off your attacks and how to avoid or manage these triggers.
- **High blood pressure.** Prolonged stress can cause an increase in a person's levels of cholesterol, the fatty substance that can block arteries. High cholesterol levels can result in high blood pressure, a condition that contributes to heart disease and stroke.
- **Weakened immune system.** Extended exposure to stress can reduce the body's ability to fight disease by weakening the immune system. When your immune system is weakened, you may be more prone to colds, flu, or more severe infections.

Mental/Emotional and Social Effects

Stress can also impact mental/emotional and social health. It can interfere with daily activities and relationships with others.

- Difficulty concentrating. It can be hard to focus during stressful situations. This can cause negative self-talk and the distorted belief that failure is inevitable.
- Mood swings. Feeling happy one moment and sad the next is a common reaction to stress. Teens may experience mood swings as a result of the hormonal changes of adolescence as well as social and academic pressures. These emotional shifts may put a strain on relationships with family and friends.

FIGURE 2–13.

If you can identify your stressors, you have a better chance of controlling them.

- Risks of substance abuse. Stress can increase a person's vulnerability to drug use. Many people give stress as the reason they started drinking or smoking. However, use of these substances actually increases stress and leads to even bigger problems.

Ways to Manage Stress

The first step in stress management is to identify the source of the stress. To help identify your personal stressors, look at what is happening around you right now. Is any of the following causing you stress?

- **Life events.** These can include getting a driver's license; graduation; moving or relocating; addition of family members by marriage, birth, or adoption; major illness; and parents' divorce or separation.
- **Physical stressors.** These can include pollution, excessive noise, physical injury, lack of rest, drug use, and excessive dieting or exercise.
- **Daily hassles.** These may include time pressures, too many responsibilities, deadlines, and conflicts with fellow students.

Stress Management Skills

To handle stress, you need a variety of **stress management skills,** or *ways to deal with and overcome problems.* One of the basic ways to manage stress is to follow a healthy lifestyle. Problems are always easier to deal with if you feel well. More specific skills for dealing with stress include:

- Knowing how and when to relax
- Keeping a positive outlook
- Learning to be assertive
- Ignoring circumstances that can't be changed
- Being physically active
- Finding a hobby you enjoy
- Avoiding drugs, alcohol, and smoking
- Getting good nutrition
- Seeking support

Relaxation

Relaxation reduces stress by slowing your heart rate and making you feel less tense. The next time you feel stressed out, try some of these tips:

- Relax your muscles. Tighten and then relax one group of muscles at a time. Start at your toes and work your way up to your head.
- Slow your breathing. Take deep, even breaths for five minutes. Inhale through your nose and exhale through your mouth.
- Get enough sleep. Feeling tired can make a stressful situation seem worse. Everything looks better after a good night's sleep!

Keep a Positive Outlook

When you are under stress, it is easy to feel hopeless. A minor problem can seem major. Remind yourself to look at the big picture and keep things in perspective. Is it really the end of the world if you don't get to stay out as late as some of your friends? Is your homework assignment really as difficult as you think? Following are some tips for keeping a positive outlook at times of stress.

- Think positively. If you tell yourself that you will fail at something, you will increase your stress. Instead, tell yourself that you will do a great job.
- Keep your sense of humor. Don't let stress prevent you from seeing the funny side of things. A good laugh is a great stress reliever.
- Have some fun. Take a little time out to do something enjoyable and relaxing. Listen to your favorite CD, read a book, or watch a funny video.

Remember that some stress can be helpful. It can motivate you to take action. Say, for example that you're nervous about doing well in team tryouts. The stress that you feel might motivate you to put in plenty of practice.

Learn to Be Assertive

To assert, according to Webster, is to "state or declare positively." Asserting implies stating confidently without need for proof. There is a distinct difference between being assertive and being aggressive. Aggression seeks to dominate. The philosophy is to win at the expense of another's self-esteem. Aggression produces mental and sometimes physical abuse. To assert is to negotiate with regard to the feelings of all concerned. There is no desire to overpower, just to be counted.

Sometimes it seems easier to let people take advantage of you than to take a stand. It is easier to remain quiet than to state your position confidently. When subjected to unacceptable deeds or words, the tendency is to suffer in silence. This action promotes stress, which contributes to emotional and physical ailments. For this reason assertiveness is a very important behavior to learn.

Learn to negotiate mutually satisfying solutions, rather than accepting the unacceptable. Being assertive builds self-esteem and confidence. It does not turn a nice person into a bully. Assertive people do not force their issues or point of view, but they calmly and positively state what has to be said. Remaining quiet when you should speak up has a way of reducing your self-respect.

Learn to speak up for your rights. Do not let others take advantage of you. Do not feel guilty when you have to say no. You have the responsibility to defend your rights as an individual.

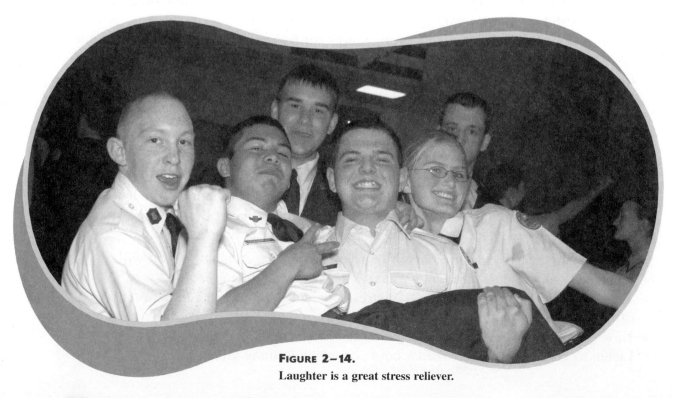

FIGURE 2–14.
Laughter is a great stress reliever.

Always be persistent if you have a valid complaint. If you feel strongly and surely about something, do not back down. Don't be afraid to disagree with someone. When the need to disagree arises, do so in an appropriate manner. It is not necessary to be loud, crude, or belligerent. Assertiveness means more than just speaking up or making demands; it also refers to negotiating with others to find solutions to problems.

If you don't understand what is expected of you, don't be afraid to ask for clarification. No question is a dumb question if there is a need to know. It is better to understand than to live in confusion.

If your rights as a person are being violated, speak up positively and intelligently. You are important simply because you are a unique being, and there is no other like you. Refer to Figure 2–15 to get an idea as to how assertive you are.

How Assertive Are You?

Fill in the blank before each sentence with the number that indicates your responses, based on the following scale:

1 All of the time   **4** Almost never
2 Most of the time   **5** Never
3 Some of the time

_____ 1. Do you keep quiet in order to avoid attention?
_____ 2. Do you let people take advantage of you?
_____ 3. Are you afraid to say no to any request for fear of hurting someone's feelings?
_____ 4. Do compliments make you uncomfortable?
_____ 5. Is it difficult to maintain eye contact when talking to others?
_____ 6. Are you hesitant about asking questions for fear of looking dumb?
_____ 7. When asked to do something you don't agree with, are you afraid to ask why?
_____ 8. Do you go out of your way to avoid making someone angry?
_____ 9. Do you feel embarrassed and out of place in social settings?

_____ **Total Score**

9–13   You are basically nonassertive.
14–23   You are somewhat assertive.
24–34   You are assertive most of the time.
35–45   You are an assertive person.

Note: This test was developed by HQ AFROTC/DOJC. Based on your total score, the test may alert you to a possible problem.

FIGURE 2–15.
Assertiveness Assessment Tool.

Ignore Circumstances That Can't Be Changed

Life offers certain circumstances that are beyond our control. When confronted with these situations, it is better to ignore them than to indulge in self-defeating behavior. It is useless to worry about something that you can't do anything about. Acknowledge that the situation exists, recognize that it is beyond your control, and proceed to things that are within your power.

Be Physically Active

Physical activity is a very good way to relieve stress. During exercise, **endorphin,** *a tranquilizing chemical,* is released in the brain, which triggers natural relaxation. Dr. Ronald Lawrence, founder and president of the American Medical Joggers Association, feels that vigorous exercise improves your total well-being. It helps people sleep better, they are better prepared to cope with stress, and work productivity is improved. In addition to the psychological benefits, physical fitness is achieved. When you look good, your self-esteem is given a boost.

Sweat Your Stress Away

When you're feeling stressed:

- Go running, bicycling, or skating.
- Play soccer, volleyball, or basketball.
- Participate in aerobic dance or martial arts.

FIGURE 2–16.

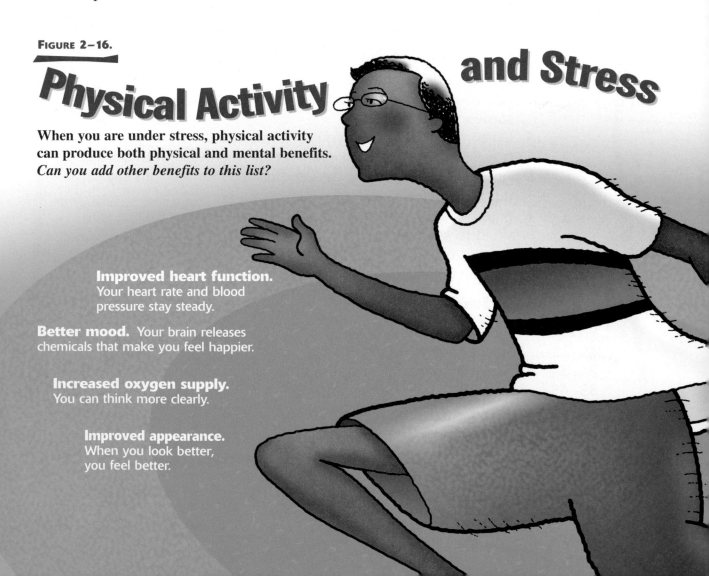

Physical Activity and Stress

When you are under stress, physical activity can produce both physical and mental benefits. *Can you add other benefits to this list?*

Improved heart function. Your heart rate and blood pressure stay steady.

Better mood. Your brain releases chemicals that make you feel happier.

Increased oxygen supply. You can think more clearly.

Improved appearance. When you look better, you feel better.

Physical activity will:

- calm you down.
- improve your mood.
- improve your appearance.
- increase your ability to handle physical and emotional stress.
- aid digestion and help you sleep better.
- help you maintain a healthy weight.
- improve immune system function.
- remind you that you are in control of your responses to life.

Find a Hobby You Enjoy

Doing something you really enjoy regularly can help reduce stress. These activities provide a creative outlet, lessen fatigue, and refresh the mind. Try to engage in extracurricular activities in your school. There should be numerous clubs and activities available in the community or the church, as well.

Many activities can be done at home. Think about what you would enjoy doing. Don't be afraid to experiment with different hobbies. Go for the gusto—try something new and different. You might find an interest you didn't know you had. As long as it is legal and does not infringe on anyone's rights, do it. You will be a healthier person for it.

Avoid Tobacco, Alcohol, and Other Drugs

Some people make the mistake of turning to tobacco, alcohol, or other drugs to relieve stress. However, using these substances does not relieve stress; it increases problems and harms health. Substance use makes the body more prone to disease and has dangerous long-term effects.

Eat Nutritious Food

Balanced nutrition is important for overall health, but it's also important in dealing with stress. Poor eating habits can actually be a source of stress by causing fatigue, weakness, and a reduced ability to concentrate. Inappropriate dieting and over- or under-eating can also put the body under additional stress. Too much stress can cause poor absorption of vitamins and minerals, which can lead to deficiencies.

Seek Out Support

Seek out support. Confide in someone you trust, such as a parent, guardian, sibling, teacher, or close friend. Just talking with someone about your problem may help you feel better about it. See Figure 2–17 for some ideas about people who may offer you support.

Health Minute

Sweat Your Stress Away

When you're feeling stressed:

- ► Go running, bicycling, or skating.
- ► Play soccer, volleyball, or basketball.
- ► Participate in aerobic dance or martial arts.

Physical activity will:

- ► calm you down.
- ► improve your mood.
- ► improve your appearance.
- ► increase your ability to handle physical and emotional stress.
- ► aid digestion and help you sleep better.
- ► help you maintain a healthy weight.
- ► improve immune system function.
- ► remind you that you are in control of your responses to life.

Good Places to Turn to for Help

Friends	Talking to friends lets you know you're not alone.
Parents and Other Adults	For example, a parent, teacher, church leader, family doctor, or school nurse may be able to offer advice or give you the information you need.
School Counselors	Counselors are trained to help with all sorts of problems.
Self-Help Groups	Find out if there's a group in your area that deals with the problems you face. For example, Alateen runs groups for teenagers who have a parent with an alcohol problem. Check with your school counselor, or look in the front of the phone book under "Mental Health."
Hotlines	These can help you right away and guide you to other sources of help. Check the front of your phone book for hotline numbers.

FIGURE 2–17.

Your Stress Management Program

Regardless of the techniques used, the ultimate purpose of all stress management programs is to demobilize the stress response as soon as it is not needed. By returning the body and mind to a more harmonious and normal state, energy can be saved for more important tasks. Develop a stress management program to address your needs and make it a part of your daily routine.

Managing Your Time

Learning time management skills can also help you reduce stress and get more done. **Time management** means *using your time wisely*. It combines planning and self-discipline.

Managing your time involves figuring out which activities are most important to you. When you have a task to finish, stay focused. Avoid distractions, such as phone calls and visitors, until you are ready to take a break. If you use your time wisely, you may be able to complete your tasks with time to spare!

Time Management Tips

- Prioritize your daily tasks, using the "ABC" system. *A* is for the tasks you *need* to do; *B* is for the tasks you'd like to get done; *C* is for tasks that can wait.
- Do it right the first time. People do learn from their mistakes. However, much time can be wasted by carelessness or by taking dangerous shortcuts.

MANAGING YOUR TIME

When you manage your time well, you reduce your stress. In this activity, you'll develop a time-management plan for the coming week.

WHAT YOU WILL NEED
- pencil
- large sheet of paper

WHAT YOU WILL DO
1. Divide your paper into seven columns, one for each day of the week. Create and label 24 rows, one for every hour of the day.
2. Pencil in the week's activities, including time for school, work, exercise, sleep, family, and friends. Include specific goals or deadlines, such as "History paper due." Include preparation time, such as "Go to library to research history paper."
3. Analyze your schedule. Are you surprised at how much time you spend on some activities? Where do you see conflicts? Are there things you'd like to do that you are not doing? Do you have adequate time to relax? To eat healthful meals and get plenty of physical activity?
4. Prioritize your tasks. Write "A" next to any task you need to do, "B" next to any you would like to get done, and "C" for any that can wait.
5. Rework your schedule. Be flexible, and remember that you may not be able to do everything. Try to consolidate tasks and delete low-priority activities.

IN CONCLUSION
Keep your time-management schedule on hand as you go through the week. At the end of the week, evaluate your schedule and change it if necessary.

- Set aside time for creative thinking. Spend a few minutes each day reviewing your goals and planning the next day's activities. This can be done before or after school, between classes, or for a short period at a scheduled time each day. It will improve your creative capacity and will help you to be innovative in planning and scheduling activities.
- Failure to listen carefully is a major barrier to using your time effectively. The average person's listening effectiveness is only 25%. If you improve your listening skills, you will avoid mistakes and misunderstandings, which will help you make better use of your time.
- Keep telephone calls short. Be polite, tactful, and helpful, but be brief. Avoid wasteful and unnecessary conversation.
- Prepare and use meeting agenda. Poorly run meetings waste everybody's time. A well-planned and followed agenda can shorten meetings and improve their quality at the same time.
- Prepare for meetings. Even if an agenda has been made, if not properly prepared, the meeting time will probably be wasted.

HEALTH SKILLS ACTIVITY

STRESS MANAGEMENT

Balance Your Schedule

One key to reducing stress is to use your time wisely and balance your schedule. Try these tips for managing a busy schedule.

- **SET PRIORITIES.** Figure out which tasks are required and which are optional.
- **PUT IT IN WRITING.** Include both required and optional tasks, but make sure you list (and do) the required tasks first.

- **PLAN YOUR TIME.** Allow enough time for each task, but also set aside some time for something you enjoy.
- **THINK AHEAD.** Think through all the details before you start a task.
- **USE REFUSAL SKILLS.** You won't always have time to do everything you want to do. Learn to say no to things you don't have time for.

- Develop plans for long-range projects. Planning is the first step in the management cycle or process. It is critical to effective time management.
- Allow time for the unexpected. No matter how well things are planned, the unexpected (problems, delays, etc.) will arise. If you plan too tightly, the unexpected will throw your entire schedule off.
- Don't do things that really don't matter. Busy work or doing low priority (C) tasks might make a person look efficient. In reality, it makes a person ineffective.
- Don't tackle too many tasks at one time. This is usually the product of failure to prioritize and poor planning.
- Don't work with unclear instructions. You will lose time checking for clear instructions or possibly make mistakes and need to redo the work.
- Finish one task before starting another. This relates to prioritizing and planning.
- Systematize work. After you prioritize your daily tasks, think about the best, most effective way the tasks can be performed.
- Don't procrastinate. What you put off today really will hurt tomorrow. Problems seldom go away. Decisions must be made. Do it when it needs to be done.
- Keep a time log. Try it for a week or two. Record all the activities you engage in during a period of time. Review the log for time wasters.
- Don't tackle the uncontrollables. Tackling the difficult is a challenge. Tackling the impossible is a waste of time.
- Deal with the causes of problems, not the symptoms. Just addressing symptoms is a real time waster. The problem will never be solved until the real cause is handled. Anything less is a waste of time.
- Don't try to involve everyone. Involve only those who really need to be involved.
- Learn how to say no. If you never say no, you will be overburdened with unnecessary work. Don't try to please everyone. Prioritize, plan, and schedule.
- Know how to reduce stress and tension.
- Learn from your mistakes—don't take it out on yourself if everything you do isn't perfect.
- Schedule difficult or most important tasks first.

Study Habits

This section will help you develop an adequate, orderly, and efficient study program. A good study program will also help you reduce stress. The suggestions and procedures are intended to serve as guides. In establishing a study program, select those methods which fit the situations. This section shows how to plan your time and direct efforts to get the greatest amount of learning in the amount of time spent studying. Studying is learning.

Effective studying is the one element guaranteed to produce good grades in school. Studying doesn't have to be boring, dull, or difficult. It can be interesting, enjoyable, and useful. If study skills are improved, studying will be more pleasant, learning will be faster, and grades will improve.

When to Study

- Schedule regular study periods. Attempt, as nearly as possible, to study the same subject at the same time in the same place each day. Some students prefer evening for studying while others find studying right after class to be more suitable. Study at the most productive time for the course. Study lecture notes right after class. If you will be called on to recite or answer questions, study right before class.
- Begin working on big assignments like science projects and term papers right away so there will be time to gather materials, prepare assignments, and make corrections and revisions.
- Take short breaks during long study sessions.
- Don't get stuck on one subject by spending too much time on it. Limit study time to approximately one hour per subject and only 20–30 minutes memorizing.
- Begin with the most boring or hardest subject and work toward the easiest or the one that is most interesting.
- Study similar subjects at separate times to avoid confusion.
- Avoid studying when tired.

FIGURE 2–18.
The OK4R method is an effective strategy for studying.

Scheduling

- A schedule saves time and energy in studying and keeps a person from forgetting important things. Feel free to change the schedule as necessary.

- Make a chart for a full week. Block in all fixed obligations: classes, meetings, meals, work, etc. Try to estimate how much time is needed each week for each subject and schedule those times.
- Weekends are good for working on longer projects. Try to keep one afternoon open for overflow work or recreation.
- Fit in these health essentials—they will help you get good results from studying:
  - Recreation
  - Sleep
  - Exercise
  - Food

How to Study

OK4R Method

Take more time for reading. One method devised by Dr. Walker Pauk is the *OK4R* method:

- **O. Overview:** Read the title, the introductory and summarizing paragraphs, and all the headings included in the reading material.
- **K. Key Ideas:** Go back and skim the text for the key ideas (usually found in the first sentence of each paragraph). Also read the italics and bold type, bulleted sections, itemizations, pictures, and tables.
- **R1.** Read assignments from beginning to end.
- **R2.** Recall: Put aside the text and say or write, in a few key words or sentences, the major points of what was read.
- **R3.** Reflect: The previous step helps to fix the material in the mind. To keep it there, relate it to other knowledge.
- **R4. Review:** This step is not done until just before the next quiz or test.

FIGURE 2–19.
In the PQRST method, it is important to state out loud what you have read.

PQRST Method

Another similar method of study which will greatly increase the learning of those who use and practice it is the *PQRST* method.

- **Preview** is the first step. Glance briefly at what is coming later, to see its general plan and idea, but not to get details. Methods for previewing material include:
  - Many authors break their material down into topics or subtopics.
  - Key sentences, which give the general ideal of what the paragraph is about, can be found at the beginning or the end of paragraphs.
  - The article or chapter may include a summary of the main ideas contained in it.
  - Scanning consists of running the eyes rapidly down a page, not reading word by word or even looking at every sentence, but picking a sentence here and there to get an idea of what the author is talking about and the general approach he or she is taking.
- **Question** is the second step in the *PQRST* method of study. While going through the *Preview* step, make up some questions which might be answered by a careful reading of the material. A list of questions may be found at the end of a chapter or reading assignment, so look for such questions first. The more you try to find the answers to good, intelligent questions while studying, the more effective learning is likely to be. The questions help concentration by focusing attention on main points. As you become skillful in making up questions while studying, you will notice that more and more of the questions appear on tests and exams. As you become familiar with the testing habits of individual instructors, it becomes easy to spot more and more of their test questions. Write down the questions while reading and study them when preparing for a test.
- **Read** is the third step in the *PQRST* method. Effective reading calls for action. The keynote of effective reading is reaction, that is, thinking hard about what is read. The extent to which your mind is alert and figuring out each point while reading is the extent to which you will learn what is being read.
- **State** is the fourth step in this method of study. This means say aloud what has been read. It is important to do this recalling verbally, by actually speaking the words aloud or quietly. The only way that you can tell whether you have a topic clearly enough in mind is to put it into words. The *State* step helps you comprehend and be able to put to use what you've studied.
- **Test** is the final step in the *PQRST* technique of study. This review step is really a shortened run through of the *State* step, but it is performed some time after the first study. Think of review in terms of testing how much is remembered and then repairing weaknesses, rather than merely looking over notes or materials. This procedure will help you remember more and be able to use the material learned.

Every step in the *PQRST* technique of study is a necessary link in a chain that leads to the most effective study. It can work no miracles. Learning will not happen without spending time and working. Here are some examples of using the method.

- **Preview:** The lesson is about . . .
- **Question:** I'll need to learn . . .
- **Read:** Get the thought of it.
- **State:** This paragraph says . . .
- **Test:** Monday's lesson said . . .

Memorizing

When an assignment calls for memorizing, try this method: Memorize actively, not passively. Use as many senses as possible. Try to visualize in concrete terms and get a picture in the mind. In addition to sight, use sound: say the words out loud and listen to the words being said. Use association: relate the fact to be learned to something personally significant or find a logical tie-in.

Ask questions in class until the lesson is understood. If the lesson is not understood, let the instructor know.

Verbalizing some types of study may be helpful. Repeat important dates, facts, etc., and write them down. Each repetition makes it easier to recall the information.

Write words, formulas, etc., which must be memorized on individual cards, and on the reverse side of each card, write the answer, meaning, etc. Study the cards until you know the material without hesitation.

Taking Notes

Taking notes helps you find and remember important ideas from your reading. It also gives you a way to quickly look up these ideas later if you don't save the article you read or if you don't have time to read the entire article again.

The temptation in taking notes is to try to write every word said. Resist it! What is needed is the important idea, not every scrap of information.

Keep these rules in mind:

- Use your own words to make notes.
- Condense information.
- Always record where the notes came from.

Learn the note-taking system the experts recommend. Use 8 1/2 by 11-inch loose-leaf paper and write on just one side. Keep notes for each course in a separate notebook or section of a notebook. Put a topic heading on each page. Then take the time to rule the page as follows:

- If the course is one in which lecture and text are closely related, use the 2-3-3-2 technique: Make columns of 2 inches down the left-hand side for recall clues, 3 inches in the middle for lecture notes, and 3 inches on the right side for text notes. Leave a 2-inch space across the bottom of the page for observations and conclusions.
- If it's a course where the lectures and the reading are not closely related, use separate pages for class notes and reading notes, following the 2-5-1 technique: 2 inches at the left for clues, 5 in the middle for notes, and an inch at the right for observations. (After a while drawing the actual lines will not be necessary.)
- In the center section or sections take your regular notes in the form you've learned during your years of school.

Hints for Good Notes

- Listen for key words.
- Listen for clues—such as "the four causes were" or "to sum up."
- Listen for transition words, such as *therefore, in conclusion, in summary*—words that indicate the instructor is leading to or repeating the main point. Do not hesitate to ask to have a point repeated.
- Listen for key words such as *because, in addition, later, therefore, also, in spite of, along with,* and *on the other hand.* They are keys to the relationships between the ideas the author or lecturer is presenting.
- Note any major conclusion if the class gets into discussion.
- If the instructor gives a point special emphasis, such as writing it on the board, put it in the notes.
- Write in script rather than in print.
- Get the point!
- Write in outline form whenever possible.
- Abbreviate words.
- In class, assume a position of physical alertness.
- Be mentally alert. Don't doodle.
- Maintain a proper mental attitude. Become involved.
- Do not be distracted by the speaker's mannerisms, his or her method of delivery, or the quality of his or her voice.
- Listen with the mind, not emotions.
- When it is appropriate to do so, raise questions in class.
- Don't let things slide. Leave blanks for words, phrases, or ideas that are missed. Fill in these gaps later.
- Study the day's assignment *before* you get to class. Then you'll know what's in the text and doesn't need taking down in your notebook. You won't waste time.
- Have plenty of notebook paper and a sharp pencil or a ready pen. If you have to stop to borrow, you lose time and could miss something important. You may become a class nuisance, besides!
- Don't try to write down everything—only the main ideas. One page of good notes is worth ten pages of trivia.
- Take notes in *your* words, not the instructor's. To do this, you must think, organize your ideas, and find your own words. If you don't understand the information well enough to express it in your own words, put a question mark in the margin and ask the instructor, after class, to explain it.

FIGURE 2–20.

Taking notes helps you find and remember important ideas from your reading.

- Copy *accurately* all formulas, rules, and assignments the instructor puts on the board.
- Develop a personal *notehand*. This is not the same as shorthand. You may wish you knew shorthand, but that *could* be a handicap because you would be tempted to take down everything. With notehand you can take down only important things, faster and better. What is notehand? It is your own personal set of symbols for words: a plus sign for *and,* a check mark that means *for,* the letter C̲ underlined for with. You will think of others. Samuel Pepys kept his famous diary in a curious notehand of his own. Woodrow Wilson developed a system of note taking when he was 14. Pope Pius XII left trunks full of notes taken in his own personal notehand.
- Leave a blank line or two as you write. That gives you room to add a thought later. Paper is cheap; don't crowd your words.
- Be sure your notes are readable. Don't scribble so fast that you can't read your notes the next day. Illegible handwriting costs businesses millions of dollars in delayed orders. Thousands of letters end up in the dead letter office because nobody can read the addresses. Students flunk exams because of unreadable notes.
- Check those ideas the instructor emphasizes. One student noted their importance with the letters *IMP.* After a test, he said proudly, "I counted my IMPs. I had marked as important 67 of the 100 exam topics."
- Include in your notes memos to yourself to dig deeper into subjects to find out more. Let's say you're studying the space program. Should we have spent these millions on earth problems, or have we had enough results from space trips to justify their cost? Get facts; seek different opinions. If you are studying Black History, find out what influence Gandhi had on Martin Luther King Jr. in the non-violent civil rights movement. What do the experts think? Take women's lib; was Joan of Arc an early example? Was Queen Elizabeth I?
- The clue column is the key to higher marks. As soon as possible after taking notes, make time to read them over—not studying them, just reading them. Check now, while it is all still fresh, to see if anything important was left out or is incorrect, and

FIGURE 2–21.
A cadet asks his instructor to explain an important topic after class.

then make changes. In the left-hand column, set down clue words to the topics in the notes. These clue words should not repeat information, but should designate or label the kind of information in the notes.

- Always record the instructor's examples. Pay close attention to note taking in the last few minutes of class time.
- Keep your notes well organized so you can quickly find what you need. These notes will make your papers clearer, your themes more interesting, your exams better illustrated. Your class discussions will become sharper and brighter, all because you are an expert taker of notes.

Outlining

The essential thing to do when outlining is to group ideas so that their relationships are clear. This means making main categories under a general topic and organizing the specific facts under them.

Outlining can come in handy when reviewing for a test. Textbook chapter headings might serve as large categories for organizing what you've learned about each topic.

Tests and Exams

The best preparation for examinations is keeping up with assignments and studying regularly. When reviewing, try to anticipate the questions the instructor might ask. Check the points the instructor seemed to emphasize in class discussions. Review the material under each heading and try to figure out what kind of questions could be asked about it.

Understand the information and relate it to what is already known.

It's good to be concerned about taking a test. It is not good to get "test anxiety"; this is excessive worry about doing well on a test and it can mean disaster.

If the test is objective (short answers), pay attention to details. An essay test might emphasize relationships among different aspects of the course material.

The most ineffective method of studying for a test is cramming—trying to learn everything at one time the night before. The loss of sleep and the disorganization of daily living habits may produce feelings of nervousness, tiredness, and confusion. The worst result of cramming is that the facts which have been so frantically accumulated will disappear in a short time.

Make use of returned examinations. Study the questions missed and analyze the wrong answers.

Read directions carefully when the instructor hands out the test. If you don't understand them, ask the instructor to explain.

Short-answer Tests

There are two important and effective steps that you can take to improve your grade on a short-answer test.

1. Make a 30-second survey of the exam to see how many questions there are, how difficult each one is, and the grade value given to each question. If the number of right answers determines the score, guess at questions you do not know. Don't guess, however, if the wrong answers will be subtracted from the right answers. In this case, the chances are guessing will hurt your final score.

2. Move along at a steady pace. Skip difficult questions and come back to them later. Don't waste time worrying about them. If you have time at the end of the exam, return to any unanswered questions. Mark the questions you skipped so you can find them easily.

Tips for Different Kinds of Tests

- **Completion:** Don't leave blanks. An answer thought to be wrong may be acceptable. Go back and check over the doubtful questions with a fresh viewpoint; this may eliminate the mental block.
- **True-False:** Guess if there is no heavy penalty on T-F questions.
- **Matching:** Answer the easy ones first to reduce the number of choices. Mark only one answer for each term.
- **Essay:** Keep these points in mind when preparing for an essay exam:
  - Read all the questions first and use the margin for noting phrases that relate to the answers. These phrases will help you write the essay answer.
  - Know the meaning of cue words such as these:
    - *Analyze*—to examine critically to show essential features.
    - *Compare*—to show differences or similarities between two or more things.
    - *Contrast*—to show differences when compared.
    - *Define*—to give a clear, not detailed, but precise meaning.
    - *Elaborate*—to develop a theme or idea in greater detail.
    - *Evaluate*—to appraise carefully, giving both the positive and negative aspects.
    - *Explain*—to clarify and interpret the details of a problem, theory, etc.
    - *Illustrate*—to explain or clarify by giving an example.
    - *List*—to set down under each other a series of facts, dates, words, names, etc.
    - *Outline*—to organize facts by arranging them in a series of headings and subheadings to show relationships.
  - Organize the answer; do not write haphazardly about the first idea that comes to mind.
  - Write legibly. Use ink unless otherwise directed by the instructor. Be sure questions are numbered correctly.
  - Read and check what you wrote before you turn it in. Be sure to answer the questions that were asked.

Libraries

Learning to use the public or school library can make studying more interesting as well as more efficient.

Most libraries also have a reference section which has dictionaries, encyclopedias, atlases, and guides to magazines and newspaper articles. Short biographies of well-known people, medical and scientific dictionaries, bibliographies (list of books on various subjects), and yearbooks are also found in the reference section. Even when not studying, the library can be a fascinating place to browse.

Additional materials that may be found in a library, such as videotapes, records, microfilms, maps, filmstrips, computers, etc., are helpful learning aids. These are great ways to make your studying more colorful and fun.

Don't hesitate to ask the librarian for help. The librarian can help locate material and make suggestions on other things you might not know.

A Final Word

To get the most out of any study program, look at the following suggestions.

- Develop a positive attitude toward study.
- Set goals and work toward achieving them.
- Study begins with attention in class.
- Turn in all assigned work on time.
- Proofread all material handed to the instructor.
- When taking notes, be sure that there is a system and order to the notes no matter what method is used.
- Review notes often—not just before a test.
- Before a test, rewrite notes in order to organize them for better study. This is not only a way to make the notes more organized, but it is a good study tool in itself.
- Take frequent breaks while studying (about every 15 minutes).
- Divide the notes into several sections. Give adequate study to all notes.
- Be aware of the areas that the instructor gives special emphasis.
- Anticipate questions that might appear on tests.
- Complete assigned reading on time. This will give you background information for classroom work.
- Set aside adequate time daily for review.

FIGURE 2–22.

Your success as a student depends on night after night of studying done by yourself.

How to Do Homework

Learning is a lonesome thing. Much of what you learn will come from the hard study you do in your own room on your homework. The assignments you study, the books you read, the TV documentaries you watch, the reports you work on, and the experiments you do—all this homework is the heart and soul of your education.

You can cram with friends for an exam. You can go out to get information about a survey. You can go to the library for a book. But your success as a student depends finally on the steady, night after night, responsible studying you do there by yourself. If you let it go, your work will show it.

Paderewski, the great pianist, said, "If I miss one day's practice, I know; if I miss two days, other musicians know; if I miss three days, my audience knows."

There are always a few smart alecks around who brag that they didn't crack a book last night. But when they want to get into a college, or get a good job, their ignorance will show.

Dr. James Conat, once president of Harvard, recommended 15 hours of homework a week. That's three hours a night if you want your weekends free! Homework is your personal responsibility, not that of your parents. You don't learn the math if your dad works the problem. A science exhibit is not really yours if your mother did most of it.

A Homework Plan

If possible, have a regular place to study, where you won't be interrupted. Study at the same place, same time, every night. That conditions your mind to *want* to study as soon as you get there. It's best to have a room of your own. It should be warm, restful, sunny in daytime and well lit at night. But you can study on the kitchen table. A famous comedian who was once an instructor says, "There were eight of us studying around the kitchen table. At one end sat Mama, sewing. At the other end sat Papa, determined that his kids should get an education. Sometimes he banged on the table so hard that all eight notebooks jiggled!" Jane Austen wrote her great novels in the parlor with the family chattering.

Get your tools ready: textbook, notebook, sharpened pencil, and everything else you need. A surgeon would not go into the operating room without his instruments. Have a map on the wall. Using a computer could make your papers more readable and easier to do. Most computers will spell check your work for you as well as define words, but if you do not have access to one, a dictionary and a set of encyclopedia are good investments, too. One student taped his lessons on a cassette at night and then listened to them on his way to school. His grades improved.

Have a good light. Eyestrain brings on fatigue and nervous tension. Get glasses if you need them. Your eyes are more wonderful than the finest camera—and only two to a customer. Take care of yours!

Let fresh air circulate through the room. It's a free study aid that keeps you from getting drowsy.

Have a personal bookshelf.

Have a bulletin board to thumbtack clippings, pictures, memos, statistics, and anything that will add to your learning. One very helpful thing is a century time chart, with each century columned in a different colored pencil, showing what events happened when. This will give you a sense of continuity.

Make a study schedule. Organize your time. Then vary your schedule only for emergencies. If your schedule says start studying at 7:30, don't put it off to go to the store, call up a friend, or watch TV. Discipline yourself. Sinclair Lewis believed that success in writing came largely from applying the seat of the pants to the seat of the chair! Same for homework.

FIGURE 2–23.

Your friends can be a helpful studying tool as long as you don't get distracted.

Have a comfortable chair, but don't slouch in it.

Have a table to spread your work on. Don't keep distracting objects there. Your sweetheart's picture could start you daydreaming. Concentrate!

Take a break. Time out is important. It freshens up your brain. Don't spend more than two hours on a single subject at a sitting. If your homework schedule is 7:30 to 10:30, try a break at 9:00. Stretch. Relax. A jog around the block may help. Go see what's in the refrigerator. But don't commute from your room to the kitchen every few minutes. Wait until your break, and don't dilly-dally about getting back.

Turn off the radio and TV when it affects concentration. If your material is fascinating, it's possible to study even with radios, friends, or a brass band in the room. When the material is dull or difficult, a pin drop could be distracting. Most learning takes everything you've got, so turn off the radio, make the friends go away, and send the brass band home. Concentrate!

Do a little rehearsing. Imagine that it's the next day and *your* turn to discuss the subject in class. Give it a trial run tonight. Watch yourself in the mirror while you speak. Record it if you like, and listen. You will see how you can improve it; next day in class you may do it superbly.

If you finish early, read something extra. If you are studying about space, read a biography of Einstein, who started the atomic age and opened our path to the moon.

This kind of extra reading will make you more interesting. Have you ever noticed that the most interesting people are those who have a little extra information?

Study your hardest subject last. Then you will go to sleep with this on your mind. Your subconscious can do wonders with it. It's like feeding facts into a computer.

When your homework is done, reward yourself!

Last: take a shower. Get your clothes and books laid out. Be ready for a calm, unhurried start tomorrow. Turn out the light and be off to your dreaming. By the way, try writing down your dreams. Somebody said, "We're all Eugene O'Neills when we sleep. Our dreams have the most complicated plots." Writing your dreams down now and then may help you understand yourself better, stimulate your imagination, and even provide fresh ideas for themes.

Tomorrow is a brand new day and you're ready for it. You know more. You feel like a disciplined, organized person. You've done your homework!

CHECKPOINTS

Lesson 2 Review

Using complete sentences, answer the following questions on a sheet of paper.

1. What are the two most common causes of stress?
2. What is the difference between eustress and distress?
3. What is the process known as the fight-or-flight response?
4. What are some of the symptoms of stress in adolescents?
5. List several illnesses that are related to stress.
6. Name four skills that can help you deal with stress.
7. What do you think the saying "Laughter is the best medicine" means?
8. Why are planning and self-discipline important to time management?
9. What does time management involve?
10. What are some things you need to do in order to manage your time more effectively?
11. List tips that can be used to help you manage your time more efficiently.
12. Why is it so important to study effectively?
13. Where are some good places to study?
14. What is the PQRST method of studying?
15. What is the advantage of taking notes during reading assignments?

Applying Health Skills

16. Make a storyboard for a teen video that demonstrates positive ways of coping with the kinds of stress that teens experience.

Behaving Positively

Making Decisions and Setting Goals

Decisions and Goals

Decision making and goal setting are two important health-related skills. Decision-making skills will help you make the best choices and find healthy solutions to problems. Goal-setting skills will help you take control over your life and give it purpose and direction.

When it comes to health, even a decision that may seem small can have great significance. Daniel, for example, persuaded his older brother to drive him to the video store. Because they were only driving around the corner, Daniel did not bother to fasten his safety belt. The car skidded on ice and Daniel hit his head against the windshield. What Daniel thought was a minor decision has left him with scars for life.

Health-related goals are also important. Goals that help you stay physically active and prevent injury will provide health benefits throughout your life. Moreover, people who set and achieve goals feel better about themselves and about their lives.

The Decision-Making Process

Decision making is *the process of making a choice or finding a solution.* It involves a series of six steps you can follow. Figure 2–24 illustrates these steps.

Step 1 is to identify the situation. What choice do you need to make? How much time do you need to make your decision? Steps 2 and 3 are to think through your options and consider the possible outcomes of each option. When evaluating your choices, you may want to follow the H.E.L.P. criteria to keep you focused:

- **H (Healthful)** Will it contribute to your health?
- **E (Ethical)** Does it show respect for yourself and others?
- **L (Legal)** Is someone your age allowed by law to do this?
- **P (Parent Approval)** Would your parents approve?

Quick Write

- List the decisions you have made since you got up this morning. Place a check next to those that had an influence on your health.

LEARN ABOUT...

- how decisions affect your health and the health of others.
- ways to make healthy, responsible decisions.
- the benefits of setting health goals.
- how body language can help you communicate.
- why "I" messages are more effective than "you" messages.
- how to improve your speaking and listening skills.
- how to use refusal skills.

VOCABULARY

- decision making
- values
- evaluate
- goal setting
- interpersonal communication
- body language
- mixed message
- eye contact
- active listening
- feedback
- refusal skills
- assertive
- prejudice
- tolerance

In Step 4 you consider your **values** and the values of society. Values are *the beliefs and ideals that guide the way a person lives.* For example, keeping a positive relationship with your family is probably one of your personal values. You know that if you decide to stay out past your curfew, family members may lose trust in you. By considering your values, and getting home on time, you show respect and earn your family's trust. Respect and trust are also core ethical values, which means they are shared by people around the world.

Evaluating Your Decision

After Step 5—making your decision and taking action—Step 6 will have you evaluate the results. **Evaluate** means *to determine the value of something.* To evaluate your decision, ask yourself the following questions:

- What was the outcome of my decision? Was it what I expected?
- How did my decision make me feel about myself?
- How did my decision affect others?
- How did my decision affect each side of my health triangle?
- What did I learn? Would I make the same decision again?

As with any skill, decision making gets easier with practice. For example, you might think about some problems that you or your family may face. Think through all six steps of the decision-making process to find a healthy solution for each problem. This practice will help you with future decisions.

Why Set Goals?

Do you feel that you do all you can do to protect your health, or are you aware that there is room for improvement? Perhaps you need to work on family relationships, or to better protect yourself from injury or infection. Setting goals will help you focus on the behaviors you want to change. **Goal setting** is *the process of working toward something you want to accomplish.* Achieving a goal requires planning and effort, and it can give you a great sense of accomplishment and pride.

Goals that you set for one area of your life often lead to the achievement of goals in other areas. For example, if you work toward the goal of becoming a black belt in karate, you will achieve fitness goals, too. Along the way, you may also reach other goals such as making new friends, gaining more self-confidence, and learning more ways to manage stress.

The Benefits of Setting Goals

Goals help you identify what you want out of life. They also help you use your time, energy, and other resources wisely. You will most likely have both long-term goals and short-term goals. Short-term goals often help you reach your long-term goals.

FIGURE 2–24.

The Decision-Making Process

What should Kendra do? Go through the six-step decision-making process to help her decide.

Kendra must make a decision. She and Michele have been best friends for a long time. Recently, Michele has been spending time with other students who ditch school. Michele has even boasted of going with them once. Now she wants Kendra to join them too. Kendra doesn't want to lose Michele's friendship, but she knows that her parents trust her to obey school rules.

1. State the situation.
2. List the options.
3. Weigh the possible outcomes.
4. Consider your values.
5. Make a decision and act.
6. Evaluate the decision.

Short-Term Goals

Some short-term goals are just that: goals that you want to achieve in the next few days or weeks. Your short-term goals may, for example, include finishing a homework assignment and writing an e-mail to your grandfather.

Other short-term goals are stepping-stones to long-term goals. Suppose, for example, that your long-term goal is to take part in a local charity 5-K run. Your short-term goals might be to run several times a week, to gradually increase the distances that you run, and to eat more nutritious foods.

DECISION MAKING

What to Do? What to Do?

Andy has been swimming since he was five years old. He loves to swim because it's fun, it makes him feel healthy, and it helps him keep physically fit. Now he has a place on the local swim team, and that requires regular practice.

However, Andy has been so busy with his sport that his grades have begun to fall. If they slip too far, he could lose his place on the team, but cheating on homework and tests could also get him kicked off. What should Andy do?

WHAT WOULD YOU DO?

Apply the six steps of the decision-making process to Andy's situation. Compare your outcome to the solutions of your classmates.

1. **STATE THE SITUATION.**
2. **LIST THE OPTIONS.**
3. **WEIGH THE POSSIBLE OUTCOMES.**
4. **CONSIDER YOUR VALUES.**
5. **MAKE A DECISION AND ACT.**
6. **EVALUATE THE DECISION.**

Long-Term Goals

Some goals take several weeks, months, or even years to achieve. For example, you might want to go on a rafting trip next summer, or to become a professional baseball player, or to go to the same college that your mother attended. These are long-term goals. They will take time, planning, and dedication. Short-term goals will help you meet these long-term goals.

Building Goal-Setting Skills

Goal setting is a skill that will benefit you in many areas of life. A good way to ensure that you reach the goals you set for yourself is to make a plan. Figure 2–25 shows the steps one teen used to reach his goal of making the school basketball team. Follow these steps when you set your own long-term goals.

Communication Skills and Leadership

Some people are much better communicators than others. They have the ability to get their message across, listen to what others have to say, and keep the lines of communication open. In short, they have good interpersonal communication skills. **Interpersonal communication** involves *the exchange of thoughts, feelings, and beliefs between two or more people.*

Like other skills, interpersonal communication must be learned and practiced. It is an important skill because you use it in all of your relationships. Think about how often you talk with family members, friends, teachers, and classmates. Effective

FIGURE 2–25.

The Goal-Setting Process

Here is one teen's plan to meet his goals.

1 **Identify a specific goal and write it down.**
Making the school basketball team.

2 **List the steps you will take to reach your goal.**
Run at least 2 miles four times each week.
Practice basketball every day.

3 **Get help and support from others.**
Ask my friends and my brother (who plays on the high school team) to play basketball with me whenever they can.
Get advice from the basketball coach about my training routine.

4 **Set up checkpoints to evaluate your progress.**
After 2 weeks of training, play a game of one-on-one against my brother.

5 **Give yourself a reward once you have achieved your goal.**
If I make the team, I will buy myself a new pair of basketball shoes.

interpersonal communication involves body language and careful word choice as well as speaking and listening skills.

Body Language

Interpersonal communication involves more than words. Your body helps to communicate your thoughts and feelings too. **Body language** is *a form of nonverbal communication.* For example, raised eyebrows might reflect curiosity, surprise, or interest. Drooping shoulders might indicate sadness, insecurity, or fear.

It is important for speakers and listeners to be aware of body language. Some forms of body language, such as smiling and nodding, encourage communication. Other forms, such as frowning and crossing arms tightly across the chest, discourage communication.

Sometimes your words and your body language don't communicate the same message. A **mixed message** occurs *when your words say one thing but your body language says another.* For example, you might say "I'm not angry," but your frown and clenched jaw convey a different message. Your body language gives your true feelings away.

Using "I" Messages

Imagine your reaction if a friend said to you, "You're never on time!" or "You're so bossy!" These types of "you" messages place blame on the other person and often cause hurt or angry feelings. Using "I" messages instead is a much more effective way to communicate. An "I" message is a statement in which a person uses the pronoun I to express an opinion or comment.

A well-crafted "I" message is a powerful communication tool. It states the situation and how you feel about the situation. It also offers an explanation for your feelings. Finally, it states what you need. For example, you might say, "When you were late for the movie I felt disappointed. I'd heard that the opening sequence was funny and I didn't want to miss it. Next time we go to the movies let's make sure we're early so we don't miss anything."

Speaking Skills

Interpersonal communication involves both giving and receiving messages. Speaking is the giving part. Good communication involves speaking clearly and carefully.

Here are some tips for improving your speaking skills.

1. **Use "I" messages.** Consider how your words will affect the other person, and express your concerns in terms of your own feelings. You'll be less likely to make others feel defensive.

2. **Make clear, simple statements.** Stick to the point and be specific. Make sure the other person understands what you're saying.

3. **Be honest with thoughts and feelings.** Say what you want to say. Be truthful and direct about your values while showing respect for your listener's values.

4. **Use appropriate body language.** Make sure your facial expressions, gestures, and posture match your message. Use **eye contact**, or *direct visual contact with another person's eyes*, to show that you are sincere.

Listening Skills

You might think that having good speaking skills means that you are a good communicator. In truth, though, good listening skills are equally important to interpersonal communication. A speaker's message has meaning only if the listener receives it. Good communication involves active listening. **Active listening** means *hearing, thinking about, and responding to the other person's message.* Here are some tips for improving your listening skills.

1. **Use appropriate body language.** Even if you disagree, stay calm and listen to what the other person has to say. Maintain eye contact, and use facial expressions and gestures that show that you are listening.

2. **Use conversation encouragers.** Show that you're listening by nodding or asking questions. Say things like "Really?" or "What happened next?" to show that you are paying attention.

3. **Mirror thoughts and feelings.** Repeat what the person said as a way of confirming what you heard. Offer feedback when appropriate. **Feedback** is *a response by the listener to what the speaker has said.*

4. **Ask questions.** After the person has finished speaking, ask questions or add your own comments or opinions.

Refusal Skills

During your teen years, there may be times when friends or acquaintances want you to do something that you do not want to do. Maybe you're just not interested. Maybe you don't have the time or the money. Maybe it's something that is unhealthy or that goes against your values. In these situations, refusal skills are useful. **Refusal skills** are *communication strategies that help you say no effectively.*

When you feel pressured to do something you don't want to do, you need to use effective refusal skills. Effective refusal skills let others know that you mean what you say. Like other skills, they take practice.

Using refusal skills will help you be true to yourself. You can resist without feeling guilty or uncomfortable. Other people will respect you for being honest about your needs and wants.

FIGURE 2–26.

Say **NO** and mean it!

Your body language can speak as loudly as your words do. These teens are likely to be understood because of their strong body language.

This teen is showing his refusal with defiant body language. This refusal will be taken seriously.

This teen's crossed arms tell others that her refusal should be taken seriously.

It's important to be assertive when you use refusal skills. **Assertive** means *behaving with confidence and clearly stating your intentions.* Show with words and actions that you mean what you say. Speak clearly, calmly, and in a firm tone of voice.

When you need to refuse someone, it is important to show that you mean what you say. Your body language, including eye contact, helps you to do this. Be sure that your body language and gestures match your words. If you stare at the floor or shift your weight from one leg to another, you won't seem very assertive. If you have a smile on your face and a teasing look in your eyes, the person pressuring you won't believe that you're serious. Instead, use eye contact, put a serious or neutral look on your face, and stand or sit up straight. Figure 2–27 illustrates how body language can show refusal.

An easy way to remember refusal skills is to keep in mind the letters in the word *stop*.

- **S**ay no in a firm voice.
- **T**ell why not.
- **O**ffer other ideas.
- **P**romptly leave.

Eliminating Communication Barriers

Have you ever heard the saying, "A chain is only as strong as its weakest link"? The same is true of communication. If one person in a relationship has good communication skills but the other person does not, the entire communication process suffers. Sometimes a person's beliefs or attitudes can make communication difficult. Examples of obstacles to clear communication include:

- **Image and identity issues.** Many teens spend at least part of their teen years searching for an identity—a sense of who they are and their place in the world. If someone is unsure of his or her values, the uncertainty can complicate the communication process.

FIGURE 2–27.

Good communications skills help you form healthy relationships.

- **Unrealistic expectations.** Avoid imposing unrealistic expectations on your listener; this may cause the individual to become frustrated or defensive.
- **Lack of trust.** Good communication is built on trust between two people. If you don't trust a person—if you believe that you can't count on him or her to tell you the truth or to keep a confidence—communication is very difficult.
- **Prejudice.** Some individuals have a **prejudice** or *an unfair opinion or judgment of a particular group of people.* Prejudice prevents a person from having an open mind and listening to new information. To avoid developing prejudices, you can demonstrate **tolerance**, or *the ability to accept others' differences and allow them to be who they are without your expressing disapproval.* Being tolerant helps you understand the differences among people and recognize the value of diversity.
- **Gender stereotyping.** Gender stereotyping is a type of prejudice that involves having an exaggerated or oversimplified belief about people of a certain gender. Assuming that all males like sports and that all females enjoy cooking are examples of gender stereotyping. Such assumptions make it difficult to communicate effectively.

HANDS-ON HEALTH

SENDING "I" MESSAGES

This activity will give you the opportunity to practice sending "I" messages. The more you practice this skill, the better communicator you will become.

WHAT YOU WILL NEED
- pencil or pen
- index cards

WHAT YOU WILL DO
1. Working in pairs, imagine everyday situations in which "you" messages might occur. Write the situation across the top of the card. Then write the "you" message below on the left. Change that same message into an "I" message, and write the "I" version on the right.
2. Here are a few sample situations:
   - Your older brother was an hour late in picking you up at the mall.
   - Your friend told a lie about you.
3. Read each "you" message to the class. Then read the corresponding "I" message.

IN CONCLUSION
1. Which types of messages did you think were the most effective? Why?
2. Think of a recent disagreement that you had with a family member or friend. How could using "I" messages have helped resolve the conflict?

CHECKPOINTS

Lesson 3 Review

Using complete sentences, answer the following questions on a sheet of paper.

1. Define the term decision making.
2. What are the six steps of the decision-making process?
3. What are three questions you can ask yourself when you evaluate a decision?
4. What are the benefits of setting goals?
5. Think of a health-related decision you made in the past month. Compare the process you used with the steps given in this lesson. Which steps did you use? Which did you not use? Would the outcome have been different if you had used all six steps?
6. What are some goals that you could set to improve your level of health?
7. Define interpersonal communication.
8. Give three examples of ways people use body language.
9. List four tips for improving speaking skills.
10. What is meant by active listening?
11. Choose someone you consider a particularly good communicator. Identify the skills that person uses to communicate so well.
12. What is the difference between an "I" message and a "you" message? Why are "I" messages generally more effective?

Applying Health Skills

13. Write a conversation a teen might have with himself or herself in which the teen decides to avoid friends who want to shoplift. Use the steps in the decision-making process. You might tape the conversation and share it with the class.
14. Make a videotape that demonstrates the power of nonverbal communication. Tape the body language of some volunteers and narrate the tape, explaining how body language sends messages. Ask the audience to interpret each person's message from his or her body language.

Mental and Emotional Health Care

Quick Write

- Briefly describe in writing two situations in which you experienced one of the following: fear, anger, love, guilt, mixed emotions.

Understanding Your Emotions

What Are Emotions?

Your **emotions** are *your feelings created in response to thoughts, remarks, and events.* The basic emotions are happiness, love, jealousy, sadness, anger, fear, anticipation, and joy. Emotions can influence most aspects of your life, including how you behave. For example, do sad movies make you cry? How do you react to being teased? How do you express extreme happiness?

Understanding Emotions

Emotions are neither good nor bad, right nor wrong. How you express your emotions is another matter. You can't always choose when an emotion will well up inside you, but you can choose how to handle it. People with good mental and emotional health seek healthy, responsible ways to express their emotions.

Important steps in learning how to express your emotions are shown in Figure 2–28.

Identifying Your Emotions

Recognizing the emotions that you experience will help you deal with them. Which emotions listed below are familiar to you?

- **Happiness** is a sense of well-being. When you are happy, you feel good about life in general.
- **Sadness** is a normal, healthy reaction to an unhappy event, such as a good friend moving away or a loved one dying. When you are sad, you may feel easily discouraged and have less energy.
- **Fear** is an emotion that can help keep you safe from danger. However, some fears, such as the fear of failure, may keep you from doing things you want or need to do.

LEARN ABOUT...

- expressing emotions in healthy ways.
- meeting emotional needs in healthy ways.
- types of mental and emotional problems.
- recognizing when a person is seriously depressed.

LEARN ABOUT...

- the warning signs of suicide.
- how to know if you need professional help for a mental or emotional problem.
- the kinds of treatments that are available.
- kinds of professionals who help people with mental health problems.

VOCABULARY

- emotions
- empathy
- anxiety
- panic
- resilience
- emotional needs
- phobia
- anxiety disorder
- personality disorder
- schizophrenia
- mood disorder
- clinical depression
- suicide
- therapy
- family therapy
- psychologist
- psychiatrist

- **Anger** is a common reaction to being emotionally hurt or physically harmed.
- **Love** is a combination of caring and affection that binds one person to another.
- **Empathy** affects your social health. **Empathy** is *the ability to understand and share another person's feelings.*
- **Sympathy** means understanding and sharing another's problems or sorrow.
- **Anxiety** can keep you from doing your best. **Anxiety** is *an overwhelming feeling of dread, much like fear.*
- **Jealousy** is a feeling of resentment or unhappiness at another's good fortune.

Expressing Emotions

People express emotions in different ways. We often learn how to express them from watching others who are close to us, such as family members. Learning to understand emotions and to express them in healthy ways is an important part of good mental and emotional health.

Expressing Anxiety and Fear

Have you ever felt anxious before giving a report or taking a test? When you are anxious or fearful, you take shorter breaths, your heart beats faster, and your muscles tense. Anxiety can help you accomplish more by releasing energy. However, too much anxiety and fear can cause you to lose sleep or even to panic. **Panic,** *a feeling of sudden, intense fear,* may be accompanied by physical symptoms such as dizziness and a pounding heart.

Sometimes just admitting to a family member or friend that you feel anxious helps. Other people may give you the reassurance and encouragement that you need. Overcoming your anxiety will help build your resilience. **Resilience** is *the ability to adapt to and recover from disappointment, difficulty, or crisis.* Resilience is also known as the "bounce-back" factor. People who develop resilience can bounce back from setbacks and disappointments.

Expressing Anger

It is normal to feel angry at times, but some people express their anger in unhealthy ways. Yelling, hitting, and threatening are not healthy ways to express anger. It is also not healthy to hold anger inside or to deny how you feel. Try these steps when you feel angry.

- Take a deep breath and stay calm.
- Focus on exactly what made you angry.
- Think of words to express your true feelings.

FIGURE 2-28.

Expressing Your Emotions

Expressing your emotions in healthy ways helps improve your overall mental health.

1 Identify the Emotion
Amy and Hannah used to be best friends. Now Amy feels angry with Hannah and avoids her. She realizes that it is because she is jealous of Hannah.

2 Understand the Cause
Amy had expected to get the lead role in the school play. Instead Hannah got the lead, and Amy just has a small part.

3 Respond in a Healthy Way
Amy recognizes that her jealousy is ruining a good friendship. She congratulates Hannah and offers to help her learn her lines.

- Calmly tell the other person how you feel and what action has caused you to feel this way.
- Tell the person what you expect from him or her in the future.

Understanding Your Emotional Needs

Everyone has physical needs, such as water, food, and sleep. You also have **emotional needs**. These are *needs that affect your feelings and sense of well-being.* Your basic emotional needs include the following:

- **The need to feel worthwhile.** You need to feel that you make a difference in the world—that you are making a contribution. Working toward short-term and long-term goals will give you a sense of accomplishment.
- **The need to love and be loved.** You need to feel that you are cared for and that you are special to people—family, friends, and classmates.
- **The need to belong.** You need to know that others accept and respect you as you are. Find friends who are accepting, reliable, and trustworthy.

Meeting Emotional Needs in Healthy Ways

Recognizing your emotional needs will help you meet them in healthy ways. You might, for example, offer to help someone without being asked. You could ask a friend how his day went and really listen to the answer. You can show affection for family members or volunteer for a good cause.

Meeting your emotional needs in healthy ways means making the choice to engage in healthful behavior. It also means abstaining from unhealthful behavior. Some teens may try to meet their emotional need for love and affection by engaging in sexual activity. This behavior carries many risks, including the risk of an unplanned pregnancy or a sexually transmitted infection. By choosing sexual abstinence teens show respect for themselves and for the health of others. Caring and affection can be shown in other positive ways, such as getting to know the other person better and sharing everyday experiences.

Mental and Emotional Problems

Everyone has problems from time to time. Most people overcome their problems and are able to function well at home, school, and work. About one person in five cannot cope, however. Such people need treatment in order to regain their mental health.

HANDS-ON HEALTH

COMMUNICATING FEELINGS

This activity will give you practice in expressing positive feelings.

WHAT YOU WILL NEED
- Paper
- Pen or pencil

WHAT YOU WILL DO
1. In a small group, develop a list of situations that could produce positive feelings for teens. An example might be receiving recognition from a coach after winning a track event.
2. Choose one of the situations on your list and write a skit in which someone expresses positive feelings to a friend.
3. Perform your skit for your classmates.
4. Have classmates evaluate your skit and, if necessary, suggest more effective ways of expressing the positive emotions.

IN CONCLUSION
1. Draw conclusions from the skits. Were students comfortable expressing positive emotions? Did the audience have useful suggestions?
2. Overall, what did you learn from this activity? How will it affect your behavior in the future?

FIGURE 2–29.

TYPES OF ANXIETY DISORDERS

Anxiety disorders can be grouped into the five categories shown here.

Disorder	Symptoms
General Anxiety Disorder	Restlessness, tiredness, difficulty concentrating, irritability, muscle tension, sleep disturbance
Panic Disorder	Pounding heart, sweating, trembling, shortness of breath, nausea, fear of losing control
Phobia	*Intense and exaggerated fear of a specific situation or object.* Examples: fear of animals, fear of flying
Obsessive-Compulsive Disorder	Obsessions such as a need to perform behaviors over and over; compulsions such as handwashing, counting, hoarding, and arranging possessions
Post-Traumatic Stress Disorder	Withdrawal or depression after a distressing experience such as sexual abuse, natural disaster, accident, or witnessing violence

The three most common types of mental health problems are anxiety disorders, personality disorders, and mood disorders. People with these disorders are troubled by worries, fears, or other emotions that interfere with their daily lives.

Anxiety Disorders

Most people experience anxiety from time to time. It's a normal reaction to challenging or worrying situations. Some people, however, have unreasonable or excessive anxiety. These people have an **anxiety disorder,** *a condition in which intense anxiety or fear keeps a person from functioning normally.* Figure 2–29 describes common anxiety disorders and their symptoms.

Personality Disorders

Personality disorders include *a variety of psychological conditions that affect a person's ability to get along with others.* People with personality disorders behave in unexpected ways. These disorders affect their thinking, moods, personal relationships, and control of sudden urges.

One of the most serious personality disorders is schizophrenia. **Schizophrenia** (skit-zoh-FREE-nee-uh) is *a severe mental disorder in which people lose contact with reality.* They may experience hallucinations in which they see or hear things that are not actually there. They may have delusions involving false personal beliefs that are unreasonable. People who have schizophrenia may not be able to sort out what is important from what is not. They may also be unable to separate what is really happening from what they imagine. For example, they may believe that they are other people, such as celebrities or historical figures.

Mood Disorders

People who feel sad when life is good, or happy for no apparent reason, may suffer from a mood disorder. A **mood disorder** is *a disorder in which a person undergoes changes in mood that seem inappropriate or extreme.* Mood disorders include bipolar disorder (also called manic-depressive disorder) and clinical depression. People with bipolar disorder go from feeling upbeat and energetic to feeling desolate and tired for no apparent reason.

Teen Depression

Everyone feels "down" or "blue" from time to time. Many teens, for example, become depressed about their looks, or about their relationships, or about getting bad grades. This kind of depression is usually short-lived and not very serious. At such times it's a good idea to identify the cause of your depression and to talk about it with someone you trust.

Clinical depression, also known as major depression, is much more serious. **Clinical depression** is *a mood disorder in which people lose interest in life and can no longer find enjoyment in anything.* The National Institute of Mental Health estimates that every year, about 5 percent of teens experience clinical depression. Some depressed teens abuse alcohol or drugs. Some try to harm themselves. Symptoms of clinical depression are described in Figure 2–30.

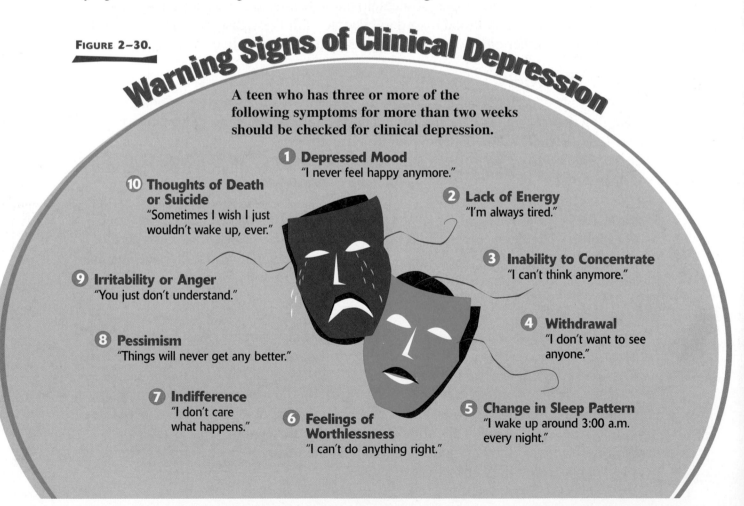

FIGURE 2–30.

Warning Signs of Clinical Depression

A teen who has three or more of the following symptoms for more than two weeks should be checked for clinical depression.

1 Depressed Mood
"I never feel happy anymore."

2 Lack of Energy
"I'm always tired."

3 Inability to Concentrate
"I can't think anymore."

4 Withdrawal
"I don't want to see anyone."

5 Change in Sleep Pattern
"I wake up around 3:00 a.m. every night."

6 Feelings of Worthlessness
"I can't do anything right."

7 Indifference
"I don't care what happens."

8 Pessimism
"Things will never get any better."

9 Irritability or Anger
"You just don't understand."

10 Thoughts of Death or Suicide
"Sometimes I wish I just wouldn't wake up, ever."

If you think that you are clinically depressed, don't just wait and hope the feeling will go away. Instead, talk to a parent, teacher, counselor, or other adult you trust, about how you feel. These adults can get you the help you need. Treatment for clinical depression involves counseling, medication, or a combination of the two. Teens who receive treatment will most likely go on to enjoy life again and feel better about themselves.

Suicide Prevention

Suicide, or *intentionally killing oneself,* is a serious problem in the United States, especially among teens. Suicide is one of the leading causes of death among young people. Every day, 14 young people between the ages of 15 and 24 years take their own lives.

Warning Signs of Suicide

You may know someone who has said things like: "The world would be better off without me," or "I'd be better off dead." Most people who commit suicide talk about it beforehand. Anyone who talks about suicide should be taken seriously. Tell a trusted adult immediately.

People who are thinking about suicide may show signs of depression at first. Once they decide to end their lives, they may feel better because they think that they have solved their problems. They may start giving away valued possessions. People who reach this point are in great danger. Other warning signs of suicide include:

- lack of energy.
- withdrawal from friends and family.
- no longer taking interest in favorite activities.
- no longer taking interest in personal appearance.
- taking unnecessary risks.
- expressing suicidal thoughts or talking a lot about death.

FIGURE 2–31.
Family and friends can be a source of help and support for teens who are having difficulty handling their problems.

What You Can Do

With most people, a suicide attempt is a cry for help. They don't really want to die, but they feel so much emotional pain that they can't see any other course of action. They need to be convinced that even though the pain seems unbearable, it will not last forever. If anyone you know talks of suicide:

- Try to react calmly and let the person talk out his or her feelings. Listen without interrupting.
- Don't make comments that challenge the person's intent, such as "You'd never have the nerve," or "You just want attention."

- Offer comfort and support. Tell the person how important she or he is to you and to other people.
- Urge the person to get help right away. Offer to tell an adult.
- Don't promise to keep a friend's talk of suicide secret. Tell an adult who will help. Telling could save a life.

Things to Remember When You're Down

Everyone has tough times and feels depressed now and then. Here are some points to remember next time you feel down.

- You are not alone. There are people who understand how you feel.
- Take care of your physical needs—get enough sleep, eat regular and healthful meals, and get plenty of physical activity.
- Avoid alcohol and other drugs, even caffeine. They will only add to your problems.
- Don't wait. Talk to someone about how you feel.

Getting Help

Talking about your thoughts and feelings may be difficult at first. You may feel frightened or embarrassed. You may feel that the adult will be shocked or annoyed at what you have to say. Realize that most adults understand and want to help. Sometimes all you need to do is let someone know that you need help. Needing help is nothing to be ashamed of. It is a mistake not to ask for help.

HEALTH SKILLS ACTIVITY

DECISION MAKING

If a Friend Seems Depressed

Leon has noticed that Keith just doesn't seem like Keith anymore. They have been friends since fifth grade. A month ago Keith's parents told him that the family will be moving to another state in the summer. At first Keith was excited about the move, but now he seems depressed about it. Nothing interests him, and he seldom smiles.

Leon is worried that Keith is showing the warning signs of suicide. However, he is afraid that if he says something, Keith might actually attempt it.

WHAT WOULD YOU DO?

Apply the skills for decision making to Leon's situation. What action would you take to find help for a friend?

1. STATE THE SITUATION.
2. LIST THE OPTIONS.
3. WEIGH THE POSSIBLE OUTCOMES.
4. CONSIDER YOUR VALUES.
5. MAKE A DECISION AND ACT.
6. EVALUATE THE DECISION.

FIGURE 2–32.

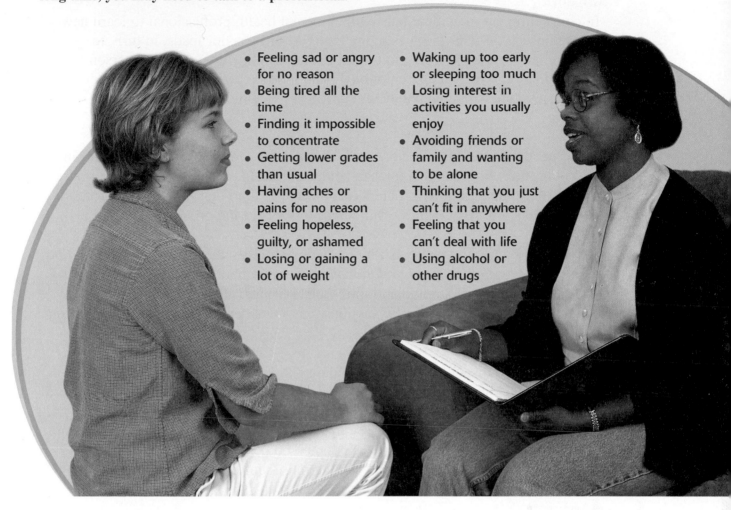

SIGNS THAT YOU MAY NEED PROFESSIONAL HELP

If you experience several of these signs, and if they last a long time, you may need to talk to a professional.

- Feeling sad or angry for no reason
- Being tired all the time
- Finding it impossible to concentrate
- Getting lower grades than usual
- Having aches or pains for no reason
- Feeling hopeless, guilty, or ashamed
- Losing or gaining a lot of weight

- Waking up too early or sleeping too much
- Losing interest in activities you usually enjoy
- Avoiding friends or family and wanting to be alone
- Thinking that you just can't fit in anywhere
- Feeling that you can't deal with life
- Using alcohol or other drugs

Seeking Professional Help

How can you tell if a problem is serious enough to discuss with a mental health professional? Learning the warning signs of mental health problems will help. Figure 2–32 shows some signs that may indicate a mental health problem for which a professional's help is needed.

Therapy Methods

There are various methods of **therapy**, or *treatment,* for mental health problems. These fall into two broad types: talk therapy and biological therapy. Talk therapy includes a variety of counseling methods. Biological therapy involves using medication to treat mental health problems.

The goal of all mental health treatment is to help patients change so that they can handle their problems better. Some professionals use only counseling, others rely mostly on medication, and still others use both types of therapy. A teen who is clinically depressed after the death of a close friend may be given medication to help improve his or her mood. The teen may also receive counseling to help her or him deal with the loss.

Counseling

In counseling, an individual talks with a mental health professional to learn new ways of thinking or behaving. Changing thoughts or behavior leads, in turn, to changes in feelings. By learning to think or behave in healthy ways, the person improves his or her mental and emotional health. Some people feel much better after just a few sessions with a mental health professional. Others may need months of counseling.

Some people choose to talk alone with a counselor. Others prefer to take part in group counseling. In group therapy, the counselor meets with several people at once who have the same or similar problems. Some people find that they benefit from the empathy and support that comes from other members of the group.

A variation on group therapy is family therapy. **Family therapy** is *counseling that seeks to improve troubled family relationships.* Family therapists are trained to help relieve family problems, strengthen family relationships, and solve small problems before they get bigger. The therapy sessions may involve all or some family members.

Counseling Methods

One form of counseling focuses on helping people think more positively about themselves. This kind of therapy can be especially helpful for people who experience depression. The professional helps the depressed person identify negative thoughts that are contributing to the depression. From that point, the person can be guided to more positive ways of thinking. Teens who are depressed because they focus on their weaknesses or mistakes, for example, can learn to focus on their strengths and achievements instead.

Another form of counseling focuses on changing behavior. This type of therapy is especially helpful to people with anxiety disorders such as phobias. The individual learns to stay calm while facing the situation he or she fears. Imagine, for example, a girl who has a severe fear of giving speeches. She might begin by learning to stay calm while giving a brief talk to a few friends. Her therapist might then encourage her to speak for a little longer and to more people. Eventually, she might be able to speak in front of a large group without feeling any fear.

Drug Treatments

Some mental health disorders can be treated with drugs. Different types of drugs are used to treat different kinds of illnesses. People with anxiety disorders may take anti-anxiety drugs, which affect the central nervous system. Those who have clinical depression may take antidepressant drugs, which affect brain activity. Drug treatment is highly individual. A drug or dose that may help one person could seriously harm another. The medications used to treat mental disorders can be prescribed only by a medical doctor.

FIGURE 2-33.
Family therapy is helping this family learn better ways to communicate with one another.

Sources of Help

People in a variety of roles and professions can help with mental health problems. Teens often seek help from the following people:

- **Parent or other adult family member.** You might be able to get all the help you need by talking with a parent or guardian, older brother or sister, or other adult family member. Family members have a special bond and care very deeply for one another.
- **Clergy member.** A leader of a church, synagogue, or mosque may have formal training in counseling. Even those who do not have such training usually have a lot of experience in counseling people of all ages.
- **Teacher or school counselor.** Many teachers and all school counselors are trained to help students with mental and emotional problems. Some counselors are specially trained to deal with problems that concern students.
- **Family counselor.** Instead of counseling individuals, family counselors see family members together. Most family counseling sessions focus on improving communication between family members.
- **School nurse.** If you are not sure what kind of help you need, a talk with the school nurse is a good place to start. School nurses are trained to deal with all health problems. A nurse can guide you to the help you need.
- **Social worker.** Many schools have social workers who help students and their families with social and personal problems that interfere with learning. They help students develop coping, social, and decision-making skills.

- **Psychologist.** A **psychologist** (sy·KAH·luh·jist) is *a mental health professional who is trained and licensed by the state to counsel.* Psychologists treat mental health problems by using one or several types of counseling.
- **Psychiatrist.** A **psychiatrist** (sy-KY-uh-trist) is *a medical doctor who treats mental health problems.* A psychiatrist is the only mental health professional who can prescribe drugs.

CHECKPOINTS

Lesson 4 Review

Using complete sentences, answer the following questions on a sheet of paper.

1. Define emotions. List five basic emotions.
2. What is the difference between empathy and sympathy?
3. Why is resilience sometimes called the "bounce-back" factor?
4. What do you need to do before you express your anger?
5. What are the basic emotional needs that everyone has?
6. Use the term *anxiety disorder* in an original sentence to show that you understand its meaning.
7. What kind of mood disorder is characterized by extreme mood swings?
8. What is the difference between clinical depression and the normal depression that most people feel from time to time?
9. Explain why clinical depression is a serious mental disorder.
10. Why do you think most people who are thinking of committing suicide talk about it?
11. Name the two broad types of therapy for mental health problems.
12. What are some of the benefits of group therapy?
13. Define the term family therapy and use it in a sentence.
14. Compare and contrast thought and behavior therapy.
15. What factors might determine which person an individual should talk to about a mental health problem?

Applying Health Skills

16. Write a public service announcement that informs students of volunteer opportunities in your community.
17. With a classmate, role-play a situation in which one person is depressed and the other reaches out to help. The person offering help should use strong communication skills.
18. Check the Yellow Pages of your local telephone book to find the mental health services that are available in your area. In which kinds of disorders do various groups and/or individual professionals specialize? Make a chart of your findings.

Avoiding and Preventing Violence

Violence in Our Society

Hitting someone is clearly an example of violence, but what about threatening to hit or hurt someone? Is that violence? What about destroying property or yelling mean and hurtful words at someone? Is that violence? The answer is yes. **Violence** is *any act that causes physical or psychological harm to a person or damage to property.* **Homicide**, *the killing of one human being by another,* is violence at its worst. In recent years the numbers of homicides and other violent acts have declined. The rates are still unacceptably high, however, and homicide remains a leading cause of death among teens.

Various factors have been suggested as causes for the high rates of violence. Some people point to the violent acts shown on television and in movies as contributing factors. Others cite changes in family structure that tend to leave children unsupervised for hours at a time. Many also believe the availability of guns to be a major cause of violence.

Violence and Teens

Much of the recent violence has involved teens. In 1998, about one-third of all victims of violent crime were ages 12 to 19. Teens are not just victims, however. Each year more than 120,000 youths are arrested for committing violent crimes. Teen violence often involves gangs, weapons, and drugs.

Gangs

Although gang activity was once associated with large cities, it is now a national problem. A **gang** is *a group of people who associate with one another to take part in criminal activity.* Typical gang activities include vandalism, graffiti, robbery, and drug dealing.

Quick Write

Write a short paragraph explaining why you think some young people resort to violence to settle differences.

LEARN ABOUT...

- factors that contribute to teen violence.
- policies to prevent violence in schools.
- ways to protect yourself from violence.

VOCABULARY

- violence
- homicide
- gang
- zero tolerance policy
- rape

Because gang members often carry weapons, they make areas unsafe for everyone. In addition, some of their actions, such as random shootings, are unpredictable. As a result, innocent people are injured or killed. The presence of gangs in a school or community causes people to live in fear instead of in safety.

Weapons

Firearm injuries are the second leading cause of death for young people ages 10 to 24. For every one person killed by a firearm, four are wounded. A survey of young people who had been shot revealed that 35 percent of them were carrying guns when they were wounded. Strategies to prevent firearm accidents include controlling gun ownership and installing safety devices on guns. Gun owners are advised to keep their firearms unloaded and to store ammunition in a separate locked place.

Drugs

Drugs and violence tend to go hand in hand. Drug users who are desperate for money to support their drug habit often turn to illegal and violent behavior. Drugs also affect a user's ability to think clearly and have good judgment. While under the influence of drugs, a person might shoplift, steal a car, or commit a violent crime.

Violence in Schools

Incidents of violence in schools have led to increased security measures. Many schools now keep all or most doors to the school locked. In some schools, students must pass through metal detectors to enter the school. School officials may search lockers and students' belongings if they have reasonable suspicion that someone is planning a violent act.

Many schools have also adopted a zero tolerance policy for weapons or weapon look-alikes, drugs, and violent behavior. A **zero tolerance policy** is a *policy that makes no exceptions for anybody for any reason.* Any student found guilty of bringing any prohibited items to school, or of violent behavior, is automatically expelled.

FIGURE 2–34.

School violence gets a lot of publicity, but the vast majority of schools experience little or no violence.

FIGURE 2–35.

Shield Yourself from Violence

Follow these precautions to protect yourself from violence.
What other actions do you usually take?

AT HOME

- Lock doors and windows when you are home alone.
- Open the door only to people you know well.
- Do not give personal information over the telephone or computer.
- Never agree to meet alone with a person you met online.
- If someone comes to the door or window and you are frightened, call 911 or the police.
- Never shoot firearms or pick them up, even if they are unloaded.
- When you come home, have your key ready before you reach the door. Do not enter if the door is ajar or appears to have been tampered with.
- Never tell a stranger that you are home alone. Instead, say that your parents are busy and can't come to the door or phone.

OUTDOORS

- Do not walk alone at night.
- Avoid poorly lit streets.
- If you think someone is following you, go into a store or other public place.
- Never hitchhike or accept a ride from strangers.
- Avoid entering an elevator alone with a stranger.
- Don't look like an easy target. Stand tall and walk with confidence.
- If someone wants your money or possessions, give them up.
- If you are attacked, scream and get away any way you can.
- Do not carry a firearm or other weapon.

Protecting Yourself from Violence

Protect yourself from violent crime by avoiding unsafe situations. Develop self-protection habits by being alert to what is going on around you and trusting your instincts. If a situation feels dangerous, it probably is. Be ready for threatening situations before they happen by planning ahead. With the adults in your family, identify some dangerous situations that could happen. Figure out what you could do to get out of those situations safely. If you suspect or hear a student talking about violence, report it to school authorities.

Choosing your friends wisely is another way to protect yourself. Avoid people who have a low commitment to school, participate in illegal activities, or use alcohol or drugs. Figure 2–35 suggests other ways to protect yourself from violence.

Protecting Yourself from Rape

Rape is *any kind of sexual intercourse against a person's will.* Over half of all rape victims know their attackers. Whenever a person is forced to have sex, whether with someone he or she knows or with a stranger, a rape has occurred. Rape is always an act of violence, and it is illegal. To protect yourself from rape, avoid situations in which an attack is possible. Here are some suggestions.

- If you go out alone with someone, make it clear that you're not interested in any sexual activity.
- Avoid secluded places.
- Don't drink alcohol or use other drugs or date people who do.
- Always carry money so you can call home or take a cab or bus if you feel unsafe.

Preventing Violence

People across the nation are making an effort to reduce and prevent violence. Here are some of the actions they have taken:

- Holding stop-the-violence rallies
- Supporting stronger gun laws

HEALTH SKILLS ACTIVITY

ADVOCACY

Help Prevent School Violence

You can help prevent school violence by acting safely and by encouraging others to play their part. Here are some actions that you can take and advocate.

- Refuse to bring a weapon or weapon look-alike to school, to carry a weapon for another person, or to keep silent about those who carry weapons.
- Immediately report any violent incidents or threats of violence to school authorities or the police.

- Learn how to manage your own anger.
- Help others settle arguments peaceably.
- Welcome new students and get to know students who are often left out.
- Sign (or start) a Peace Pledge in which students promise to settle disagreements peaceably and to work toward a safe campus.

WITH A GROUP
Work with classmates to create a brochure that encourages all students to play their part in keeping the school safe.

- Installing lighting in parks and playgrounds
- Breaking up gang control of public parks
- Starting Neighborhood Watch programs
- Supporting teen curfews
- Teaching nonviolent conflict resolution
- Assigning more police to street patrols

CHECKPOINTS

Lesson 5 Review

Using complete sentences, answer the following questions on a sheet of paper.

1. Define violence and homicide.
2. What is the purpose of a zero tolerance policy?
3. What are three basic ways you can protect yourself from violence?
4. Why do you think that violent crime levels in the United States remain unacceptably high?
5. What could be done in your community to discourage teens from joining gangs?

Applying Health Skills

6. Work with other students to research antiviolence organizations on the Internet. Make a list of the violence prevention methods they suggest. Create a handout based on your findings, and distribute it to your class.

UNIT 3

Wellness and Fitness

Unit Chapters

Chapter 3   Be Health Smart

Chapter 4   Physical Activity and Fitness

Chapter 5   Making Safe, Drug-Free Decisions

In Your Home and Community

Practicing Healthful Behaviors

Work with your family to create a family wellness plan. Start by identifying your family health care providers. Discuss your need for good nutrition and regular physical activity. Then create a family fitness plan and brainstorm ways to help and encourage each other to be active.

CHAPTER 3

Be Health Smart

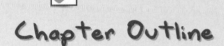

Chapter Outline

- Lesson 1   Health Care
- Lesson 2   Nutrition
- Lesson 3   First Aid

Quick Write

Briefly describe how you decide what to eat. Do you think that your eating plan is well balanced? Why or why not?

Health Care

The Role of Health Care

David is having a physical examination as required by his school. After checking David's immunization record, Dr. Lee gives him a booster shot for tetanus. When David tells her that he is having pain in his right knee, Dr. Lee carefully examines the knee. Then she writes out an order for tests on David's knee at the hospital X-ray department.

Dr. Lee, the hospital, and the X-ray technician are all part of the health care system. A **health care system** includes *all the medical care available to a nation's people, the way they receive the care, and the way the care is paid for.* The original focus of the health care system in the United States was to treat people who were sick or injured. Today the focus has expanded to include **preventive care**, which involves *keeping disease or injury from happening or getting worse.*

The Health Care System

To be an informed consumer of health care services, you need to understand how the health care system works. Physicians, nurses, dentists, dental hygienists, optometrists, pharmacists, and laboratory technicians are just a few of the professionals who work in the health care system. Health care providers work in a variety of settings.

Who Provides Health Care?

Health care can be divided into general care and specialized care. **Primary care physicians** are *the medical doctors who provide physical checkups and general care.* School nurses, nurse practitioners, and physician's assistants are also part of primary care.

Patients who need a specific type of care are referred to specialists. **Specialists** are *doctors trained to handle particular kinds of patients or medical conditions.* Pediatricians (peed·ee·uh·TRISH·uhnz), for example, deal with infants and

Quick Write

Make a list of the people who provide you and your family with health care. Beside each name, write what that person does.

LEARN ABOUT...

- different kinds of health care providers.
- why teens need regular checkups.
- how people pay for health care.
- the role of government agencies in protecting public health.
- the public health role of state and local agencies.
- nongovernmental health organizations.

children, and dermatologists deal with problems and diseases of the skin. Have you had experience with a health specialist?

You and Your Health Care

It is recommended that teens get annual checkups for preventive care. Sometimes called wellness checks, these visits are designed to promote wellness and detect any health problems early. The recommended ages for these physicals are between 11 and 14 years, between 15 and 17 years, and between 18 and 21 years.

A preventive medical checkup for teens might include:

- Testing hearing and vision.
- Checking for sports injuries, especially in the knee.
- Checking for scoliosis, which is a disorder of the spine.
- Screening for high blood pressure.
- Screening for eating disorders and obesity.

In addition to the annual wellness checkup, teens need to get other regular checkups and to receive whatever health care is recommended. Types of health care teens might receive are listed in Figure 3–1.

VOCABULARY

- health care system
- preventive care
- primary care physician
- specialist
- health insurance
- health maintenance organization (HMO)
- preferred provider organization (PPO)
- point of service plan (POS)
- public health
- Medicare
- Medicaid

FIGURE 3–1.

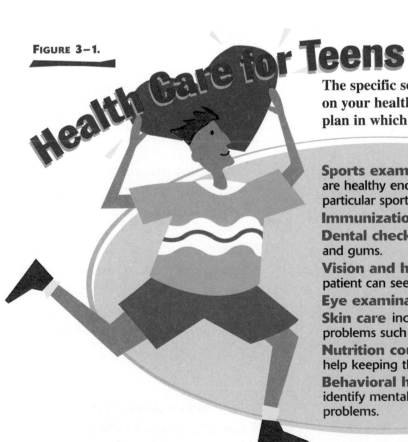

Health Care for Teens

The specific services that you receive will depend on your health and, possibly, on the health care plan in which you are enrolled.

Sports exams ensure that teens are healthy enough to participate in a particular sport.

Immunizations protect against specific diseases.

Dental checkups examine the health of the teeth and gums.

Vision and hearing testing determine how well the patient can see and hear.

Eye examinations check for eye diseases and disorders.

Skin care includes screening and treatment for problems such as acne or skin cancer.

Nutrition counseling assists those who need help keeping their weight within a healthy range.

Behavioral health assessment helps identify mental and emotional problems.

Where Do You Go for Health Care?

Health care facilities provide inpatient care and outpatient care. Inpatient care is for patients who have a serious illness or injury and who need to stay at the facility. A person recovering from major surgery, or one who needs constant monitoring, would receive inpatient care. Outpatient care is for less serious conditions or procedures. Examples are treating sprains, putting stitches on wounds, and extracting teeth. Patients get the care they need and then return home. Many routine tests are also provided on an outpatient basis.

Health services are available in most communities in a variety of forms. Facilities in your community may include the following:

- **Clinics.** Primary care physicians and specialists may provide outpatient care in a community clinic. Local clinics often receive government funding.
- **Private practice.** Primary care physicians and specialists who work in private practice work for themselves.
- **Group practice.** Often two or more physicians join together to offer health care in a group practice. Doctors in group practice share office space, equipment, and support staff.
- **Hospitals.** Most hospitals offer both inpatient and outpatient care. Some doctors work only in a hospital. Others have offices elsewhere and use the hospital facilities when their patients need them.

How People Pay for Health Care

Many people have some form of **health insurance**, which is *a plan in which private companies or government programs pay for part of a person's medical costs.*

With private insurance, a person pays a monthly fee to the insurance company. In return, the company pays part of most of the person's medical costs. Many people have private insurance through their employers. Common types of private insurance plans include:

- **Health Maintenance Organizations (HMOs).** An **HMO** is *an organization that provides health care for a fixed price.* People who belong to an HMO pay a monthly fee regardless of how much health care they need. Usually they must see only doctors who have signed a contract with the HMO.
- **Preferred Provider Organizations (PPOs).** A **PPO** is *a type of insurance in which medical providers agree to charge less for members of the plan.* Members who choose doctors outside the plan pay more.
- **Point of Service (POS) plans.** A **POS** is *a health plan that allows members to choose providers inside or outside the plan.* Choosing an outside provider often results in a greater out-of-pocket cost to members.

Public Health

Certain aspects of health need to be managed as part of a larger effort. This larger effort, managed by federal, state, and local governments, is referred to as public health. **Public health** involves *the protection and promotion of health at the*

HEALTH SKILLS ACTIVITY

ACCESSING INFORMATION

Health Care in the Community

Most communities have a variety of health care services. Examples include:

- home nursing care for patients who need medical help in their own home.
- relief support for people who are caring for an ill or injured family member.
- Alateen and Al-Anon groups for family members who live with alcoholics.
- community health screenings.
- flu shots for the elderly and other at-risk individuals.
- recreational sports and activity programs, providing supervised physical activity sessions.

WITH A GROUP
Make a list of health care resources offered at your school and in your community. You can obtain the information from parents and from local media. Then create a brochure that includes the name and number of each resource you found.

community level. In this context, the community may be a small town, a large city, a state, or even the nation. Many organizations are involved in administering public health at these different levels.

Federal Health Agencies: Medicare and Medicaid

The main health organization of the federal government is the Department of Health and Human Services (HHS). HHS is responsible for more than 300 programs that protect the health of all Americans. These programs include two federal health insurance programs—Medicare and Medicaid. Figure 3–2 lists some of the HHS public health divisions.

Medicare and Medicaid were begun in 1965 to provide health coverage for seniors and people who could not afford health care. **Medicare** *covers people age 65 and over and some people younger than 65 who have medical disabilities or other specific conditions.* Medicare is a fee-for-service plan. People who use Medicare see doctors who accept Medicare patients and pay part of the cost of their care. The rest of the costs are paid by Medicare.

People with limited income and financial resources may qualify for Medicaid. **Medicaid** is *a joint federal and state program that helps pay medical costs* for people who qualify. Medicaid programs vary from state to state. Medicaid may cover some things that Medicare doesn't cover, such as nursing home care, home health care, and some prescription drugs.

FIGURE 3–2.

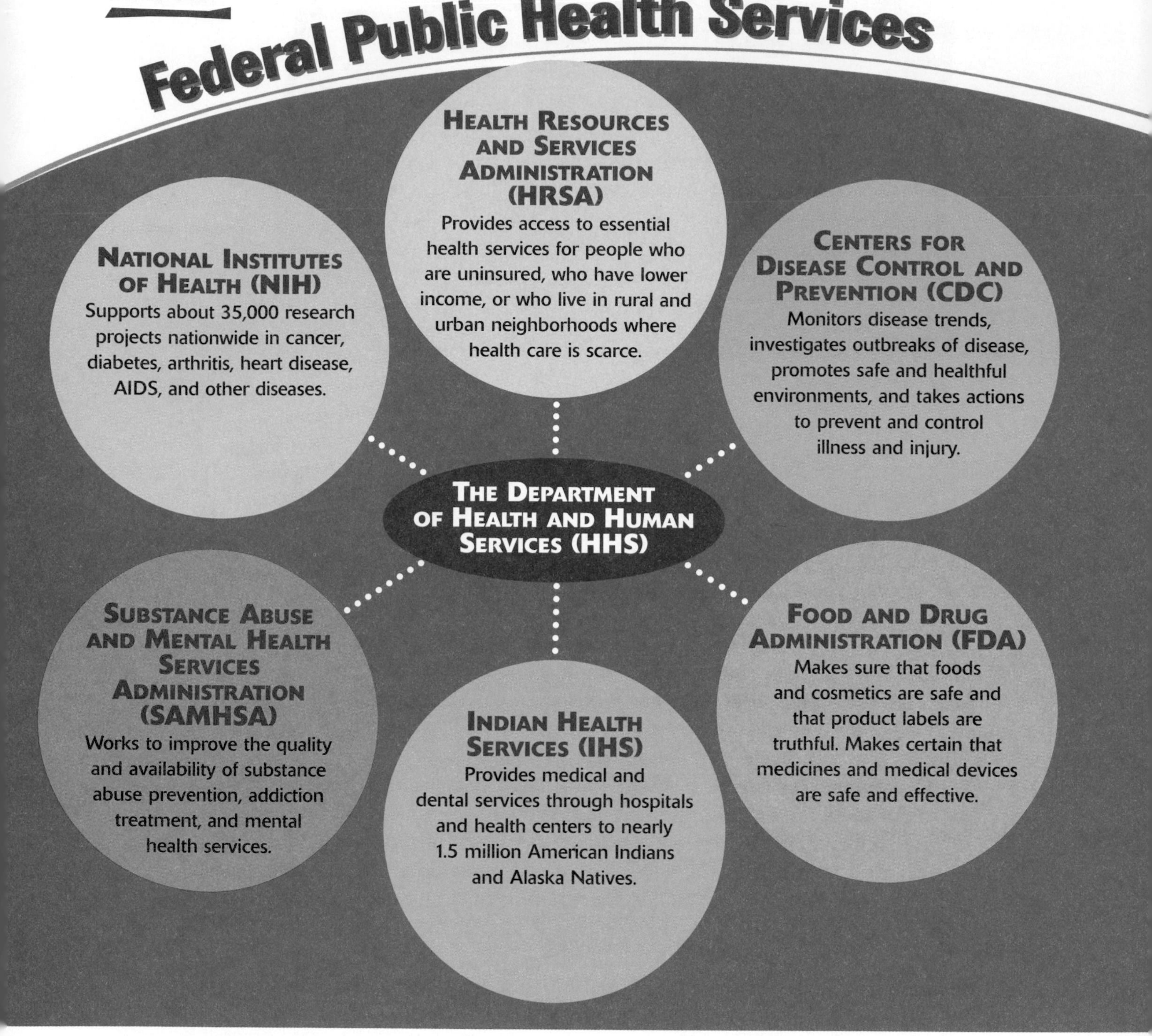

Federal Public Health Services

HEALTH RESOURCES AND SERVICES ADMINISTRATION (HRSA)
Provides access to essential health services for people who are uninsured, who have lower income, or who live in rural and urban neighborhoods where health care is scarce.

NATIONAL INSTITUTES OF HEALTH (NIH)
Supports about 35,000 research projects nationwide in cancer, diabetes, arthritis, heart disease, AIDS, and other diseases.

CENTERS FOR DISEASE CONTROL AND PREVENTION (CDC)
Monitors disease trends, investigates outbreaks of disease, promotes safe and healthful environments, and takes actions to prevent and control illness and injury.

THE DEPARTMENT OF HEALTH AND HUMAN SERVICES (HHS)

SUBSTANCE ABUSE AND MENTAL HEALTH SERVICES ADMINISTRATION (SAMHSA)
Works to improve the quality and availability of substance abuse prevention, addiction treatment, and mental health services.

INDIAN HEALTH SERVICES (IHS)
Provides medical and dental services through hospitals and health centers to nearly 1.5 million American Indians and Alaska Natives.

FOOD AND DRUG ADMINISTRATION (FDA)
Makes sure that foods and cosmetics are safe and that product labels are truthful. Makes certain that medicines and medical devices are safe and effective.

Other Federal Agencies That Protect Consumer Rights
Other federal agencies work to protect and enforce consumer rights. These include:

- **Consumer Product Safety Commission (CPSC).** The CPSC works to reduce the risk of injury or death from unsafe products. It can ban products it finds dangerous and can order manufacturers to notify people who have bought an unsafe product.
- **Food Safety and Inspection Service (FSIS).** The FSIS oversees the safety of meat and poultry.

- **Federal Trade Commission (FTC).** The FTC protects consumers from unfair trade practices. It also regulates advertising in order to prevent advertisers from presenting misleading information.

State and Local Health Agencies

State and community health organizations also offer services independently. All states and most cities have health departments. The work of these departments varies from place to place, but all help to control and prevent disease. Some of the tasks performed by local health departments include the following:

- Provide basic health care services to people with low incomes.
- Monitor the safety of water and sewage systems.
- Make sure that garbage is removed and properly handled and disposed of.
- Set standards of cleanliness and sanitation for restaurants.
- Offer health education and promotion programs.

HEALTH SKILLS ACTIVITY

ADVOCACY

Public Health

Use your advocacy skills to influence others to support a public health-related law, ordinance, goal, or project. Here are some of the many ways that teens can practice public health advocacy:

- Set an example by following health and safety laws and ordinances.
- Never take an action that could endanger the health or safety of others.
- Volunteer to help charitable organizations sponsoring events that promote public health.
- Learn which groups in your community deal with public health issues. Identify their current goals and support them.
- If you notice a condition or activity that threatens public health, notify the proper authorities.

WITH A GROUP

Brainstorm a list of public health issues in your community. From your list, choose one issue to work on. Make an advocacy plan to bring about change. Carry out your plan.

Nongovernmental Health Organizations

Governmental public health organizations are funded by the taxes people pay. Nongovernmental health organizations rely mostly on contributions and volunteers to provide important public health services. Some of these organizations focus on one type of disease. Examples are the American Heart Association, the Asthma and Allergy Foundation of America, and the American Cancer Society. They pay for research for ways to prevent and cure the disease. They also help people who have the disease, and they provide programs that teach ways to prevent it.

The American Red Cross is one of the first organizations on the scene after a natural disaster. Its workers are trained to respond quickly to a large-scale emergency. The Red Cross collects blood from volunteers and distributes it to hospitals for people who need transfusions. It also offers courses on first aid, safety, and health.

CHECKPOINTS

Lesson 1 Review

Using complete sentences, answer the following questions on a sheet of paper.

1. Define the term *preventive care* and use it in an original sentence.
2. What is the difference between a *primary care physician* and a *specialist?*
3. What is the difference between the ways HMOs, PPOs, and POS plans pay for health care?
4. Why do you think there is more emphasis on preventive care now than there was in the past?
5. Name four things a typical teen could expect his or her doctor to check for during a preventive medical checkup.
6. Define the term *public health* and use it in an original sentence.
7. What is the name of the main health organization of the federal government?
8. Which federal agency is authorized to ban the sale of unsafe products?
9. Name the HHS division you would contact for information on safe ways to store and prepare food.
10. Which nongovernmental health organizations would you contact for information on the latest cancer research? On where to find a safe place to stay after a serious storm?

Applying Health Skills

11. You have learned of the importance of preventive care for teens. Prepare a brief announcement in which you explain why teens, no matter how healthy they appear to be, need to get checkups. If possible, arrange for your announcement to be delivered at school.
12. Interview the manager of your school cafeteria or the manager of a local public swimming pool. Find out what state and local health laws the manager must obey. Share your information with your classmates.

Nutrition

Why You Need Nutritious Food

When you drink a cool glass of milk or bite into a crisp apple, you probably are thinking about the taste and texture of the foods. Yet while you're enjoying the pleasures of eating, the foods you eat are influencing your overall health and wellness. When you make healthy choices about foods, you're more likely to look your best and perform at your peak.

One important reason you eat is to take in calories. **Calories** are *units of heat that measure the energy used by the body and the energy that foods supply to the body.* You need this energy for everything you do—from running laps to doing your homework. Food also provides **nutrients**, *substances in food that your body needs.* Nutrients have many important roles, including

- giving you energy.
- building new tissues and repairing cells.
- helping your body's processes and systems run smoothly.

Different foods contain different types and amounts of nutrients. You need a wide variety of healthful foods to get all the nutrients your body needs.

Nutrition is *the process of using food and its substances to help your body have energy, grow, develop, and work properly.* Good nutrition is one of the main factors in building and maintaining good health.

What Influences Your Food Choices?

What are your favorite foods? Do you know why you make these food choices? Chances are that you eat a variety of foods and that your food choices are influenced by many different factors. Figure 3–3 describes some of these factors.

Appetite and Hunger

When you smell popcorn, do you want to try some? Does the sight of fresh strawberries make your mouth water? Do you love

Quick Write

What's your idea of a healthful meal or snack? Create a menu for what you consider a day of healthful foods you would enjoy.

LEARN ABOUT...

- why your body needs nutritious food.
- what influences your food choices.
- the difference between appetite and hunger.
- getting the nutrients you need.
- how your body uses different nutrients.
- the sources of different nutrients.
- the need for water and fiber in your meals and snacks.
- substances in food that should be limited.
- resources that can help you make wise food choices.

LEARN ABOUT...

- balancing the different foods you eat.
- using the nutrition information on food labels.

VOCABULARY

- calories
- nutrients
- nutrition
- appetite
- hunger
- nutrient deficiency
- carbohydrates
- proteins
- amino acids
- saturated fats
- unsaturated fats
- triglycerides
- vitamins
- minerals
- fiber
- trans fatty acids
- cholesterol
- Dietary Guidelines for Americans
- foodborne illness
- Percent Daily Value

to crunch on fresh carrots? These are signs of your appetite at work. Your **appetite** is *the psychological desire for food.* It may be stimulated by the smell, sight, or texture of food.

Appetite is different from hunger. **Hunger** is *the physical need for food.* When you are hungry, your brain sends a signal to find food. You may hear your stomach growl or feel it contract. You may also feel tired or light-headed. These signs indicate that your body's supply of food energy and nutrients is running low.

When you eat, the hunger gradually goes away. Your stomach needs about 20 minutes to send a message back to the brain to turn off the hunger switch. Eating slowly allows time for your brain to receive the message. Many people overeat when they eat too fast.

Food and Emotions

Food can meet emotional needs too. Do certain foods that you associate with special events bring you happy memories? Perhaps you have favorite foods that comfort you when you are feeling ill or sad. Using food as a way of dealing with negative emotions is not a healthy way to respond to these feelings. People who eat to relieve stress or boredom need to develop more appropriate coping skills.

Getting the Nutrients You Need

Everyone needs the same nutrients to maintain good health, but the amount of nutrients needed depends on a person's age, gender, state of health, and level of activity. When you do not get enough of a particular nutrient, you could have a **nutrient deficiency**, *a shortage of a nutrient.*

As a teen, you need more calcium than you did before for building strong and growing bones. However, suppose you don't eat enough foods that supply calcium. Over time, the calcium deficiency could affect the strength of your teeth and bones. A food plan that includes calcium-rich foods helps prevent osteoporosis, a disease in which bones become brittle and more liable to break. You also need more iron because your body makes more red blood cells as you grow. A shortage of iron can lead to a blood disease called anemia. In general, teens need more of most nutrients to support growth and satisfy energy needs.

Most people in the United States get plenty of food, yet many still do not get the nutrients they need. This is partly the result of lifestyles that tend to encourage fast foods and promote foods that are high in fat and sugar. Eating low-nutrient, high-fat foods, along with overeating, can lead to long-term health problems such as heart disease, cancer, and diabetes. Your nutritional knowledge and healthy eating habits are your best defense against poor nutrition.

FIGURE 3-3.

FACTORS THAT INFLUENCE FOOD CHOICES

Factors	Description
Family and friends	You may prefer certain foods, like burritos or vegetable stir-fry, because you have grown up eating them at home. At the same time, your friends may persuade you to try new and different foods.
Cultural background	Different cultures have different traditions about what they eat, and perhaps where, how, and with whom they eat. For example, Mexican American families may eat beans, corn, and tortillas, while Italian American families may favor pasta dishes. Many Americans enjoy trying a variety of ethnic foods. What cultural foods are part of your eating pattern?
Food availability	Some foods are regional, growing only in certain areas. Some are seasonal and available only in certain months. Fresh blueberries, for example, are plentiful in summer but hard to find in the winter months. Still, modern transportation and growing methods have expanded the food supply. Many foods that were once regional or seasonal are now available in many areas year-round.
Time and money resources	Schedules and budgets affect a family's food choices. Eating fast foods or convenience foods often takes less time. Some families may look for bulk foods that provide more for the dollar.
Advertising	Have you ever tried a food because you heard about it from a television or magazine ad? Ads can influence our choices of certain brands and products and may persuade us to try new foods.
Knowledge of nutrition	The more you know about the nutrients in different foods, the better able you are to choose foods that supply the health benefits that you need.
Personal preferences	Your personal likes and dislikes and overall health goals contribute to your food choices. Some people have allergies or medical conditions that affect their food choices. Among the foods that most often cause allergic reactions are milk, peanuts, wheat, and shellfish.

The Six Types of Nutrients

Food nourishes you with more than 40 different nutrients. These nutrients are grouped into six categories: carbohydrates, proteins, fats, vitamins, minerals, and water. Eating a variety of foods to provide these nutrients is essential to good health.

Carbohydrates

Carbohydrates are *the sugars and starches that provide your body with most of its energy.* Carbohydrates can be either simple or complex. Simple carbohydrates, or sugars, are found in fruit, milk, and honey. Sugar is also added to candy, cookies, and other foods. Complex carbohydrates, or starches, are found in breads, cereals, pasta, rice, potatoes, dry beans, corn, and other starchy vegetables. As your body digests complex carbohydrates, it breaks them down into simple sugars, which are absorbed into the bloodstream to provide energy. Nutritionists recommend that 45 to 65 percent of your daily calories come from carbohydrates derived from fiber-rich fruits, vegetables, and whole grains.

Proteins

Proteins are *nutrients your body uses to build, repair, and maintain cells and tissues.* They also help your body fight disease, and they provide energy when your body doesn't get enough from other sources.

Amino acids are *small units that make up protein.* Your body can produce most amino acids on its own. The remaining ones, called essential amino acids, must come from food you eat.

Foods from animal sources, such as meat, fish, poultry, eggs, milk, and yogurt, contain complete proteins. They provide all the essential amino acids. Foods from plant sources, such as soybeans, nuts, peas, and dry beans, contain incomplete proteins. They lack one or more of the essential amino acids. Vegetarians can combine foods from plant sources to make complete proteins. Consuming a variety of plant foods, such as beans, rice, nuts, and peas, gives you complete proteins and provides the essential amino acids. You don't need to eat these foods at the same meal to get the benefit. Just have a good variety throughout the whole day.

Fats

Fats are nutrients that provide energy and perform many functions for your body. They carry fat-soluble vitamins and promote healthy skin and normal growth. Foods that are high in fats tend to be high in calories. For this reason, health experts generally recommend that your eating plan include only moderate amounts of fat.

Saturated fats are *fats that are solid at room temperature.* They are found mostly in animal and dairy products such as butter, red meat, cheese, and whole milk. An eating pattern that includes too many saturated fats can increase a person's risk of heart disease.

FIGURE 3-4.

Combining beans, rice, and a green leafy vegetable can provide complete protein and essential vitamins and minerals.

Unsaturated fats are *fats that remain liquid at room temperature.* They come mainly from plant sources. Foods containing mostly unsaturated fats include vegetable oils, nuts, avocados, and olives. Unsaturated fats lower cholesterol levels and are considered healthier than saturated fats.

Triglycerides are *the chemical form in which most fat exists in food and the chief form of fat storage in the body.* Triglycerides are derived from fats eaten in foods or made in the body from other energy sources such as carbohydrates. Triglycerides are long chains of fatty acids that provide much of the energy your body's cells need to function. Too high levels of triglycerides circulating in the bloodstream have been linked to heart disease in some people.

Vitamins

Vitamins are *substances needed in small quantities to help regulate body functions.* Vitamins help your body fight infections, use other nutrients, and perform other tasks. Water-soluble vitamins, such as vitamin C and B vitamins, dissolve in water, cannot be stored in your body, and should be part of your daily eating pattern. Fat-soluble vitamins, including vitamins A, D, E, and K, dissolve in fat and can be stored in body fat until needed. See Figure 3–5 for more information about functions and sources of selected vitamins.

Minerals

Minerals are *elements needed in small quantities for forming healthy bones and teeth, and for regulating certain body processes.* Calcium, phosphorus, and magnesium help build strong bones and teeth. Iron plays a vital role in making red blood cells. Potassium is involved in both chemical and cellular functions in the body. For example, it is necessary for building muscles, normal body growth, and proper functioning of nerve cells in the brain and throughout the body. See Figure 3–5 for more information about functions and sources of selected minerals.

Water

Water is a nutrient that is vital to your life and health. It makes up over half of your body and serves many important functions. Water transports nutrients through your body, helps you digest food, lubricates your joints, removes wastes, and helps regulate body temperature.

You lose water every day in urine and sweat, and you need to replace it continually. A combination of thirst and normal drinking behavior—especially consuming fluids with meals—usually is enough to maintain normal hydration. However, if it's particularly hot or you're involved in prolonged physical activity, it's important to consume fluid regularly during the activity and to drink several glasses of water or other fluid after the physical activity is completed. Choose liquids such as plain drinking water, fruit juices, milk, and soup. Beverages with caffeine or added sugar are not the best choices.

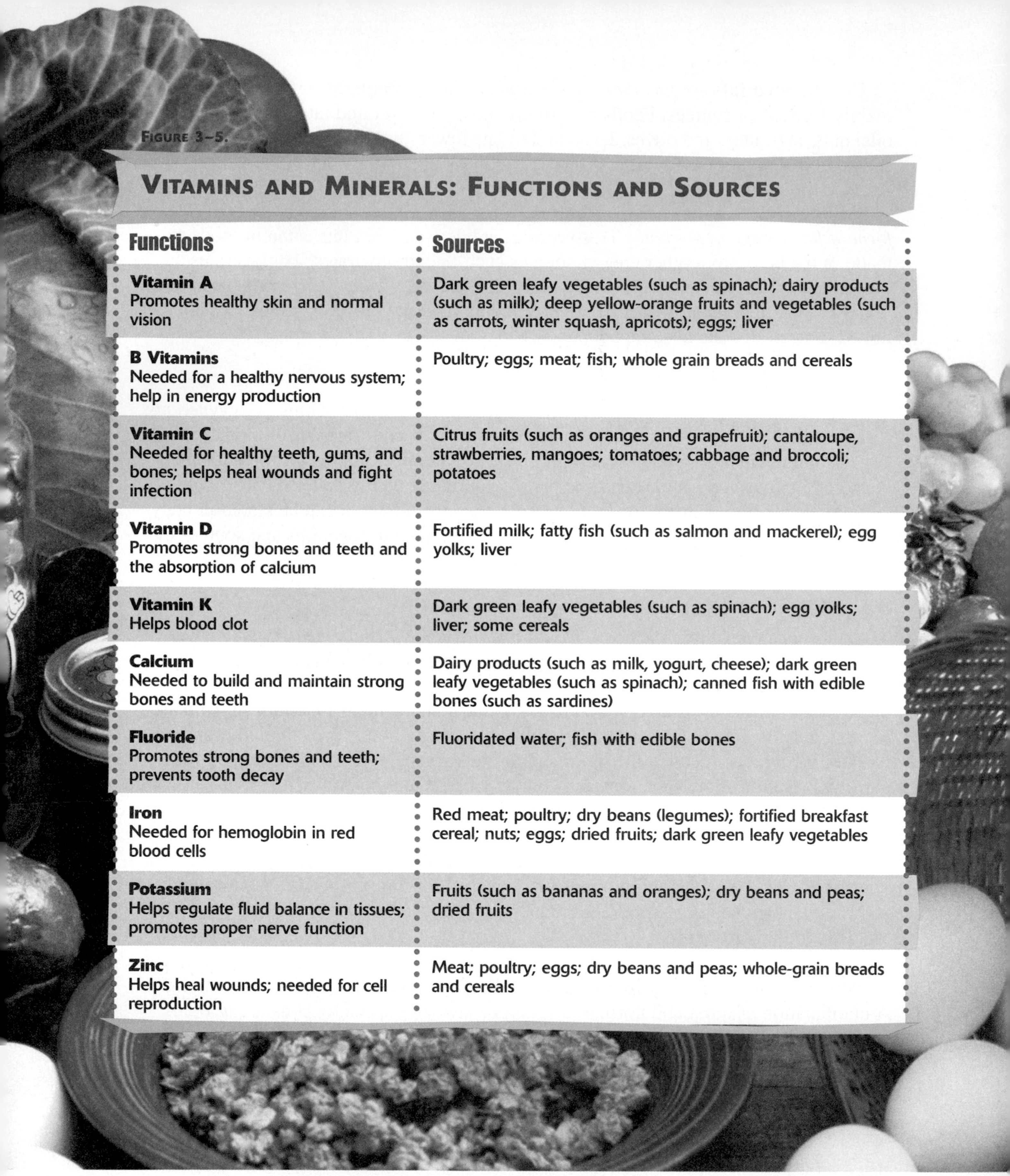

FIGURE 3–5.

VITAMINS AND MINERALS: FUNCTIONS AND SOURCES

Functions	Sources
Vitamin A Promotes healthy skin and normal vision	Dark green leafy vegetables (such as spinach); dairy products (such as milk); deep yellow-orange fruits and vegetables (such as carrots, winter squash, apricots); eggs; liver
B Vitamins Needed for a healthy nervous system; help in energy production	Poultry; eggs; meat; fish; whole grain breads and cereals
Vitamin C Needed for healthy teeth, gums, and bones; helps heal wounds and fight infection	Citrus fruits (such as oranges and grapefruit); cantaloupe, strawberries, mangoes; tomatoes; cabbage and broccoli; potatoes
Vitamin D Promotes strong bones and teeth and the absorption of calcium	Fortified milk; fatty fish (such as salmon and mackerel); egg yolks; liver
Vitamin K Helps blood clot	Dark green leafy vegetables (such as spinach); egg yolks; liver; some cereals
Calcium Needed to build and maintain strong bones and teeth	Dairy products (such as milk, yogurt, cheese); dark green leafy vegetables (such as spinach); canned fish with edible bones (such as sardines)
Fluoride Promotes strong bones and teeth; prevents tooth decay	Fluoridated water; fish with edible bones
Iron Needed for hemoglobin in red blood cells	Red meat; poultry; dry beans (legumes); fortified breakfast cereal; nuts; eggs; dried fruits; dark green leafy vegetables
Potassium Helps regulate fluid balance in tissues; promotes proper nerve function	Fruits (such as bananas and oranges); dry beans and peas; dried fruits
Zinc Helps heal wounds; needed for cell reproduction	Meat; poultry; eggs; dry beans and peas; whole-grain breads and cereals

Other Substances in Food

Food contains many substances in addition to the major nutrients. Some of these substances, such as fiber, are important to your health and should be part of your everyday food choices. For good health, try to limit fats, cholesterol, added sugars, and salt. Go easy on drinks with caffeine, too.

Fiber

Fiber is *the part of fruits, vegetables, grains, and beans that your body cannot digest.* It helps move food particles through your digestive system. Including high-fiber foods in your eating plan may help lower your risk of certain types of cancer and reduce your risk of heart disease. Foods high in fiber include whole-grain breads and cereals, fruits and vegetables, and dry beans and peas.

Hidden Fats

Health experts recommend that no more than 25 to 35 percent of teens' daily calories come from fat. It's easy to cut down on the fats you can see. For example, put a smaller amount of butter on your baked potato, or trim fat from meat. Fats are often hidden in processed and prepared foods. It's harder to cut down on hidden fats, but it can be done. Go easy on fried foods and switch from whole to low-fat milk. Read the labels on packaged foods to check for fats and oils.

Trans fatty acids, or trans fats, are *artificial fats made when hydrogen gas reacts with oil.* They can be found in cookies, crackers, icing, potato chips, margarine, and microwave popcorn. Trans fats pose a higher risk of heart disease than saturated fats, which were once believed to be the worst kind of fats. Trans fats not only raise total cholesterol levels, they also deplete good cholesterol (HDL), which helps protect against heart disease. Trans fats are also called hydrogenated fats.

Cholesterol

Cholesterol is *a waxy substance used by the body to build cells and hormones and to protect nerve fibers.* Most cholesterol is produced in your liver and circulates in the blood. Cholesterol is also found in foods of animal origin, including meats, chicken, egg yolks, and dairy products. Eating high-cholesterol foods can affect the levels of cholesterol in your blood. There are two types of cholesterol in your blood. Low-density cholesterol, or LDL, is a "bad" form that can leave deposits on the walls of your blood vessels. This buildup raises the risk of heart attack or stroke. High-density cholesterol, or HDL, is a "good" form that can help lower LDL levels. To help reduce LDL levels in your blood, limit your intake of foods that are high in fat and cholesterol. Regular physical activity also helps prevent LDL buildup.

Added Sugar

You may be surprised to learn that the average American eats about 100 pounds of sugar a year! Sugar occurs naturally in fruit and milk, and it provides food energy. It is also added to many prepared foods such as soft drinks, cookies, candy, breakfast cereal, and even spaghetti sauce. Sugar is not harmful in moderate amounts. However, you might develop health problems if you eat too many foods high in added sugar.

Sodium

Sodium is a necessary nutrient that helps control the balance of fluids in the body. It occurs naturally in salt, in various foods, and in many prepared sauces. It is also used extensively in processed foods to flavor or preserve the food.

Most Americans eat much more sodium than they need. For some people, too much sodium may contribute to high blood pressure and fluid retention. You can lower your sodium intake by using spices instead of salt and by using food labels as a guide.

Caffeine

Caffeine is a substance that stimulates the nervous system and can become habit-forming. It is an ingredient in "power drinks," cola, some other soft drinks, coffee, tea, and chocolate. Caffeine stimulates the heart rate and the appetite. It can perk you up, but then it makes you feel drowsy so that you want more. For this reason, it's best to limit your intake of products containing caffeine.

HANDS-ON HEALTH

JARS OF SUGAR

Do you know how much sugar you consume when you grab a quick drink or snack? The following table lists the amount of sugar, in grams, that you might find in several popular foods.

Food	Grams of Sugar
Cola (12 oz.)	42
Fat-free, fruit yogurt (8 oz.)	35
Light popcorn (1 c.)	0
Fruit punch drink (8 oz.)	27
Sweetened breakfast cereal (¾ c.)	15
Three reduced-fat chocolate sandwich cookies	14
Chocolate candy bar (1.55 oz.)	40

WHAT YOU WILL NEED
- seven empty baby food jars
- container of sugar
- set of measuring spoons

WHAT YOU WILL DO
1. Note that 5 grams of sugar is equivalent to 1 level teaspoon of sugar; 1 gram is just under ¼ teaspoon; 2 grams is a little under ½ teaspoon.
2. Calculate how many teaspoons of sugar each listed product contains.
3. Using the spoons, measure the amount of sugar in each product. Place that amount in a jar and label the jar.

IN CONCLUSION
1. Evaluate your findings.
2. Take time out to determine the nutrient content of the foods in each list. Which foods offer the best nutritional value?

Nutrition Guidelines

How do you know you're getting the nutrients you need? The U.S. government has developed nutrition tools to help Americans make wise food choices. Two such tools are the Dietary Guidelines for Americans and the Nutrition Facts panel.

Dietary Guidelines for Americans

The **Dietary Guidelines for Americans** are *recommendations about food choices for all healthy Americans age 2 and over.* The guidelines were revised in 2005. The guidelines highlight three keys to a healthy lifestyle:

- Make smart choices from every food group.
- Find your balance between food and physical activity.
- Get the most nutrition out of your calories.

Make Smart Choices from Every Food Group

The best way to give your body the balanced nutrition it needs is by eating a variety of nutrient-packed foods every day. Just be sure to stay within your daily calorie needs. A healthy eating plan is one that

- emphasizes fruits, vegetables, whole grains, and fat-free or low-fat milk and milk products.
- includes lean meat, poultry, fish, beans, eggs, and nuts.
- is low in saturated fats, trans fats, cholesterol, salt (sodium), and added sugars.

Don't Give in When You Go Out

It's important to make smart food choices and watch portion sizes wherever you are—at the grocery store, in your favorite restaurant, or running errands. Try these tips:

- At the store, plan ahead by buying a variety of nutrient-rich foods for meals and snacks throughout the week.
- When grabbing lunch, have a sandwich on whole-grain bread and choose low-fat or fat-free milk, water, or other drinks without added sugars.
- In a restaurant, choose grilled, steamed, or broiled dishes instead of those that are fried or sautéed.
- On a long trip, pack some fresh fruit, cut-up vegetables, string cheese strips, or a handful of unsalted nuts—to help you avoid impulsive, less healthful snacks.

FIGURE 3–6.

It is important to make smart food choices wherever you are.

Mix Up Your Food Choices within Each Food Group

- **Focus on fruits.** Eat a variety of fruits—whether fresh, frozen, canned, or dried—rather than a fruit juice for most of your fruit choices. For a 2,000 calorie diet, you will need two cups of fruit each day (for example, one small banana, one large orange, and one-quarter cup of dried apricots or peaches).
- **Vary your veggies.** Eat more dark green vegetables such as broccoli, kale, and other dark leafy greens; orange vegetables such as carrots, sweet potatoes, pumpkins, and winter squash; and beans and peas, such as pinto beans, kidney beans, black beans, garbanzo beans, split peas, and lentils.
- **Get your calcium-rich foods.** Get three cups of low-fat or fat-free milk—or an equivalent amount of low-fat yogurt and/or low-fat cheese (one-and-a-half ounces of cheese equals one cup of milk)—every day. If you don't or can't consume milk, choose lactose-free milk products and/or calcium fortified foods and beverages.
- **Make half your grains whole.** Eat at least three ounces of whole-grain cereals, breads, crackers, rice, or pasta every day. One ounce is about one slice of bread, one cup of breakfast cereal, or one-half cup of cooked rice or pasta. Look to see that grains such as wheat, rice, oats, or corn are referred to as "whole" in the list of ingredients.
- **Go lean with protein.** Choose lean meats and poultry. Bake it, broil it, or grill it. And vary your protein choices—with more fish, beans, peas, nuts, and seeds.

Find Your Balance between Food and Physical Activity

Becoming a healthier you isn't just about eating healthy—it's also about physical activity. Regular physical activity is important for your overall health and fitness. It also helps you control body weight by balancing calories you take in as food with the calories you expend every day.

- Aim for a healthy weight. Maintaining your weight helps you look and feel good. It also lowers your risk for heart disease, some cancers, and diabetes. Check with your health care provider to determine if you are at a healthy weight for your height and age.
- Be physically active for 60 minutes every day, or almost every day.
- For even greater health benefits and to help control body weight, increase the intensity or the amount of time that you are physically active. About 60 minutes a day may be needed to prevent weight gain.

Get the Most Nutrition out of Your Calories

Active female teens should consume 2,400 calories a day. Active male teens should consume 2,800 to 3,200 calories a day. The Dietary Guidelines define *active* as a lifestyle that includes physical activity equivalent to walking more than three miles per day at a pace of three to four miles per hour, in addition to the light physical activity associated with typical day-to-day life. You could use up your entire calorie requirements on a few high-calorie items, but chances are you won't get the full range of vitamins and nutrients your body needs to be healthy.

Go easy on foods that are high in fats, sugars, and salt. Follow these guidelines to get the most nutrition out of your calories.

- Choose the most nutritionally rich foods you can from each food group each day—those packed with vitamins, minerals, fiber, and other nutrients, but lower in calories. Pick foods like fruits, vegetables, whole grains, and fat-free or low-fat milk and milk products more often.
- Choose foods that are low in saturated fat, trans fat, and cholesterol, and moderate in total fat. Foods high in saturated fat (such as butter and whole milk) and trans fat (such as cookies, chips, and margarine) raise blood cholesterol levels.
- Choose beverages and foods to moderate your intake of sugars. Soft drinks provide many calories but few nutrients. They can also contribute to tooth decay. Try to limit your intake of drinks and foods containing added sugar. Check the ingredient list on packaged foods. If sucrose, corn syrup, honey, fructose, or other sweeteners are listed first or second, these foods are high in sugars.
- Choose and prepare foods with less salt. High salt or sodium intake can contribute to high blood pressure and cause calcium loss. If you normally add salt to food, try using herbs such as basil or oregano, or spices such as paprika instead.

HEALTH SKILLS ACTIVITY

ACCESSING INFORMATION

Reading a Food Label

The following information is provided on all Nutrition Facts panels. Use this information to compare foods and choose wisely.

- **SERVING SIZE.** The serving size is the portion that most people eat. Portion sizes allow for easy comparison of similar foods.
- **CALORIES.** Active female teens should consume 2,400 calories per day, and active male teens should consume between 2,800 and 3,200 calories per day. Consider what percentage of this amount one serving of the food provides for you. Also consider how many of the calories in a serving come from fat.
- **NUTRIENTS.** Use the nutrient information to limit your intake of total fat, saturated fat, cholesterol, and sodium. Get enough dietary fiber, vitamins A and C, calcium, and iron.

- **PERCENT DAILY VALUE.** Determine how much the nutrients in a serving contribute to your total daily eating plan. Use the "5–20 rule." Look for foods that provide 5 percent Daily Value or less of fat, cholesterol, and sodium. Choose foods that provide 20 percent Daily Value or more of dietary fiber, vitamins, and minerals.

1. How many grams of fat does one serving of the product contain? How much saturated fat does it have?
2. What percentage of your total daily sodium allowance does one serving contain?
3. What Percent Daily Value of vitamin A does one serving provide? Vitamin C? Is the product a good source of these vitamins?

ON YOUR OWN
Use the sample label in Figure 3–7 to help answer these questions. Assume that you take in about 2,500 calories a day.

Play it Safe with Food

Know how to prepare, handle, and store food safely. Part of wise nutrition involves making sure that foods are safe from harmful bacteria and other contaminants. Doing so reduces the risk of **foodborne illness**, which is *a sickness that results from eating food that is not safe to eat.*

- Clean hands, food-contact surfaces, fruits, and vegetables. To avoid spreading bacteria to other foods, meat and poultry should *not* be washed or rinsed.
- Separate raw, cooked, and ready-to-eat foods while shopping, preparing, or storing.
- Cook meat, poultry, and fish to safe internal temperatures to kill microorganisms.
- Chill perishable foods promptly and thaw foods properly.

Nutrition Labeling

Perhaps you have noticed that all packaged foods carry a label titled "Nutrition Facts." These labels provide valuable information for making healthful food choices. Food labels compare products to the **Percent Daily Value**. This figure is *the percent of the recommended daily amount of a nutrient provided in a serving of food.* The Percent Daily Value is based on an intake of 2,000 calories per day. Understanding how to read a food label, like the one shown in Figure 3–7, can help you select nutritious foods and balance your eating pattern.

FIGURE 3–7.

WHAT THE FOOD LABEL TELLS YOU

Food labels provide important nutritional information that can help you make sensible food choices.

A The nutrient content of the food is calculated according to its serving size. The serving size on the food label may differ from sizes shown on the Food Guide Pyramid.

B The amount of total fat in one serving is listed, followed by the amount of saturated fat. The calories from fat are shown to the right of the total calories per serving.

C Major vitamins and minerals are shown, along with their Percent Daily Value.

Nutrition Facts

Serving Size 1/2 cup (114g)
Servings Per Container 4

Amount Per Serving	
Calories 90	Calories from Fat 30
	% Daily Value*
Total Fat 3g	**5%**
Saturated Fat 0g	0%
Cholesterol 0mg	**0%**
Sodium 300mg	**13%**
Total Carbohydrate 13g	**4%**
Dietary Fiber 3g	12%
Sugars 3g	
Protein 3g	

Vitamin A	80%	•	Vitamin C	60%
Calcium	4%	•	Iron	4%

* Percent Daily Values are based on a 2,000 calorie diet. Your daily values may be higher or lower depending on your calorie needs:

	Calories	2,000	2,500
Total Fat	Less Than	65g	80g
Sat Fat	Less Than	20g	25g
Cholesterol	Less Than	300mg	300mg
Sodium	Less Than	2,400mg	2,400mg
Total Carbohydrate		300g	375g
Dietary Fiber		25g	30g

Calories per gram:
Fat 9 • Carbohydrate 4 • Protein 4

D Major nutrients are listed in milligrams (mg) or grams (g) and as a percentage of the recommended amount for a person consuming 2,000 calories per day.

E Dietary fiber and sugar are given under Total Carbohydrate.

A Information provided on the lower part of the Nutrition Facts panel is the same from product to product. It contains advice about the amounts of certain nutrients that should be eaten each day. Amounts are given for both a 2,000-calorie and a 2,500-calorie diet.

Vegetarianism

A vegetarian is a person who eats mostly or only plant foods. Some people are vegetarians for religious or cultural reasons. Others make this choice because of their concern for the environment or for how food animals are raised or slaughtered. Many people become vegetarians for health reasons. By cutting out the saturated fats and cholesterol found in many or all animal products, vegetarians may reduce their risk of cardiovascular disease and some cancers. Also, vegetarians may consume more fruits, vegetables, and whole grains—foods that are linked to a reduced risk of many health problems. Figure 3–9 describes four vegetarian eating styles.

FIGURE 3–8.
Many people become vegetarians for health reasons.

FIGURE 3–9.

VEGETARIAN EATING PLANS

No matter which plan a person follows, a vegetarian eating style still involves choosing nutritious foods.

Plan Name	Foods Included
Lacto-ovo vegetarianism	• Dairy *(lacto)* foods and eggs *(ovo)* in addition to foods from plant sources.
Lacto vegetarianism	• Dairy foods in addition to foods from plant sources.
Ovo vegetarianism	• Eggs and foods from plant sources. Fortified soy milk and soy cheese are often substituted for dairy products.
Vegan	• Foods from plant sources only. Fortified soy milk and soy cheese are often substituted for dairy products.

CHECKPOINTS

Lesson 2 Review

Using complete sentences, answer the following questions on a sheet of paper.

1. What are *calories?* What do they measure?
2. What is *nutrition?* What is the relationship between nutrition and health?
3. What is the difference between appetite and hunger?
4. Why is calcium important in a teen's food choices?
5. How is it possible to have plenty of food and yet be poorly nourished?
6. Define carbohydrates. Give two examples of foods that contain simple carbohydrates and two examples of foods that contain complex carbohydrates.
7. Explain why your body needs protein.
8. What is the difference between saturated fats and unsaturated fats?
9. What kinds of foods contain added sugars?
10. What are two tools developed by the government to help Americans make wise food choices?
11. What are the three keys to a healthy lifestyle outlined in the Dietary Guidelines for Americans?
12. Define foodborne illnesses. How can foodborne illness be prevented?
13. Name two foods in each of the five food groups identified in the Dietary Guidelines for Americans.
14. Why do you think people tend to eat too much fat and too much sugar? What might be done to change this situation?
15. Select two of these four food substances: fiber, sodium, caffeine, and sugar. Explain whether or not they are components of your daily food and drink choices.
16. Think about your own food choices. What food groups do you need to eat more from in your eating plan? What food groups do you need to cut down on?

Applying Health Skills

17. By now you are probably aware that you could make changes in your eating patterns to improve your health. Perhaps you could include more fiber or cut back on fatty foods. Write a nutritional goal and list the steps needed to attain it.
18. If available, read the Nutrition Facts panel on the label of the foods you eat during a typical day. Compare the nutritional content with that recommended in the Dietary Guidelines for Americans. How does your daily intake compare? Write a short report summarizing your findings.

First Aid

What Is First Aid?

First aid is *the immediate temporary care given to an injured or ill person until he or she can get professional help.* Knowing what to do during certain common emergencies can prevent further damage and may even speed recovery. Equally important, though, is knowing what not to do. In serious cases, providing the correct first aid can make the difference between life and death. Any time first aid is needed, it's important to stay calm. Doing so will allow you to better help the victim.

Be Prepared

First aid might be needed anywhere, at any time, and without warning. Learning basic first aid skills will help you handle most common emergencies. Another way to be prepared is to keep a list of emergency numbers near all phones. All family members should know where family health records are kept. If a family member has certain allergies, for example, that information may be needed during an emergency.

It is also important to keep first-aid supplies at home and in the car and to know how to use them. You can assemble your own first-aid kit or buy a packaged kit. Figure 3–10 provides suggestions for basic first-aid supplies. If a family member has a medical condition, specific medicines may need to be added to the kit.

Universal Precautions

People infected with HIV or hepatitis B carry the virus in their blood. Because these diseases are communicable, touching contaminated blood carries a risk. For this reason, it is important to protect yourself when giving first aid. Follow **universal precautions**, which are *actions taken to prevent the spread of disease by treating all blood as if it were contaminated.*

Quick Write

Suppose that you witnessed a car accident. List the actions you would take to provide help and the order in which you would take them.

LEARN ABOUT...

- how to be prepared for emergencies.
- how to take universal precautions when giving first aid.
- the basic steps to follow in emergencies.
- how to recognize and evaluate common emergencies.
- first-aid treatments for common emergencies.
- when to call for medical assistance.
- how to deal with life-threatening emergencies.

LEARN ABOUT...

- shock, and why it must be considered in any emergency.
- how to provide rescue breathing.
- the ABCs of CPR.

VOCABULARY

- first aid
- universal precautions
- sprain
- fracture
- heat cramps
- heat exhaustion
- heatstroke
- abdominal thrusts
- shock
- CPR

Universal precautions include wearing protective gloves when treating a victim. Use a face mask or shield when giving first aid for breathing emergencies. Cover any open wounds on your body with sterile dressings. Avoid touching any object that had contact with the victim's blood. Always wash your hands thoroughly after giving first aid.

The First Steps

Every emergency situation is unique. However, there are four steps to take for most emergencies. The sequence of steps is as follows: recognize the signs of an emergency, decide to act, call for help, and provide care until help arrives.

Recognize the Signs of an Emergency

Your senses of hearing, sight, and smell will alert you to most emergencies. Listen if you hear people calling out. Are they in trouble? Be alert to sudden loud or unusual noises, such as shattering glass.

Sometimes the first sign of an emergency is an odor such as the smell of smoke. Also be alert for any strong smell that makes your eyes sting, causes you to cough, or makes breathing difficult. These sensations can signal a chemical spill or toxic gas release.

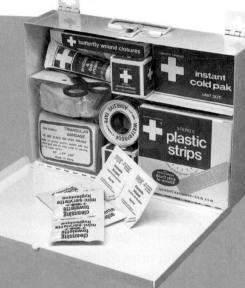

FIGURE 3–10.

FIRST AID SUPPLIES

Keeping a first aid kit in your home will help your family be prepared for emergencies. *What other supplies might you add to this kit?*

Instruments: tweezers, scissors

Equipment: thermometer, cotton swabs, blanket, cold pack

Medications: antiseptic ointment, sterile eyewash, activated charcoal, syrup of ipecac

Dressings: gauze pads, adhesive tape, adhesive bandages, triangular bandage

Miscellaneous: small flashlight, tissues, hand cleaner, disposable gloves, face mask, plastic bags

Decide to Act

In an emergency, evaluate the situation and decide what action is needed. Then consider your strengths and limitations before you act. For example, unless you are trained in lifesaving, don't dive into a lake to rescue someone who is drowning. Instead, you might throw the person a life preserver or some other object that floats. Your first responsibility in any situation is to protect your own safety. Never put your own life in danger to help someone else.

Some people hesitate to help others because they are afraid of doing something wrong. Almost all states have Good Samaritan laws, which protect rescuers who act responsibly from legal action. In an emergency, one action that is always beneficial is to call for help. Getting help is often the best and only action for you to take, and this alone can save a life.

Call for Help

In most of the United States, the number to call for all emergencies is 9–1–1. Dialing 0 for the operator is also an option and may be necessary in some small towns. When you call, stay calm. Be ready to tell the emergency operator the nature of the emergency and the street address or location. The operator will notify the police, fire department, or emergency medical services. If you don't know the address, you can describe the location by using landmarks. Stay on the phone until the operator has the necessary information and tells you that you can hang up.

Provide Care Until Help Arrives

Once you have called for help, provide care by staying with the injured person and protecting him or her from further injury. Help the person maintain normal body temperature by providing a coat or blanket for warmth. Carefully loosen any tight clothing, and provide shade from the sun if necessary. Reassure the victim that help is on the way.

FIGURE 3–11.
It's a good idea to take along a first-aid kit; you never know when you will need it.

In general, you should not try to move a victim. Moving the person could cause pain or further injury. Wait for professional help to arrive. The only situation in which a victim should be moved is if he or she is in danger, such as in the path of oncoming traffic.

If the victim is unconscious and unresponsive, cardiopulmonary resuscitation (CPR) is needed. This technique for dealing with life-threatening emergencies is described at the end of this lesson.

What to Do: Common Emergencies

Sprains, bruises, and broken bones are a few of the common emergencies you may experience. Others include insect bites, burns, poisoning, foreign objects in the eye, nosebleed, fainting, heat cramps, and heatstroke. Learn how to properly treat these conditions. Also recognize the difference between a minor condition that you can treat and a more serious condition that needs professional medical assistance.

Sprains

A **sprain** is *a condition in which the ligaments that hold the joints in position are stretched or torn.* Sprains usually result from a sudden force, often a twisting movement. Ankles and knees are the most commonly sprained joints. Swelling and bruising often accompany a sprain. Serious sprains should be treated by a physician. To treat minor sprains, use the R.I.C.E. method:

- **Rest.** Rest the affected joint for 24 to 48 hours.
- **Ice.** Apply ice to reduce swelling and pain. Place a cloth between the skin and the bag of ice in order to reduce discomfort.
- **Compression.** Compress the injured part by wrapping it in an elastic bandage.
- **Elevation.** Elevate, or raise, the injured part above the level of the heart to reduce swelling.

Broken Bones

A **fracture** is *a break in a bone.* An open fracture is a complete break with one or both sides of the bone piercing the skin. A closed fracture does not break the skin and may be difficult to identify. Typical signs of a closed fracture include pain, swelling, and misshapen appearance. Sometimes, however, a broken bone causes no immediate pain. The only way to be sure a bone is broken is to have it X-rayed.

FIGURE 3–12.

Ankles and knees are the most commonly sprained joints.

Insect Bites and Stings

Insect bites or stings often cause pain and swelling at the site of the bite or sting. For people who are allergic to bites and stings, however, the situation is much more serious, and possibly life-threatening. If a person develops a rash, has difficulty breathing, shows signs of

FIGURE 3–13.

HOW TO REMOVE A TICK

If you find a tick on your body, have an adult follow the method shown to remove it.

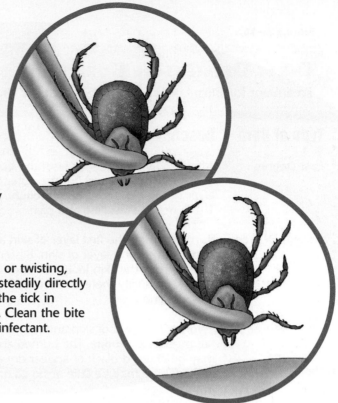

1 Using a pair of pointed, smooth-tipped tweezers, grasp the tick by the head or mouth parts right where they enter the skin. Do not grasp the tick by the body.

2 Without jerking or twisting, pull firmly and steadily directly outward. Place the tick in alcohol to kill it. Clean the bite wound with disinfectant.

shock, or is known to be allergic to stings, he or she needs professional medical help immediately.

First aid for insect bites involves washing the affected area and applying a special lotion for bites. For insect stings, you first need to remove the stinger by scraping against it with your fingernail. Once the stinger is out, apply ice or a cold pack to relieve pain and prevent swelling. If a person is bitten by a tick, the tick will burrow into the skin and needs to be removed very carefully. Figure 3–13 shows the correct procedure for removing ticks.

Burns

First aid for burns depends on the amount of skin burned, the location of the burn, and the depth of the burn. Burns to the eye or airway and burns caused by chemicals or electricity require special first aid procedures, which are not covered here. Figure 3–14 explains how to recognize and treat three classifications of burns.

Poisoning

A poison is a substance that causes harm when swallowed, breathed in, absorbed by the skin, or injected into the body. About half of all poisonings involve medicines or household products. Anyone who has been poisoned needs immediate treatment. Call the nearest poison control center, a 24-hour hot line that provides emergency medical advice on treating poisoning victims. Be prepared to give information about the victim and about the suspected poison. The person at the poison control center will tell you what action to take. You may be instructed to give the victim large amounts of water or milk to dilute the poison. For some types of poison, you may be told to give the victim something to induce vomiting.

Figure 3–14.

THREE DEGREES OF BURNS

Treatment for burns depends on the severity of the burn.

Type of Burn	Description	Treatment
First-Degree	Affects only the outer layer of the skin. The skin is usually red but the outer layer has not been burned through. There may be swelling and pain.	Cool the burn with running water, immerse the burn in cold water, or apply cold compresses for at least 15 minutes. Cover the burn with a sterile bandage.
Second-Degree	Burns through the first layer of skin and burns the second layer of skin. Blisters develop and the skin looks red and splotchy. Usually there is severe pain and swelling.	A burn no larger than 2 to 3 inches in diameter can be treated as a first-degree burn. If the burn is larger, or is on the hands, feet, face, groin, buttocks, or a major joint, get medical help immediately.
Third-Degree	Involves all layers of skin and may affect fat, muscle, and bone. The burned area may be charred black or appear dry and white. There may be little or no pain felt at this stage.	Call for medical help. While you are waiting, treat the victim for shock. Do not remove burned clothing. Cover the area of the burn with a cool, moist sterile bandage or clean cloth. Do not apply cold water to the burns. Keep the victim still and help him or her to sip fluids.

If the skin comes into direct contact with a poisonous chemical such as a pesticide or household cleaning agent, remove any clothing that has come into contact with the chemical. Remove as much of the chemical from the surface of the skin as you can by flooding with water for 15 minutes. While the skin is being flooded, call the nearest poison control center.

Foreign Object in the Eye

If you get a foreign object in your eye, don't rub the eye. Rubbing can cause injury. Try to flush the object out of your eye with clean water. Hold the rim of a small, clean glass filled with water against the base of your eye socket. Keeping your eye open, gently pour the water into the eye. If the object isn't washed out, repeat the process. If you cannot clear your eye, get assistance.

To help somebody else who has a foreign object in the eye, first locate the object. Gently pull the lower lid downward while the person looks up. If you do not see the object, hold the upper lid open and examine the eye while the person looks down. If the object is floating on the surface of the eye, lightly touch the object with a moistened cotton swab or the corner of a clean cloth. If you cannot remove the object, seek medical assistance immediately.

Nosebleed

Nosebleeds can be caused by an injury, by being in a very dry place, or even by a cold. If you experience a nosebleed, pinch your nose shut with your thumb and index finger and breathe through your mouth. Keep the nose pinched for 5 to 10 minutes. If bleeding lasts more than 15 minutes or if there is a lot of blood, get medical assistance immediately.

Fainting

Fainting occurs when the blood supply to the brain is cut off for a short amount of time. A person who faints loses consciousness briefly. If you feel faint, lie down or sit down and place your head between your knees. If someone else faints, follow these steps.

- Leave the person lying down. Check the airway. If the person is breathing, raise the legs above the level of the head.
- Loosen any tight clothing.
- If the person does not regain consciousness in 1 to 2 minutes, call for help. If the person is not breathing, call for help and start CPR if you are trained (see the end of this lesson).
- Losing consciousness after a head injury is not fainting—call for help if this occurs. Immediate CPR is needed if there are no signs of life.

Heat-Related Illnesses

Heat-related illnesses include heat cramps, heat exhaustion, and heatstroke. **Heat cramps** are *painful, involuntary muscle spasms that usually occur during heavy exercise in hot weather.* People who experience heat cramps should rest, cool down, and drink water or a sports drink that contains electrolytes. Gentle stretching exercise and gentle massage may help relieve the cramps.

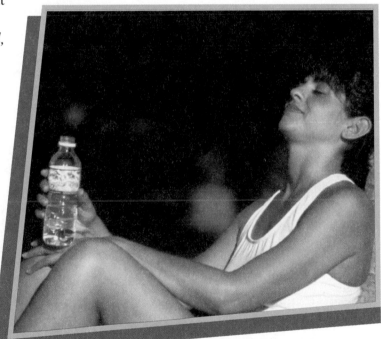

FIGURE 3–15.
It is important to rest, cool down, and drink water when suffering heat cramps.

Heat exhaustion is *a condition characterized by faintness, nausea, rapid heartbeat, and hot, red, dry, or sweaty skin.* If you are with someone who shows signs of heat exhaustion, take the person to a shady or air-conditioned place. Have the person lie down and slightly elevate the feet. Loosen clothing. Have the person drink cold, but not iced, water. Cool the person by spraying him or her with cool water and by fanning. Keep careful watch. Heat exhaustion can quickly become **heatstroke**, which is *the most serious form of heat illness.*

FIGURE 3–16.

FIRST AID FOR A CHOKING ADULT OR OLDER CHILD

Before you perform abdominal thrusts, determine if the person is choking. *Why is asking if a person can speak a good test for choking?*

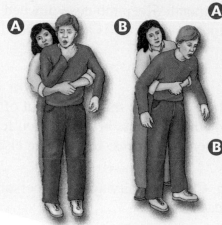

A Stand behind the person who is choking. Wrap your arms around the person's waist and tip the person slightly forward. Make a fist. Place the fist just above the person's navel but below the breastbone. Position the fist so the thumb side is against the victim's abdomen. Grasp your fist with your other hand.

B Quickly, thrust inward and upward. The motion is similar to one you would use if you were trying to lift the person off the ground. Repeat thrusts until the food or object is dislodged. If the person becomes unresponsive, call for medical help and begin CPR.

Heatstroke is potentially life-threatening because the body's normal processes for dealing with heat, including sweating, close down. The main sign of heatstroke is a marked increase in body temperature—generally greater than 104°F. Rapid heartbeat and rapid and shallow breathing are other signs. If heatstroke is a possibility, treat the person as for heat exhaustion and call immediately for emergency medical assistance.

When Minutes Count: Severe Emergencies

In a life-threatening emergency, a person may have only minutes to live unless the right treatment is provided. If you can provide appropriate first aid in such a situation, you may save a life. For all life-threatening emergencies, try to stay calm, and call for help.

Choking

More than 3,000 people die from choking every year. Choking occurs when a person's airway becomes blocked by a piece of food or some other object. If the object is not removed, air will not reach the lungs and the person could die. A choking person usually has an expression of fear and may clutch his or her throat—the universal sign for choking. He or she may wheeze or gasp, turn reddish purple, have bulging eyes, and will be unable to speak. If the person can speak or cough, it is not a choking emergency.

A choking person needs immediate help. You may be able to clear the object from an adult's or child's throat by using the technique shown in Figure 3–16. The technique shown is the **abdominal thrusts** technique, which uses *quick, upward pulls into the diaphragm to force out an obstruction blocking the airway.* The first aid procedure for a choking infant is different from the adult technique. Check with a first aid manual to learn how to help infants.

If you are choking and are alone, give yourself an abdominal thrust. There are two ways to do this. First, make a fist and position it slightly above your navel. Grasp your fist with your other hand and thrust inward and upward into your abdomen until the object pops out. The second technique is to lean over a firm object, such as the back of a chair, and press your abdomen into it.

Shock

Shock is *a life-threatening condition in which the circulatory system fails to deliver enough blood to vital tissues and organs.* The many causes of shock include injury, burns, severe infection, heat, poisoning, blood loss, and heart attack. Because shock can result from a medical emergency, you should look for signs of it when providing first aid.

Signs of shock to watch for include cool, clammy, pale or gray skin; weak and rapid pulse; and slow, shallow breathing. The pupils may be dilated, and the eyes may have a dull look. If conscious, the victim of shock may feel faint, weak, confused, and anxious.

If you think the victim is in shock or in danger of shock, call for medical help and take these precautions.

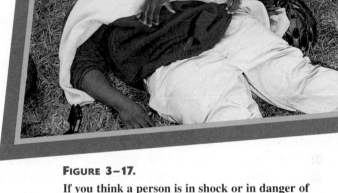

FIGURE 3–17.

If you think a person is in shock or in danger of shock, call for medical help immediately.

- Have the person lie down on his or her back. Raise the feet higher than the head. Try to keep the person from moving.
- Loosen tight clothing.
- Keep the person warm. Use a blanket, coat, or whatever is available as a cover.
- Do not give the person anything to drink.
- If the person vomits or bleeds from the mouth, roll the person to his or her side to help prevent choking.

Severe Bleeding

To stop severe bleeding, have the person lie down. If possible, raise the site of the bleeding above the level of the heart. When treating bleeding, use protective gloves whenever possible. Bleeding can usually be stopped by applying direct pressure to the wound, using a clean cloth. If that is unsuccessful, apply pressure to the artery that supplies blood to the area of the wound. See Figure 3–18.

FIGURE 3–18.

PRESSURE POINT BLEEDING CONTROL

This illustration shows the areas on arms and legs that can be pressed against a bone to stop circulation to the arm or leg.

Arm

Use four fingers to press on the inside of the upper arm at the area circled in the diagram. You will press the artery at this point against the arm bone. To find the artery, feel for a pulse below the round muscle of the biceps.

Leg

Keeping your arm straight, use the heel of your hand to press the groin at the area shown in the diagram. You will press the artery at this point against the pelvic bone. You may need to use both hands to apply enough pressure.

HANDS-ON HEALTH

LOCATING PRESSURE POINTS

In addition to the arteries leading to the arms and legs, there are two pressure points on either side of the neck. The carotid arteries, which supply blood to the head and brain, run just below the skin here. Knowing where pressure points are can help you be prepared to quickly check pulse or stop severe blood flow.

WHAT YOU WILL DO

1. Referring to **Figure 3–18**, locate the pressure points for your left and right arm and left and right leg arteries. Feel for the pulse.
2. Referring to the photograph, feel for the pulse at your right carotid. Then find the pulse at your left carotid. The carotid arteries have the strongest pulse.

IN CONCLUSION

1. Name the pressure point you would press to stop severe blood flow from the following: left calf, right forearm, right wrist, right ankle.
2. If you needed to check someone's pulse, which pressure point would you use? Why?

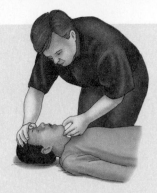

THE ABCs OF CPR

The first steps of CPR involve assessment and rescue breathing. If you have an available breathing mask, follow the directions that came with the mask.

❶ Airway. Look inside the victim's mouth. If you see anything blocking the airway, remove it. Lay the person flat on a firm surface. Gently tilt the head back with one hand and lift the chin with the other. If you suspect head or neck injuries, do not move the victim's head. Open the airway by lifting the jaw instead.

❷ Breathing. Look, listen, and feel to find out if the victim is breathing. *Look* for chest movement. *Listen* at the victim's mouth for breathing sounds. *Feel* for exhaled air on your cheek. If the victim is not breathing, begin rescue breathing. Pinch the person's nostrils shut, take a normal breath and place your mouth over the victim's, forming a seal. Give two slow breaths, each about 2 seconds long. The victim's chest should rise with each breath.

❸ Circulation. Check for circulation by watching for some response to your rescue breaths, such as breathing, coughing, or movement. If there are no signs of circulation, a person trained in CPR should begin chest compressions immediately (see **Figure 3–20**). If the victim responds but is not breathing normally, give a rescue breath every 5 seconds.

What Is Cardiopulmonary Resuscitation (CPR)?

Imagine that you are in an emergency situation in which somebody loses consciousness. You gently shake the victim and shout "Are you OK?" but the victim does not respond. If a victim is unresponsive, he or she needs cardiopulmonary resuscitation (CPR) immediately. **CPR** is *a first aid procedure that combines rescue breaths with chest compressions to restore breathing and circulation.* Only people who have received the proper training should perform CPR.

The first steps of CPR, as recommended by the American Heart Association, are known as the ABCs—airway, breathing, and circulation. The ABC technique to use for adults and older children is shown in Figure 3–19. Check a first aid manual to learn how to help younger children and infants. Figure 3–20 illustrates the process for combining rescue breaths with chest compressions.

Figure 3–20.

CPR FOR ADULTS

CPR involves both chest compressions and rescue breaths. It should be administered only by people who are properly trained.

❶ Position your hands. Prepare to start chest compressions by finding a spot on the lower half of the victim's breastbone. Place the heel of one hand on that point, and interlock the fingers with the fingers of the other hand. Do not allow your fingers to rest on the victim's ribs.

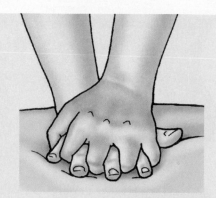

❷ Begin chest compressions and rescue breathing. Lean over the victim until your shoulders are over your hands. Lock your elbows, then press down firmly and release, allowing the chest to spring back. Without pausing, give 15 chest compressions at a rate of about 100 per minute. Pause to give 2 rescue breaths (see **Figure 3–19**). Check for signs of circulation after 4 cycles, then every few minutes as you continue. Give CPR until the victim revives or help arrives.

FIGURE 3–21.
Cadets chat with instructor.

Lesson 3 Review

Using complete sentences, answer the following questions on a sheet of paper.

1. Define the term *first aid*.
2. What are four universal precautions to take when giving first aid?
3. List the first four steps to take when an emergency occurs.
4. Give three examples of ways you can provide help to an injured person until professional help arrives.
5. Define the terms *sprain* and *fracture*. Use both terms in a sentence that demonstrates their meanings.
6. Explain the process for removing a tick from a person's body.
7. What should you do to help someone who has swallowed a poisonous substance?
8. What action should you take if you feel faint?
9. Define the term *abdominal thrust* and explain when it should be used.
10. What are the signs of shock?
11. What actions should you take to stop severe bleeding?
12. What is CPR? In what circumstances should it be used?
13. Why is it so important to know basic first aid?
14. If you come upon an injured person on a jogging path, should you try to drag the person to the side of the path? Why or why not?
15. What would you do for a burn about 1½ inches in diameter that had burned through the first layer of skin and burned the second layer of skin? Explain your answer.
16. How does the treatment for heatstroke differ from that for heat cramps?
17. A driver walks out after a car crash and says that he is all right. However, his skin is gray, his pupils are dilated, and his breathing is shallow. From what condition might the driver be suffering? What should you do?

Applying Health Skills

18. With family members, discuss your family's preparedness for emergencies. Begin by listing possible emergencies. Then decide what should be done for each situation and how prepared every member is to act. Make a plan of the steps you could take to become more prepared.
19. With a classmate, write a scenario for dealing with a common emergency. Act out your scenario for the class.

CHAPTER 4

Physical Activity and Fitness

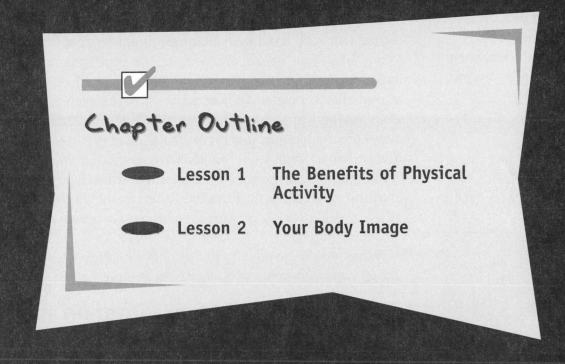

✓

Chapter Outline

Quick Write

How would you describe your physical activity and fitness habits? Explain how you stay active every day.

The Benefits of Physical Activity

Quick Write

How would you measure a person's fitness level? According to your criteria, are you physically fit?

LEARN ABOUT...

- what it means to be physically fit.
- the benefits of physical activity.
- kinds of activities that will help you stay fit.
- the four elements of physical fitness.
- ways to test your physical fitness.
- how to set and achieve fitness goals.
- writing an activity plan.
- the three stages of an exercise session.
- checking your fitness progress.
- choosing sports activities that are right for you.
- preparing yourself to take part in sports.
- minimizing your risk of injury in sports.

Physical Activity, Exercise, and Physical Fitness

The terms *physical activity, exercise,* and *fitness* are closely related, but each has a particular meaning. **Physical activity** refers to *any kind of movement that uses up energy.* Physical activity includes exercising and playing sports. It also includes the movements associated with an active lifestyle, such as biking to the store, raking leaves, or walking up and down the stairs. **Exercise** is *a specifically planned and organized session of physical activity that you do to improve or maintain your physical fitness.* By combining regular exercise with an active lifestyle and sound nutrition, you can be fit. **Physical fitness** is *the ability to handle the physical demands of everyday life without becoming overly tired.*

When you're physically fit, you have enough energy to do the things you want to do, plus energy in reserve for the unexpected.

Benefits of an Active Lifestyle

Physical activity benefits you in both body and mind. Besides promoting your overall health, physical activity helps you look and feel better. Since many physical activities involve other people, you'll also get social benefits.

Physical activity provides mental and emotional benefits, too. Being active lets you clear your mind and "burn off" stress. In addition, the physical and social benefits that you get help you feel good about yourself as a person. Figure 4–1 shows some of the mental/emotional, physical, and social benefits of physical activity.

Physical Activity and Weight Control

The CDC reports that more than one-half of American adults and 14 percent of teens are overweight. This situation can be traced to a sedentary lifestyle and overeating. To stay within a weight range that is healthy for you, it's important to develop good eating habits and be physically active on a regular basis.

Understanding how the food you eat gets converted into energy can help you maintain a healthy weight. **Metabolism** is *the process by which your body gets energy from food.* Food's energy value is measured in units of heat called calories. Your body needs a sufficient number of calories each day to function properly. Additional calories must be burned through physical activity or they will be stored in the body as fat. When you are physically active, your metabolic rate rises and your body burns more calories than when it is at rest. The number of calories burned depends in part on the nature of the activity. When you stop being active, your metabolic rate slowly returns to normal. For several hours afterward, however, you continue to burn more calories than you did before you began the activity.

Increasing Your Level of Fitness

How can you increase your level of physical fitness? The first step toward physical fitness is to recognize that physical activity is important to your lifelong health and well-being. The next step is to move more! Make physical activity part of your daily life.

Becoming more active is as easy as seeing the opportunities for physical activity that are all around you. Instead of using elevators and escalators, take the stairs. Walk or ride a bike to the mall rather than asking your parents for a lift.

In addition to looking for everyday opportunities, plan regular sessions of exercise. Start by exercising 10 to 15 minutes at a time and gradually work up to about 60 minutes on most days of the week. If you feel that you do not have time to spare, try breaking your physical activity down into smaller sessions during the day. Three 10-minute sessions provide the same benefit as one 30-minute activity.

Choosing the Right Activities

It is important to choose activities that give you the benefits you want. There are two main types of exercise: aerobic and anaerobic. **Aerobic exercise** is *rhythmic, nonstop, moderate to vigorous activity that requires large amounts of oxygen and works the heart.* Running, biking, and swimming are forms of aerobic exercise. **Anaerobic exercise** is *intense physical activity that requires little oxygen but uses short bursts of energy.* Sprinting and gymnastics are examples of anaerobic exercise.

Each type of exercise benefits the body in a particular way. You can combine both types of exercise to achieve optimum fitness. By choosing a variety of activities, you can receive the benefits of both types of exercise.

Stay Active: A Key to Fitness

Technology has made life simpler, easier, and more fun. As wonderful as technology is, though, it has a downside. It has replaced many of the physical

FIGURE 4–1.

Benefits of Physical Activity

Mental/Emotional Benefits
- Feel more alert and energetic
- Reduce stress
- Learn new things
- Get a sense of accomplishment
- Lessen mental fatigue
- Build a positive self-image
- Increase self-confidence and self-esteem

Physical Benefits
- Strengthen heart and lungs
- Strengthen bones
- Manage weight
- Control blood sugar
- Control blood pressure
- Increase strength and stamina
- Improve flexibility and muscle tone
- Improve balance, the feeling of stability and control over your body
- Develop coordination, the smooth and effective working together of your muscles and bones
- Improve reaction time
- Increase body's defense to diseases
- Improve sleep

Social Benefits
- Engage in enjoyable activities
- Meet and interact with new people
- Use abilities to work with others as a team
- Get support from friends
- Share goals and achievements with others

activities that were once part of daily life. People ride instead of walk. They use machines to do the work that used to be done by hand. They sit at home, watching sports on TV, instead of playing ball in the park. They send e-mail instead of walking over to a friend's house.

Think about your own lifestyle. Estimate how many hours a week you watch television or sit at a computer screen. Now estimate the number of hours you spend doing something physically active. Compare the totals. Are you active most of the time or inactive? Because you know that physical activity and exercise are essential to fitness, this comparison may make you stop and think about how you spend your time.

STRESS MANAGEMENT

Relaxation Exercises

Physical activity is an effective way to relieve stress and help you unwind. You might also do relaxation exercises to reduce feelings of stress. Here are some examples:

- **LIE ON YOUR BACK.** Make fists and tense your arms. Hold for a moment, then relax. In turn, tense and then relax your neck, shoulders, legs, feet, and abdomen.

- **LIE ON YOUR SIDE, WITH BOTH ARMS ABOVE YOUR HEAD.** Tense your whole body, then completely relax, letting your arms and legs fall where they may, as though you were a rag doll. Turn to your other side and repeat.

- **SIT QUIETLY.** Close your eyes, take a slow, deep breath, and let it out slowly. Repeat two more times. Open your mouth, move your jaw to the right, and hold for a few seconds. Then move it to the left and hold. Repeat several times.

ON YOUR OWN
Try each of these exercises. Did they reduce your body tension? Which exercise had the greatest effect?

Endurance, Strength, and Flexibility: The Elements of Fitness

Exercise can be used to develop four elements of fitness: heart and lung endurance, muscle strength and endurance, body composition, and flexibility.

Heart and Lung Endurance

Endurance is your ability to engage in vigorous physical activity over time without tiring too easily or quickly. **Heart and lung endurance** refers to *how effectively your heart and lungs work when you exercise and how quickly they return to normal when you stop.* Heart and lung endurance is important in all kinds of exercise—biking, jumping rope, swimming, and playing ball. Figure 4–2 shows one way to measure heart and lung endurance. Before performing the test in Figure 4–2, practice walking or jogging for six to eight weeks and learn to pace yourself so that you can walk or jog continuously.

The best way to build up heart and lung endurance is through sustained moderate to vigorous exercise lasting at least 60 minutes on most days. This kind of physical activity is called cardiovascular exercise because it raises your breathing rate and heartbeat and benefits your cardiovascular system.

Some cardiovascular exercises are:

- **Walking/Jogging/Running**. Start off slowly, and then gradually increase your pace. Work up to a 30-minute walk, or alternate walking and jogging until you can jog or run for 20 minutes.
- **Swimming.** Swimming provides a total body workout. Gradually work up to 20 minutes of continuous swimming. Swim at a steady pace and vary your routine by using different strokes.

FIGURE 4-2.

DETERMINING HEART AND LUNG ENDURANCE

For this test, you'll see how far you can walk in 30 minutes or jog in 20 minutes.

1 Team up with a partner. Go to a track or running area with quarter-mile markers. Warm up with walking and gentle stretching exercises for 5 to 10 minutes.

2 Walk for 30 minutes or jog for 20 minutes. Have your partner record the distance that you cover. Cool down afterward by walking slowly and doing gentle stretching exercises.

3 Switch roles and repeat the exercise.

4 Caution: If you have a heart or lung disease, check with your doctor before attempting this test.

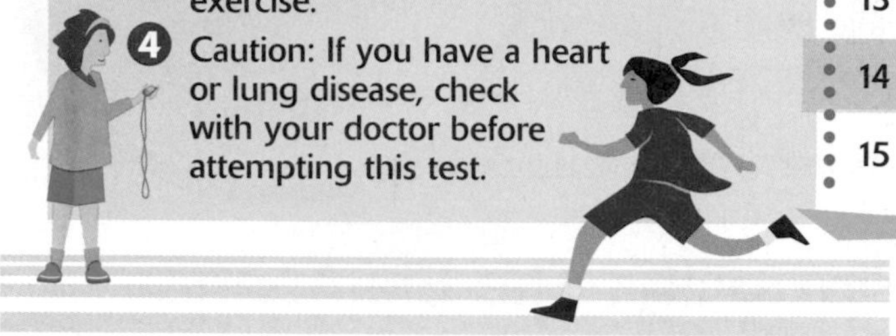

Scoring (miles)

If you score within the range given for your age and gender, your heart and lung endurance is acceptable. If not, continue to practice walking or jogging until you can score in the acceptable range.

Age	Females Walking	Jogging	Males Walking	Jogging
12	2–2.2	1.6–1.8	2.2–2.4	1.8–2.0
13	2–2.2	1.6–1.8	2.2–2.4	1.8–2.0
14	2–2.2	1.6–1.8	2.2–2.4	1.8–2.0
15	2–2.2	1.6–1.8	2.2–2.4	1.8–2.0

Source: Modified with permission from *Foundations of Personal Fitness: Any Body Can . . . Be Fit!*, by D. Rainey and T. Murray.

- **Jumping Rope.** As you jump, guard your joints against unnecessary strain by raising your feet just high enough to allow the rope to pass.

It's a good idea to vary your exercise routines. *Switching between different exercises* is known as **cross-training** and has benefits over doing one exercise all the time. Whatever exercises you choose, don't overdo it.

Muscle Strength and Endurance

The ability of your muscles to exert a force is called strength. **Muscle strength** measures *the most weight you can lift or the most force you can exert at one time.* **Muscle endurance** is *the ability of a muscle to repeatedly exert a force over a prolonged period of time.* The greater your muscle strength, the more force your muscles can exert. The greater your muscle endurance, the longer your muscles can exert their strength.

There are many ways to build and measure muscle strength (see Figures 4–3 and 4–4). Three basic strengthening exercises are push-ups, curl-ups, and step-ups.

- **Do push-ups to strengthen muscles in your arms and chest.** Lie facedown on the floor. Bend your arms and place your palms flat on the floor beneath your shoulders. Straighten your arms, pushing your entire body upward, and then lower your body to the floor. Repeat.

FIGURE 4–3.

DETERMINING ABDOMINAL MUSCLE STRENGTH AND ENDURANCE

You can test the strength and endurance of your abdominal muscles by measuring your ability to do bent-knee curl-ups.

❶ Team up with a partner.

❷ Partner A lies on mat with knees bent and feet flat on the floor. Partner B holds partner A's feet.

❸ Partner A curls up slowly with arms crossed over the chest, and chin tucked to the chest so that the head never touches the mat. The curl-up is completed when partner A's shoulder blades return to the testing surface.

❹ Partner A should do curl-ups at the rate of about 20 per minute, stopping when he or she can no longer continue, or has completed 60 curl-ups.

❺ Partners A and B switch roles and repeat the exercise.

Scoring (number completed)

If you score within the range given for your age and gender, your abdominal strength and endurance is acceptable. If you do not score within the range, continue to practice your curl-ups until you can score in the acceptable range.

Age	Females	Males
12	20–35	25–40
13	25–40	30–45
14	25–40	30–45
15	25–40	30–45

Source: Modified with permission from *Foundations of Personal Fitness: Any Body Can . . . Be Fit!*, by D. Rainey and T. Murray.

FIGURE 4–4.

DETERMINING UPPER BODY STRENGTH AND ENDURANCE

You can test your upper body strength and endurance by measuring the time you can hang from a bar with your chin above the bar.

❶ Team up with a partner.

❷ Partner A grasps horizontal bar with palms facing in, and raises body to position where chin is above bar, elbows are flexed, and chest is close to the bar. Partner B spots Partner A and stops Partner A from swinging.

❸ Partner B starts stopwatch. Partner A remains in position for as long as possible.

❹ Watch is stopped when Partner A's chin touches bar, head tilts backward, or chin falls below level of bar.

❺ Partners A and B switch roles and repeat the exercise.

Scoring (seconds)

If you score within the range given for your age and gender, your upper body strength and endurance is acceptable. If you do not score within the range, continue to practice your static arm hang until you can score in the acceptable range.

Age	Females	Males
12	7–14	7–14
13	7–14	12–20
14	7–14	12–20
15	7–14	12–20

Source: Modified with permission from *Foundations of Personal Fitness: Any Body Can . . . Be Fit!*, by D. Rainey and T. Murray.

- **Do curl-ups to strengthen your abdominal muscles.** Lie on your back with your knees bent and your heels on the floor. Cross your arms over your chest. Curl your upper body forward so that both shoulder blades come off the floor. Uncurl and repeat.
- **Do step-ups to strengthen your leg muscles.** Step up onto a step with your left foot and then bring your right foot up. Step down with your left foot and bring the right foot down. Repeat, alternating between feet.

Many students your age become interested in weight training. Weight training is a good way to build muscle strength. Lift light weights multiple times, and make sure you learn from an expert, such as a fitness instructor.

Body Composition

A third element of fitness is body composition. **Body composition** is *the ratio of body fat to lean body tissue, such as bone, muscle, and fluid.* One way to measure body composition is to use the skinfold test. It involves pinching a fold of skin on your upper arm and on your calf. The fold is measured with an instrument called a skinfold caliper, and the two numbers are added together. Ask your fitness instructor about the skinfold test.

Body composition tells you if you are carrying too much body fat. Eating nutritious, low-fat foods and participating in regular physical activity can help you maintain a healthy body composition.

Flexibility

The fourth element of fitness, **flexibility**, is *the ability of your body's joints to move easily through a full range of motion.* When you have good flexibility, you can easily bend, turn, and stretch your body. People with limited flexibility may move stiffly or strain parts of their body. Figure 4–5 shows how to measure the flexibility of muscles in your lower back and the back of your legs.

You can improve your flexibility through regular stretching, bending, and twisting exercises. Move slowly and gently, and improve the flexibility of different muscle groups gradually.

Your Fitness Level

After reading this section and completing the physical fitness tests described, you should have a clearer idea of your heart and lung endurance, muscle strength and endurance, body composition, and flexibility. Are you as physically fit as you should be? Are you as fit as you would like to be?

If you want to raise your level of physical fitness, you'll need to set goals for yourself and then decide how to achieve these goals. Remember to consider your limits, though. Some people improve faster than others, and some people have a higher fitness potential than others.

FIGURE 4–5.

DETERMINING FLEXIBILITY

Warm up with some light-and-easy stretches. When you take the test, move slowly and smoothly. Don't strain your muscles.

❶ Remove shoes and sit down in front of 12-inch high box. There should be a ruler on top with the "zero" end against the edge nearest you. Extend both legs with feet flat against box. Arms should extend over ruler with one hand on top of the other.

❷ Reach forward with hands along the ruler four times. Hold position of the fourth reach for at least one second.

❸ Record number of inches your fingers reach on the ruler.

Scoring

Females	Males	Rating
Reach beyond toes at least 1 inch	Reach beyond toes at least 1 inch	Acceptable Flexibility
Cannot reach toes	Cannot reach toes	Low Flexibility

Source: Modified with permission from *Foundations of Personal Fitness: Any Body Can . . . Be Fit!*, by D. Rainey and T. Murray.

HANDS-ON HEALTH

YOUR TARGET PULSE RATE

Exercise should increase your heartbeat to at least 50 percent of your maximum rate to provide a benefit for your heart and lungs. The heartbeat rate that will safely provide the greatest benefit is between 60 and 80 percent of your maximum rate. This is your target pulse rate (also known as target heart rate). In this activity, you will find your target pulse rate.

WHAT YOU WILL NEED
• watch with a second hand

WHAT YOU WILL DO
1. Determine your maximum heartbeat rate by subtracting your age from the number 220.
2. Multiply your maximum heartbeat rate by 60 percent and then by 80 percent.

Compare the range of your target pulse rate with those in the chart.
3. For the next two weeks, take your pulse while exercising. Write down the activity you are doing and your pulse rate.

IN CONCLUSION
Was your heartbeat rate generally within the range of your target pulse rate? Which activities produced the highest rate? The lowest?

AGE	MAXIMUM PULSE RATE	TARGET PULSE RATE
12	208	125–166
13	207	124–166
14	206	124–165
15	205	123–164

Heredity and overall health both play important roles in a person's physical abilities. For example, someone with asthma may become short of breath when exercising. A person with a physical impairment may not be able to participate in all activities. To develop a realistic plan that is right for you, check with your doctor before pursuing your fitness goals.

Setting Fitness Goals

Starting a fitness plan can be confusing. You may wonder which activities will best help you reach your fitness goals. Maybe you're not sure how to do an exercise. As a teen, you can turn to a fitness instructor, your physical education teacher, or a coach. Any of these experts can show you how to get started, what equipment to use, and how to exercise safely. An expert can also help you stay motivated. Figure 4–6 compares different types of activities.

Being Active Every Day

Whatever your fitness goals may be, try to do one or more forms of physical activity or exercise each day. Include a mixture of activities during the week, and vary your routine in order to develop different parts of your body.

FIGURE 4–6.

RATING DIFFERENT ACTIVITIES

The ratings in this chart show the benefits of activities done for 30 minutes or more.

Exercise	Flexibility	Muscle Strength and Endurance	Heart and Lung Endurance
Handball	High	High	High
Swimming	High	Medium	High
Jogging	Medium	High	High
Bicycling	Medium	High	High
Tennis	High	Medium	Medium
Brisk walking	Medium	High	High
Slow walking	Low	Medium	Medium
Softball	Medium	Low	Low
Weight training	Low	High	Low

To become fit and stay fit, you need different types of physical activity. Here are some ideas for developing an active lifestyle.

- **Daily activity.** Look for opportunities to be active every day. Take the stairs instead of the elevator. Bike to a friend's home. Walk to the store. Rake leaves. Shovel snow. Wash and wax the car.
- **Aerobic exercise.** Aim to do at least 60 minutes of moderate to vigorous physical activity most days of the week. Swim laps. Join the track team. Take a brisk walk. Ride a stationary bike. Jump rope.
- **Sports, recreation, leisure activities.** Spend half an hour or more several times a week participating in activities that are fun and get your blood moving. Play soccer, racquetball, volleyball, or basketball. Hike a mountain trail. Take a dance class. Go skating or bowling.

Preparing an Activity Plan

To achieve your fitness goals, you may find it helpful to make a weekly physical activity plan like the one in Figure 4–7. A written plan will keep you on track and help you exercise consistently. To develop your plan, first write down all scheduled physical activities or exercise sessions, such as gym periods, team practices, and dance classes. Next, pencil in a variety of physical activities and exercises.

Try to balance your schedule so that every day contains some activities but no single day is overloaded. Also, be flexible, and include some choices. For example, you might write, "Jog or bike ride," and then decide which activity you prefer when that day comes. Keep in mind that your activity plan should meet your personal fitness goals. Your friends' goals and activities may differ from yours.

FIGURE 4–7.

A SAMPLE WEEKLY ACTIVITY PLAN

A written plan will help you include a balance of activities in your weekly schedule.

Sunday	Monday	Tuesday	Wednesday	Thursday	Friday	Saturday
29	**30**	**31**	**1**	**2**	**3**	**4**
Bike ride 1 hr.	Gym class 30 min. Soccer practice 1 hr. Walk home from practice 20 min.	Basketball or jog after school 40 min. Karate class 1 hr.	Gym class 30 min. Soccer practice 1 hr.	Basketball or bike ride after school 40 min. Karate class 1 hr.	Gym class 30 min. Walk home from school 20 min.	Soccer game 50 min. Karate class 1 hr.
Total: 1 hour	Total: 1 hour 50 min.	Total: 1 hour 40 min.	Total: 1 hour 30 min.	Total: 1 hour 40 min.	Total: 50 min.	Total: 1 hour 50 min.

Exercise Stages

Your exercise workouts should have three stages: the beginning warm-up, the workout itself, and then the cool-down. Each of these stages is discussed on the following pages. Because all three stages are important, it's wise not to skip any of them.

Warming Up

A **warm-up** is *a period of low to moderate exercise to prepare your body for more vigorous activity.* You should start every exercise session with a warm-up lasting about ten minutes. During this period, your heartbeat rate gradually increases, and your body temperature starts to rise. As the flow of blood to your muscles increases, they become more flexible, which makes them less prone to injury during exercise.

Begin a warm-up with gentle aerobic activities, such as a fast walk, followed by stretching exercises. When you stretch, move slowly and stretch the muscles little by little. Be careful not to overstretch or bounce as you stretch, which can damage body joints or tissues. Figure 4–8 shows two typical stretching exercises. Some stretches are not good for your joints. Ask your fitness instructor for a good stretching routine.

FIGURE 4–8.

Stretching Exercises

Different stretching exercises benefit different parts of the body. The exercises in these pictures stretch calves and shoulders. *How do you warm up before you exercise?*

Calf stretch
Stand near a wall, and lean toward it with your palms flat against the surface. Bend one leg, and keep the other leg extended. While keeping the heel of the extended leg on the ground, move your hips forward until you feel a stretch in the calf muscle.

Shoulder stretch
Lean against a wall for support, as shown. Keep your arms straight while moving your upper body downward. Keep your feet under your hips and your knees slightly bent.

Another way to warm up is to do the actual movements of your planned activity but at a slow and easy pace. For example, if you plan to play racquetball, you might warm up by gently hitting the ball back and forth with your opponent and then doing a variety of stretching exercises.

Working Out

Once you have warmed up, you're ready to work out. Your workouts should start off at a comfortable level of physical activity and build up gradually. Some guidelines for starting and increasing your workout program include:

- **Frequency.** Gradually increase the number of times you exercise per week. Start by exercising two or three times the first week and work your way up to exercising daily.
- **Intensity.** This refers to the difficulty of your physical activity or exercise session. The most common way of gauging intensity is in terms of heartbeat rate. You can usually increase intensity by speeding up—running faster, for example, or doing more sit-ups in less time. You can also increase intensity by making yourself work harder. For example, it's harder to bike up a hill than along a flat road.
- **Duration.** Limit your workout sessions to about 10 to 15 minutes at first. Gradually increase the time until you're exercising for about 30 to 45 minutes each session. Remember to aim for 60 minutes of physical activity on most days.
- **Order.** If you're doing both aerobic and strength-building exercises during a workout session, perform the aerobic exercise first. Your muscles will work more smoothly after aerobic activity.

If you want to build on your workout, do it gradually. Change only one element at a time. For example, if you increase the duration of your workout, keep intensity and frequency the same.

Cooling Down

Just as a warm-up should precede your workout, a cool-down should follow it. A **cool-down** is *a period of low to moderate exercise to prepare your body to end a workout session.* Cooling down helps return blood circulation and body temperature to normal.

If you end a workout abruptly, your muscles may tighten up and you may feel faint or dizzy. To avoid such effects, slow your body down gradually. Continue the movements of your workout activity, but at a slower, easier pace. A cool-down should last about ten minutes, and it should include gentle stretching exercises.

Checking Your Progress

As you work toward your fitness goals, you'll want to monitor your progress. Remember that change comes gradually. Don't expect to cut 30 seconds off your mile time after a week of working out. Here are some suggestions for evaluating your progress.

- Keep an exercise log or journal. Making performance notes after each workout will help you keep track of exercise sessions.

- After four to eight weeks of workouts, you should observe some improvement in your overall fitness. Depending on the exercises you've been doing, you should feel stronger, have more endurance, or have greater flexibility. You may also find that you feel better overall, look fitter, and have more energy.
- If you see no significant change after eight weeks, you need to evaluate the situation. Have you been exercising regularly? Do you need to modify your fitness goals?
- Another measure of fitness is your resting heartbeat rate, the number of times per minute your heart beats when your body is at rest. The average heartbeat rate ranges from 72 to 84 beats per minute. A resting heartbeat rate less than 72 is generally associated with physical fitness.
- Once you reach your fitness goals, consider setting new goals for yourself.

Choosing the Right Activity

To choose the right sports for you, consider the kinds of activities you enjoy most. While both individual and team sports provide personal satisfaction and a way to stay active, one sport may suit your needs better than others. Of course, many teens take part in both individual and team sports.

Individual Sports

Individual sports are *physical activities that you can do on your own or with a friend.* You don't need to be part of a team to participate in individual sports. For example, biking, running, walking, swimming, golf, and skating are all sports you can do by yourself.

What are the advantages of individual sports? They are more flexible than team sports. You can do them whenever you feel like it, and you can do them for as long as you wish.

That's also one possible disadvantage of individual sports. You have to find the time and the motivation to take part in your chosen sport. Some people find it hard to stick to a plan if they have to do it on their own.

FIGURE 4–9.
Walking is a popular individual sport.

Team Sports

Many teens enjoy **team sports**—*organized physical activities with specific rules, in which groups of people play together against other groups.* There are many different team sports to choose from, including baseball, soccer, basketball, volleyball, and football. Dual sports, requiring only two to four players, include tennis and racquetball. Team sports may be offered by

- schools.
- city or town recreation departments.
- community centers.
- teen clubs and organizations.
- sports and fitness centers.
- church and synagogue youth programs.

Playing on a team can be a positive and enjoyable experience. Many teens like the excitement of competition. Whether or not your team wins, you have the companionship and support of your teammates and coaches as you work together toward a common goal. Playing on a team also gives you an opportunity to develop communication and social skills. You learn about cooperation, compromise, and good sportsmanship.

Of course, team sports are not suitable for everyone. Some teens don't like having a set schedule, which typically requires them to attend several practices and games a week, after school and on weekends. Perhaps their family circumstances prevent them from committing themselves to a team. For these people, individual sports offer a better fitness alternative.

Sports Conditioning

Whether you choose an individual sport or a team sport, you need to be physically fit to do your best. **Sports conditioning** is *regular physical activity or exercise to strengthen and condition muscles for a particular sport.* It takes time and effort. You'll also need to eat healthful foods, learn safety rules, and obtain appropriate equipment.

Sports and Nutrition

An important part of sports conditioning is eating a balanced, nutritious diet. Your choices should include a variety of foods and a limited amount of fat. Here are other guidelines.

- **Get enough carbohydrates.** Your body needs extra energy to play sports. Fruits, vegetables, pasta, and whole-grain breads provide carbohydrates, an excellent energy source.
- **Get enough vitamins and minerals.** Be sure to get plenty of calcium, potassium fiber, magnesium, and vitamin E. These nutrients are essential to a balanced diet and to sports conditioning. Calcium, for example, strengthens bones, while iron helps provide muscles with oxygen during physical activity.
- **Don't eat too much protein.** Athletes need protein, but no more than anyone else, provided they are eating enough nutritious foods. Even though protein helps to build

muscle tissue, it is only through exercise and training that you can develop your muscles.

- **Drink water!** If you play sports, your body will lose water through perspiration. To maintain fluid balance, consume fluid regularly during the activity and drink several glasses of water or other fluid after you're done playing sports. Your goal is to avoid **dehydration**, *excessive water loss from the body,* which can lead to dizziness, muscle cramps, and heatstroke.

Safety First

Whenever you exercise or participate in sports, you increase your risk of injury. The three basic aspects of safety are safe behavior, safe and proper equipment, and knowing your limits.

Safe Behavior

Many sports-related injuries can be prevented by thinking ahead. Here are some tips.

- **Exercise where and when it's safe.** A soft, even surface is easier on your legs, knees, and feet than a hard or uneven surface. Exercise with another person and avoid deserted places. Protect yourself during hot weather by exercising in the cooler mornings or evenings. Remember to wear sunscreen outdoors.
- **Always warm up and cool down.** Gradually get your body ready to begin exercising. End your workout by cooling down.
- **Practice your sport regularly.** Team practices help you maintain your physical fitness levels and help you and your teammates learn to work together effectively and safely.
- **Learn the proper techniques and rules of the game.** Following the rules and regulations of a sport promotes both safety and good sportsmanship.
- **Keep your emotions under control.** Anger or frustration can lead to unsafe or unwise actions. Try to stay calm and relaxed.

Safe Equipment

What you wear when you exercise or play sports is important to your safety. Here are some clothing and equipment guidelines.

- **Wear loose-fitting or stretchable clothes.** For some sports, clothing that fits loosely gives you freedom of movement and helps you stay cooler. For other sports, tight, stretchable clothes are more appropriate.
- **If you exercise outdoors, make yourself visible.** Wear light-colored and reflective clothing so you'll be visible to drivers.
- **When exercising in cold weather, dress in layers.** You can easily add or remove layers as needed during your workout.
- **Wear protective equipment.** Different sports require protection for different parts of the body. Always wear the necessary gear.

- **Choose shoes carefully.** Shoes should fit properly, feel comfortable, provide adequate support, and be suitable for the activity you have chosen.
- **Select your equipment wisely.** Whether you're picking skates, a helmet, or a baseball glove, take the time to make a wise choice.

Know Your Limits

When exercising or playing sports, it's important to recognize your limits. Here are some suggestions that will help.

- **Listen to your body.** Exercise can cause discomfort, like mild breathlessness or tired muscles, but pain is not normal. If you're feeling pain, your body is telling you to slow down, rest, or stop completely. If pain persists, see a doctor.
- **Stop if you get injured or feel ill.** If you get hurt while exercising or while playing in a game, don't continue until someone checks you out. Consult a coach, fitness instructor, or doctor. Also, don't play sports if you're not feeling well.
- **Use the R.I.C.E. formula.** If you have a minor sports injury such as a sprained ankle, follow the Rest, Ice, Compression, Elevation formula. See the First Aid lesson in Chapter 3 for details.

Avoiding Harmful Substances

Anabolic steroids are *drugs that cause muscle tissue to develop at an abnormally fast rate.* Although steroids and certain other drugs may increase strength, the use of these drugs is both dangerous and illegal. Here are some of the side effects users may experience:

- Liver and brain cancers
- Weakening of tendons, leading to joint or tendon injuries
- Cardiovascular damage and high blood pressure, raising the risk of heart attack
- Mental and emotional effects, such as anxiety, severe mood swings, uncontrolled rage, and delusions
- Severe acne
- Trembling
- Bone damage
- Facial hair growth in females and breast development in males

Anabolic steroids and other performance-enhancing drugs have no place in a healthy fitness plan. Besides damaging your body, they can destroy your athletic career.

FIGURE 4–10.
Avoid using steroids and other harmful substances to stay healthy and perform well.

CHECKPOINTS

Lesson 1 Review

Using complete sentences, answer the following questions on a sheet of paper.

1. Define *physical activity, exercise,* and *physical fitness.*

2. Using your own words, tell what it means to be physically fit.

3. Give three examples of the mental/emotional benefits of physical activity and three examples of the social benefits.

4. What is the difference between aerobic exercise and anaerobic exercise?

5. Define *heart and lung endurance.* What is the best way to build heart and lung endurance?

6. What is the difference between muscle strength and muscle endurance?

7. Which part of your body is strengthened by curl-ups? By step-ups?

8. What are the advantages of good flexibility?

9. What should you keep in mind when preparing an activity plan?

10. What are the three stages of an exercise workout?

11. Define *warm-up* and *cool-down.* What are their similarities and differences?

12. Why would it be unwise to skip the cool-down stage?

13. Explain the meaning of *sports conditioning.*

14. What is *dehydration?* Why is it dangerous?

15. List three ways to practice safe behavior in sports.

16. What are the dangers of using anabolic steroids?

17. Would you describe yourself as physically fit? Think back to last week and write down your physical activities. What do you conclude from your list?

18. How might staying fit help you manage stress? How has physical activity provided you with an outlet for tension or anger?

19. Your friend wants to improve her physical fitness. When she exercises, she rarely raises her heartbeat above 50 percent of her maximum heartbeat rate. What advice would you offer her? Why?

20. How are strength, endurance, and flexibility related?

21. What adjustments do you need to make in frequency, intensity, and time to meet your personal workout needs?

22. Why is it important to set fitness goals before starting an exercise program?

23. What advice would you give to a teammate who often misses practice or arrives late?

24. Carlton borrows his older brother's protective gear and his sports shoes, even though his brother is much bigger. How is he risking injury?

Applying Health Skills

25. Survey classmates, family members, and adult friends who are physically active. Ask each person why he or she maintains an active lifestyle. Write down the answers and compare them to the benefits shown in Figure 4–1. Present your survey findings to the class.

26. Look through magazines to find photos of people performing different types of physical activity or exercise. Cut them out and make a collage on a poster. Explain in captions how these activities contribute to these people's overall physical fitness. Share your poster with the class.

27. Make a weekly activity plan like the one shown in Figure 4–7. Exchange plans with another student. Offer suggestions to each other for changing, improving, or expanding the plan.

28. With a partner, make a list of all the places in your community that provide opportunities to join a sports team. Include on your list information about the hours they are open and fees they charge. Share your list with your classmates.

FIGURE 4–11.
Living an active lifestyle helps you feel good about yourself.

Your Body Image

Quick Write

How are teens' body images portrayed in magazines and other media? Are they realistic? Write down your opinions on this issue.

LEARN ABOUT...

- the relationship between weight, growth, and health.
- how eating and physical activity habits affect weight.
- ways to maintain your healthy weight.
- why some people develop eating disorders.
- the health risks associated with eating disorders.
- where a teen with an eating disorder can get help.

Body Image

How do you react when you look at yourself in the mirror? How do you feel about your appearance? *The way you see yourself* is called your **body image**. A person who feels good about the way she or he looks is more likely to have a positive self-image.

Trying to look the same as a model, an athlete, or anyone else is not a healthy approach to body image. No individual weight or body type is ideal at any age. Your body will grow and change throughout your teen years. A few extra pounds now, for example, could disappear in a few months after you grow an inch. Someone who feels too skinny may fill out after he or she stops growing taller.

Your Appropriate Weight

Many factors influence your **appropriate weight**, or *the weight that is best for your body.* These factors include your gender, height, age, and body frame (small, medium, or large), and, during your teen years, your growth pattern. At your appropriate weight, you are more likely to feel good about yourself and have the energy you need for peak performance.

You can find out if your weight is appropriate by using the Body Mass Index chart in Figure 4–12. The **Body Mass Index (BMI)** is *a measurement that allows you to assess your body size, taking your height and weight into account.*

Weight Problems

Being overweight or underweight is unhealthy. People who are **overweight** are *more than the appropriate weight for gender, height, age, body frame, and growth pattern.* People who are **underweight** are *less than the appropriate weight for gender, height, age, body frame, and growth pattern.* Many teens are concerned that they have a weight problem. In reality, most teens don't need to lose or gain weight. In fact, unwise dieting can interfere with normal growth and development.

Overweight

Eating empty-calorie foods or eating more food than needed leads to weight gain. Busy teens tend to grab food on the run from fast-food places and convenience stores. Much of this food is high in fat and calories. Some food comes in supersize portions, which attract consumers with a bargain price. Weight gain is also linked to a sedentary, or inactive, lifestyle. Many people spend their day sitting at a desk. At home they may watch television, play video games, or use a computer. These activities burn fewer calories than those involving movement.

Excess weight puts strain on the heart and lungs. Overweight people have an increased risk of developing high blood pressure, diabetes, heart disease, cancer, and stroke. If you think that you are overweight, check with your health care professional. You may just be gaining a few pounds before getting taller. This is the body's way of storing up extra energy for growing.

VOCABULARY

- body image
- appropriate weight
- Body Mass Index (BMI)
- overweight
- underweight
- eating disorders
- anorexia nervosa
- malnutrition
- bulimia
- binge eating disorder

FIGURE 4–12.

Body Mass Index

To find your place on the chart, first calculate your BMI by following the formula given below. Then trace an imaginary line straight up from your age to the BMI you calculated. The point where your age and BMI meet tells you the approximate weight range you fall into. However, since people grow at different rates, this is only an estimate.

To calculate your BMI:

1. Multiply your weight in pounds by 0.45.

2. Multiply your height in inches by 0.025. Square the result.

3. Divide your answer to step 1 by your answer to step 2. The answer is your BMI.

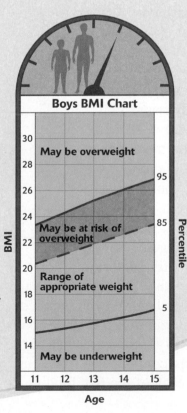

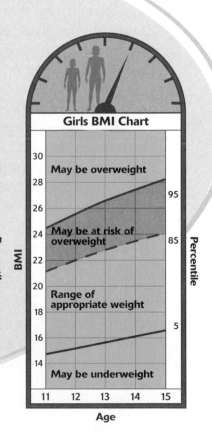

Underweight

If you appear skinny during your teenage growth years, you are not necessarily underweight. You may simply be growing taller first. After reaching a certain height, your body may take time to catch up and add shape and muscle.

Some people are underweight because they do not consume enough nutrients. Others are underweight because of extreme dieting or excessive exercise. Both reasons pose serious health risks. People who are underweight may not have enough body fat to cushion the body's organs and bones. They may often feel tired due to insufficient food energy, and they have little body fat as an energy reserve. Underweight people are also more likely to develop disorders related to a low food intake, such as anemia.

The Role of Calories

The calories you take in and use every day affect your weight. As you know, calories measure both the energy available in food and the energy your body uses. The more calories a food contains, the more energy it provides.

You consume calories whenever you eat. When you take in the same number of calories that your body burns, your weight remains the same. When your body burns more calories than you take in, you lose weight. When you take in more calories than your body burns, you gain weight. Your body stores the extra calories as fat.

On average, teen females require 2,200–2,400 calories per day, and teen males require 2,800–3,200. Do not worry if you eat too much or too little in a given day. It is more important to focus on your average intake over the long term.

Healthy weight management requires more than counting calories. You'll want to consider the nutrient value of the foods you eat. A healthful eating plan is based on foods with high nutrient density. These foods contain large amounts of nutrients relative to the number of calories they contain. The following are examples of foods with high nutrient density from each of the five food groups.

FIGURE 4–13.

When you're thirsty, choose water instead of a soft drink. A 12-ounce can of cola may have 150 empty calories.

- **Grain Group:** whole wheat pasta and breads, rice, tortillas, bagels
- **Fruit Group:** all fruits
- **Vegetable Group:** all vegetables
- **Meat and Beans Group:** tofu, chicken, lean beef, tuna, beans
- **Milk Group:** low-fat and fat-free milk, yogurt, cheese

Reaching Your Appropriate Weight

If you think that you might be above or under your appropriate weight, check with a health care professional. He or she can determine if you need to lose or gain weight while you are growing, and can suggest the best approach for you. Most successful weight-change programs combine increased physical activity with a healthful eating plan, including mostly nutrient-dense foods.

Adjusting Calorie Intake

To reduce calorie intake, eat smaller servings. Instead of eating fried foods, choose foods that are broiled, baked, or steamed. Add flavor by using herbs and spices instead of oils or cream sauces. Drink fewer soft drinks and more water.

To increase calorie intake, eat more servings of lean and low-fat foods, including those with complex carbohydrates, such as breads, pastas, and vegetables. Whether you want to reduce or increase calorie intake, use the Dietary Guidelines as a guide.

Increasing Physical Activity

Physical activity plays a key role in keeping a healthy weight. It helps tone muscle and reduce fat. You can also burn calories by increasing your level of activity. Figure 4–14 lists some of the other benefits of regular physical activity.

FIGURE 4–14.

PHYSICAL ACTIVITY AND YOUR WEIGHT

Physical activity helps you manage your weight and stay healthy. *How do you stay physically active?*

Physical Activity . . .

A Helps your heart and lungs work better.

B Can help strengthen and firm your muscles.

C Burns calories and helps you maintain a healthy weight.

D Helps you manage stress.

E Helps you feel good, have more energy, and develop higher self-esteem.

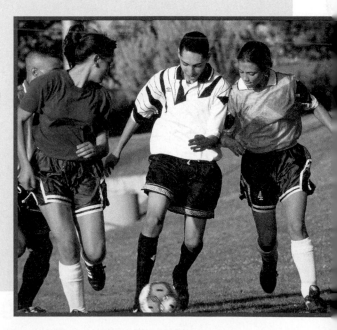

Managing Weight Change

Fad diets, pills, and other "procedures" that promote quick weight loss cannot replace informed, healthful choices about weight change. In fact, they may lead to loss of water and lean muscle rather than fat.

The majority of fad diets promote eating very few calories, eliminating certain healthful foods, or skipping meals altogether. Most of these "diets" are ineffective and perhaps unsafe. They can lead to serious nutritional deficiencies. Fasting, or not eating for long periods of time, is also dangerous. Side effects of fasting can include loss of muscle tissue, heart damage, digestive problems, and stunted growth. Diet pills can be addictive and can have serious side effects. Body wraps cause water loss rather than loss of fat. With all these methods, weight may drop temporarily but returns quickly.

Recognize the Risks

These behaviors may put your health at risk:

- Following weight-loss programs that promise quick results
- Relying on special products or formulas
- Trying to lose more than 1/2 to 1 pound per week
- Eating fewer than 2,200 calories a day for a female, or 3,000 for a male
- Skipping meals

Weight-Management Tips

To maintain a healthy weight, learn to eat smart and stay active for a lifetime. The following tips will help you manage your weight safely.

- Work with a health care professional to develop a safe weight-management program.
- Set realistic goals.
- Burn calories through fun physical activities, such as bike riding, dancing, skating, and swimming.
- Develop healthful eating habits; follow the Dietary Guidelines for Americans to help you select nutrient-dense foods.
- Plan your meals and snacks so that you take in the same number of calories that you burn.
- Watch your portion sizes so you know how much you're eating.

FIGURE 4–15.
Developing healthful eating habits will help you maintain a healthy weight.

The Risks of Eating Disorders

Many teens spend a great deal of time worrying about their weight. Some even try to lose weight. Sometimes these worries and efforts get out of control. Obsession with food intake, coupled with mental and emotional problems, can lead to eating disorders. **Eating disorders** are *extreme and damaging eating behaviors that can lead to sickness and even death.*

Eating disorders can be triggered by many psychological factors, including low self-esteem, poor body image, and depression. Teens are at risk because of the normal stresses during the teen years and the natural growth patterns of their bodies. Eating disorders are serious; they can be fatal. People with eating disorders need professional help.

Anorexia Nervosa

Anorexia nervosa is *an eating disorder characterized by self-starvation leading to extreme weight loss. Anorexia* means "without appetite," and *nervosa* means "of nervous origin." Most people who develop anorexia nervosa are teenage girls and young women. Men and teenage boys can also have the disorder, however. People with anorexia nervosa have a distorted body image. Most also have trouble coping with everyday stresses, such as high expectations, the need to achieve, or the need to be popular.

HANDS-ON HEALTH

CALCULATING FAT INTAKE

The Dietary Guidelines recommend that you receive no more than 35 percent of your calories from fat. In this activity, you will learn how to calculate the percentage of calories from fat in a given food.

WHAT YOU WILL NEED
- pencil and notebook
- calculator (optional)
- 3 Nutrition Facts food labels

WHAT YOU WILL DO
1. Choose one of your food labels. Divide the amount in the "calories from fat" category by the amount in the "total calories" category. For example, a 200-calorie granola bar might contain 80 calories from fat. Divide 80 by 200 and you get 0.4.

2. Multiply the result by 100 to express the figure as a percentage. 0.4 times 100 is 40. The granola bar derives 40 percent of its calories from fat.
3. Repeat this procedure with your other food labels and record the results.

IN CONCLUSION
1. Which, if any, of the foods provides over 35 percent of its calories from fat?
2. Save labels from as many foods you eat in a day as possible. Use the formula to determine the percentage of calories from fat of each.
3. How can you use the formula to make healthy choices in your daily food intake?

Most people with anorexia nervosa eat very little. Some develop **malnutrition**, *a condition in which the body doesn't get the nutrients it needs to grow and function properly.* They may also develop shrunken organs, bone loss, low body temperature, low blood pressure, and a slowed metabolism. In some people with anorexia, an irregular heartbeat may lead to cardiac arrest.

Treatment for anorexia nervosa sometimes requires a stay at a hospital or clinic. There, the person will get the nutrients needed to restore physical health. She or he will also receive counseling to address the underlying problems causing the disorder.

FIGURE 4-16.

Even when they are very thin, people with anorexia nervosa see themselves as overweight.

Bulimia

Another type of eating disorder is bulimia, or bulimia nervosa. **Bulimia** is *a condition in which a person eats large amounts of food and then tries to purge.* Many people with bulimia force themselves to vomit. Others take laxatives to force the food quickly through their body. Although bulimia is most common among young women and teenage girls, young men and teenage boys can also develop the disorder.

People with bulimia are extremely concerned about being thin and attractive. They have an overwhelming need to maintain control over their bodies. They might gorge on large amounts of food. Then, fearing that they are losing control of their bodies, they may take drastic steps to regain control. Some go on crash diets, including fasting, to try to make up for overeating.

Bulimia damages the body in many ways. Stomach acids from frequent vomiting can damage teeth and injure the mouth and throat. Vomiting can also cause the stomach to rupture. Repeated use of laxatives can damage the kidneys and liver, causing long-term health problems. Many people with bulimia suffer from malnutrition as a result of emptying the body of nutrients.

Binge Eating Disorder

Another eating disorder is **binge eating disorder**, or *compulsive overeating.* This disorder may be the most common eating disorder, affecting between 1 million and 2 million Americans. People with binge eating disorder eat unusually large amounts of food at a time. Unlike people with bulimia, though, they do not rid their bodies of the food. Afterward, they often feel a sense of guilt and shame.

People with binge eating disorder may use food as a way of coping with depression and other mental/emotional problems. However, the guilt and shame they feel after bingeing adds to the depression. This creates a cycle that can be difficult to break without professional help. Because binge eating disorder often leads to excess weight, it contributes to many health problems, such as obesity, diabetes, and heart disease.

Help for People with Eating Disorders

People who have eating disorders usually need professional help. Sometimes this help can come from a counselor or psychologist. Help is also available through clinics and support groups such as Overeaters Anonymous, which are found in many communities. If a friend develops an eating disorder, you might want to speak to a school nurse or counselor. It is natural to want to solve your friend's problem by yourself. However, you can help most by showing support and guiding him or her to a health professional.

Family and friends can also provide much-needed support for a person with an eating disorder. Often their role is to encourage the person to seek help. Figure 4–17 takes a closer look at the role that family and friends can play.

FIGURE 14–17.

HELPING SOMEONE WITH AN EATING DISORDER

Someone you know may have an eating disorder. Following these steps may enable you to help him or her.

A **Encourage the person to seek help.**
A person with an eating disorder may not be aware of the seriousness of the condition. The person may also deny that the problem exists and may not want to be helped.

B **Tell an adult.**
You can talk to your parent or guardian, the school nurse, a counselor, or another trusted adult to see if they can help the person get the needed help.

C **Get professional help.**
Psychological problems are usually the cause of eating disorders. The person with the disorder requires professional

help. Sometimes family members are also encouraged to meet with the counselor.

D **Encourage the person to join a support group.**
Support groups provide encouragement to people with eating disorders and help them on the road to recovery.

E **Recommend a follow-up.**
Eating disorders can recur and could become lifelong problems. Follow-up visits to counselors and support groups are an important part of the recovery process.

DECISION MAKING

Helping a Friend

Recently, Jasmine has become concerned about her best friend Maria. At lunch, Maria barely touches her food. She doesn't have the energy for riding her bike anymore. She has become very thin. Yet when Jasmine and Maria went shopping recently, Maria complained about being fat, even though small-sized clothes were too big for her.

Jasmine is worried that Maria may have anorexia nervosa. Jasmine has tried to share her concerns with Maria, but Maria denies that she has a problem. Jasmine has thought about talking to Maria's mother, but she doesn't want to make Maria angry by going behind her back.

WHAT WOULD YOU DO?

Apply the decision-making process to Jasmine's situation. With a classmate, role-play a conversation in which Jasmine expresses her concerns to Maria. Then role-play a conversation between Jasmine and Maria's mother. What other options does Jasmine have?

1. **STATE THE SITUATION.**
2. **LIST THE OPTIONS.**
3. **WEIGH THE POSSIBLE OUTCOMES.**
4. **CONSIDER YOUR VALUES.**
5. **MAKE A DECISION AND ACT.**
6. **EVALUATE THE DECISION.**

CHECKPOINTS

Lesson 2 Review

Using complete sentences, answer the following questions on a sheet of paper.

1. Define body image. Use the term in an original sentence.
2. What is the definition of overweight?
3. Give two reasons why teens might become overweight.
4. What are four tips for reaching or maintaining a healthy weight?
5. What is an eating disorder?
6. Name four ways in which anorexia and bulimia can harm the body.
7. What is the difference between bulimia and binge eating disorder?
8. What kinds of people can help a person with an eating disorder?
9. Why are teens generally advised not to try to lose weight during their growing years?
10. Your friend Ronnie wants to go on a crash diet to lose weight. What advice would you give him?

Applying Health Skills

11. Develop a plan to make healthful food choices and increase physical activity over the next three days.

12. Find a magazine article or book about someone with bulimia or anorexia nervosa. Read the article or book and write a brief summary of it. What influences or pressures contributed to the disorder? Were the influences internal or external?

FIGURE 4–18.
Cadets perform morning drill.

CHAPTER 5

Making Safe, Drug-Free Decisions

Chapter Outline

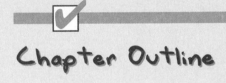

- Lesson 1   Medicines and Drugs
- Lesson 2   Tobacco
- Lesson 3   Alcohol

Quick Write

In what ways have medicines and drugs helped people lead healthier lives? In what ways have they created problems?

Medicines and Drugs

The Difference between Medicines and Drugs

What do you think of when you hear the words *medicines* and *drugs?* Many people use the terms interchangeably. However, there is a difference. **Drugs** are *substances other than food that change the structure or function of the body or mind.* **Medicines** are *drugs that are used to treat or prevent diseases and other conditions.* All medicines are drugs, but not all drugs are medicines.

Medicine Safety

In the United States, the Food and Drug Administration (FDA) is responsible for ensuring that all medicines are safe and effective. The FDA approval process includes the following steps.

1. A potential new medicine is discovered.

2. Researchers conduct experiments to help decide how the new medicine might be used to treat an illness. Early testing is conducted on animals to determine if the medicine has any harmful effects.

3. The FDA reviews the preliminary research and test results. If approved, the new medicine is studied in humans.

4. If the FDA decides that the medicine is safe and effective for its intended use, the FDA approves it.

5. Once approved, the medicine can be made available for physicians to prescribe or for consumers to purchase.

Releasing Medicines to the Public

One function of the FDA is to determine how the health consumer can obtain a medicine. There are two ways.

Prescription Medicines

Some medicines are very strong and potentially harmful, so doctors must write special orders for them. These **prescription medicines** are *medicines that can be sold only with a written*

Quick Write

Briefly describe the most important reason teens should avoid drug use.

LEARN ABOUT...

- how medicines differ from drugs.
- types of medicines.
- how medicines are used.
- how medicines affect the body.
- the difference between drug misuse and drug abuse.
- how narcotics affect the body.
- the effects of stimulants on the body.
- what depressants do to the body.
- the risks of using marijuana.
- the dangers of hallucinogens.
- how inhalants affect the body.

order from a physician. Figure 5–1 shows the information that must appear on all prescription medicine labels. Always read the instructions before you start taking any kind of medication.

Over-the-Counter (OTC) Medicines

Have you ever used cough syrup or nasal spray when you had a cold? These **over-the-counter (OTC) medicines** are *medicines that are safe enough to be taken without a written order from a physician.* OTC medicines may cause harm if not used as directed.

OTC medicines are available at pharmacies, supermarkets, and other stores that sell medicine. Always check with an adult before using any OTC or other medicine. Be sure to read and understand the information provided on an OTC medicine label.

Types of Medicines

There are different types of medicines, and each type affects the body in specific ways. The most common uses for medicines include preventing disease, fighting infection, and relieving pain.

Medicines to Prevent Diseases

Some medicines, known as vaccines, prevent a disease from developing. Traditional **vaccines** contain *a preparation of dead or weakened germs that causes the immune system to produce antibodies.* **Antibodies** are *proteins that attack and kill or disable specific germs that cause disease.*

Common vaccines given today include those that protect you from diphtheria, whooping cough, measles, mumps, rubella, chicken pox, pneumonia, and hepatitis A and B. These vaccines provide long-lasting protection. Other vaccines, such as the flu shot, must be administered periodically.

Medicines to Fight Infection

Many germs and diseases cannot be prevented with vaccines. Instead, certain medicines are used to restore health. **Antibiotics** (an·ti·by·AH·tiks) are *medicines that reduce or kill harmful bacteria in the body.* Each type of antibiotic fights only certain types of bacteria. For example, penicillin (pen·uh·SI·luhn) is highly effective in killing the bacteria that cause strep throat and pneumonia.

Medicines to Relieve Pain

Many people take medicines to relieve pain. When the body feels pain, such as that from a headache or toothache, pain messages travel along the nerves and spinal cord to the brain. The role of pain medicines is to block these pain messages or lessen their effect.

LEARN ABOUT...

- what club drugs and steroids do to the body.
- ways to avoid drugs.
- how drug users can kick the habit.
- where people who abuse drugs can get help.
- alternatives to using drugs.

VOCABULARY

- drugs
- medicines
- prescription medicines
- over-the-counter (OTC) medicines
- vaccine
- antibodies
- antibiotics
- side effect
- tolerance
- narcotics
- addiction
- stimulants
- amphetamine
- methamphetamine
- depressants
- hallucinogens
- psychological dependence
- inhalant
- physical dependence
- withdrawal
- detoxification

FIGURE 5–1.

PRESCRIPTION MEDICINE LABEL

Medicine labels provide important information. *How many times can this prescription be refilled?*

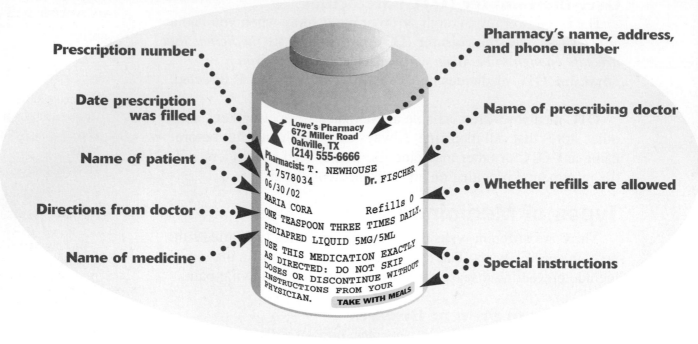

Prescription number •

Date prescription was filled •

Name of patient •

Directions from doctor • • •

Name of medicine •

Pharmacy's name, address, and phone number

Name of prescribing doctor

Whether refills are allowed

Special instructions

Lowe's Pharmacy
672 Miller Road
Oakville, TX
(214) 555-6666
Pharmacist: T. NEWHOUSE
R 7578034   Dr. FISCHER
06/30/02
MARIA CORA   Refills 0
ONE TEASPOON THREE TIMES DAILY.
PEDIAPRED LIQUID 5MG/5ML
USE THIS MEDICATION EXACTLY
AS DIRECTED: DO NOT SKIP
DOSES OR DISCONTINUE WITHOUT
INSTRUCTIONS FROM YOUR
PHYSICIAN.   TAKE WITH MEALS

Aspirin is one of the most commonly used medicines for treating minor pain. Aspirin substitutes, such as acetaminophen and ibuprofen, are also popular. These pain medicines are widely available and do not require a doctor's prescription. Occasionally, a serious illness or a chronic disease will cause serious pain. In this case, a doctor may prescribe stronger medicines such as codeine or morphine.

Other Medicines

A variety of medicines is available to treat people with certain health problems or conditions. Specific medicines are used by people with chronic conditions, including heart and blood pressure problems, diabetes, and allergies.

Medicine in the Body

The effects of a medicine in the body depend on the type and amount of medicine taken. The way a medicine is taken will also affect how quickly it begins to work in the body. Figure 5–2 illustrates the four main ways in which medicines can enter the body.

Medicines will affect each person differently. That is why it is important for medicine to be used only as prescribed or directed, and only by the person who needs the medicine.

FIGURE 5–2.

HOW MEDICINES ENTER THE BODY

The way medicines enter the body depends on their form.

Ingestion

Medicine in the form of pills, tablets, capsules, and liquids is ingested, or swallowed. The medicine moves through the stomach and small intestine and is absorbed into the bloodstream and circulated throughout the body. You can take cold medicines this way.

Injection

Medicine given through injection goes directly into the blood. Some injections are given in a vein, others under the skin or into a muscle. If you have diabetes, you may need to give yourself daily injections.

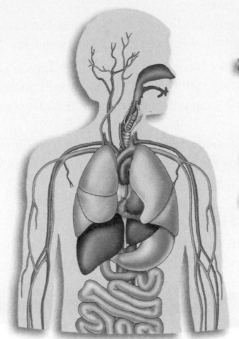

Inhalation

When a liquid medicine is changed into a fine mist, it can be inhaled, or breathed in. If you have asthma, you may need an inhaler.

Absorption

Creams and ointments are applied to the skin or scalp and absorbed by the body. Skin patches are applied to the skin and release medicine over time. If you have a cold, you may rub ointment on your chest to clear your lungs.

Side Effects

In addition to its intended effect, some medicines also cause one or more side effects. A **side effect** is *any effect of a medicine other than the one intended.* Common side effects include headaches, an upset stomach, and drowsiness. If you have side effects with a medicine, talk to your doctor, nurse, or pharmacist. Some side effects, such as kidney failure, can be serious. Others may stop after the body adjusts to the medicine. Some people may be allergic to certain medicines and may need to see a doctor about a replacement.

Tolerance

When used over a long period of time, certain medicines can cause a person to develop a tolerance. **Tolerance** is *a condition in which a person's body becomes used to the effect of a medicine and needs greater and greater amounts of it in order for it to be effective.* In some cases, the medicine ceases to be effective and the doctor must prescribe a different type of medicine.

Overuse of Medicines

If medicines are overused, they can lose their ability to fight diseases. For example, the use of penicillin became widespread in the 1940s. Within just a few years, new strains of bacteria had developed. The new bacteria were resistant to penicillin. The more often antibiotics are used, the more likely it is that bacteria will develop a resistance to them. This is another reason why medicines must always be used wisely and in moderation.

Mixing Medicines

When two or more medicines are taken at the same time, the combined effects may be dangerous. The following reactions are possible.

- Each medicine may have a stronger effect than it would have if taken alone.
- The medicines may combine to produce unexpected effects.
- One medicine may cancel out the expected effects of the other.

Because mixing medicines can produce unpredictable and sometimes even deadly results, it is vital for people to let their physician know about any and all medicines they are presently taking.

Drug Misuse and Abuse

People can harm themselves by not using drugs properly. Drug misusers take legal drugs in an improper way. Drug abusers take substances that are against the law or are

HEALTH SKILLS ACTIVITY

PRACTICING HEALTHFUL BEHAVIORS

Medicine Safety in the Home

How much do you know about medicine safety? Follow these tips to store, use, and dispose of medicines safely.

- Store medicines in a cool, dry place.
- Keep medicines safely sealed in childproof containers, and keep them out of the reach of children.

- Do not share prescription medicines. They could cause serious harm to someone else.
- Do not use nonprescription medicines for more than ten days at a time unless you check with your doctor.
- Before taking two or more medicines at the same time, get your doctor's approval.
- Know what medicines are in your home and what they are used to treat. Keep only those that are currently needed.
- Do not use medicines that have passed their expiration date.
- To safely dispose of outdated or unused liquids or pills, flush them down the toilet.

WITH A GROUP
Create a "Medicine Safety Checklist" suitable for home use. Review the completed checklist with your family. Post the list in an appropriate place in your home.

not supposed to be taken into the human body. They may also use legal drugs for nonmedical purposes. The following are forms of drug misuse and drug abuse.

Drug Misuse

- Using a drug without following the directions
- Combining medicines without a physician's advice
- Taking more of a drug than the doctor ordered
- Using a drug prescribed for someone else
- Giving your prescription to someone else
- Using a drug for longer than a physician advises

Drug Abuse

- Using any illegal drug
- Using a medicine when you do not need it
- Taking a substance that was not meant to enter the body
- Using a drug for purposes other than medical treatment
- Faking health problems to obtain or renew a prescription

Narcotics

Narcotics are *specific drugs that are obtainable only by prescription and are used to relieve pain.* Doctors may prescribe the narcotics morphine or codeine, for example, to treat extreme pain. Narcotics can be safe when taken under a physician's supervision, but they are so addictive that their sale and use is controlled by law. People with an **addiction** have a *physical or psychological need for a drug.* Pharmacists must keep records of all sales of narcotics.

Heroin

Heroin (HEHR·uh·win) is an illegal narcotic that is made from morphine. It is the most commonly abused narcotic and is highly addictive. When users do not get the heroin they need, they feel severe pain. Heroin depresses the central nervous system and can lead to coma or death.

Because drug users often share dirty needles, users of heroin and other injected drugs are at increased risk of contracting HIV. According to recent CDC data, half of all new infections with HIV occur among abusers of injected drugs.

Stimulants

Stimulants (STIM·yuh·luhnts) are *substances that speed up the body's functions.* Stimulants make the heart beat faster, increase breathing rate, and raise blood pressure. The effects of some stimulants are so mild that people may not even realize they are using a drug. Caffeine is a stimulant found in cocoa, coffee, tea, and many soft drinks.

Some stimulants may be prescribed to help people with certain physical or emotional problems. Stimulant abuse can be very dangerous, however. High doses of strong stimulants may cause blurred vision, dizziness, anxiety, loss of coordination, or collapse. Stimulants such as amphetamine, cocaine, and crack can also become habit-forming, and users can become addicted quickly. Figure 5–3 describes some common stimulants and their harmful effects.

Amphetamine

Amphetamine (am·FE·tuh·meen) is *a drug that stimulates the central nervous system.* Doctors may prescribe amphetamines to treat hyperactive children. Amphetamines are highly addictive, however. People who use or abuse amphetamines can develop a dependence on the drugs, needing larger and larger doses to get the desired effect.

Methamphetamine

Methamphetamine is *a stimulant similar to amphetamine.* Doctors prescribe methamphetamines to treat diseases such as narcolepsy, Parkinson's disease, and obesity. In recent years, methamphetamines have appeared in "club drugs"—dangerous, illegal substances available at dance clubs and all-night parties.

Cocaine

Cocaine is a powerful, illegal stimulant. Its abuse has become a major health problem in the United States. Some people use cocaine because it makes them feel happy and energetic. This feeling is short-lived, however, and is followed by

FIGURE 5–3.

EFFECTS OF STIMULANTS

Stimulants come in a variety of forms, all of which can be very dangerous if abused.

Substance	Other Names	Forms	Methods of Use	Harmful Effects
Amphetamine	Crystal, ice, glass, crank, speed, uppers	Pills, powder, chunky crystals	Swallowed, snorted up the nose, smoked, injected	Uneven heartbeat, rise in blood pressure, physical collapse, stroke, heart attack, and death
Methamphetamine	Meth, crank, speed, ice	Pills, powder, crystals	Swallowed, snorted up the nose, smoked, injected	Memory loss, damage to heart and nervous system, seizures, death
Cocaine	Coke, dust, snow, flake, blow, girl	White powder	Snorted up the nose, injected	Damage to nose lining, liver, and heart; heart attack, seizures, stroke, and death
Crack	Crack, freebase rocks, rock	Off-white rocks or chunks	Smoked, injected	Damage to lungs if smoked, seizures, heart attack, and death

depression as the drug wears off. Users often take more cocaine to relieve the depression, thus forming an addiction to it. Cocaine is a dangerous drug, and an overdose can be fatal.

Crack

Crack is a concentrated form of cocaine that can be smoked. Smoking crack has the same effects on the body as using cocaine, only stronger. Crack reaches the brain within seconds and produces an intense high. The high lasts only for a few minutes, though, and is followed by an equally intense low. The user then craves more of the drug to relieve the intense bad feelings. For these reasons, crack is one of the most addictive and dangerous drugs used in the United States today.

Depressants

Depressants are *substances that slow down the body's functions and reactions.* These substances, which are often called sedatives, lower blood pressure and slow down heart rate and breathing. Doctors sometimes prescribe depressants for relief of anxiety, tension, nervousness, and sleeplessness. There are three main kinds of depressants.

- **Tranquilizers** (TRAN·kwuh·ly·zerz), when used as prescribed by a physician, can help reduce anxiety and relax muscles.
- **Barbiturates** (bar·BI·chuh·ruhts) are powerful sedatives that produce a feeling of relaxation.
- **Hypnotics** (hip·NAH·tiks) are very strong drugs that bring on sleep.

Depressants should be taken only under a doctor's supervision. If taken over an extended period, they can cause dependence and a need for more and more of the drug.

Depressants produce effects similar to those produced by alcohol, which itself is a form of depressant. When depressants are combined with alcohol, the effects increase and the risks multiply. The results can be deadly. Figure 5–4 provides more information about depressants and their effects on the body.

Street Drugs

Companies that manufacture drugs sold as medicines must follow strict government regulations. These laws ensure that the medicines are pure and consistent in strength, known risks, and side effects.

Any drug that is made or sold outside of these laws is considered a street drug. Street drugs include illegally made, packaged, or sold legal drugs, such as amphetamines. Street drugs also include illegal drugs, such as heroin and marijuana. There are no laws to protect the purity and content of street drugs. People who use them don't know how much of the drug they are taking. As a result, they risk being poisoned and dying of accidental overdose.

FIGURE 5–4.

EFFECTS OF DEPRESSANTS

If abused, depressants can have many harmful effects on the body, up to and including death.

Substance	Other Names	Forms	Methods of Use	Harmful Effects
Tranquilizer	Valium, Librium, Xanax	Pills or capsules	Swallowed	Anxiety; reduced coordination and attention span. Withdrawal can cause tremors and lead to coma or death.
Barbiturate	Downers, barbs, yellow jackets, reds	Pills or capsules	Swallowed	Causes mood changes and excessive sleep. Can lead to coma.
Hypnotic	Quaaludes, Ludes, Sopor	Pills or capsules	Swallowed	Impaired coordination and judgment. High doses may cause internal bleeding, coma, or death.

Marijuana

Marijuana is the most commonly used street drug. The main active chemical in marijuana is THC (tetrahydrocannabinol), which affects the brain. Hashish, which is made from the same plant, is much stronger than marijuana because it contains more THC. Figure 5–5 lists the effects of marijuana.

Although some users mix marijuana with food and eat it, most choose to smoke it. As a result, marijuana smokers experience many of the same lung problems as tobacco smokers. These include persistent coughing, bronchitis symptoms, and frequent colds. Marijuana smoke contains three to five times the amount of tar and other cancer-causing substances found in tobacco smoke.

Hallucinogens

Hallucinogens (huh·LOO·suhn·uh·jenz) are *drugs that distort moods, thoughts, and senses.* Physical effects of hallucinogens include increased heart rate and blood pressure and lack of muscle coordination. Hallucinogens can also cause decreased sensitivity to pain, which can result in serious self-injury.

Taking a hallucinogen may cause the user to hallucinate, or see things that are not really there. Sometimes it can trigger uncontrolled, violent behavior. Hallucinogens also cause people to lose their sense of direction, distance, and time. These effects often lead to misjudgments that result in serious injuries and death.

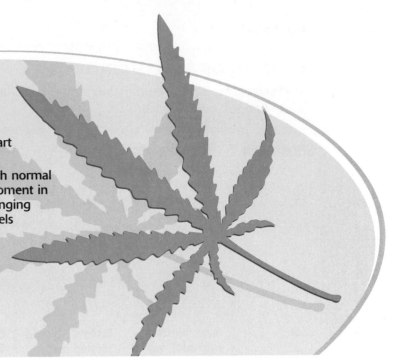

FIGURE 5–5.

EFFECTS OF MARIJUANA

Common street names for marijuana include pot, grass, weed, joint, and herb.

- Reduces memory, reaction time, and coordination, and impairs judgment
- Reduces initiative and ambition
- Increases heart rate and appetite and lowers body temperature

- Damages heart and lungs
- Interferes with normal body development in teens by changing hormone levels
- May cause addiction

PCP

Phencyclidine (fen·SI·kluh·deen), commonly called PCP, is a powerful and dangerous hallucinogen whose effects last a long time. PCP produces strange, destructive behavior, which causes many users to end up in hospital emergency rooms. PCP use often leads to **psychological dependence**, *an addiction in which the mind sends the body a message that it needs more of a drug.* Figure 5–6 provides more information about PCP.

LSD

LSD is an abbreviation for lysergic (luh·SER·jik) acid diethylamide (dy·e·thuh·LA·myd), another powerful hallucinogen. Use of LSD often produces rapid mood swings and hallucinations. Some users have terrifying thoughts and feelings, such as fear that they are dying or going crazy. Many LSD users experience flashbacks. During a flashback, the effects of LSD may recur days, months, or years after the drug was taken. Figure 5–6 gives additional information about LSD.

Inhalants

Any substance whose fumes are sniffed and inhaled to produce mind-altering sensations is considered an **inhalant**. Household products that come in aerosol spray cans are commonly used as inhalants. These products include spray paint, cleaning fluid, lighter fluid, hair spray, nail polish remover, and other harmful substances. These substances are not meant to be taken into the body and can be very dangerous.

When inhalants are breathed in, their harmful fumes go directly to the brain. These fumes commonly cause headache, nausea, vomiting, and loss of coordination. A single use can result in sudden death. Inhalant use can lead to **physical dependence**, *a type of addiction in which the body itself feels a direct need for a drug.* Long-term inhalant use can damage the liver, kidneys, and brain.

FIGURE 5–6.

EFFECTS OF HALLUCINOGENS

Hallucinogens can have many harmful effects on the body,
up to and including death.

Substance	Other Names	Forms	Methods of Use	Harmful Effects
PCP	Angel dust, supergrass, killer weed, rocket fuel	White powder; liquid	Applied to leafy materials and smoked	Loss of coordination; increase in heart rate, blood pressure, and body temperature; convulsions, heart and lung failure, or broken blood vessels; bizarre or violent behavior; temporary psychosis; false feeling of having super powers.
LSD	Acid, blotter, microdot, white lightning	Tablets; squares soaked on paper	Eaten or licked	Increase in blood pressure, heart rate, and body temperature; chills, nausea, tremors, and sleeplessness; unpredictable behavior; flashbacks; false feeling of having super powers.

Club Drugs

Club drugs are drugs that are associated with nightclubs, concerts, and all-night dance parties called raves. Other terms for drugs associated with these activities are *designer drugs* and *look-alike drugs.* The term *designer drug* often refers to a synthetic version of a natural drug. *Look-alike drugs* are drugs that resemble and are passed off as another drug.

Some club drugs are colorless, tasteless, and odorless. These properties have led to the dangerous practice of drug slipping. Drug slipping occurs when a drug is placed in someone's food or beverage without that person's knowledge. Because drug slipping has been used to aid in committing rape, some club drugs are sometimes called date rape drugs. Commonly used club drugs include:

- **Ecstasy**, also called E, X, and XTC, is a stimulant and a hallucinogen in pill form. Users may experience confusion, depression, anxiety, nausea, faintness, chills, or sweating. Ecstasy can cause permanent brain damage.
- **GHB** is a depressant, and its street names include Liquid Ecstasy, Liquid X, Georgia Home Boy, and Grievous Bodily Harm. Available in powder and liquid form, GHB is especially dangerous when taken with alcohol or other drugs. The combination may result in sleep, coma, and death.
- **Rohypnol** is a powerful sedative. It's also called the date rape drug, Roofies, and R-2. Rohypnol is typically a small white tablet, which when dissolved in liquid, has no taste or odor. The drug's short-term effect is a sleepy, relaxed feeling that lasts 2 to 8 hours. The user might also black out.

- **Ketamine** is an anesthetic used for medical purposes, mostly in treating animals. Misused as a club drug, Ketamine is often sold as a white powder to be snorted, like cocaine, or injected. The drug is also smoked with marijuana or tobacco products. Ketamine causes hallucinations and dreamlike states. Its use may result in death through respiratory failure.

Anabolic Steroids

Some athletes mistakenly believe that drugs will improve their performance. They may start using steroids, which bulk up muscle at an abnormally fast rate. In time, the harmful effects of steroids become obvious. They include acne, mood swings, nausea, liver damage, brain cancers, and shortening of final adult height when taken by children and teens. Athletes are routinely tested for illegal drugs. If they have bccn using steroids or other drugs, they face stiff penalties and may lose their right to compete.

FIGURE 5-7.

The best way to improve your athletic performance is to practice. *How could drug use ruin, rather than help, an athlete's career?*

HEALTH SKILLS ACTIVITY

REFUSAL SKILLS

Refusing Drugs

Megan is thrilled when Nina invites her to "join the crowd" at her home after school. It isn't often that a junior like Nina would even talk to Megan, a freshman.

When Megan gets to Nina's house, she sees that there are five or six girls from school but no adults. Nina brings out a little bag of tablets and tells the girls that the pills are a cool new club drug. She says that all the kids are taking the pills at dance parties. She starts to pass the pills around. Megan sits frozen in her chair.

WHAT WOULD YOU DO?

Apply refusal skills to Megan's situation. With a classmate, role-play a scenario in which Megan used S.T.O.P. to refuse Nina's offer of a club drug.

SAY NO IN A FIRM VOICE.
TELL WHY NOT.
OFFER OTHER IDEAS.
PROMPTLY LEAVE.

Staying Drug Free

You have the responsibility to be the healthiest person you can be. The best way to meet that responsibility is to make wise choices that have a positive effect on your health. One of the most important decisions you can make is to be drug free. Figure 5–8 shows some of the many advantages of avoiding drugs. What can you add to the list?

Kicking the Habit

Kicking the drug habit once it has been established is much harder than resisting the pressure to start. The first step is for the drug user to recognize that a problem exists. The next step is to start the recovery process.

If the person has become physically or psychologically addicted to a drug, then the recovery process involves withdrawal. **Withdrawal** includes *the physical and*

FIGURE 5–8.

Reasons to be Drug Free

- You will not be breaking the law.
- You will have better concentration and memory.
- You will make wiser decisions.
- You will be able to focus on improving your talents and enjoying your interests.
- You will have more natural energy.
- You can reach your full growth potential.
- You can be as healthy as possible.
- You will look better because drugs will not ruin your appearance.
- You will have better control of your feelings and actions.
- You will not regret foolish actions caused by drug-impaired judgment.
- You will not waste money on drugs.
- You will have better relationships with family members.
- You will respect yourself for taking care of your body and mind.
- You will be able to succeed in education.
- Your mental and emotional development will be on time, not delayed.

psychological symptoms that occur when someone stops using an addictive substance.
Withdrawal symptoms vary depending on the drug used, but may include vomiting,
headaches, chills, and hallucinations.

Withdrawal is often a painful process, and medications are usually given to ease the
withdrawal symptoms. In addition to ridding one's body of the addictive substance,
the recovering drug user must change his or her thinking and the habits that led to the
drug use. Although withdrawing from drugs is difficult, the benefits of becoming drug
free are well worth the effort.

Getting Help

Drug users need help to recover from their addiction. Most communities offer
support groups and treatment programs for drug addiction. A
support group is a group of people who share a
common problem and work
together to help one another
cope and recover. Common
support groups for drug
addiction include Narcotics
Anonymous and Cocaine
Anonymous. Nar-Anon
provides help for those who
have been affected by someone
else's drug use.

A good drug treatment
program has trained experts who
provide education and support and
who can help the user through the
withdrawal period. Withdrawal
often requires **detoxification**
(dee·tahk·si·fi·KAY·shuhn), *the
physical process of freeing the body
of an addictive substance.* "Detox"
also involves helping the user overcome
psychological dependence on the substance and
regain health. A variety of treatment centers are available to help people recover from
drug abuse.

FIGURE 5-9.

Being drug free allows you to have more success
in your education.

- **Detox units** are usually part of a hospital or other treatment center. Addicts remain
  under a doctor's care while going through detoxification.
- **Inpatient treatment centers** are places where people stay for a month or more to
  fully concentrate on recovery.
- **Outpatient treatment centers** are places where people get treatment for a few
  hours each day. Then they return to their homes and regular surroundings.

Living Drug Free

Choosing to live drug free will provide lifelong benefits. You will find that there are many exciting ways to spend your time.

If you feel lonely, depressed, or bored:

- Learn a new sport or hobby or join a club.
- Start a regular physical activity routine.
- Volunteer to help people in your community.

If you need help solving personal problems:

- Talk to an adult you trust.
- Contact a hot line or support group.

If you are tense and anxious:

- Learn relaxation techniques like yoga or tai chi.
- Get enough rest and physical activity, and eat properly.
- Use time management skills to avoid overscheduling your time.

FIGURE 5–10.

Learning a new hobby is just one drug-free way to feel better about yourself.

DRUG-FREE CAMPAIGN

Kicking a drug habit is much harder than resisting the pressure to start using drugs. You can help spread this important message to young people. Work with a small group of classmates to create an advertising campaign that promotes staying drug free. Design your campaign to reach younger students.

WHAT YOU WILL NEED
- art supplies and paper
- computer access, if possible

WHAT YOU WILL DO
1. Decide what media you will include in your campaign. For example, you might create a poster or a Web page for the school Web site.
2. Choose an advertising technique to use. You might create an informational, persuasive, or sensational ad.
3. Brainstorm ideas for an effective ad. Then divide the work so that each group member has a task to complete.
4. Post your ads in the classroom, in the school newspaper, or on the school Web site, as appropriate.

IN CONCLUSION
1. As a class, evaluate the effectiveness of each group's ad campaign. How well was the message conveyed?
2. What are some other ways to encourage younger students to stay drug free?

CHECKPOINTS

Lesson 1 Review

Using complete sentences, answer the following questions on a sheet of paper.

1. Give three reasons people take medicines.
2. What is the difference between antibodies and antibiotics?
3. What is a *side effect?*
4. List the three possible reactions that can result from taking more than one medicine at the same time.
5. What are three forms of drug misuse and three forms of drug abuse?
6. What is *addiction?* Use it in a complete sentence.
7. How is heroin use related to the spread of HIV?

8. List two types of stimulants, and describe their effects on the body.

9. Define the terms *hallucinogen* and *inhalant*. Explain the relationship between the two terms.

10. Name two hallucinogens known by their initials.

11. What is the difference between *psychological dependence* and *physical dependence?*

12. Why are club drugs especially dangerous?

13. List five reasons to be drug free that are most important to you.

14. Define the term *withdrawal.*

15. In your own words, describe what detoxification does.

16. Name the three types of drug treatment programs.

17. Explain the difference between prescription medicines and over-the-counter medicines.

18. Every day, Rose took the same dose of the same medicine to manage her arthritis pain. After taking the medicine for two years, it no longer helped. What might have happened?

19. How do the effects of stimulants differ from those of depressants?

20. How would you refuse an offer to try crack?

21. How can the feeling of having super powers make the use of PCP and LSD dangerous?

22. Why are teens more likely than adults to abuse inhalants?

23. Why do you think more and more teens are deciding to stay drug free?

24. Your cousin Ian says that he uses marijuana to relax. Name three alternatives that you could suggest to him.

Applying Health Skills

25. Write a letter to the editor of your school or community newspaper promoting the responsible use of antibiotics. Be sure to mention the problems caused by overuse of antibiotics.

26. Some people use illegal drugs because they think that drugs will help them manage stress. Write down five examples of healthful ways to manage stress without using drugs.

27. Use library or reliable online resources to find out what is currently known and being researched about marijuana's effects on the body. Prepare a chart showing the risks marijuana poses to various body systems, such as the lungs, brain, and immune system.

28. With a partner, collect information about reliable programs available in your school and community to help teens become or stay drug free. Report your findings to your class.

Tobacco

What Is Tobacco?

Tobacco is a plant that grows best in warm, humid climates. The leaves of a tobacco plant are dried, aged for two or three years, mixed with chemicals, and then used to make various products for smoking or chewing.

Tobacco contains a powerful drug that changes the brain's chemistry. This change makes the tobacco user want more and more tobacco. Tobacco use is harmful to people's health and is a major cause of early and preventable death. Nonetheless, many people use some form of tobacco on a regular basis.

Types of Products

Tobacco products come in many different forms, including cigarettes, cigars, and smokeless tobacco. Regardless of the form, all tobacco products are harmful. That's why there are laws to control the advertising and sale of tobacco products.

Cigarettes

Cigarettes are the most common form of tobacco. In the United States, millions of people smoke cigarettes. Cigarettes put smokers at risk for emphysema and other lung and heart diseases, cancer, infertility, and stroke. Each year more than 430,000 people in the U.S. die from diseases caused by cigarette smoking.

Cigars and Pipes

Cigars contain the same dangerous substances as cigarettes but in much larger quantities. One large cigar can contain as much tobacco as a pack of cigarettes. Cigar smokers are 4 to 10 times more likely to contract cancer of the mouth, larynx, and esophagus than nonsmokers, and they have a greater risk of dying from heart disease.

Some people smoke pipes, using loose tobacco. Pipe smokers usually inhale less than cigarette smokers, but they still increase

Quick Write

Why do some teens begin using tobacco? List all the reasons you can think of.

LEARN ABOUT...

- the different forms in which tobacco is sold and consumed.
- the harmful substances in all forms of tobacco.
- the damage tobacco does to body systems.
- the negative effects that tobacco may have on appearance.
- why people become addicted to tobacco.
- how tobacco use harms other people.
- the costs to society of tobacco use.
- reasons some teens start using tobacco.
- strategies for avoiding tobacco use.
- ways to quit using tobacco.

their risk of cancer. Cancers of the lip, mouth, and throat are common among pipe smokers.

Smokeless Tobacco

Smokeless tobacco is tobacco that is chewed or sniffed. Common names for it are spit, chew, and snuff. Many people believe that smokeless tobacco is safer than other tobacco products because the user doesn't inhale tobacco smoke. This is not true. Users of smokeless tobacco still absorb poisonous substances through the mouth or nose. Smokeless tobacco has been linked to cancers of the mouth, esophagus, larynx, stomach, and pancreas. Chewing tobacco also stains the teeth and causes tooth loss and gum disease. Moreover, tobacco chewers need to spit out tobacco juice from time to time—a habit that many people find offensive.

Specialty Cigarettes

The use of bidis and cloves has increased in the United States. Bidis are flavored, unfiltered cigarettes from India. Clove cigarettes, which are made in Indonesia, contain tobacco and ground cloves. Bidis and cloves are often sold in health food stores, which may give people the impression that they are safe to smoke. These specialty cigarettes can, however, be even more dangerous than regular cigarettes. Some bidis contain pure tobacco with seven times as much nicotine and twice as much tar as regular cigarettes.

What Is in Tobacco?

Tobacco and tobacco smoke contain approximately 4,000 chemicals. Over 200 of them are known to be dangerous to humans, especially nicotine, tar, and carbon monoxide.

Nicotine is *an addictive drug found in tobacco leaves and in all tobacco products.* An **addictive** drug is one that is *capable of causing a user to develop intense cravings*

FIGURE 5–11.

Despite the fact that tobacco use is harmful, tobacco companies continue to produce billions of tobacco products every year. *What creates the demand for tobacco products?*

for it. When smoked or chewed, nicotine takes less than 7 seconds to reach the brain, where it creates a feeling of stimulation. About 30 minutes later, when the chemicals have left the brain, the user begins to feel discomfort. The desire to recapture the feeling and avoid the feeling of discomfort causes the user to crave more tobacco.

Tar is *a dark, thick, sticky liquid that forms when tobacco burns.* When smokers inhale, tar gets into their lungs. It leaves a residue that destroys **cilia**, the *tiny, hairlike structures that protect the lungs.* Over time, it also destroys the air sacs in the lungs. The presence of tar can make breathing difficult. It is known to cause emphysema, other lung diseases, and cancer.

Carbon monoxide is *a colorless, odorless, poisonous gas that is produced when tobacco burns.* The carbon monoxide in smoke passes through the lungs into the bloodstream. There, it reduces the amount of oxygen the blood cells can carry. A reduced oxygen supply weakens muscles and blood vessels, which, in turn, may lead to heart attacks and stroke.

How Tobacco Affects the User's Body

The chemicals in tobacco and tobacco smoke cause damage to most of the body's systems. Tobacco use is particularly damaging to teens because their bodies are still growing and developing. Some of the effects of tobacco use are evident almost immediately. Others become apparent over time. Figure 5–12 shows both the short-term and the long-term harmful effects of tobacco use on body systems.

Tobacco and Appearance

Most of the damage caused by tobacco use occurs inside the body. However, tobacco use also harms a person's outer appearance. Every time a person uses a tobacco product, the smell of tobacco lingers on his or her hands, breath, hair, and clothing.

Over time, tobacco use can lead to stained teeth and fingers. Tobacco users often look older more quickly because their skin wrinkles. With shortness of breath and frequent coughing, smokers are generally less physically fit than nonsmokers. Smokeless tobacco users often develop cracked lips, inflamed gums, and sores in their mouths.

A tobacco user's appearance can affect his or her social relationships. Many people are offended by a tobacco user's smelly breath, hair, and clothing, and they don't want to get close to him or her.

Who Buys Tobacco?

Tobacco is a big business in the United States. In one year, tobacco companies spend over $6.8 billion on marketing and advertising campaigns. That's more than $18.5 million every day! In spite of all this advertising, tobacco use among adults has declined over 40 percent since 1965. Today, the majority of adults—about 75 percent—don't use tobacco.

FIGURE 5–12.

SHORT TERM AND LONG-TERM EFFECTS OF TOBACCO USE

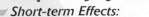

A Nervous System
Short-term Effects:
Changes take place in brain chemistry. Withdrawal symptoms (nervousness, shakes, headaches) may occur as soon as 30 minutes after the last cigarette. The heart rate and blood pressure increase.

Long-term Effects: There is an increased risk of stroke due to decreased flow of oxygen to the brain.

B Circulatory System
Short-term Effects:
Heart rate is increased. Energy is reduced because less oxygen gets to body tissues.

Long-term Effects: Blood vessels are weakened and narrowed. Cholesterol levels increase. Blood vessels are clogged due to fatty buildup. Oxygen flow to heart is reduced. Risk of heart disease and stroke is greater.

C Respiratory System
Short-term Effects:
User has bad breath, shortness of breath, reduced energy, coughing, and more phlegm, (mucus). Colds and flu are more frequent. Allergies and asthma problems increase. Bronchitis and other serious respiratory illnesses increase.

Long-term Effects:
Risk of lung cancer, emphysema, and other lung diseases increases.

D Digestive System
Short-term Effects: User has upset stomach, bad breath, stained teeth, dulled taste buds, and tooth decay.

Long-term Effects: Risk of cancer of the mouth and throat, gum and tooth disease, stomach ulcers, and bladder cancer increases.

Tobacco companies want to attract new users to replace those who have either quit or died. In the eyes of the tobacco industry, children and teens represent the most profitable market. People who become addicted to nicotine as teens are likely to spend thousands of dollars on tobacco products in their lifetime. As a result of lawsuits settled in 1998, tobacco companies have agreed not to use cartoon characters and other advertising methods that might attract children and teens. Nevertheless, the industry continues to find ways to lure young smokers.

REFUSAL SKILLS

Choose to Refuse Tobacco

Elena, an eighth grader, attends a school that includes grades seven through twelve. One day Phoebe, a popular junior, stops to talk to her on the way home from school. Elena feels flattered by the older girl's attention. Her good mood turns to alarm, however, when Phoebe offers her a bidi.

Elena's health class has just finished a unit on tobacco, and she knows that bidis are harmful. She decides to use the S.T.O.P. refusal skills to deal with the situation.

WHAT WOULD YOU DO?

Apply the S.T.O.P. refusal skills to Elena's situation. With a classmate, role-play a conversation between Elena and Phoebe. Reverse roles and do the role-play again. Were you comfortable using the S.T.O.P. refusal skills? Why or why not?

SAY NO IN A FIRM VOICE.
TELL WHY NOT.
OFFER OTHER IDEAS.
PROMPTLY LEAVE.

Expensive Habit

Tobacco use is not only an unhealthy habit but also an expensive one. People who use tobacco frequently pay higher health insurance rates. They generally have more doctor and dental bills because of tobacco-related illnesses. There is also the cost of the tobacco product itself. A pack of cigarettes costs around $2.75. At that rate, smokers who smoke a pack a day will spend over $1,000 each year just on cigarettes.

Tobacco Addiction

Despite the high personal costs and health risks of tobacco use, a number of people continue to smoke or chew tobacco. They may want to stop but find it difficult or frustrating. This is because they have formed an addiction to the nicotine in tobacco. An **addiction** is *a physical or psychological need for a drug.* Addiction develops from regular use of a drug. Nicotine addiction can occur in a short amount of time. Nicotine causes two types of addiction.

- **Physical dependence** is *a type of addiction in which the body itself feels a direct need for a drug.* Nicotine affects body temperature, heart rate, digestion, and muscle tone. Once the nicotine level drops or the nicotine leaves the body's systems, the body craves more. Tobacco users don't feel normal unless their bodies are under the influence of nicotine.

- **Psychological dependence** is *an addiction in which the mind sends the body a message that it needs more of a drug.* Certain events, situations, and habits trigger a desire to use tobacco. Teens might think they need to smoke a cigarette to help them relax at a party or to help them be more alert before a test. Many smokers feel the need for a cigarette every time they talk on the telephone or finish a meal.

According to the Centers for Disease Control and Prevention, nicotine addiction is the most common form of drug addiction in the United States. Nicotine is more addictive than heroin or cocaine. Teens are more likely to develop a severe level of addiction than people who begin to use tobacco at a later age.

You Can Quit!

Two-thirds of the adults who smoke say that they would like to quit, and teen smokers are as eager to quit as adults are. In the year 2000, 70 percent of teen smokers said they regretted having started. Despite the difficulties associated with quitting, approximately 44 million American adults are now former smokers.
Figure 5–13 shows the number of former smokers in the United States population between 1970 and 1998.

FIGURE 5–13.

LOOK WHO'S NOT SMOKING

The number of Americans who don't smoke, either because they never started or because they quit, has been rising steadily.

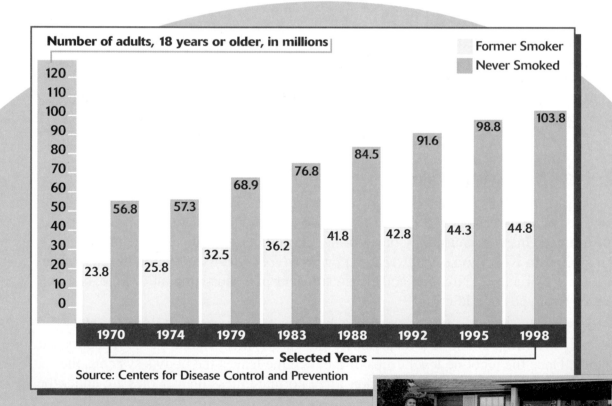

Source: Centers for Disease Control and Prevention

Withdrawal

In order to quit, tobacco users have to go through **withdrawal**, *the physical and psychological symptoms that occur when someone stops using an addictive substance.* Physical symptoms of nicotine withdrawal include the craving to use nicotine, headaches, shakiness, fatigue, increased appetite, and nausea. Psychological symptoms include feeling irritable, nervous, anxious, and sad. People going through withdrawal may have trouble thinking during the day and sleeping during the night. The intensity of withdrawal symptoms and the length of time they last vary from person to person. An inability or reluctance to cope with withdrawal is often the main obstacle to quitting tobacco use.

Costs to Society

Individuals who use tobacco are not the only ones harmed by its effects. Smoke from cigarettes, cigars, and pipes also threatens the health of nonsmokers. In addition, the harm tobacco causes adds up to serious costs for families and society.

Secondhand Smoke

Secondhand smoke is *air that has been contaminated by tobacco smoke.* There are two kinds of secondhand smoke. **Mainstream smoke** is *smoke that a smoker inhales and then exhales.* **Sidestream smoke** is *smoke given off by the burning end of a cigarette, cigar, or pipe.* Sidestream smoke contains twice as much tar and nicotine as mainstream smoke.

Nonsmokers can develop respiratory illnesses such as pneumonia and bronchitis as a result of secondhand smoke. Infants and young children who are constantly exposed to secondhand smoke have more colds, ear infections, allergies, and asthma than children who grow up in smoke-free homes. Secondhand smoke can also lead to lung disease, heart disease, and cancer in nonsmokers.

Public Health Costs

Tobacco-related illnesses increase the cost of medical care for everyone. Consumers must pay higher rates for health care insurance in order to cover these costs. Taxpayers must also pay the medical bills of patients who lack health insurance.

Costs to the Nation's Economy

People who miss work because of tobacco-related illnesses produce fewer goods and services. As a result, companies earn less money. Productive time is also lost when tobacco users leave their workstations to have a cigarette. Tobacco use costs the United States almost $100 billion each year in health care costs and lost productivity.

Pregnancy and Tobacco

Women who smoke during pregnancy increase their risk of having a low birth weight baby and a premature delivery. Nicotine and carbon monoxide keep needed nutrients and oxygen from the fetus. The incidence of Sudden Infant Death Syndrome (SIDS) is also higher in homes where parents smoke.

TOBACCO FACTS PAMPHLETS

Antitobacco programs in schools have been very successful in reducing tobacco use among young people. In this activity you will use your knowledge to help other teens stay away from tobacco.

WHAT YOU WILL NEED
- sheet of paper
- pen and colored markers

WHAT YOU WILL DO
1. Think of a group to whom you would like to deliver an antitobacco message. It should be a group you know well, such as your scout troop, your soccer teammates, or friends in your community.
2. Fold a sheet of paper into thirds to make a six-page pamphlet.
3. Put a catchy title for your pamphlet on the cover.
4. Use the other pages to list facts that may persuade the group to stay tobacco free.
5. Illustrate your pamphlet with antitobacco drawings, cartoons, or logos.
6. Photocopy your pamphlet so you have enough copies for everyone in the group.

IN CONCLUSION
Give your pamphlet to the members of the group. Ask them to share the pamphlet with other groups of teens.

Why Some Teens Start to Use Tobacco

The good news is that the majority of young teens—about 65 percent—don't smoke. In addition, smoking among high school students began to decline in 1998. The bad news is that each day, 4,800 teens smoke their first cigarette. Of this group, 2,000 will become regular smokers. One-third of these will eventually die of smoking-related illnesses.

Internal Influences

Teens may start using tobacco because of internal influences.

- **Stress.** Teens may think that tobacco will help them relax and cope with stress. They don't realize that the symptoms of withdrawal from nicotine, which occur as often as every 30 minutes, will add to their daily stresses.
- **Weight.** Some teens wrongly believe that using tobacco will help them maintain a healthy weight. In reality, its use reduces a person's capacity for aerobic exercise and sports.
- **Image.** Using cigarette lighters and blowing smoke makes some teens feel grown up. Teens who are really mature know that they don't want to give up lifelong health just to look "cool."
- **Independence.** Tobacco use may seem to be a sign of independence. However, it's really just the opposite. Tobacco users become dependent on their unhealthy and costly habit.
- **Peer acceptance.** Teens may think they need to smoke in order to fit in with their peer group. However, most teens today don't want anything to do with tobacco users.

FIGURE 5–14.
The best way to maintain a healthy weight is to stay active and eat a healthful diet. *Why doesn't tobacco fit in to a healthy weight-management plan?*

External Influences

External influences may also cause teens to start smoking.

- **Imitate role model.** Some teens want to be like a friend, a celebrity, or some other role model who uses tobacco. They don't realize that their role models wish they could quit their tobacco habit.
- **Peers.** Peers, siblings, and friends are powerful influences. Many teens try their first cigarette with a friend who already smokes.
- **Entertainment.** Movies and television shows often portray tobacco use in ways that appeal to teens. Tobacco companies pay millions of dollars to have their products featured in movies.
- **Advertising.** There is strong evidence that tobacco advertising influences teens. One study found that 86 percent of kids who smoke prefer the three most heavily advertised brands.
- **Family members and other adults.** Some teens see their parents and other adults using tobacco and think that it's all right for them to use it, too.

How Not to Start

The best way to lead a tobacco-free life is never to start using tobacco products. About 90 percent of adult smokers began smoking before the age of 21, and half of them had become regular smokers by age 18. If you avoid using tobacco during middle school or high school, there's a good chance you'll never start.

Resisting peer pressure to use tobacco can be difficult. However, you can use several strategies to help you.

- **Choose friends who don't use tobacco.** If you don't spend time with people who use tobacco, you won't be pressured to use it yourself.
- **Avoid situations where tobacco products may be used.** You may be invited to a party where you know your peers will be smoking or chewing tobacco. Give your reasons for not going and then do something fun with your tobacco-free friends instead.
- **Use refusal skills.** If tobacco users urge you to try tobacco, you can simply say no. If the pressure continues, however, you can explain your reasons for avoiding tobacco products. Figure 5–16 shows some ways to refuse tobacco. Remember to be assertive. If your peers continue to pressure you, leave.

Strategies for Quitting

A variety of strategies are available to help someone break the tobacco habit. One way is to quit gradually by reducing the number of cigarettes smoked, or the frequency of using chew, over a period of time. Another way to quit is **cold turkey**, or *stopping all at once.* Cold turkey is thought to be more effective than trying to quit gradually.

Tobacco users, no matter what age, may need products such as a nicotine patch or nicotine gum to help them through withdrawal. The **nicotine patch** is *a medication that allows tobacco users to give up tobacco right away while gradually cutting down on nicotine.* The patch is available both by prescription and over-the-counter. Nicotine gum is available over-the-counter, and it works in a similar way as the patch.

Tobacco users who want to quit may seek help from local support groups and organized programs or from professional counselors. The American Lung Association, the American Heart Association, and the American Cancer Society, as well as hospitals and health groups, offer programs to help tobacco users quit.

FIGURE 5–15.

Choosing friends who don't use tobacco helps you avoid the peer pressure to use tobacco.

FIGURE 5–16.

Ways to Refuse Tobacco

"I'll get into trouble with my parents."

"I just washed my hair, and I don't want to smell it up."

"How about chewing a stick of gum instead?"

"No, I need to stay fit."

"I don't like the taste of cigarettes."

"That big tobacco wad in my mouth would look gross!"

HEALTH SKILLS ACTIVITY

ANALYZING INFLUENCES

Be Prepared

When you can recognize internal and external influences on your personal health behavior, you'll be ready to handle them. Here are some examples of people, events, and situations that might tempt teens to use tobacco.

- A stressful day at school.
- Constantly being exposed to ads for tobacco products on the Internet or in a convenience store.
- Curiosity about what it would feel like to smoke.
- Discovering that a highly respected person used tobacco.
- Seeing a tobacco ad that features young adults having fun.
- Hearing that smoking helps keep weight down.

ON YOUR OWN

Draw up your own list of internal and external influences that might pressure you to start using tobacco. Make a plan showing how you would deal with each one.

Lesson 2 Review

Using complete sentences, answer the following questions on a sheet of paper.

1. Name five forms in which tobacco is sold.

2. Why is smoking cigars or using smokeless tobacco just as harmful as smoking cigarettes?

3. Define *nicotine*. Explain what *addictive* means.

4. Describe some long-term effects that tobacco has on the respiratory system and the digestive system.

5. Define the term *addiction*. Use it in an original sentence.

6. How do physical dependence and psychological dependence differ?

7. What are three symptoms of nicotine withdrawal?

8. Identify the two types of smoke that nonsmokers might inhale.

9. List internal and external influences that affect tobacco use.

10. What are three strategies for resisting peer pressure to use tobacco?

11. What does it mean to quit *cold turkey?*

12. What resources are available to help tobacco users quit?

13. Why do you think cigarettes are more commonly used than other forms of tobacco?

14. Explain why tobacco use can negatively affect a person's social relationships.

15. What would you say to a friend who just wants to "experiment" with smoking?

16. Why are pregnant women advised not to smoke?

17. Why are efforts to prevent teens from using tobacco so important?

Applying Health Skills

18. Find a local chapter of the American Cancer Society, American Heart Association, American Dental Association, or American Lung Association on the Internet. Request information about the effects of smoking or using smokeless tobacco. Use this information to prepare a display for the school library or nurse's office on what tobacco does to the body.

19. Make a poster showing the effects of secondhand smoke on nonsmokers. Your poster should express a point of view about the rights of nonsmokers. Be sure to include the facts to support your point of view. Display your poster in the classroom.

20. Interview family members, neighbors, and friends about how they have stayed tobacco free, how they quit smoking or using chew, or why they want to quit. Compile your findings into a report titled "How Not to Use Tobacco."

Alcohol

Alcohol and the Body

Alcohol is *a drug that is produced by a chemical reaction in fruits, vegetables, and grains.* It is a depressant that has powerful effects on the body. In the United States, the law prohibits alcohol use by minors. Adults, however, can choose whether or not to drink alcohol. To make responsible decisions about alcohol use, people need to understand how alcohol affects the body.

Alcohol, like other depressant drugs, slows down the functions of the brain and other parts of the nervous system. It also affects the digestive and urinary systems. Excessive use of alcohol over a long period can damage almost every organ in the body.

FIGURE 5–17.

Avoiding alcohol will help you concentrate and stay focused. *What day-to-day activities in your life require precision and skill?*

Figure 5–18 shows some of the short-term and long-term effects of alcohol consumption.

Alcohol and the Individual

The effect that alcohol has on a person is influenced by a number of factors, including:

- **Body size.** The same amount of alcohol has a greater effect on a small person than it does on a larger person.
- **Gender.** In general, alcohol moves into the bloodstream faster in females.

Quick Write

Write a refusal statement that you can use to avoid the pressure to use alcohol.

LEARN ABOUT...

- the effects of alcohol on the body.
- why alcohol affects each individual differently.
- the effects of alcohol on a fetus.
- the problems alcohol causes in teens.
- the dangers of drinking.
- the disease called alcoholism.
- how alcoholics can recover.
- sources of help for alcohol addiction.
- the reasons some teens use alcohol.
- the reasons to avoid alcohol use.
- how the media influence our view of alcohol.
- alternatives to alcohol for fun and relaxation.

Vocabulary

- alcohol
- blood alcohol concentration (BAC)
- cirrhosis
- intoxicated
- binge drinking
- fetal alcohol spectrum disorders (FASD)
- alcoholism
- recovery
- detoxification
- sobriety
- alternatives

- **Time Frame.** A person who drinks a lot in a short period of time is more likely to become intoxicated. Rapid drinking overwhelms the liver's ability to break down the alcohol.
- **Amount.** Drinking a large quantity of alcohol causes alcohol levels in the bloodstream to rise. If the levels become too high, alcohol poisoning can occur. Figure 5–19 shows the alcohol content of some common alcoholic beverages.
- **Food.** Food in the stomach slows down the passage of alcohol into the bloodstream.
- **Medicine.** Alcohol can interfere with the effects of medicines, and medicines can intensify the effects of alcohol.

Blood Alcohol Concentration

The amount of alcohol in a person's bloodstream is referred to as the **blood alcohol concentration (BAC)**. BAC is expressed as a percentage of total blood volume. For example, if a person's BAC is 0.1 percent, then 1/10 of 1 percent of the fluid volume of his or her blood is actually alcohol. A person's BAC depends on the amount of alcohol consumed as well as body size and the other factors discussed earlier.

Figure 5–18.

Effects of Alcohol on the Body

Short-term effects occur within minutes of drinking alcohol. Long-term effects develop over time.

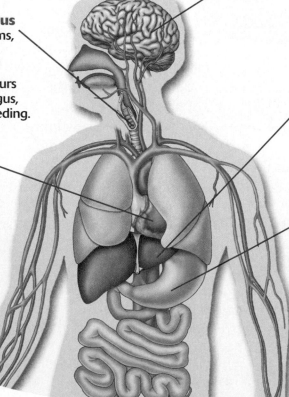

Brain and Nervous System
Short term: Speech is slurred and vision is blurred. Drinker has difficulty walking.

Long term: Brain cells, many of which cannot be replaced, are destroyed. Damage occurs to nerves throughout the body, resulting in numbness in the hands and feet.

Mouth and Esophagus
Short term: Tongue, gums, and throat are affected; breath smells of alcohol.

Long term: Damage occurs to tissues of the esophagus, resulting in possible bleeding.

Heart and Blood Vessels
Short term: Perspiration increases and skin becomes flushed.

Long term: High blood pressure and damage to the heart muscle is common. Blood vessels harden and become less flexible.

Liver
Short term: Liver changes alcohol into water and carbon dioxide.

Long term: Liver is damaged, possibly resulting in **cirrhosis** (suh·ROH·sis), *scarring and destruction of the liver.*

Stomach and Pancreas
Short term: Stomach acids increase, which often results in nausea and vomiting.

Long term: Irritation occurs in the stomach lining, causing open sores called ulcers. Pancreas becomes inflamed.

FIGURE 5–19.

ALCOHOL CONTENT OF DIFFERENT DRINKS

Each of the following contains the same amount of alcohol—about 0.5 oz. of pure alcohol. Beer and wine contain a lower percentage of alcohol by volume than distilled liquors such as vodka or whiskey.

Beer 12 oz.	Wine 4 oz.	Vodka or Whiskey 1.5 oz.
5% alcohol by volume	12-15% alcohol by volume	40% alcohol by volume

A person with a BAC of 0.1 percent—or in some states, 0.08 percent—is considered legally **intoxicated**, or *physically and mentally impaired by the use of alcohol*. Driving while intoxicated can result in a jail term and, in some states, loss of driver's license. For anyone under 21, a BAC above 0 percent is illegal.

Binge drinking—*the consumption of several alcoholic drinks in a very short period of time*—is especially dangerous. Because alcohol is a depressant, it slows body systems down. If the BAC of a binge drinker rises sharply enough, the person will stop breathing and will die.

Fetal Alcohol Spectrum Disorders

When a pregnant woman drinks alcohol, it passes from her body into her developing baby's bloodstream. A fetus exposed to alcohol in this way may be born with fetal alcohol spectrum disorders. **Fetal alcohol spectrum disorders (FASD)** is *a range (spectrum) of alcohol-related birth defects that include both physical and mental problems*.

FASD is the leading known cause of mental retardation and birth defects in the United States. The good news is that it is entirely preventable. Since even small amounts of alcohol can harm a fetus, the only safe decision for a pregnant woman is not to drink any alcohol at all.

Alcohol and Teens

Alcohol can interfere with a teen's growth process. Studies show that teens who abuse alcohol have poorer language skills than other teens. New research also suggests that exposure to alcohol during the teen years reduces levels of certain hormones essential to normal development. It may also delay the onset of the menstrual cycle and affect other aspects of sexual maturity.

Teen alcohol use also has many other serious consequences:

- Up to two-thirds of suicides on college campuses involve alcohol.
- Almost one-half of all traffic deaths of people under age 25 involve alcohol.
- Nearly a quarter of all violent crimes committed by teens involve alcohol.
- Between one-third and two-thirds of date rape cases among teens and college students involve alcohol.

Alcohol: A Threat to Everyone

Alcohol use is widespread in American society. Nearly 14 million adult Americans have physical, social, and psychological problems related to alcohol use. It causes premature death from a variety of diseases. It also contributes to unnecessary deaths and injuries on the roads and in the home.

Drinking and Injuries

Drinking and driving are a dangerous, and potentially deadly, combination. Drinking alcohol impairs a person's vision, reaction time, and physical coordination. Consequently, a person who has been drinking should never get behind the wheel of a car.

Alcohol causes other kinds of unintentional injuries as well. It impairs a person's ability to ride a bicycle, skateboard, or scooter. About one-third of all bicyclists and pedestrians who die in motor vehicle collisions have been drinking. Alcohol is also linked to about one-third of all drowning deaths and about half of all deaths by fire.

Alcoholism

Alcohol can become addictive. **Alcoholism** is *a progressive, chronic disease involving a mental and physical need for alcohol.* People with this disease are called alcoholics. Alcoholics cannot control their drinking. They drink even when they know they are harming their health and hurting others.

An addiction to alcohol is both psychological and physical. With psychological addiction, the mind sends the body a message that it needs more and more alcohol. With physical addiction, the body develops a direct need for the drug. Either way, an alcoholic feels very uncomfortable when alcohol is withheld for even a brief period.

FIGURE 5–20.
More than half of the drivers killed in nighttime automobile collisions are legally drunk. *What could be done to prevent drunk driving in your community?*

Stages of Alcoholism

Alcoholism develops in three stages. These stages develop over time and are not the same for each alcoholic.

- **Stage 1.** A person starts using alcohol to relieve stress or to relax. Soon the person needs alcohol to cope with daily life. He or she begins to lie or make excuses about drinking.
- **Stage 2.** As the person continues to drink, the body develops a need for more and more alcohol. The drinker may be absent from school or work but continues to deny that there is a problem.
- **Stage 3.** In the final stage of alcoholism, the problem is clear to other people. The drinker's body is strongly addicted, and the drinking is now out of control.

Help for the Dependent Person

A person who is addicted to alcohol is dependent on it. The addiction can be treated, however. *The process of learning to live an alcohol-free life* is called **recovery**. The steps of recovery are shown in Figure 5–21.

Recovering from alcoholism is difficult, but it can be done. As with drug addiction, the recovery process may involve withdrawal. Withdrawal symptoms include nausea, sweating, shakiness, and anxiety. Treatment for alcoholism depends on the severity of the alcoholism and the resources available in your community. Treatment may include

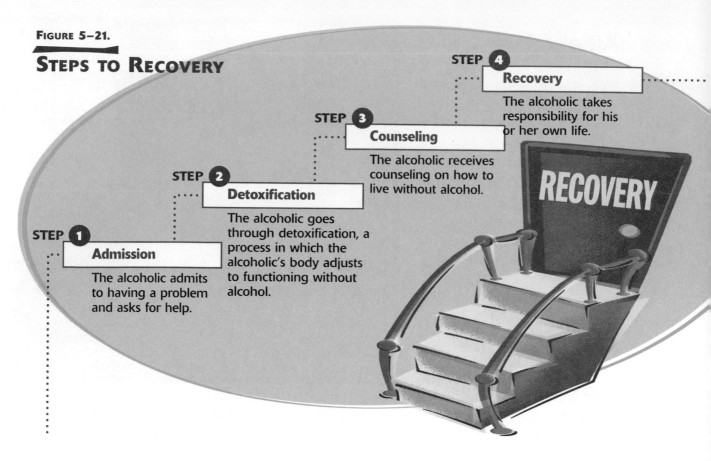

FIGURE 5-21.

STEPS TO RECOVERY

STEP 1
Admission
The alcoholic admits to having a problem and asks for help.

STEP 2
Detoxification
The alcoholic goes through detoxification, a process in which the alcoholic's body adjusts to functioning without alcohol.

STEP 3
Counseling
The alcoholic receives counseling on how to live without alcohol.

STEP 4
Recovery
The alcoholic takes responsibility for his or her own life.

RECOVERY

detoxification, *the physical process of freeing the body of an addictive substance.* "Detox" also involves helping the user overcome psychological dependence on the substance and regain health. A variety of treatment centers are available to help people recover from alcoholism.

- **Detox units** are usually part of a hospital or other treatment center. Alcoholics remain under a doctor's care while going through detoxification.
- **Inpatient treatment centers** are places where people stay for a month or more to fully concentrate on recovery.
- **Outpatient treatment centers** are places where people get treatment for a few hours each day. Then they return to their homes and regular surroundings.

Treatment may also include taking prescribed medications to help prevent a return to drinking (or relapse) once drinking has stopped and individual and/or group counseling. Such counseling often involves teaching alcoholics to identify situations and feelings that trigger the urge to drink and to find new ways to cope that do not include alcohol use.

Many alcoholics join support groups to help them be successful. One of the best known of these support groups is Alcoholics Anonymous (AA). AA is an organization of recovering alcoholics who know firsthand the difficulty of beating alcohol addiction. Most cities have chapters of AA. Listings for AA and other support groups for alcoholism can be found in the Yellow Pages of the phone book, usually under the heading Alcoholism. **Sobriety,** which is *living without alcohol,* is a lifelong challenge.

Help for the Family

The harmful effects of alcohol do not affect only the drinker. The drinker's family members and friends suffer as well. One in four families in the United States is affected by alcoholism. Alcohol abuse is a factor in the breakup of many families. Many cases of spousal abuse and child abuse involve someone who has been drinking.

A growing number of young people are living with a person who is addicted to alcohol. These teens may not realize that they need help for themselves as well as for the problem drinkers in their lives. The first step to take is to admit that the problem exists. The second is to reach out for help.

Many alcohol treatment centers offer help to family members of the alcoholic. These programs teach family members about alcoholism and provide individual and family therapy. Some family members join support groups where they can talk with other people who have faced the same problems. Two of these support groups are described here.

- **Al-Anon** helps family members and friends of alcoholics. Al-Anon members learn how to help themselves as well as the person dependent on alcohol.
- **Alateen** helps young people cope with having a family member or friend who is an alcoholic. Its members share their experiences and work together to improve their lives.

Listings for Al-Anon, Alateen, and other support groups for family members and friends of alcoholics can be found in the Yellow Pages of the phone book, usually under the heading Alcoholism.

How You Can Help

If a friend or family member has a problem with alcohol, he or she needs help. Always remember, however, that your most important responsibility is to yourself. If you are close to an alcoholic, try not to let that person's drinking problem change your own behaviors and attitudes. Here are some ways you may be able to help an alcoholic.

- When the drinker is sober, talk calmly with him or her about the harm that alcohol does.
- Tell the drinker how concerned you are, and encourage her or him to seek help. Let the person know that the drinking worries you.
- Help the drinker feel good about quitting, and provide information about groups that can help.

Why Some Teens Drink Alcohol

You have learned that alcohol will harm your physical and mental/emotional health, and that drinking alcohol is against the law for teens. Why, then, do some young people experiment with alcohol? Here are some statements teens may give, followed by what they should know about alcohol.

DRUNK-DRIVING STATISTICS

You probably have seen public service announcements about drunk driving on television and billboards. Find out whether these campaigns help reduce alcohol-related collisions.

WHAT YOU WILL NEED
- pencil
- ruler
- sheet of graph paper

WHAT YOU WILL DO

Study the following statistics from the National Highway Traffic Safety Administration. The statistics show the percentage of people killed in traffic accidents involving a person who was legally drunk, out of the total number of people killed in all traffic accidents.

Create a line graph to examine the data. Divide the horizontal x-axis into 10 1-year segments, and label each year from 1990 to 1999. Label the vertical y-axis with percent values in increments of 5, ranging from 25 percent at the bottom to 45 percent at the top. Graph the data. Then answer the questions that follow.

YEAR	PEOPLE KILLED IN ALCOHOL-RELATED ACCIDENTS
1990	39.6 percent
1991	38.4 percent
1992	36.3 percent
1993	34.9 percent
1994	32.2 percent
1995	32.5 percent
1996	32.0 percent
1997	30.3 percent
1998	30.0 percent
1999	30.0 percent

IN CONCLUSION

Examine your graph and determine how the data changed over a 10-year period. Did alcohol-related fatalities increase, decrease, or stay the same? What factors may have caused a change in the rate of alcohol-related fatal collisions?

What Teens May Say

- "I'll look more grown-up with a drink in my hand."
- "If I drink, I'll be able to forget my problems."
- "I'm stressed out about this test. A drink will help me relax."

- "My friends keep pressuring me to try alcohol."
- "The ads make drinking look like fun."

What Teens Should Know

- You won't look mature getting in trouble for illegal underage drinking.
- The problems will still be there when the effects of the alcohol wear off.
- Alcohol does not relieve stress; it disrupts sleep and can create more stress.
- Real friends won't pressure you to do something harmful.
- Alcohol companies want people to spend money on their products.

Reasons to Refuse Alcohol

At least one-third of Americans do not drink alcohol at all, and many who used to drink have stopped. As people become aware of the physical and emotional damage that drinking can cause, fewer choose to start drinking. More and more young people are choosing not to drink also. Here are some of their reasons:

- **It is illegal.** Drinking is against the law for anyone under age 21. Obeying the law makes your life easier and safer.
- **It interferes with your activities.** As a teen, your life is full of activities. You go to school, and you have family responsibilities and friendships. Teens who choose not to drink will be better able to meet these challenges.
- **It promotes foolish behaviors.** Drinking can make people sick. It can also cause them to embarrass or endanger themselves.
- **It is not smart.** Smart teens know that drinking does not enhance popularity. Drinking does not make a person more mature. Acting responsibly is a sign of maturity.
- **It disappoints those who care about you.** Teens who drink alcohol have to hide their behavior. Many young people would rather not have to be dishonest with people they care about.
- **It harms your health.** Drinking alcohol harms body organs, particularly the liver, and increases the chance for injuries.

Figure 5–22.

Refusing alcohol is one of the healthiest decisions you can make. *How does being alcohol free help your performance in school?*

Seeing Through Media Messages

Television, magazines, and billboards often show attractive, healthy people drinking alcohol. Beer advertisements often link drinking with sporting events, fast cars, popularity, and fun. If you were to believe the hidden messages, you might think that it is normal, smart, and sophisticated to drink. You might also notice that the models often look very young. Why do you think that the beer manufacturers might want that young look?

Keep in mind that alcohol companies spend billions of dollars each year promoting their products. Their advertisements focus on people's activities while using these products, rather than on the products themselves.

When you see ads for alcohol, use your own judgment to evaluate them. Will an alcoholic drink really make you more attractive or more popular? Will your relationships be successful and problem free as a result of drinking? The harsh realities of alcohol use are not shown by alcohol manufacturers. You must dig deeper to find the facts.

Alternatives to Drinking Alcohol

Why do some teens give in to the pressure to drink alcohol? One reason is that they have not thought about alternatives. **Alternatives** are *other ways of thinking or acting.* There are plenty of alternatives to drinking. A few of them are suggested here.

- **Become good at something that requires a steady hand.** Assemble a model airplane, play a video game, or paint a picture. Then congratulate yourself—a person whose senses are dulled by alcohol could not accomplish what you have.
- **Join other teens for alcohol-free fun.** Plan an alcohol-free party or outing, or have a basketball or volleyball game. Make sure all invited know that alcohol use will not be tolerated.
- **Volunteer to help others.** Volunteer at a hospital or nursing home, or lend a hand to a community improvement organization such as Habitat for Humanity.
- **Learn something new.** You might learn a musical instrument, computer program, or foreign language. Learn a sport you have never tried before, such as karate or kickboxing.
- **Advocate.** Volunteer to speak to an elementary school class about the dangers of alcohol and the benefits of remaining alcohol free. Younger children look up to teens like you as role models.

HEALTH SKILLS ACTIVITY

REFUSAL SKILLS

Saying No to a Drink

Antonio has just transferred to a new school. He loves living in a bigger city, but does not know many people. One day, he and a classmate named Noel start talking about computer games. They both love to play, and they begin to spend a lot of time at Noel's house after school.

Antonio feels great about his new friend. He becomes uneasy, however, when Noel goes to the refrigerator and offers Antonio a beer. Antonio wants to refuse, but does not want to risk ruining the friendship. What should he say?

What Would You Do?

Write down three responses that Antonio can make to Noel using the S.T.O.P. guidelines. Share them with your classmates and decide which seem most effective.

SAY NO IN A FIRM VOICE.
TELL WHY NOT.
OFFER ANOTHER IDEA.
PROMPTLY LEAVE.

CHECKPOINTS

Lesson 3 Review

Using complete sentences, answer the following questions on a sheet of paper.

1. Define the term *alcohol*. Use it in an original sentence.
2. What kind of drug is alcohol? How does it affect the nervous system?
3. List three factors that will influence the way an individual is affected by alcohol.
4. What is BAC short for? What does it measure?
5. In what ways does alcohol impair a person's ability to drive?
6. Define the term *alcoholism*. Use it in an original sentence.
7. Name the two kinds of addiction involved in alcoholism.
8. What happens during the first stage of alcoholism?
9. Name three factors that might influence a teen to drink alcohol.
10. Why is it a bad idea to use alcohol to relieve stress?
11. Define the term *alternatives*. Use it in an original sentence.
12. Which alternative to drinking makes you a positive role model to younger students?
13. Why is a small female who drinks the same amount of alcohol as a large male more likely to experience a stronger effect from the alcohol?
14. Why are pregnant women generally advised to avoid all alcohol during their pregnancy?
15. What could be done to reduce the number of collisions resulting from drinking and driving?
16. Why do you think family members of alcoholics are advised not to make excuses to others for the alcoholic's behavior?
17. How might drinking create more problems for a teen who is already troubled?
18. List six fun ways to relax that do not involve alcohol.

Applying Health Skills

19. Do your part to advocate against binge drinking. Prepare a public service announcement in which you emphasize the extreme dangers of binge drinking by teens. If possible, record your announcement and arrange to have it played at school.
20. Play your part to stamp out drunk driving. Check out the Web site for Students Against Destructive Decisions (SADD). Use some of the information and ideas you find there to prepare your personal campaign to advocate against drinking and driving.
21. List all the reasons you can think of for not drinking alcohol. Organize your list into three parts to correspond to the three sides of your health triangle: physical, mental/ emotional, and social.

UNIT
4

Citizenship in the United States

Unit Chapter

Chapter 6   **Foundations of United States Citizenship**

In Your Home and Community

Assessing Information

Find out the purposes of your government firsthand. Contact a government leader, such as a state representative, a city council member, or a school board member, and ask how the government he or she represents serves American citizens.

Foundations of United States Citizenship

Chapter Outline

- Lesson 1 — **The American Flag and Other Symbols**
- Lesson 2 — **Civics**
- Lesson 3 — **The Constitution of the United States**
- Lesson 4 — **The Bill of Rights**
- Lesson 5 — **U.S. National Government**
- Lesson 6 — **Comparing Systems of Government**

Quick Write

What does it mean to you to be a United States citizen? Write what you think are some of the rights and responsibilities of United States citizens.

The American Flag and Other Symbols

Quick Write

Make a list of everything you know about the design of the American flag. Then write down what you know about how to display it, treat it, and show it respect. What do the American flag and other patriotic symbols mean to you?

LEARN ABOUT...

- the history of the American flag.
- flag laws and regulations.
- displaying and using the flag.
- customs and courtesies to the American flag and the National Anthem.
- the Pledge of Allegiance.
- the Great Seal of the United States and the Air Force Seal.

History of the American Flag

The Second Continental Congress officially adopted the American flag, also called the "Stars and Stripes" and "Old Glory," in Philadelphia on June 14, 1777. This action was the result of a resolution offered by the Congressional Marine Committee, which read:

Resolved: that the flag of the United States be thirteen stripes, alternate red and white; that the union be thirteen stars, white in a blue field representing a new constellation.

The number 13 represents the original Thirteen Colonies. The resolution gave no instruction as to how many points the stars should have or how to arrange the stars on the blue union. The **union** is *the upper left corner of the flag.* Some flags had stars scattered on the blue field without any specific design, some had the stars arranged in rows, and some in a circle. The first Navy Stars and Stripes had the stars arranged in staggered formation, in alternate rows of threes and twos on a blue field. Other Stars and Stripes flags had stars arranged in alternate rows of four, five, and four. Some stars had six points while others had eight.

There is strong evidence that Francis Hopkinson of New Jersey, a signer of the Declaration of Independence, was responsible for the stars in the American flag. At the time that the flag resolution was adopted, Hopkinson was the Chairman of the Continental Navy Board's Middle Department. Hopkinson also helped design other devices for the government, including the Great Seal of the United States.

The Betsy Ross Flag

During the Revolutionary War, several patriots made flags for our new nation. Some of the makers were Cornelia Bridges,

FIGURE 6–1.
The Betsy Ross Flag.

Elizabeth (Betsy) Ross, and Rebecca Young, all from Pennsylvania, and John Shaw of Annapolis, Maryland. Betsy Ross was the best known of these persons. She made flags for 50 years, and the claim that she designed the first flag of the United States is based on family traditions. We know that she made flags for the Pennsylvania State Navy in 1777. The flag known as the "Betsy Ross flag," in which the stars were arranged in a circle, did not appear until the early 1790s.

William J. Canby, a grandson of Betsy Ross, brought her to public attention in 1870. In a paper he read before a meeting of the Historical Society of Pennsylvania, Canby stated:

> *It is not* tradition, *it is* report *from the lips of the principal participator in the transaction, directly told not to one or two, but a dozen or more living witnesses, of which I myself am one, though but a little boy when I heard it.*
>
> *. . . Colonel Ross with Robert Morris and General Washington, called on Mrs. Ross and told her they were a committee of Congress, and wanted her to make a flag from the drawing, a rough one, which, upon her suggestions, was redrawn by General Washington in pencil in her back parlor. This was prior to the Declaration of Independence. I fix the date to be during Washington's visit to Congress from New York in June, 1776 when he came to confer upon the affairs of the Army, the flag being no doubt, one of these affairs.*

The Grand Union Flag

The first flag of the colonists that looked like the present Stars and Stripes was the Grand Union Flag. This is sometimes referred to as the Congress Colors, the First Navy Ensign, and the Cambridge Flag. An **ensign** is *a national flag displayed on ships and aircraft, often with the special insignia of a branch or unit of the armed forces.*

The Grand Union flag had 13 stripes, alternately red and white, representing the original Thirteen Colonies. It had a blue field in the upper left corner, bearing the red cross of St. George of England with the white cross of St. Andrew of Scotland. As the flag of the revolution, it was used on many occasions. The ships of the Colonial Fleet were the first to display this flag on the Delaware River. On December 3, 1775, John Paul Jones, a Navy lieutenant, raised this flag aboard Captain Esek Hopkin's flagship *Alfred.* Later, the flag was raised on the liberty pole at Prospect Hill, which was near George Washington's headquarters in Cambridge, Massachusetts. It was our unofficial national flag and ensign of the Navy until June 14, 1777. At that time, the Continental Congress authorized the Stars and Stripes.

FIGURE 6–2.
Grand Union Flag.

The Final Flag Design

The first change in the flag's design was in 1794, when Congress passed an act requiring that the flag consist of 15 white stars on a blue field and 15 stripes, alternating red and white. This change was due to Vermont (in 1791) and Kentucky (in 1792) being admitted as states of the union. This flag, which was the official flag from 1795 to 1818, played a role in many historic events. It inspired Francis Scott Key to write "The Star Spangled Banner" when Fort McHenry was being attacked in 1814. It was the first flag to be flown over a fortress of the Old World when American Marine and Naval forces raised it above the pirate stronghold in Tripoli on April 27, 1805. It was the ensign of American forces in the Battle of Lake Erie in September of 1813. It was flown by General Jackson in New Orleans in January of 1815.

FIGURE 6–3.
Stars and Stripes.

However, realizing that the flag would become difficult to carry if it had a stripe for each new state, Capt. Samuel C. Reid, USN, suggested to Congress that the stripes remain 13 in number to represent the Thirteen Colonies. He also suggested that a star be added to the blue field for each new state coming into the union. On April 4, 1818, President Monroe accepted a bill requiring that the American flag have a union of 20 stars, white on a blue field. The bill also stated that each time a new state came into the union, one star would be added to the union of the flag on the Fourth of July following its date of admission. The 13 alternating red and white stripes would remain unchanged. This act set the basic design of the flag while making sure that the growth of the nation would be properly symbolized.

Eventually, the growth of the country resulted in a flag with 48 stars, when Arizona and New Mexico were admitted to the union in 1912. Alaska added a 49th star in 1959, and Hawaii a 50th star in 1960. With the 50-star flag came a new design and arrangement of the stars in the union, a requirement met by President Eisenhower in Executive Order number 10834, issued August 21, 1959. At that time a national banner with 50 stars became the official American flag. The colors used in the American flag are white for purity and innocence, red for hardness and valor, and blue for vigilance, perseverance, and justice. This flag was raised for the first time at 12:01 A.M. on July 4, 1960, at the Fort McHenry National Monument in Baltimore, Maryland.

Traditionally a symbol of liberty, the American flag has carried the message of freedom to many parts of the world. Sometimes the same flag that was flying at a crucial moment in our history has been flown again in another place to symbolize continuity in our struggles for the same cause of liberty. One of the most memorable is the flag that flew over the Capitol in Washington on December 7, 1941, when Pearl Harbor was attacked. This same flag was raised again on December 8 when war was declared on Japan and three days later when war was declared against Germany and Italy. President Roosevelt called it the "flag of liberation" and carried it with him to the Casablanca Conference and on other historic occasions. It flew from the mast of the *USS Missouri* during the formal Japanese surrender on September 2, 1945. It also was used in 1945 at the United Nations Charter meeting in San Francisco, California, and at the Big Three Conference at Potsdam, Germany.

The Flag Today
Today's American flag has 13 horizontal stripes—seven red and six white, alternating—and a union of white stars of five points on a blue field. The blue field is in the upper quarter of the flag next to the staff, and extends to the lower edge of the fourth red stripe from the top. The number of stars equals the number of states in the Union.

Flag Laws and Regulations
The United States Code contains the laws relating to the American flag. Title 4, Chapter 1 is about the flag and seal, seat of government, and the states. Title 18, Chapter 33 is about crimes and criminal procedures. Title 36, Chapter 10 is about patriotic customs and observances. Executive orders and presidential proclamations add to these laws.

Displaying and Using the Flag
The flag is usually displayed only from sunrise to sunset on buildings and on stationary flagstaffs in the open. However, you can display the flag 24 hours a day for

a patriotic effect. A law signed on July 7, 1976, permits the display of an all-weather American flag all day and night, if properly lit during hours of darkness.

The flag should be hoisted briskly and lowered ceremoniously. It should not be displayed in bad weather, except when using an all-weather flag. The flag can be displayed on all days, especially on the following holidays:

- New Year's Day, January 1
- Inauguration Day, January 20
- Dr. Martin Luther King's Birthday, January 15
- Abraham Lincoln's Birthday, February 12
- Presidents' Day (George Washington's Birthday), third Monday in February
- Easter Sunday (the exact date varies each year)
- Mother's Day, second Sunday in May
- Armed Forces' Day, third Saturday in May
- Memorial Day (half-staff until noon), the last Monday in May
- Flag Day, June 14
- Independence Day, July 4
- Labor Day, first Monday in September
- Constitution Day, September 17
- Columbus Day, second Monday in October
- Navy Day, October 27
- Veteran's Day, November 11
- Thanksgiving Day, fourth Thursday in November
- Christmas Day, December 25
- Other days as proclaimed by the President of the United States
- State birthdays (date of admission and state holidays)

The flag should be displayed daily on or near the main administration building of every public institution. It should be displayed in or near every polling place on election days, and it should be displayed during school days in or near every schoolhouse.

Ways to Position and Display the Flag

When carrying the flag in a procession with another flag or flags, make sure it is either on the marching right—that is, the flag's own right—or, if there is another line of flags, in the front and center of that line. Other guidelines for proper display of the flag include:

- Do not display the flag on a float in a parade, except from a staff or suspended with folds falling free.
- Do not drape the flag over the hood, top, sides, or back of a vehicle, railroad train, or boat. When displaying the flag on a motorcar, fix the staff firmly to the chassis or clamp it to the right fender.
- Do not place any other flag or pennant above or, if on the same level, to the right of the American flag. The only exception is during church services conducted by Naval

chaplains at sea, when the church pennant may be flown above the flag during church services for Navy personnel.

- Do not fly any flag or pennant above the American flag, except the United Nations flag at the United Nations Headquarters.

- When using the national colors for ceremonies by motorized and mechanized organizations, make sure they are carried on vehicles specifically designed for color and color guards. The position in line from right to left will be as follows: the national colors, the organizational flag, and the individual's flag (displayed only when a general officer is commanding).

FIGURE 6-4.
Color guard collage.

- When displaying the American flag with another flag against a wall from crossed staffs, make sure the American flag is on the right—the flag's own right—and that its staff is in front of the staff of the other flag.

- In general, display the American flag flat or hanging free. Do not drape it over doorways or arches, tie it in a bow, or fashion it into any other shape.

- When the American flag is among a group of flags—of states or localities, or pennants of societies—that are displayed from staffs, make sure the American flag is at the center, highest point of the group.

- The American flag should always be at the peak when flown on the same halyard with flags of states, cities, and localities (or pennants of societies). A **halyard** is *a rope for hoisting and lowering things.* When the flags are on adjacent staffs, hoist the American flag first and lower it last. Do not place any other flag or pennant above the American flag or to its right.

- When displaying flags of two or more nations, fly them from separate staffs of the same height. Make sure the flags are approximately equal in size. International usage forbids the display of the flag of one nation above that of another nation in time of peace.

- When displaying the American flag from a staff that projects horizontally or at an angle from a windowsill, balcony, or front of a building, place the union of the flag at the peak of the staff unless the flag is at half-staff.

- When the flag is suspended over a sidewalk from a rope extending from a house to a pole at the edge of the sidewalk, hoist the flag out from the building, union first.

| With other flags or pennants | With other flags | From a building | Against a wall |

FIGURE 6–5.

The American Flag displayed in various positions.

- When displaying the flag horizontally or vertically against a wall, make sure the union is uppermost and to the flag's own right—that is, to the observer's left. The same applies when displaying the flag in a window.

- When displaying the flag over the middle of the street, suspend it vertically with the union to the north in an east-west street, or to the east in a north-south street.

- When using the flag displayed flat on a speaker's platform, display it above and behind the speaker. When displaying the flag from a staff in a church or public auditorium, make sure it holds the position of superior prominence. The position should be in front of the audience and in the position of honor at the right of the clergyman or speaker as he or she faces the audience. Place any other flag to the left of the clergyman or speaker, or to the right of the audience.

- The flag should be a distinctive feature of a ceremony for unveiling a statue or monument. Never use it as the covering for the statue or monument.

- When flying the flag at half-staff, first hoist it to the peak for an instant, and then lower it to the half-staff position. Raise the flag to the peak again before it is lowered for the day. **Half-staff** means *the position of the flag when it is one-half the distance between the top and bottom of the staff.* On Memorial Day, display the flag at half-staff until noon only, then raise it to the top of the staff.

- By order of the president, fly the flag at half-staff upon the death of principal figures of the United States Government, as a mark of respect to their memory. Do the same for the governor of a state, territory, or possession. In the event of the death of other officials or foreign dignitaries, display the flag at half-staff. Follow the instructions or orders set by the president, or follow customs or practices that are consistent with law. If a present or former official of the government of any state, territory, or possession of the United States dies, the governor of that state, territory, or possession may decide to

FIGURE 6–6.

Airmen at Andrews AFB lower the flag to half staff. *(Courtesy of Staff Sgt. Bennie J. Davis III)*

fly the national flag at half-staff. The rule is to fly the flag at half-staff in the following situations:

- For thirty days after the death of the president or a former president.
- For ten days after the day of death of the vice president, the chief justice, a retired chief justice of the United States, or the speaker of the house of representatives.
- From the day of death until internment of an associate justice of the Supreme Court, a secretary of an executive or military department, a former vice president, or the governor of a state, territory, or possession. **Executive or military department** means *any agency listed under sections 101 and 102 of title 5, United States Code.*
- On the day of death and the following day for a member of Congress. **Member of Congress** means *a senator, a representative, a delegate, or the resident commissioner from Puerto Rico.*
- When using the flag to cover a casket, place it with the union at the head and over the left shoulder. Do not lower the flag into the grave or let it touch the ground.

Displaying the United Nations Flag

When the American flag and the United Nations flag are on display together, the American flag is on the right—best identified as "the marching right." The American flag will be equal in size or larger, in the position of honor on the right (observer's left), and above the United Nations flag. The United Nations flag will be carried only for occasions honoring the United Nations or its high dignitaries. When carried in this way, the United Nations flag will be on "the marching left" and below the United States flag.

Showing Respect for the American Flag

Always show respect to the American flag. Never dip the flag to any person or thing. Only regimental colors, state flags, and organization or institutional flags are dipped as a mark of honor. The only circumstance in which the American flag would be dipped is when a U.S. Naval vessel receives this type of salute from a vessel registered by a nation formally recognized by the United States.

- Never display the flag with the union down, except as a signal of dire distress when extreme danger to life or property exists.
- Never let the flag touch anything beneath it, such as the ground, the floor, water, or merchandise.
- Never carry the flag flat or horizontally; always carry it aloft and free.
- Never use the flag as wearing apparel, bedding, or drapery. Always allow it to fall free. Never put things on it, pull it back or up, or drape it in folds.
- When using the bunting of blue, white, and red, always arrange it with the blue above, the white in the middle, and the red below. A **bunting** is *a lightweight, loosely woven fabric used mainly for flags and festive decorations.* Some common uses for bunting are for covering a speaker's desk, draping the front of a platform, and decoration in general.
- Never fasten, display, use, or store the flag a way in which it can be easily torn, soiled, or damaged in any way.
- Never use the flag as a ceiling covering.

- Do not place or attach any mark, insignia, letter, word, figure, design, picture, or drawing on the flag.
- Never use the flag as a receptacle for receiving, holding, carrying, or delivering anything.
- Never use the flag for advertising purposes. Do not embroider it on cushions, handkerchiefs, and other personal items. Do not put it on paper napkins, boxes, or anything that is used temporarily and discarded. Do not fasten advertising signs to a staff or halyard from which the flag is flying.
- Do not use any part of the flag as a costume or athletic uniform. However, a flag patch may be affixed to the uniform of military personnel, firemen, policemen, and members of patriotic organizations. The flag represents a living country and is itself considered a living thing. Since the lapel flag pin is a replica, wear it on the left lapel near the heart.
- If a flag is worn out and is no longer fit for display, destroy it in a dignified way, preferably by burning. First cut the blue field from the flag, then cremate the two pieces. Always perform this ceremony with respect and feeling.

FIGURE 6–7.
Always treat the flag with respect.

Customs and Courtesies to the American Flag and the National Anthem

The American Flag and National Anthem are symbols of all the people, their land, and their institutions. When we salute these symbols, we are saluting the nation. Air Force personnel follow specific procedures to show their respect to the flag and the National Anthem. We show the same respect to flags and national anthems of friendly foreign nations.

Flag ceremonies occur during parades, reveille, retreat, and prior to special events. **Reveille** is *the signal for the start of the official duty day.* **Retreat** *signals the end of the official duty day and also serves as a ceremony for paying respect to the flag.*

The National Anthem is played at most flag ceremonies. Sometimes "To the Colors," a bugle call, is used instead, and it is given the same respect as the National Anthem. "To the Colors" can be used when a band is not available or during bad weather. During these ceremonies, all military and civilian personnel render the proper courtesies.

Courtesies to the Flag

When in Uniform and in Formation. When you are in uniform and in formation, but not part of a ceremony, the unit commander commands "present arms" during the National Anthem or "To the Colors." The unit should be facing the flag before being given "present arms."

When in Uniform, but Not in Formation. At any outdoor ceremony that uses the American flag, come to attention, face the flag in the ceremony, and salute. At sporting events, if the flag is visible, face the flag and salute. If the flag is not visible, face the band and salute in its direction. If the music is recorded, face the front and salute. At all other outdoor occasions follow the same general principle: come to attention, face the flag (if it is visible), and salute. If the flag is not visible, face the music and do the same.

When Indoors and the National Anthem or "To the Colors" is Played. When you are indoors and the National Anthem or "To the Colors" is played, face the flag (if it is present) and assume the position of attention. If no flag is present, assume the position of attention while facing the music. Do not salute unless under arms.

When Outdoors in Uniform. When you are in uniform and the National Anthem or "To the Colors" is played, stand at attention, face the flag, and render the military salute. If the flag is not visible, face the music. Salute on the first note of music and hold the salute until the last note.

When Outdoors in Civilian Clothes. When in civilian clothes and the National Anthem or "To the Colors" is played, stand at attention, face the flag, and place your right hand over your heart. If the flag is not visible, face the music and do the same. A male cadet removes his headdress with the right hand and holds it at his left shoulder with his right hand over his heart. A female cadet salutes by standing at attention and placing her right hand over her heart. Male cadets without hats salute in the same way as female cadets.

To an Escorted Flag Outdoors. If you are at any outdoor event and an uncased flag is escorted past you, stand at attention, face the front, and render the appropriate salute. Render the salute approximately six paces before the flag is even with you, and hold the salute until the flag is approximately six paces past you.

On a Stationary Flagstaff. Salute flags on stationary flagstaffs only at reveille, retreat, and special occasions. Do not salute small flags, flags at half-staff, or cased and folded flags.

When Indoors in Civilian Clothing. When in civilian clothing indoors, render the civilian salute by standing at attention and placing the right hand over the heart.

During Indoor Ceremonies. During indoor ceremonies, when the National Anthem or "To the Colors" is played, face the flag and come to attention. If the flag is not visible, come to attention and face the music or the front. Do not salute unless under arms. When you are indoors and the ceremony is outdoors, you do not need to face the flag or salute. The same rule applies during ceremonies that are broadcast over radio or on television.

By Vehicle Passengers. At the first sound of the music, all vehicles come to a complete stop. Occupants of a civilian or military vehicle, including the driver, should sit quietly until the music ends.

At Half-Staff. When the flag is at half-staff, it is to honor and pay respect to deceased people of national importance. The Chief of Staff of the Air Force sets the number of days or periods to keep the flag at half-staff. The flag is flown at half-staff on all bases that make up the command of the deceased commander. Deceased cadets may also be honored in the same way.

Miniature Flags. Do not salute miniature flags, such as those displayed at downtown parades and sporting events.

Conduct During Hoisting, Lowering, or Passing of the American Flag. During the ceremony of hoisting or lowering the flag, or when the flag is passing in a parade or in review, everyone except those in uniform should face the flag and stand at attention with the right hand over the heart. Those in uniform should render the military salute. Cadets who are not in uniform should remove their headdress with their right hand and hold it at the left shoulder with the hand over the heart. When the flag in is in a moving column, salute at the moment the flag passes.

Conduct During the National Anthem. When the flag is displayed during the National Anthem, all present except those in uniform should stand at attention facing the flag with the right hand over the heart. Cadets not in uniform should remove their headdress with their right hand and hold it at the left shoulder with the hand over the heart. People in uniform should render the military salute at the first note of the anthem and stay in this position until the last note. When the flag is not displayed, those present should face toward the music and act in the same way they would if the flag were displayed.

The National Anthem

Francis Scott Key, a 34-year-old lawyer and poet, wrote the National Anthem in 1814. During the night of September 13, 1814, the British fleet bombarded Fort McHenry in the harbor at Baltimore, Maryland. Francis Scott Key watched the attack from the deck of a British prisoner-exchange ship. He had gone to seek the release of a friend, but they were refused permission to go ashore until after the attack. As the battle stopped on the following morning, Key turned his telescope to the fort and saw that the American flag was still waving. The sight so inspired him that he pulled a letter from his pocket and began to write a poem, "The Star-Spangled Banner," which was eventually adopted as the National Anthem of the United States. Key returned to Baltimore, and later that day he rented a room at a tavern where he completed the poem. Following are the words to the National Anthem, as originally written by Francis Scott Key in 1814.

The Star-Spangled Banner

O! say can you see, by the dawn's early light,
What so proudly we hail'd at the twilight's last gleaming?
Whose broad stripes and bright stars, thro' the perilous fight,
O'er the ramparts we watched were so gallantly streaming?
And the rockets' red glare, the bombs bursting in air,
Gave proof thro' the night that our flag was still there.
O! say does that Star-Spangled Banner yet wave
O'er the land of the free and the home of the brave?

On the shore, dimly seen thro' the mist of the deep,
Where the foe's haughty host in dread silence reposes,
What is that which the breeze, o'er the towering steep,
As it fitfully blows, half conceals, half discloses?
Now it catches the gleam of the morning's first beam,
In full glory reflected now shines on the stream.
'Tis the Star-Spangled Banner. O long may it wave
O'er the land of the free and home of the brave.

And where is that band who so vauntingly swore,
That the havoc of war and the battle's confusion
A home and a country should leave us no more?
Their blood has wash'd out their foul footstep's pollution.
No refuge could save the hireling and slave
From the terror of flight or the gloom of the grave,
And the Star-Spangled Banner in triumph doth wave
O'er the land of the free and the home of the brave.

O thus be it e'er when freemen shall stand
Between their lov'd home and war's desolation,
Blest with vict'ry and peace, may the Heav'n-rescued land
Praise the pow'r that hath made and preserv'd us a nation.
Then conquer we must, when our cause it is just,
And this be our motto, "In God is our Trust."
And the Star-Spangled Banner in triumph shall wave
O'er the land of the free and the home of the brave.

The Pledge of Allegiance

The Pledge of Allegiance recited today was developed from the original. The original one was drawn up in August 1892 in the offices of *Youth's Companion* magazine in Boston, Massachusetts. It was written to celebrate the 400th anniversary of the discovery of America and was first published in the September 8, 1892 issue of the magazine. Public schools first used it to celebrate Columbus Day on October 12, 1892.

Two people claimed to be the author of the first draft. One was James B. Upham, a partner in the firm that published the magazine. The other was Francis M. Bellamy, a former minister and a member of the magazine staff at the time. Although this is still debated, the 79th Congress recognized Mr. Bellamy as the author in December 1945. At that time, his work was officially designated as the Pledge of Allegiance to the Flag by Public Law 287. In 1942, when the 77th Congress set rules pertaining to the use and display of the flag, the Pledge of Allegiance was granted official recognition.

FIGURE 6–8.
The flag is known around the world as a symbol of liberty and freedom. *(Courtesy of Jack Star/PhotoLink/Getty Images)*

In its original version, the pledge read "my flag" instead of "the flag of the United States." The National Flag Conference in 1923 adopted the change in the wording. The change was made to help foreign-born children and adults to think of the American flag when reciting the Pledge, instead of the flags of their native lands.

The final change, authorized by an Act of Congress on June 14, 1954, added the words "under God." Signing the act, President Eisenhower remarked that:

> *. . . in this way we are reaffirming the transcendence of religious faith in America's heritage and future; in this way we shall constantly strengthen those spiritual weapons which forever will be our country's most powerful resource in peace and war.*

The Pledge is a vital, thrilling expression of every American's patriotism and loyalty to the flag. It is also an expression of the magnificent free nation it represents—a nation that recognizes God as its superior and the source of its strength. The Pledge should keep us ever mindful of our solemn duty to preserve, at any cost, our precious heritage of liberty and justice for all citizens. The Pledge should be recited daily in classrooms and at all meetings and ceremonies at which the flag is displayed.

The stance for reciting the Pledge of Allegiance is to come to attention and face the flag. When not in uniform, cadets should remove their headdress with their right hand and hold it at the left shoulder. Cadets in uniform should remain silent, stand at attention, face the flag, and salute if outdoors; if indoors, stand at attention. Uniformed members may also recite the Pledge, if civilians are present.

The Pledge of Allegiance to the Flag

I pledge allegiance to the flag of the United States of America *(pause),* and to the republic for which it stands *(pause),* one nation under God *(pause),* indivisible *(pause),* with liberty and justice for all.

I: You and me; an individual; a person.

PLEDGE: Take a vow; an oath; a promise.

ALLEGIANCE: Duty owed to your country; observance of obligation.

TO THE FLAG: A symbol of liberty; freedom; that which we as free men and women do so cherish.

OF THE UNITED STATES: Joined together; combined; produced by two or more persons; a union our forefathers put together in 1776 to make us a united people free of a tyrant or an oppressor.

OF AMERICA: A land blessed with brotherhood from sea to shining sea; a land full of natural resources; a land where anyone can do what he or she wants as long as it does not violate the rights of another.

AND TO THE REPUBLIC: A state in which the supreme power rests in the body of citizens entitled to vote and is exercised by elected representatives.

FOR WHICH IT STANDS: A flag known throughout the world as a symbol of freedom; a nation in which people can worship as they please, speak and not be afraid of being censored for what they say, express an opinion in writing and not be afraid of being arrested for writing what they feel.

ONE NATION: A body of people associated with a particular territory, who are conscious of their unity; one body of people speaking the same language and yet opening doors to those foreign to us and saying, "Welcome."

UNDER GOD: Meaning we have been so blessed.

INDIVISIBLE: Incapable of being divided; even with our own internal problems, our people, when sensing someone trying to take away our freedom, will answer the call to put down an adversary; we will unite.

WITH LIBERTY: Freedom from outside control; freedom from captivity; freedom from dictatorship; the right to choose our own government.

AND JUSTICE: The quality of being just; equitable, fair treatment for all, regardless of social background or economic standing; the right to be heard, to see our accusers, and to question why.

FOR ALL: Not for just a chosen few, but for everyone in the land.

Flag Presentation

Presentation of the flag during a ceremony should be preceded by a brief talk emphasizing the importance of the occasion. Following the presentation, all present should salute the flag, recite the Pledge of Allegiance, and sing the National Anthem.

Flag Day

Each year on June 14, we celebrate the birthday of the Stars and Stripes, which came into being on June 14, 1777. At that time, the Second Continental Congress authorized a new flag to symbolize the new nation, the United States of America.

The Stars and Stripes first flew in a Flag Day celebration in Hartford, Connecticut, in 1861, during the first summer of the Civil War. The first national observance of Flag Day was June 14, 1877, the centennial of the original flag resolution.

By the mid 1890s, the observance of Flag Day on June 14 was a popular event. Mayors and governors began to issue proclamations in their jurisdictions to celebrate this event.

In the years to follow, public sentiment for a national Flag Day observance greatly increased. Many patriotic societies and veterans groups got involved with the Flag Day movement. Since their main objective was to inspire patriotism among the young, schools were the first to become involved in flag activities.

In 1916, President Woodrow Wilson issued a proclamation calling for a nationwide observance of Flag Day on June 14. In 1949, Congress made this day a permanent observance by resolving: "That the 14th day of June of each year is hereby designated as Flag Day." President Harry Truman signed the measure into law. Although Flag Day is not celebrated as a federal holiday, Americans everywhere continue to honor the history and heritage it represents.

The Great Seal of the United States

On July 4, 1776, the Continental Congress passed a resolution authorizing a committee to devise a seal for the United States of America. This mission was designed to reflect the Founding Fathers' beliefs, values, and sovereignty of the new Nation. It did not become a reality until June 20, 1782.

In heraldic devices, such as seals and insignias, each element has a specific meaning. Even colors have specific meanings. The colors red, white, and blue did not have meanings for the Stars and Stripes when it was adopted in 1777. However, the colors in the Great Seal did have specific meanings. Charles Thompson, Secretary of the Continental Congress, reported to Congress on the Seal. He stated:

> *The colors of the pales (the vertical stripes) are those used in the flag of the United States of America; white signifies purity and innocence; red, hardiness and valour; and blue, the color of the chief (the broad band above the stripes) signifies vigilance, perseverance and justice.*

Some people in Pennsylvania did not want Charles Thomson to be a delegate to the First Continental Congress. Thomson had actively and publicly resisted Britain's attempts to control the North American Colonies. On the first day of assembly, however, the Congress unanimously elected Thomson as secretary. He served in that post through the duration of the Continental Congresses—from 1774 through 1789. Thomson is the little-known designer of the Great Seal of the United States.

Charles Thomson

The obverse of the Great Seal—which is used 2,000 to 3,000 times a year—authenticates the president's signature on many official documents. **Obverse** means *the front of an official seal or insignia.* **Authenticate** means *to establish or prove as real or true.* Some of the documents on which the obverse of the Great Seal appears are treaty ratifications, international agreements, appointments of ambassadors and civil officers, and communications from the president to heads of foreign governments. **Ratification** is *an approval or sanction.*

FIGURE 6–9.

The Obverse of the Great Seal. *(Courtesy of the U.S. Government Printing Office)*

FIGURE 6–10.

The Reverse of the Great Seal. *(Courtesy of the U.S. Government Printing Office)*

The American bald eagle is prominently featured on the obverse of the Great Seal. The eagle supports a shield composed of 13 red and white stripes (pales), representing the Thirteen Original States, with a blue bar (chief) uniting the shield and representing Congress. The motto of the United States, *E Pluribus Unum* (meaning out of many, one), refers to this union. The olive branch and 13 arrows grasped by the eagle symbolize peace and war and the powers solely vested in the Congress. The constellation of stars symbolizes the new nation taking its place among the sovereign powers.

The design of the obverse of the Great Seal is the U.S. coat of arms. It can be shown on coins, postage stamps, passports, monuments and flags, and in many other ways. The American public sees both the obverse and less familiar reverse—which is never used as a seal—every day when exchanging the one-dollar bill. The pyramid on the reverse of the Great Seal signifies strength and duration. The eye over it and the motto, *Annuit Coeptis* (meaning He [God] has favored our undertakings), allude to the many interventions of Providence in favor of the American cause. The Roman numerals below are the date of the Declaration of Independence. The words under it, *Novus Ordo Seclorum* (meaning a new order of the ages), signify the beginning of the new American era in 1776.

The Great Seal die, counter die, press, and cabinet in which they are housed are located inside a locked glass enclosure at the Exhibit Hall of the Department of State. An officer from the department's presidential appointments staff does the actual sealing of documents after the secretary of state has countersigned the president's signature.

The Air Force Seal

Like the American flag, the design of the Air Force Seal is based on historic tradition and symbolism. The official Air Force colors of ultramarine blue and Air Force yellow appear prominently on the Air Force Seal. The circular background of the seal is ultramarine blue. The trim is Air Force yellow. The coat of arms in the center of the seal has two parts. The crest consists of the eagle, wreath, and cloud formation. The American bald eagle, which symbolizes the United States and its air power, appears in its natural colors. The wreath under the eagle is made up of six alternate folds of metal, (white, representing silver) and light blue. This repeats the metal and color used in the shield. The white clouds behind the eagle show the start of a new sky—the Department of the Air Force.

FIGURE 6–11.
The Air Force Seal.

The shield below the eagle is divided horizontally into two parts by a nebulous line representing clouds. The top part bears an Air Force yellow thunderbolt with flames in natural color that shows striking power through the use of aerospace.

The 13 white encircling stars represent the original Thirteen Colonies. The Air Force yellow numerals under the shield are 1947, the year the Department of the Air Force was established. The band encircling the whole design is white-edged in Air Force yellow with black lettering. The inscriptions read "Department of the Air Force" on the top part and "United States of America" on the lower part.

The American's Creed

I believe in the United States of America as a Government of the people, by the people, for the people; whose just powers are derived from the consent of the governed; a democracy in a republic, a sovereign nation of many sovereign states; a perfect union, one and inseparable; established upon those principles of freedom, equality, justice, and humanity for which American patriots sacrificed their lives and fortunes.

I, therefore believe it is my duty to my country to love it; to support its constitution; to obey its laws; to respect its flag; and to defend it against all enemies.

William Tyler Page of Friendship Heights, Maryland, wrote the American's Creed in 1918 during the course of a nationwide contest on the subject. Page was a descendant of President John Tyler and Representative John Page, who served in the Congress from 1789 to 1797.

William Tyler Page began his government career as a congressional page in December of 1881. In 1919, he was elected clerk of the House of Representatives and held that position until December of 1931. A new post, Emeritus Minority Clerk, was then created for him, which he occupied until his death on October 20, 1942.

CHECKPOINTS

Lesson 1 Review

1. What was the name of the first flag to resemble the present Stars and Stripes? What were the elements in its design?

2. Name the president who accepted a bill on April 4, 1818, requiring that the flag of the United States have a union of 20 stars, white on a blue field. What process did he establish for adding stars to the union and when they should be added?

3. What event prompted Francis Scott Key to write the National Anthem?

4. The admission of what two states in 1912 resulted in a flag with 48 stars?

5. What were the 49th and 50th states, and when were they added to the union?

6. Why was Executive Order No. 10834 issued and who issued it?

7. What do the colors used in the flag symbolize?

8. What should you do if you are in uniform and the National Anthem or "To the Colors" is played?

9. When and where was the flag raised for the first time?

10. Describe the present American flag.

11. Where are the laws found that govern the American flag?

12. When the United Nations flag and the American flag are on display together, what is the position of the American flag?

13. List several days during the year when the flag is displayed.

14. What is the significance of The Great Seal of the United States?

15. Who wrote the American's Creed and in what year?

Applying Citizenship Skills

16. Write a letter to the editor of your school or community newspaper explaining how to show proper respect for the American flag.

FIGURE 6–12.
Cadets lower the flag at the end of a school day.

Civics

What Is Civics?

Civics is *the study of the rights and duties of citizens.* The concept of citizenship dates back more than 2,500 years to ancient Greece and Rome. In those days, only a few people—men with property—could be citizens. This elite group helped govern the city and enjoyed other privileges that the common people did not share.

Today gender and wealth are no longer requirements for citizenship. Indeed, most people are citizens of the country in which they live. Citizens have certain rights and duties. **Citizens** are *community members who owe loyalty to the government and are entitled to protection from it.* However, being a citizen means much more than just living in a country. American citizens who live abroad are still citizens of the United States. Citizens are a

Quick Write

Write down what you know about our democratic government. Consider how living in a democracy affects your life.

LEARN ABOUT...

- civics and the need for government.
- the functions of government, including security and public services.
- the different levels of government and democracy.
- citizenship and the naturalization process.
- aliens in America.
- duties and responsibilities of citizenship, including volunteerism.

AMERICANS IN ACTION

When Americans vote or serve on a jury, their actions are based on ideas that people had in the fourth century B.C. In examining how people act, Aristotle wrote these words: "If liberty and equality, as is thought by some, are chiefly to be found in democracy, they will be best attained when all persons alike share in the government to the utmost."

Aristotle teaches

part of a country. They may share a common history, common customs, or common values. They agree to follow a set of rules and to accept the government's authority.

The Need for Government

A **government** is *the ruling authority for a community*. Any organization that has the power to make and enforce laws and decisions for its members acts as a government.

For hundreds of years, people have formed governments. Thomas Hobbes, an English political thinker during the 1600s, believed that without government life would be "solitary, poor, nasty, brutish, and short." Hobbes claimed that human beings naturally compete for territory, resources, and power. If each of us could do just as we pleased, fighting would be common, and survival would depend on strength and cunning.

Think about trying to play basketball with no rules or referees. How would players know what to do and what not to do? How would the winner be determined? The game would probably be a chaotic free-for-all. Similarly, if there were no government to make and enforce laws, we would live in a state of confusion, violence, and fear. We would also struggle to meet our needs entirely on our own. Fortunately, government can make it possible for people to live together peacefully and productively.

The Functions of Government

Governments serve many purposes and offer citizens many benefits. They help keep order, settle conflicts, and protect the community. They provide services that individuals could not supply independently. They also guide the community and plan for its future by setting policies, making budgets, and interacting with other communities.

Keeping Order and Providing Security

Conflicts are unavoidable when people live together in a community. Citizens may disagree on all sorts of matters—their choice of leaders, the best way to raise or spend money, the rightful owner of certain property, and so on. Governments make laws to help prevent conflicts and to settle the conflicts that arise. Governments have the power to enforce the laws. For example, to make sure that drivers obey traffic regulations, police officers are empowered to ticket or arrest violators. Courts decide whether those accused of crimes are guilty and how to set punishment if found guilty.

Along with the need for law and order come concerns about community security—defending citizens and their land from enemies. Arrangements must be made to fight

VOCABULARY

- civics
- citizens
- government
- public policy
- budget
- dictatorship
- democracy
- direct democracy
- representative democracy
- political party
- majority rule
- naturalization
- aliens
- immigrants
- deport
- responsibilities
- duties
- draft
- tolerance
- community
- bureaucracies
- welfare
- volunteerism

off possible threats. For this reason, governments set up armed forces and agencies that watch for likely sources of trouble.

Providing Public Services

Governments provide many services that would not be available without cooperation and coordination. Governments create and manage libraries, schools, hospitals, parks, and recreation centers. They develop systems to provide mass transit and supply water to our homes and businesses. Government workers build and repair streets, erect bridges, collect garbage, and deliver the mail.

FIGURE 6–13.
Apple Valley High School students in Minnesota recite the Pledge of Allegiance. *How do you think reciting the pledge reflects citizenship?*

Many government services are aimed at keeping the public healthy and safe. Local communities set up fire departments and ambulance services, for example. States license drivers and doctors. Other government agencies protect us from dangerous drugs or spoiled food. Government inspectors check for safety problems in everything from factories to day care centers to amusement park rides.

Governments also give help to needy people. For example, in each of the 50 states, poor families and people who are out of work can receive food aid or cash. Government agencies also supply affordable housing, health care, job training, and special programs for people with disabilities.

FIGURE 6–14.
A banner created by American students after the terrorist attacks of September 2001.

Guiding the Community

Another function of government is to develop public policy. **Public policy** is *a course of government action to achieve community goals.* For example, when government leaders decide they want to protect consumers or strengthen national security, they are setting public policy goals. When they pass laws or develop guidelines to reach these goals, they are making public policy.

Most public policy decisions involve some financial planning, as well. Governments have limited amounts of money, and they must be careful to use it wisely. Creating a budget is key to the success of the community. A **budget** is *a plan for collecting and spending money.*

Another part of guiding the community is developing relations with the community's neighbors and other outsiders. Governments often take responsibility for communicating and cooperating with other governments for the benefit of their citizens. International trade, travel, and military pacts or agreements are all part of public policy. These would all be impossible if national governments were not concerned about foreign relations.

Levels of Government

Within a single country, there may be many levels of government. Each level exercises authority over a different group of people. The highest level in the United States is the national government, centered in the nation's capital, Washington, D.C. The national government makes and enforces laws for the entire country. Each of our 50 states has its own government as well, which decides matters for the people in that state. The level of government closest to Americans is local government.

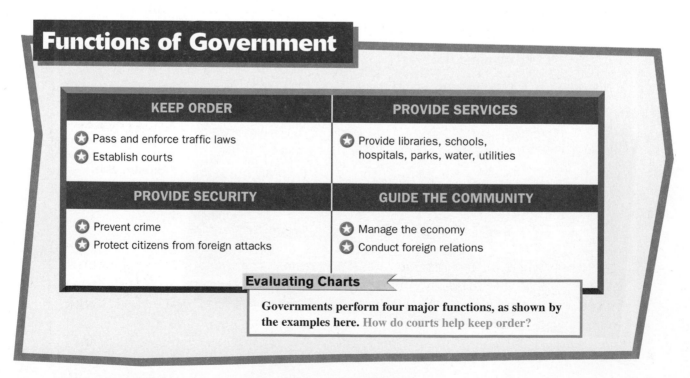

Functions of Government

KEEP ORDER	PROVIDE SERVICES
★ Pass and enforce traffic laws ★ Establish courts	★ Provide libraries, schools, hospitals, parks, water, utilities

PROVIDE SECURITY	GUIDE THE COMMUNITY
★ Prevent crime ★ Protect citizens from foreign attacks	★ Manage the economy ★ Conduct foreign relations

Evaluating Charts

Governments perform four major functions, as shown by the examples here. How do courts help keep order?

Local governments include counties, cities, and towns. Your school may have a student government, and if you choose to belong to a club, you respect that organization's governing body, too.

When people speak of "the government," they usually mean the national government. State and local governments, as well as governments of organizations, cannot take actions that go against the laws and authority of the national government.

Democratic Government

In some parts of the world, governmental power lies in the hands of just a small group or even a single person. For example, the government of Cuba is a dictatorship. A **dictatorship** is *a government controlled by one person or a small group of people.* In the United States, all citizens share in governing and being governed. This kind of government, *in which the people rule,* is called a **democracy**. The foundations of democracy are more than 2,500 years old. Democracy began in ancient Greece, most famously in the city of Athens. Every citizen of Athens had the right and responsibility to participate in the city's government, and all citizens had an equal voice. This was a **direct democracy**—*all the citizens met to debate government matters and vote firsthand.* Direct democracy is not practical for most countries today because of their large sizes and large populations. Many countries have representative democracies instead. In **representative democracies**, *the citizens choose a smaller group to represent them, make laws, and govern on their behalf, but the people remain the source of the government's authority.*

The United States is the oldest representative democracy in the world. For more than 225 years, Americans have elected presidents, members of Congress, and other leaders to speak for them. Citizens express their views in person, over the phone, by e-mail and regular "snail" mail, and through public opinion polls and political groups.

Principles of American Democracy

Abraham Lincoln, America's sixteenth president, described our democracy as a "government of the people, by the people, for the people." His words make three important points. First, the power of the government comes from the citizens. Second, Americans themselves, acting through their representatives, run their government. Third, the purpose of the government is to make the United States a better place for those who live here.

Because democratic governments exist by the people, all genuine democracies have free, fair, and competitive elections. Through free elections, people have the chance to choose their leaders and voice their opinions about various issues.

What makes an election fair and free? First, everyone's vote must carry the same weight. This principle is often expressed in the phrase "one person, one vote." Second, all candidates have the right to express their views freely to the public. Citizens are free to support candidates or issues. There can only be a minimum of legal requirements for voting. For example, our voting laws center on age, residence, and citizenship. Other factors, like race and ethnic and religious background, cannot be used to restrict voting. Finally, citizens may vote freely by secret ballot, without fearing punishment for their voting decisions.

Competitive elections and competing political parties are important parts of democracies. A **political party** is *a group of individuals with broad, common interests who organize to support candidates for office and determine public policy.* Competing political parties give voters a choice among candidates. Also, the parties out of power help make those in power more responsible to the needs of the people.

In a democracy, individuals are free to develop their own capacities. This means that the government works to promote equality, and all people have an equal opportunity to develop their talents.

Of course, you can't please all the people all the time. Another principle of our democracy is majority rule. **Majority rule** means that *when differences of opinion arise, we will abide by what most people want.* At the same time, we insist on respect for the rights of those in the minority.

Respect for minority rights is sometimes difficult to maintain, especially if society is under a great deal of stress. For example, the United States government imprisoned more than 100,000 Japanese Americans in relocation camps during World War II. Government leaders feared that these Americans would be disloyal. This relocation program caused severe hardships for many Japanese Americans and deprived them of basic liberties. In 1988 Congress recognized the "grave injustice" of the relocation camps and offered payments of $20,000 to those Japanese Americans still living who had been relocated.

After the terrorist attacks of 2001, President George W. Bush realized that many people might turn their anger against Muslims in the United States. So soon after the attacks, he visited the Islamic Center in Washington, D.C. He explained that Islam is a peaceful religion and urged Americans to treat Muslim Americans fairly.

FIGURE 6–15.
A town meeting in Warren, Vermont.

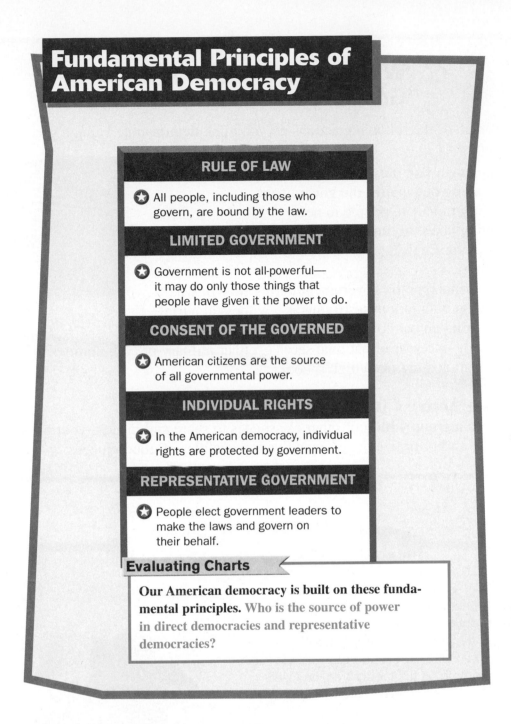

Fundamental Principles of American Democracy

RULE OF LAW

★ All people, including those who govern, are bound by the law.

LIMITED GOVERNMENT

★ Government is not all-powerful—it may do only those things that people have given it the power to do.

CONSENT OF THE GOVERNED

★ American citizens are the source of all governmental power.

INDIVIDUAL RIGHTS

★ In the American democracy, individual rights are protected by government.

REPRESENTATIVE GOVERNMENT

★ People elect government leaders to make the laws and govern on their behalf.

Evaluating Charts

Our American democracy is built on these fundamental principles. Who is the source of power in direct democracies and representative democracies?

Who Are America's Citizens?

Citizens are people with certain rights and duties under a government, who owe allegiance to that government. Every country has rules about how people gain citizenship. In the United States, the Fourteenth Amendment defines a U.S. citizen as anyone "born or naturalized in the United States." Therefore, the U.S. Constitution establishes two ways to become a citizen: by birth and by naturalization. **Naturalization** is *the legal process by which foreigners can choose to become American citizens.*

What Does It Mean to Be a "Good Citizen" of a Country?

Which of the following actions do you think demonstrate being a good citizen?

- Hanging a flag outside the home or on the car
- Speaking out against the government
- Giving money to people in need
- Paying taxes on time
- Speaking English
- Voting
- Not criticizing the government during time of war
- Serving on a jury or testifying as a witness at a trial
- Swearing an oath of allegiance to the United States
- Serving one year of national service, either military or community service, after graduating from high school

Be An Active Citizen

Form a group with four other classmates to share and discuss your priorities. Identify and prioritize the group's five top qualities of good citizens.

AMERICANS IN ACTION

He thought he was an American citizen. He was drafted in 1969 and served two years in the U.S. Army during the Vietnam War; but when Tom Castillo carried out some research on his family tree, he made a discovery. He had been born in Mexico. When Castillo was about five, he, his mother, and two siblings moved from Mexico to Texas. His mother kept his birthplace a secret, wanting him to grow up American. Now, at age 52, Castillo has become a naturalized citizen of the United States. It was a natural step for Castillo, who says, "I've always considered myself an American first."

American soldier during the Vietnam War

Citizenship by Birth

If you were born in any of the 50 states or the District of Columbia, you automatically became an American citizen at birth. The same is true if you were born outside the country but in American territory, such as Puerto Rico or Guam or on a U.S. military base overseas. Even if you were born elsewhere, you could still claim American citizenship if your parents are both citizens or if one parent is a citizen who has actually lived in the United States.

Children born on American soil to non-U.S. citizens also become U.S. citizens at birth. An exception to this rule is made for children born to foreign diplomats—official government representatives—living in the United States. Such children keep the citizenship of their parents.

Under some circumstances, Americans may hold dual citizenship. This means that they enjoy rights in the United States and in another country at the same time. For example, a child born abroad to American parents may be both a U.S. citizen and a citizen of the country of his or her birth.

The Naturalization Process

Several million aliens live in the United States. **Aliens** are *people who are not citizens.* Some come to study, to work, or to visit relatives for awhile. They remain citizens of their own countries and eventually return home. Other aliens, however, plan to settle here and become naturalized citizens. More than half a million immigrants gain American citizenship each year. **Immigrants** are *people who move permanently to a new country.*

Aliens who want to become United States citizens must first sign a statement saying just that. This Declaration of Intention is then filed with the Immigration and Naturalization Service (INS), an agency of the national government. For most aliens, the next step comes after living in the United States at least five years. (Aliens who are married to citizens wait only three years.) During this time, many immigrants take special classes to prepare for citizenship. At this time, if they are at least 18 years old and have lived for at least three months in the state where they seek naturalization, they may file an application for citizenship.

After the paperwork is checked, the alien has an interview with an INS official. Agency officials want to be sure the alien meets the necessary requirements and has a good moral character. The applicant must also take a citizenship exam that consists of questions about reading, writing, and speaking English. It also has basic facts about the history and government of the United States. Afterward, the INS makes its decision.

If the application is granted, the final step in naturalization is attending a ceremony and pledging an oath of allegiance. The alien swears to be loyal to this country above all others, to obey the Constitution and other laws, and to perform military or other duties if needed. Then the person signs a document and is declared a citizen of the

United States. If he or she has children under 18, they automatically become naturalized citizens, too.

A Lifelong Privilege

Whether they are naturalized or native-born, most Americans keep their citizenship forever. Only the federal government can both grant citizenship and take it away. Although state governments can deny a convicted criminal some of the privileges of citizenship, such as voting, they do not have the power to deny citizenship itself. The government may strip naturalized citizens of their citizenship if it was not obtained properly. However, in most cases, the only way to lose U.S. citizenship is to voluntarily give it up. This must be done in a foreign country, with a formal oath signed before an appropriate American official.

There is no going back for those who take this step. They cannot later change their minds and regain citizenship. They also remain liable for old debts and any crimes they may have committed in the United States.

> ### OATH OF ALLEGIANCE TO THE UNITED STATES
>
> I hereby declare, on oath, that I absolutely and entirely renounce and abjure [reject] all allegiance and fidelity to any foreign prince, potentate, state, or sovereignty, to whom or which I have heretofore been a subject or citizen; that I will support and defend the Constitution and laws of the United States of America against all enemies, foreign and domestic; that I will bear true faith and allegiance to the same; that I will bear arms on behalf of the United States when required by law; that I will perform noncombatant service in the armed forces of the United States when required by law; that I will perform work of national importance under civilian direction when required by law; and that I take this obligation freely without any mental reservation or purpose of evasion; so help me God.

FIGURE 6–16.

All citizenship applicants must take the citizenship oath. *What step in the naturalization process comes just before taking the citizenship oath?*

Aliens in America

The United States restricts the number of immigrants who can enter the country. Millions apply, but only about 675,000 are accepted each year. Traditionally, the relatives of U.S. citizens and people with needed job skills received the highest priority. Family members still get special consideration. But because of the Immigration Act of 1990, emphasis has shifted toward welcoming "those who want to work and produce and contribute," as one member of Congress put it. The new policy benefits people with particular skills, talents, or the money to invest in our economy.

Illegal Aliens

Despite immigration limits, approximately 5 to 6 million aliens are living in the United States illegally. Some were refused permission to immigrate; others never applied for permission because they feared a long, slow process or being turned down.

Illegal aliens come to the United States in a variety of ways. A few enter the country as temporary visitors and never leave. Others risk capture and arrest by illegally crossing our borders with Mexico and Canada. Other illegal aliens are foreigners who have stayed in the United States after their legal permits have expired.

Whatever the method, the reason is usually the same. "I came for work and for a better life," explained one Mexican immigrant; yet illegal aliens often have a difficult time in the United States. Many have no friends or family here, no place to live, and no sure way to earn money. It is against the law to hire illegal aliens, and those who do find work usually receive little pay and no benefits. Every day they live with the fear that government officials will discover and deport them. To **deport** people is *to send them back to their own country.*

The United States Border Patrol is the law-enforcement unit of the INS. Its main responsibility is to detect and prevent the illegal entry of aliens into the United States. The Border Patrol patrols the 6,000 miles of Mexican and Canadian international land borders and 2,000 miles of coastal waters surrounding the Florida Peninsula and the island of Puerto Rico.

Legal Aliens

Aliens who have entered the United States legally lead lives much like those of American citizens. Aliens—both legal and illegal—may hold jobs, own property, attend public schools, and receive other government services. They pay taxes and are entitled to legal protection.

Aliens do not have full political rights, however. They may not vote in elections or run for office. They may not serve on juries or work in most government jobs. In addition, unlike U.S. citizens, aliens must carry identification cards at all times.

American Biographies

EMMA LAZARUS (1849–1887)

Emma Lazarus wrote the poem that today captures the meaning of the Statue of Liberty. Lines from "The New Colossus," written in 1883, appear at the statue's base.

In words now famous, Lazarus declared:

Give me your tired, your poor,

Your huddled masses yearning to breathe free.

Lazarus, the fourth of seven children, grew up in one of the oldest and most respected Jewish families in New York City. She published her first book at age 17 and by age 25 was a well-known writer.

All around her, Lazarus saw a city alive with immigration. New York more than doubled in size as millions of immigrants came to the United States in the late 1800s. Lazarus felt strong ties with Jews driven from Russia because of their religion. She started classes in English and helped Russian Jews find housing.

To Lazarus, the United States was the "golden door" to freedom. She hoped that the Statue of Liberty, erected in 1886, would serve as a beacon of liberty to the entire world.

On September 11, 2001, terrorist acts killed thousands of Americans. President George W. Bush led the nation during this troubled time, and in 2002 proclaimed: " . . . After America was attacked, it was as if our entire country looked into a mirror and saw our better selves. We were reminded that we are citizens, with obligations to each other, to our country, and to history. We began to think less of the goods we can accumulate and more about the good we can do. . . . In the sacrifice of soldiers, the fierce brotherhood of firefighters, and the bravery and generosity of ordinary citizens, we have glimpsed what a new culture of responsibility could look like. We want to be a nation that serves goals larger than self. We have been offered a unique opportunity, and we must not let this moment pass."

Proud Americans

A Citizen's Legal Duties

When you think of your community, do you think of your neighborhood or perhaps your town? Actually, each of us belongs to many communities—our school or workplace; our church, synagogue, or mosque; our state; and our country. On the broadest level, we are also members of the global community, more connected than ever before to people around the world.

We all have a stake in making our communities safe and successful. Thus we all have certain responsibilities to fulfill. **Responsibilities** are *things we should do; they are obligations that we fulfill voluntarily.* As American citizens, we also have legal duties that we are required to perform. **Duties** are *things that we must do.*

National, state, and local governments require Americans to perform certain duties established by laws. If we fail to perform them, we are subject to legal penalties, such as fines or imprisonment. By accepting all of these responsibilities and duties, we strengthen our communities and help secure our rights. Some countries require their citizens to perform many duties, such as serving a certain number of years in the military. Although the U.S. government asks less of its citizens, it does require that they fulfill the following duties.

Obey Laws

Following the law is a citizen's most important duty. Our laws are designed for specific purposes—to help people get along, to prevent accidents, to see that resources are used fairly, and so on. If we do not obey the law, then governments cannot maintain order or protect our health, safety, and property.

Pay Taxes

Taxes pay for the government's activities. Without them, the federal government could not pay its employees, maintain armed forces to defend the country, and help those in need. Your local government could not hire police officers or firefighters, and your state could not pave roads or maintain prisons.

Citizens pay taxes in several ways. The federal government and some states and cities collect income taxes—a percentage of what people earn. Most states and some cities collect taxes on the sale of goods and services. Most local governments collect taxes on the residential and commercial property within school districts.

Defend the Nation

In the United States, all men aged 18 through 25 are required to register with the government in case the country needs to draft them. To **draft** means *to select for military service.* Since the end of the Vietnam War, there has been no draft, and America's military has been made up of volunteers. Still, the government has the authority to use the draft if the country should suddenly have to go to war.

Serve in Court

In criminal cases and most civil matters, the Constitution guarantees the right to a trial by jury. To ensure this, every adult citizen must be prepared to serve on a jury. People can be excused from jury duty if they have a good reason, but service is usually rewarding. People involved in court cases depend on their fellow citizens to reach a fair verdict. Another duty of citizens is to serve as witnesses at a trial if called to do so.

Attend School

Most states require young people to attend school until age 16. This benefits both you and the government. You need knowledge and skills to make wise decisions, and our democratic system of government needs informed citizens to operate well. In school you gain an understanding of history, government, and other important subjects. You also learn to think through problems, form opinions, and express your views clearly.

Civic Responsibilities

Several responsibilities of citizenship are voluntary obligations rather than legal duties. If you ignore these, you won't be arrested or punished. If you fulfill them, you help our democracy flourish and reap personal benefits as well.

Be Informed

Every day government leaders make decisions that affect your life. The state legislature, for example, might pass a law changing the rate of sales tax you pay. Your school board might vote to start the school day earlier. Your town council might set aside funds for a new recreation center. As a citizen, you have a responsibility to know what the government is doing so that you can voice your opinions on matters you feel strongly about.

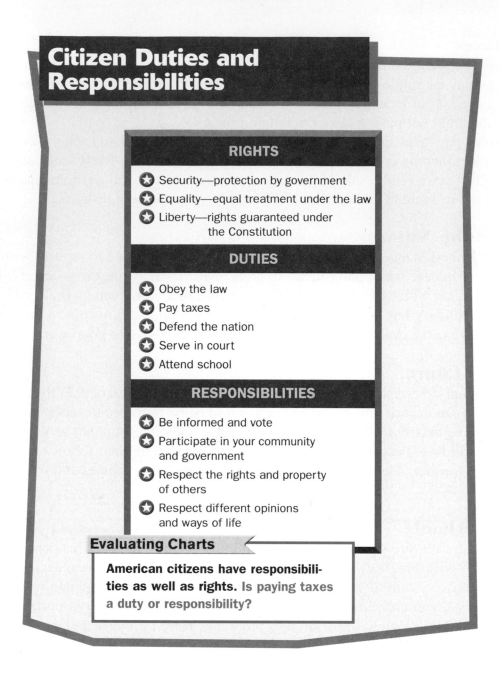

Citizen Duties and Responsibilities

RIGHTS

- ⭐ Security—protection by government
- ⭐ Equality—equal treatment under the law
- ⭐ Liberty—rights guaranteed under the Constitution

DUTIES

- ⭐ Obey the law
- ⭐ Pay taxes
- ⭐ Defend the nation
- ⭐ Serve in court
- ⭐ Attend school

RESPONSIBILITIES

- ⭐ Be informed and vote
- ⭐ Participate in your community and government
- ⭐ Respect the rights and property of others
- ⭐ Respect different opinions and ways of life

Evaluating Charts

American citizens have responsibilities as well as rights. Is paying taxes a duty or responsibility?

To learn about issues and leaders, you can read books, newspapers, and magazines. You can listen to the news on radio and television and talk with your teachers, family, and friends. You can also find useful information on the Internet.

Being informed includes knowing your rights. For example, people accused of crimes have the right to be represented by a lawyer. If people were unaware of that right, they might not receive fair trials.

Speak Up and Vote

The Founders of our nation set up a government based upon the principle of popular sovereignty, or "consent of the governed." People are the source of any and all governmental power; that is, government exists to serve you. But you must make your concerns known if you expect public officials to act in your interests. Call, write, or send e-mail to your elected representatives. Join a political party or a group working for a particular cause. Above all, vote.

Voting is one of a citizen's most important rights and responsibilities. By electing political leaders and voting for or against proposed measures, Americans give their consent to the government. As former President Franklin D. Roosevelt said,

"The ultimate rulers of our democracy are not a president and senators and congressmen and government officials, but the voters of this country."

Thoughtful voters study the candidates and issues carefully before marking their ballots. They also regularly check on what elected leaders are doing. If an official's performance falls short, it is up to the voters to choose someone else in the next election. Voting responsibly ensures that leadership is changed in a peaceful and orderly manner.

Respect Others' Rights

To enjoy your rights to the fullest, you must be prepared to respect other people's rights. For example, if you own a dog, you have an obligation to keep it from becoming a nuisance to your neighbors. If you're in the library, you should not interfere with anyone's right to work quietly.

Citizens also have a responsibility to show respect for public property and for the property of others. Some people might claim that "no one gets hurt" when they litter in a park or paint graffiti on a school wall. Yet, such public property belongs to us all, and we all pay if it is damaged.

Vandalism and littering are actually more than disrespectful acts; they are crimes. Many of our laws have been enacted to encourage people to respect others' rights. If you have a party that gets out of hand, for example, you could be arrested for disturbing the peace.

Respect Diversity

In a democratic society like ours, with such a diverse population, it is especially important to respect the civil liberties of others. Although you may disagree with people or disapprove of their lifestyles, they have an equal right to their beliefs and practices. *Respecting and accepting others, regardless of their beliefs, practices, or differences,* is called **tolerance**. Treating others politely and respectfully is thus part of being a good citizen. One of America's strengths has always been the diversity of its people.

Immigrants have brought a variety of religions, traditions, and lifestyles to this country, and they continue to do so. As citizens, we have a responsibility to respect the practices and traditions of others when they are different from our own, just as we expect them to respect our differences. There are no degrees of citizenship in the United States. All citizens are equal and entitled to be treated the same.

Contribute to the Common Good

Responsible citizens care about others. They are willing to contribute time, effort, and money to help other people and to improve community life for everyone.

Think about what your community would be like if no one donated to charities, volunteered in after-school programs, or lent a hand at the local health clinic. What if no one even spoke out about community problems? Communities and governments need people to participate. If we want our communities to thrive, all American citizens must be active participants and not just idle bystanders.

FIGURE 6–17.

As Americans, we have a responsibility to respect the practices and traditions of others. Thai Americans celebrate the Thai New Year during a Songkran Festival in New York City in April.

The Need for Citizens' Involvement

Why did Korczak Ziolkowski do so much work and not accept payment? He was a volunteer. Another volunteer, John Gatus, a retired steamfitter who volunteered in an anti-gang neighborhood patrol, explained, "Volunteer work brings real change, change you can be a part of, change you can see with your own eyes. You don't need politicians or police to tell you things are better. You can see it and feel it for yourself and know you were a part of it. . . . There's a real pride involved. We're part of a community."

Every year more than half of all Americans do volunteer work to help make their communities better places to live. A **community** is *a group of people who share the same interests and concerns.* These volunteers include more than 14 million students in grades 6 through 12. Without the efforts of so many private citizens, many pressing social needs simply would not be met.

In the United States, governments provide a wealth of services. We rely on government for everything from local police protection to national defense, from collecting household trash to ensuring clean water and air nationwide. Citizens, though, also share responsibility for meeting community needs.

The government, after all, has limited resources. In addition, governments are **bureaucracies**—*complex systems with many departments, many rules, and many people in the chain of command.* Because of this, government cannot always respond

Without Korczak Ziolkowski, there would be no Crazy Horse Memorial. Ziolkowski, born of Polish descent in Boston, became famous as a mountain carver, but it is his life and dedication that have inspired the people who learn about him. Ziolkowski assisted Gutzon Borglum at Mount Rushmore, and then dedicated the rest of his life to sculpting the Crazy Horse Memorial. Crazy Horse was a Native American leader who bravely defended his people and their way of life. Ziolkowski carved Crazy Horse as a memorial to the leader's spirit. Ziolkowski worked on the memorial—the world's largest sculpture—for 36 years, until his death in 1982. He refused to be paid for his work. Ziolkowski's wife and family continue his work on the Crazy Horse Memorial.

Honoring Crazy Horse

quickly or efficiently to social problems. In many cases, the best solutions come from private citizens. Good citizens are concerned about the welfare—*the health, prosperity, and happiness*—of all members of the community.

In 1961 President John F. Kennedy issued his famous challenge, "Ask not what your country can do for you; ask what you can do for your country." In 2001 President George W. Bush called for a renewed commitment to community service. He noted that we can show " . . . the world the true values of America through the gathering momentum of a million acts of responsibility and decency and service."

Donating Time and Money

People contribute to their communities in countless ways, working independently or as part of volunteer groups, both large and small. You probably know a mom or dad who is active in the PTA (Parent Teacher Association) or leads a Scout troop. Neighbors might spend a Saturday afternoon cleaning up a vacant lot or preparing holiday baskets for needy families. Retirees mentor schoolchildren, record books on audiotapes and CD-ROMs for the blind, and lead museum tours. You or your fellow students might visit nursing home patients, volunteer in an animal shelter, or collect canned goods for a local food pantry.

Contributing your time to work on community projects is the heart of volunteerism—*the practice of offering your time and services to others without payment.* However, Americans may also support worthy causes by contributing money. In 2000, individual Americans gave more than $152 billion to charity. Much of this money came from small donations by average citizens. The typical American donates about two percent of his or her income to charity.

Many companies, too, believe in giving something back to the community. Small businesses may sponsor a recreational sports team or donate prizes for a charity's fund-raiser. Large companies often contribute thousands of dollars to community projects, like building a new public swimming pool or putting on a free concert. They frequently match the charitable donations of their employees, chipping in a dollar of corporate funds for every dollar that a worker gives to charity.

Many companies make a special commitment to investing in young people. They may offer college scholarships to students or give their employees time off to volunteer in the schools.

Volunteers in Action

Community involvement tends to be rooted in individual action and informal groups. People are more likely to participate when they feel a personal connection to a cause or know others involved. Thus, they join their Neighborhood Watch or become active at their child's school. They reach out to the community through their religious congregations or service clubs like the Lions and Kiwanis. Some people, however, volunteer through more formal channels.

Charitable Organizations

More than one million charities are officially registered with the federal government. Many are small and locally based. They often work on one or two projects, such as helping the victims of domestic abuse or preserving historic landmarks. Other organizations, such as the United Way, the Boys and Girls Clubs of

American Biographies

JUSTIN DART, JR. (1930–2002)

Justin Dart, Jr., had a message to deliver: "People with disabilities are fully equal." To spread that message, he traveled to all 50 states at least four times and to nations around the world. Stricken with polio at age 18, Dart used a wheelchair and knew personally the hurdles people with disabilities must overcome. He worked to tear down these hurdles by launching, along with his wife Yoshiko Saji Dart, the disability rights movement.

Dart advised governors, presidents, and the U.S. Congress on the subject of disabilities. However, he relied on grassroots support—the support of ordinary people—to bring about change. "Get into politics as if your life depended on it," he told one audience.

In 1990 Dart's grassroots army won the passage of the Americans with Disabilities Act. The act prohibits discrimination against people with disabilities. In 1998 Dart received the Presidential Medal of Freedom, the nation's highest civilian award. At the beginning of the twenty-first century, Dart announced a new goal—to carry the disability rights movement worldwide.

America, and Big Brothers Big Sisters, are large, national bodies with varied activities serving millions of people.

All of these groups depend on ordinary people who give their time freely. Most, however, also have some paid staff who help set organizational goals, manage the budget, and oversee operations.

School-Based Programs

Across the country, more than half of all schools now arrange community service for students in grades 6 through 12. Several hundred school districts even require it. In Atlanta, Chicago, and the entire state of Maryland, for example, high school students must volunteer a set number of hours to earn a diploma.

Some people believe that community service is less meaningful when it is obligatory. According to one school official in Atlanta, however, the "students think it's a neat idea, and for many of them it is nothing new." Many have already been active volunteers in the community.

National Service Programs

Over the years, the federal government has created various national programs to encourage volunteerism. In 1961, for example, the Peace Corps was launched to help people in the poorest corners of the world. The Peace Corps has sent tens of thousands of Americans to 135 countries, where they advise farmers, teach children, dig wells, help start small businesses, and fight the spread of AIDS and other serious diseases. Here in the United States, the government provides community service opportunities through AmeriCorps and the Senior Corps.

More than 50,000 Americans participate each year in AmeriCorps. Most work through local and national organizations to meet community needs. Under the guidance of the American Red Cross, for example, volunteers help victims of floods, fires, earthquakes, and other disasters. Working with other groups, they might clean up polluted rivers, immunize children, or assist people with disabilities. In return for a year of full-time service, AmeriCorps volunteers receive an allowance to live on and money to help pay for college.

The Senior Corps provides volunteer opportunities to Americans aged 55 or older. These senior citizens take part in three main programs. Foster Grandparents work one on one with children with special needs. Senior Companions help other seniors meet their daily needs while living in their own homes. The Retired and Senior Volunteer Program (RSVP) links volunteers to service opportunities right in their backyards. For example, they might deliver hot meals with Meals on Wheels, help plant and tend a neighborhood garden, or teach English to immigrants.

On January 29, 2002, in his annual State of the Union Address, President Bush asked Americans to join together and help, saying, "If you aren't sure how to help, I've got a good place to start." Bush went on to describe a new program, called USA

Freedom Corps. The program brought together the Peace Corps, AmeriCorps, and Senior Corps. Bush added another component called "Citizen Corps." Citizen Corps is an important part of the USA Freedom Corps. It was created to help coordinate volunteer activities that will make our communities safer, stronger, and better prepared to respond to any emergency situation. President Bush stated that the purpose of Freedom Corps was a focus on three "areas of need: responding in case of crisis at home, rebuilding our communities, and extending American compassion throughout the world." Bush appealed to Americans to serve their neighbors and their nation. You can find more information about the Citizen Corps on their Web site at:
http://www.usafreedomcorps.gov/content/programs/citizencorps/index.asp

FIGURE 6–18.
President Bush proposes the Freedom Corps.

The Benefits of Volunteering

The United States has always been a nation of volunteers. When Alexis de Tocqueville, a French political writer, visited America in the 1830s, he was amazed to see citizens pitching in to solve community problems rather than relying on the government. He explained it as "self-interest rightly understood." In other words, by banding together to serve the community, we also serve ourselves.

By volunteering we make our communities better places to live and gain new opportunities to learn, make friends, and improve our teamwork, leadership, and problem-solving skills. It is satisfying to know that you can make a difference in someone else's life.

FIGURE 6–19.

Working together in emergencies. Workers formed a human chain to transport supplies to boats, which carried them to Manhattan to help recovery efforts at the World Trade Center in 2001.

American Volunteers in Action

PERCENTAGE OF ADULTS ACTIVE IN VOLUNTEER WORK

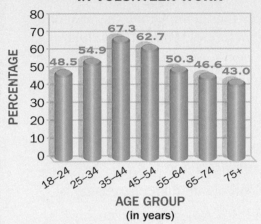

Source: *Statistical Abstract of the United States, 2000.*

VALUE OF U.S. VOLUNTEERS, 1987–1998
(Total Value of Volunteer Time)

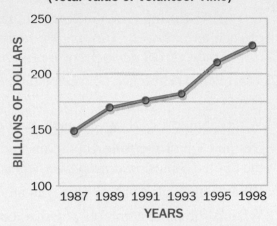

Source: www.childstats.gov

HOW CAN YOU VOLUNTEER?

Places to Volunteer	Sample Volunteer Activities
★ Homeless shelters	★ Prepare and distribute meals
★ Food banks	★ Help organize a food drive
★ Hospices and hospitals	★ Talk with families and kids
★ Special Olympics	★ Help raise funds or lead activities
★ Habitat for Humanity	★ Help build a house
★ State and local parks	★ Clean up trails or pick up trash
★ City parks	★ Assist with recreational activities
★ Schools or after-school programs	★ Tutor a child or new immigrant
★ Libraries	★ Read to children or reshelve books
★ Senior citizen centers	★ Deliver meals to homebound seniors
★ Animal shelters	★ Take care of animals
★ Environmental organizations	★ Lead hikes or lobby for a cause
★ Political campaigns	★ Lend a hand at the campaign office or join a letter-writing campaign
★ Red Cross and Salvation Army	★ Help out in an emergency
★ Local charities and organizations	★ Create a Web site
★ Your school or community government	★ Hold an elective office, attend a city council or school board meeting or public hearing and voice your opinion

WHY SHOULD YOU VOLUNTEER?

- ★ To help others
- ★ To learn something new about an activity or organization
- ★ To meet people and make friends
- ★ To beat boredom
- ★ To better deal with a loss you have experienced (such as the death of a loved one)
- ★ To learn something new about life
- ★ To explore careers

Analyzing Graphs

There are many volunteering opportunities in your local community. All volunteers are valuable resources to their communities. Which age group of Americans has the highest percentage of people volunteering?

Lesson 2 Review

1. Use the following terms in complete sentences that demonstrate the meaning of each term: *civics, citizen, government, public policy, budget, dictatorship, democracy, direct democracy, representative democracy, majority rule*.

2. What is the difference between a direct democracy and a representative democracy?

3. What three levels of government exist in the United States?

4. Define each of the following terms and explain how it relates to citizenship in the United States: *naturalization, alien, immigrant, deport*.

5. What is dual citizenship? How can an American obtain dual citizenship?

6. What is the most common way that a person loses American citizenship? Explain the process by which this happens.

7. Define *draft* and *tolerance*, and use them in sentences related to U.S. citizenship.

8. When was the last time the United States had a military draft?

9. Why is it important for citizens of the United States to be informed about issues and about their political leaders? How can you become informed?

10. Define *bureaucracy, community*, and *welfare*, and use them in sentences related to *volunteerism*.

11. Why does our government need people to volunteer in their communities? What ways can you volunteer?

12. What program was launched in the early 1960s to assist people in the poorest parts of the world? What types of activities do volunteers with this organization perform? How do these activities help people in other countries?

Applying Citizenship Skills

13. Interview an American who became a citizen through the naturalization process. What reasons brought him or her to the United States? Why did he or she want to become an American citizen?

14. Contact a local volunteer organization. Find out what projects or problems they are working on in your community and how they use volunteers. Report your findings to the class.

The Constitution of the United States

A Remarkable Document

The Constitution of the United States is truly a remarkable document. It was one of the first written constitutions in modern history. The Framers wanted to devise a plan for a strong central government that would unify the country, as well as preserve the ideals of the Declaration of Independence. The document they wrote created a representative legislature, the office of president, a system of courts, and a process for adding amendments. For over 200 years, the flexibility and strength of the Constitution has guided the nation's political leaders. The document has become a symbol of pride and a force for national unity.

The entire text of the Constitution and its amendments follows. For easier study, those passages that have been set aside or changed by the adoption of amendments are printed in blue. Also included are explanatory notes to help clarify the meaning of each article and section.

Quick Write

How do you think the Constitution of the United States protects your rights and freedom as an American citizen? Write down five ways the Constitution protects you.

LEARN ABOUT...

- the parts of the Constitution and what they mean.
- amending the Constitution.
- interpreting the Constitution.

VOCABULARY

- Preamble
- Bill of Rights
- income tax

FIGURE 6-20.
James Madison, author of the Constitution.

Preamble

We the People of the United States, in Order to form a more perfect Union, establish Justice, insure domestic Tranquility, provide for the common defence, promote the general Welfare, and secure the Blessings of Liberty to ourselves and our Posterity, do ordain and establish this Constitution for the United States of America.

Article I

Section 1

All legislative Powers herein granted shall be vested in a Congress of the United States, which shall consist of a Senate and House of Representatives.

Section 2

[1.] The House of Representatives shall be composed of Members chosen every second Year by the People of the several States, and the Electors in each State shall have the Qualifications requisite for Electors of the most numerous Branch of the State Legislature.

[2.] No person shall be a Representative who shall not have attained to the Age of twenty five Years, and been seven Years a Citizen of the United States, and who shall not, when elected, be an Inhabitant of that State in which he shall be chosen.

[3.] Representatives and direct Taxes shall be apportioned among the several States which may be included within this Union, according to their respective Numbers, which shall be determined by adding to the whole Number of free Persons, including those bound to Service for a Term of Years, and excluding Indians not taxed, three fifths of all other Persons. The actual Enumeration shall be made within three Years after the first Meeting of the Congress of the United States, and within every subsequent Term of ten Years, in such Manner as they shall by Law direct. The Number of Representatives shall not exceed one for every thirty Thousand, but each State shall have at Least one Representative; and until such enumeration shall be made, the State of New Hampshire shall be entitled to chuse three; Massachusetts eight, Rhode-Island and Providence Plantations one, Connecticut five, New-York six, New Jersey four, Pennsylvania eight, Delaware one, Maryland six, Virginia ten, North Carolina five, South Carolina five, and Georgia three.

[4.] When vacancies happen in the Representation from any State, the Executive Authority thereof shall issue Writs of Election to fill such Vacancies.

[5.] The House of Representatives shall chuse their Speaker and other Officers; and shall have the sole Power of Impeachment.

The Preamble introduces the Constitution and sets forth the general purposes for which the government was established. The Preamble also declares that the power of the government comes from the people.

The printed text of the document shows the spelling and punctuation of the parchment original.

What It Means
Article I. The Legislative Branch The Constitution contains seven divisions called articles. Each article covers a general topic. For example, Articles I, II, and III create the three branches of the national government—the legislative, executive, and judicial branches. Most of the articles are divided into sections.

What It Means
Representation The number of representatives from each state is based on the size of the state's population. Each state is entitled to at least one representative. *What are the qualifications for members of the House of Representatives?*

Vocabulary

preamble: *introduction*
constitution: *principles and laws of a nation*
enumeration: *census or population count*
impeachment: *bringing charges against an official*

John Adams, the first vice president

Vocabulary

president pro tempore: *presiding officer of Senate who serves when the vice president is absent*
indictment: *charging a person with an offense*
quorum: *minimum number of members that must be present to conduct sessions*
adjourn: *to suspend a session*
immunity privilege: *members cannot be sued or prosecuted for anything they say in Congress*
emoluments: *salaries*
bill: *draft of a proposed law*
revenue: *income raised by government*

Section 3

[1.] The Senate of the United States shall be composed of two Senators from each State, chosen by the Legislature thereof, for six Years; and each Senator shall have one Vote.

[2.] Immediately after they shall be assembled in Consequence of the first Election, they shall be divided as equally as may be into three Classes. The Seats of the Senators of the first Class shall be vacated at the Expiration of the second Year, of the second Class at the Expiration of the fourth Year, and of the third Class at the Expiration of the sixth Year, so that one third may be chosen every second Year; and if Vacancies happen by Resignation, or otherwise, during the Recess of the Legislature of any State, the Executive thereof may make temporary Appointments until the next Meeting of the Legislature, which shall then fill such Vacancies.

[3.] No Person shall be a Senator who shall not have attained to the Age of thirty Years, and been nine Years a Citizen of the United States, and who shall not, when elected, be an Inhabitant of that State for which he shall be chosen.

[4.] The Vice President of the United States shall be President of the Senate, but shall have no Vote, unless they be equally divided.

[5.] The Senate shall chuse their other Officers, and also a President pro tempore, in the Absence of the Vice President, or when he shall exercise the Office of the President of the United States.

[6.] The Senate shall have the sole Power to try all Impeachments. When sitting for that Purpose, they shall be on Oath or Affirmation. When the President of the United States is tried, the Chief Justice shall preside: And no Person shall be convicted without the Concurrence of two thirds of the Members present.

[7.] Judgment in Cases of Impeachment shall not extend further than to removal from Office, and disqualification to hold and enjoy any Office of honor, Trust or Profit under the United States: but the Party convicted shall nevertheless be liable and subject to Indictment, Trial, Judgment and Punishment, according to Law.

Section 4

[1.] The Times, Places and Manner of holding Elections for Senators and Representatives, shall be prescribed in each State by the Legislature thereof; but the Congress may at any time by Law make or alter such Regulations, except as to the Places of chusing Senators.

[2.] The Congress shall assemble at least once in every Year, and such Meeting shall be on the first Monday in December, unless they shall by Law appoint a different Day.

Section 5

[1.] Each House shall be the Judge of the Elections, Returns and Qualifications of its own Members, and a Majority of each shall constitute a Quorum to do Business; but a smaller Number may adjourn from day to day, and may be authorized to compel the Attendance of absent Members, in such Manner, and under such Penalties as each House may provide.

[2.] Each House may determine the Rules of its Proceedings, punish its Members for disorderly Behaviour, and, with the Concurrence of two thirds, expel a Member.

[3.] Each House shall keep a Journal of its Proceedings, and from time to time publish the same, excepting such Parts as may in their Judgment require Secrecy; and the Yeas and Nays of the Members of either House on any question shall, at the Desire of one fifth of those Present, be entered on the Journal.

[4.] Neither House, during the Session of Congress, shall, without the Consent of the other, adjourn for more than three days, nor to any other Place than that in which the two Houses shall be sitting.

Section 6

[1.] The Senators and Representatives shall receive a Compensation for their Services, to be ascertained by Law, and paid out of the Treasury of the United States. They shall in all Cases, except Treason, Felony and Breach of the Peace, be privileged from Arrest during their Attendance at the Session of their respective Houses, and in going to and returning from the same; and for any Speech or Debate in either House, they shall not be questioned in any other Place.

[2.] No Senator or Representative shall, during the Time for which he was elected, be appointed to any civil Office under the Authority of the United States, which shall have been created, or the Emoluments whereof shall have been encreased during such time; and no Person holding any Office under the United States, shall be a Member of either House during his Continuance in Office.

Section 7

[1.] All Bills for raising Revenue shall originate in the House of Representatives; but the Senate may propose or concur with Amendments as on other Bills.

[2.] Every Bill which shall have passed the House of Representatives and the Senate, shall, before it become a Law, be presented to the President of the United States; If he approve he shall sign it, but if not he shall return it, with his Objections to that House in which it shall have originated, who shall enter the Objections at large on their Journal, and proceed to reconsider it. If after such Reconsideration two thirds of that House shall agree to pass the Bill, it shall be sent, together with the Objections, to the other House, by

Senate gavel

What It Means
Congressional Salaries To strengthen the federal government, the Founders set congressional salaries to be paid by the United States Treasury rather than by members' respective states. Originally, members were paid $6 per day. In 2001, all members of Congress received a base salary of $145,100.

What It Means
Where Tax Laws Begin All tax laws must originate in the House of Representatives. This ensures that the branch of Congress that is elected by the people every two years has the major role in determining taxes.

What It Means
How Bills Become Laws A bill may become a law only by passing both houses of Congress and by being signed by the president. The president can check Congress by rejecting—vetoing—its legislation. *How can Congress override the president's veto?*

which it shall likewise be reconsidered, and if approved by two thirds of that House, it shall become a Law. But in all such Cases the Votes of both Houses shall be determined by yeas and Nays, and the Names of the Persons voting for and against the Bill shall be entered on the Journal of each House respectively. If any Bill shall not be returned by the President within ten Days (Sundays excepted) after it shall have been presented to him, the Same shall be a Law, in like Manner as if he had signed it, unless the Congress by their Adjournment prevent its Return, in which Case it shall not be a Law.

[3.] Every Order, Resolution, or Vote to which the Concurrence of the Senate and House of Representatives may be necessary (except on a question of Adjournment) shall be presented to the President of the United States; and before the Same shall take Effect, shall be approved by him, or being disapproved by him, shall be repassed by two thirds of the Senate and House of Representatives, according to the Rules and Limitations prescribed in the Case of a Bill.

Section 8

[1.] The Congress shall have the Power To lay and collect Taxes, Duties, Imposts and Excises, to pay the Debts and provide for the common Defence and general Welfare of the United States; but all Duties, Imposts and Excises shall be uniform throughout the United States;

[2.] To borrow Money on the credit of the United States;

[3.] To regulate Commerce with foreign Nations, and among the several States, and with the Indian Tribes;

[4.] To establish an uniform Rule of Naturalization, and uniform Laws on the subject of Bankruptcies throughout the United States;

[5.] To coin Money, regulate the Value thereof, and of foreign Coin, and fix the Standard of Weights and Measures;

[6.] To provide for the Punishment of counterfeiting the Securities and current Coin of the United States;

[7.] To establish Post Offices and post Roads;

[8.] To promote the Progress of Science and useful Arts, by securing for limited Times to Authors and Inventors the exclusive Right to their respective Writings and Discoveries;

[9.] To constitute Tribunals inferior to the supreme Court;

[10.] To define and punish Piracies and Felonies committed on the high Seas, and Offences against the Law of Nations;

[11.] To declare War, grant Letters of Marque and Reprisal, and make Rules concerning Captures on Land and Water;

[12.] To raise and support Armies, but no Appropriation of Money to that Use shall be for a longer Term than two Years;

[13.] To provide and maintain a Navy;

[14.] To make Rules for the Government and Regulation of the land and naval Forces;

[15.] To provide for calling forth the Militia to execute the Laws of the Union, suppress Insurrections and repel Invasions;

Civil War money

Vocabulary

resolution: *legislature's formal expression of opinion*

naturalization: *procedure by which a citizen of a foreign nation becomes a citizen of the United States.*

tribunal: *a court*

letter of marque: *authority given to a citizen to outfit an armed ship and use it to attack enemy ships in time of war*

reprisal: *taking by force property or territory belonging to another country or to its citizens*

insurrection: *rebellion*

[16.] To provide for organizing, arming, and disciplining, the Militia, and for governing such Part of them as may be employed in the Service of the United States, reserving to the States respectively, the Appointment of the Officers, and the Authority of training the Militia according to the discipline prescribed by Congress;

[17.] To exercise exclusive Legislation in all Cases whatsoever, over such District (not exceeding ten Miles square) as may, by Cession of particular States, and the Acceptance of Congress, become the Seat of Government of the United States, and to exercise like Authority over all Places purchased by the Consent of the Legislature of the State in which the Same shall be, for the Erection of Forts, Magazines, Arsenals, dock-Yards, and other needful Buildings, — And

[18.] To make all Laws which shall be necessary and proper for carrying into Execution the foregoing Powers, and all other Powers vested by this Constitution in the Government of the United States, or in any Department or Officer thereof.

Section 9

[1]. The Migration or Importation of such Persons as any of the States now existing shall think proper to admit, shall not be prohibited by the Congress prior to the Year one thousand eight hundred and eight, but a Tax or duty may be imposed on such Importation, not exceeding ten dollars for each Person.

[2.] The Privilege of the Writ of Habeas Corpus shall not be suspended, unless when in Cases of Rebellion or Invasion the public Safety may require it.

[3.] No Bill of Attainder or ex post facto Law shall be passed.

[4.] No Capitation, or other direct, Tax shall be laid, unless in Proportion to the Census or Enumeration herein before directed to be taken.

[5.] No Tax or Duty shall be laid on Articles exported from any State.

[6.] No Preference shall be given by any Regulation of Commerce or Revenue to the Ports of one State over those of another: nor shall Vessels bound to, or from, one State, be obliged to enter, clear, or pay Duties in another.

[7.] No Money shall be drawn from the Treasury, but in Consequence of Appropriations made by Law; and a regular Statement and Account of the Receipts and Expenditures of all public Money shall be published from time to time.

[8.] No Title of Nobility shall be granted by the United States: And no Person holding any Office of Profit or Trust under them, shall, without the Consent of the Congress, accept of any present, Emolument, Office, or Title, of any kind whatever, from any King, Prince, or foreign State.

What It Means

Elastic Clause The final enumerated power is often called the "elastic clause." This clause gives Congress the right to make all laws "necessary and proper" to carry out the powers expressed in the other clauses of Article I. It is called the elastic clause because it lets Congress "stretch" its powers to meet situations the Founders could never have anticipated.

What does the phrase "necessary and proper" in the elastic clause mean? Almost from the beginning, this phrase was a subject of dispute. The issue was whether a strict or a broad interpretation of the Constitution should be applied. The dispute was first addressed in 1819, in the case of *McCulloch* v. *Maryland*, when the Supreme Court ruled in favor of a broad interpretation.

What It Means

Habeas Corpus A writ of habeas corpus issued by a judge requires a law official to bring a prisoner to court and show cause for holding the prisoner. A bill of attainder is a bill that punished a person without a jury trial. An "ex post facto" law is one that makes an act a crime after the act has been committed. *What does the Constitution say about bills of attainder?*

[1.] No State shall enter into any Treaty, Alliance, or Confederation; grant Letters of Marque and Reprisal; coin Money; emit Bills of Credit; make any Thing but gold and silver Coin a Tender in Payment of Debts; pass any Bill of Attainder, ex post facto Law, or Law impairing the Obligation of Contracts, or grant any Title of Nobility.

[2.] No State shall, without the Consent of the Congress, lay any Imposts or Duties on Imports or Exports, except what may be absolutely necessary for executing it's inspection Laws: and the net Produce of all Duties and Imposts, laid by any State on Imports and Exports, shall be for the Use of the Treasury of the United States; and all such Laws shall be subject to the Revision and Controul of the Congress.

[3.] No State shall, without the Consent of Congress, lay any Duty of Tonnage, keep Troops, or Ships of War in time of Peace, enter into any Agreement or Compact with another State, or with a foreign Power, or engage in War, unless actually invaded, or in such imminent Danger as will not admit of delay.

Article II
Section 1

[1.] The executive Power shall be vested in a President of the United States of America. He shall hold his Office during the Term of four Years, and, together with the Vice President, chosen for the same Term, be elected, as follows

[2.] Each State shall appoint, in such Manner as the Legislature thereof may direct, a Number of Electors, equal to the whole Number of Senators and Representatives to which the State may be entitled in the Congress: but no Senator or Representative, or Person holding an Office of Trust or Profit under the United States, shall be appointed an Elector.

[3.] The Electors shall meet in their respective States, and vote by Ballot for two Persons, of whom one at least shall not be an Inhabitant of the same State with themselves. And they shall make a List of all the Persons voted for, and of the Number of Votes for each; which List they shall sign and certify, and transmit sealed to the Seat of the Government of the United States, directed to the President of the Senate. The President of the Senate shall, in the Presence of the Senate and House of Representatives, open all the Certificates, and the Votes shall then be counted. The Person having the greatest Number of Votes shall be the President, if such Number be a Majority of the whole Number of Electors appointed; and if there be more than one who have such Majority, and have an equal Number of Votes, then the House of Representatives shall immediately chuse by Ballot one of them for President; and if no person have a Majority,

---

What It Means
Limitations on the States Section 10 lists limits on the states. These restrictions were designed, in part, to prevent an overlapping in functions and authority with the federal government.

What It Means
Article II. The Executive Branch Article II creates an executive branch to carry out laws passed by Congress. Article II lists the powers and duties of the presidency, describes qualifications for office and procedures for electing the president, and provides for a vice president.

United States coins

Vocabulary

appropriations: *funds set aside for a specific use*
emolument: *payment*
impost: *tax*
duty: *tax*

then from the five highest on the List the said House shall in like Manner chuse the President. But in chusing the President, the Votes shall be taken by States, the Representation from each State having one Vote; A quorum for this Purpose shall consist of a Member or Members from two thirds of the States, and a Majority of all the States shall be necessary to a Choice. In every Case, after the Choice of the President, the Person having the greatest Number of Votes of the Electors shall be the Vice President. But if there should remain two or more who have equal Votes, the Senate shall chuse from them by Ballot the Vice President.

[4.] The Congress may determine the Time of chusing the Electors, and the Day on which they shall give their Votes; which Day shall be the same throughout the United States.

[5.] No Person except a natural born Citizen, or a Citizen of the United States, at the time of the Adoption of this Constitution, shall be eligible to the Office of President; neither shall any Person be eligible to that Office who shall not have attained to the Age of thirty five Years, and been fourteen Years a Resident within the United States.

[6.] In Case of the Removal of the President from Office, or of his Death, Resignation, or Inability to discharge the Powers and Duties of the said Office, the Same shall devolve on the Vice President, and the Congress may by Law provide for the Case of Removal, Death, Resignation or Inability, both of the President and Vice President, declaring what Officer shall then act as President, and such Officer shall act accordingly, until the Disability be removed, or a President shall be elected.

[7.] The President shall, at stated Times, receive for his Services, a Compensation, which shall neither be encreased nor diminished during the Period for which he shall have been elected, and he shall not receive within that Period any other Emolument from the United States, or any of them.

[8.] Before he enter on the Execution of his Office, he shall take the following Oath or Affirmation:—"I do solemnly swear (or affirm) that I will faithfully execute the Office of President of the United States, and will to the best of my Ability, preserve, protect and defend the Constitution of the United States."

Section 2

[1.] The President shall be Commander in Chief of the Army and Navy of the United States, and of the Militia of the several States, when called into the actual Service of the United States; he may require the Opinion, in writing, of the principal Officer in each of the executive Departments, upon any Subject relating to the Duties of their respective Offices, and he shall have Power to grant Reprieves and Pardons for Offences against the United States, except in Cases of Impeachment.

What It Means

Previous Elections The Twelfth Amendment, added in 1804, changed the method of electing the president stated in Article II, Section 3. The Twelfth Amendment requires that the electors cast separate ballots for president and vice president.

What It Means

Qualifications The president must be a citizen of the United States by birth, at least 35 years of age, and a resident of the United States for 14 years.

What It Means

Vacancies If the president dies, resigns, is removed from office by impeachment, or is unable to carry out the duties of the office, the vice president becomes president. The Twenty-fifth Amendment sets procedures for presidential succession.

What It Means

Salary Originally, the president's salary was $25,000 per year. The president's current salary is $400,000 plus a $50,000 nontaxable expense account per year. The president also receives living accommodations in two residences—the White House and Camp David.

What It Means

The Cabinet Mention of "the principal officer in each of the executive departments" is the only suggestion of the president's cabinet to be found in the Constitution. The cabinet is an advisory body, and its power depends on the president. Section 2, Clause 1 also makes the president—a civilian—the head of the armed services. This established the principle of civilian control of the military.

What It Means

Presidential Powers An executive order is a command issued by a president to exercise a power which he has been given by the U.S. Constitution or by a federal statute. In times of emergency, presidents sometimes have used the executive order to override the Constitution of the United States and the Congress. During the Civil War, President Lincoln suspended many fundamental rights guaranteed in the Constitution and the Bill of Rights. He closed down newspapers that opposed his policies and imprisoned some who disagreed with him. Lincoln said that these actions were justified to preserve the Union.

Impeachment ticket

What It Means

Article III. The Judicial Branch The term *judicial* refers to courts. The Constitution set up only the Supreme Court, but provided for the establishment of other federal courts. The judiciary of the United States has two different systems of courts. One system consists of the federal courts, whose powers derive from the Constitution and federal laws. The other includes the courts of each of the 50 states, whose powers derive from state constitutions and laws.

What It Means

Statute Law Federal courts deal mostly with "statute law," or laws passed by Congress, treaties, and cases involving the Constitution itself.

[2.] He shall have Power, by and with the Advice and Consent of the Senate, to make Treaties, provided two thirds of the Senators present concur; and he shall nominate, and by and with the Advice and Consent of the Senate, shall appoint Ambassadors, other public Ministers and Consuls, Judges of the supreme Court, and all other Officers of the United States, whose Appointments are not herein otherwise provided for, and which shall be established by Law: but the Congress may by Law vest the Appointment of such inferior Officers, as they think proper, in the President alone, in the Courts of Law, or in the Heads of Departments.

[3.] The President shall have Power to fill up all Vacancies that may happen during the Recess of the Senate, by granting Commissions which shall expire at the End of their next Session.

Section 3

He shall from time to time give to the Congress Information of the State of the Union, and recommend to their Consideration such Measures as he shall judge necessary and expedient; he may, on extraordinary Occasions, convene both Houses, or either of them, and in Case of Disagreement between them, with Respect to the Time of Adjournment, he may adjourn them to such Time as he shall think proper; he shall receive Ambassadors and other public Ministers; he shall take Care that the Laws be faithfully executed, and shall Commission all the Officers of the United States.

Section 4

The President, Vice President and all civil Officers of the United States, shall be removed from Office on Impeachment for, and Conviction of, Treason, Bribery, or other high Crimes and Misdemeanors.

Article III

Section 1

The judicial Power of the United States, shall be vested in one supreme Court, and in such inferior Courts as the Congress may from time to time ordain and establish. The Judges, both of the supreme and inferior Courts, shall hold their Offices during good Behaviour, and shall, at stated Times, receive for their Services, a Compensation, which shall not be diminished during their Continuance in Office.

Section 2

[1.] The judicial Power shall extend to all Cases, in Law and Equity, arising under this Constitution, the Laws of the United States, and Treaties made, or which shall be made, under their Authority;—to all Cases affecting Ambassadors, other public Ministers and Consuls;—to all Cases of admiralty and maritime Jurisdiction;—to Controversies to which the United States shall be a Party;—to Controversies between two or more States;—between a State and Citizens of another State;—between Citizens of different States,—between Citizens of the same State claiming Lands under Grants of different States, and between a State, or the Citizens thereof, and foreign States, Citizens or Subjects.

[2.] In all Cases affecting Ambassadors, other public Ministers and Consuls, and those in which a State shall be Party, the supreme Court shall have original Jurisdiction. In all the other Cases before mentioned, the supreme Court shall have appellate Jurisdiction, both as to Law and Fact, with such Exceptions, and under such Regulations as the Congress shall make.

[3.] The Trial of all Crimes, except in Cases of Impeachment, shall be by Jury; and such Trial shall be held in the State where the said Crimes shall have been committed; but when not committed within any State, the Trial shall be at such Place or Places as the Congress may by Law have directed.

Section 3

[1.] Treason against the United States, shall consist only in levying War against them, or in adhering to their Enemies, giving them Aid and Comfort. No Person shall be convicted of Treason unless on the Testimony of two Witnesses to the same overt Act, or on Confession in open Court.

[2.] The Congress shall have Power to declare the Punishment of Treason, but no Attainder of Treason shall work Corruption of Blood, or Forfeiture except during the Life of the Person attainted.

Article IV
Section 1

Full Faith and Credit shall be given in each State to the public Acts, Records, and judicial Proceedings of every other State. And the Congress may by general Laws prescribe the Manner in which such Acts, Records and Proceedings shall be proved, and the Effect thereof.

Section 2

[1.] The Citizens of each State shall be entitled to all Privileges and Immunities of Citizens in the several States.

[2.] A Person charged in any State with Treason, Felony, or other Crime, who shall flee from Justice, and be found in another State, shall on Demand of the executive Authority of the State from which he fled, be delivered up, to be removed to the State having Jurisdiction of the Crime.

What It Means
The Supreme Court A Court with "original jurisdiction" has the authority to be the first court to hear a case. The Supreme Court has "appellate jurisdiction" and mostly hears cases appealed from lower courts.

What It Means
Article IV. Relations Among the States Article IV explains the relationship of the states to one another and to the national government. This article requires each state to give citizens of other states the same rights as its own citizens, addresses admitting new states, and guarantees that the national government will protect the states.

Vocabulary
original jurisdiction: *authority to be the first court to hear a case*
appellate jurisdiction: *authority to hear cases that have been appealed from lower courts*
treason: *violation of the allegiance owed by a person to his or her own country, for example, by aiding an enemy*

Vocabulary

extradition: *surrender of a criminal to another authority*
amendment: *a change to the Constitution*
ratification: *process by which an amendment is approved*

[3.] No Person held to Service of Labour in one State, under the Laws thereof, escaping into another, shall, in Consequence of any Law or Regulation therein, be discharged from such Service or Labour, but shall be delivered up on Claim of the Party to whom such Service or Labour may be due.

Section 3

[1.] New States may be admitted by the Congress into this Union; but no new State shall be formed or erected within the Jurisdiction of any other State; nor any State be formed by the Junction of two or more States, or Parts of States, without the Consent of the Legislatures of the States concerned as well as of the Congress.

[2.] The Congress shall have Power to dispose of and make all needful Rules and Regulations respecting the Territory or other Property belonging to the United States; and nothing in this Constitution shall be so construed as to Prejudice any Claims of the United States, or of any particular State.

Section 4

The United States shall guarantee to every State in this Union a Republican Form of Government, and shall protect each of them against Invasion; and on Application of the Legislature, or of the Executive (when the Legislature cannot be convened) against domestic Violence.

Article V

The Congress, whenever two thirds of both Houses shall deem it necessary, shall propose Amendments to this Constitution, or, on the Application of the Legislatures of two thirds of the several States, shall call a Convention for proposing Amendments, which, in either Case, shall be valid to all Intents and Purposes, as Part of this Constitution, when ratified by the Legislatures of three fourths of the several States, or by Conventions in three fourths thereof, as the one or the other Mode of Ratification may be proposed by the Congress; Provided that no Amendment which may be made prior to the Year One thousand eight hundred and eight shall in any Manner affect the first and fourth Clauses in the Ninth Section of the first Article; and that no State, without its Consent, shall be deprived of its equal Suffrage in the Senate.

Article VI

[1.] All Debts contracted and Engagements entered into, before the Adoption of this Constitution, shall be as valid against the United States under this Constitution, as under the Confederation.

[2.] This Constitution, and the Laws of the United States which shall be made in Pursuance thereof; and all Treaties made, or which shall be made, under the Authority of the United States, shall be the supreme Law of the Land; and the Judges in every State shall be bound thereby, any Thing in the Constitution or Laws of any State to the Contrary notwithstanding.

[3.] The Senators and Representatives before mentioned, and the Members of the several State Legislatures, and all executive and judicial Officers, both of the United States and of the several States, shall be bound by Oath or Affirmation, to support this Constitution; but no religious Test shall ever be required as a Qualification to any Office or public Trust under the United States.

What It Means
Article VI. National Supremacy Article VI contains the "supremacy clause." This clause establishes that the Constitution, laws passed by Congress, and treaties of the United States "shall be the supreme Law of the Land." The "supremacy clause" recognized the Constitution and federal laws as supreme when in conflict with those of the states.

Article VII

The Ratification of the Conventions of nine States, shall be sufficient for the Establishment of this Constitution between the States so ratifying the Same.

Done in Convention by the Unanimous Consent of the States present the Seventeenth Day of September in the Year of our Lord one thousand seven hundred and Eighty seven and of the Independence of the United States of America the Twelfth. In witness whereof We have hereunto subscribed our Names,

What It Means
Article VII. Ratification Article VII addresses ratification and declares that the Constitution would take effect after it was ratified by nine states.

Signers

George Washington, **President and Deputy from Virginia**

New Hampshire
John Langdon
Nicholas Gilman

Massachusetts
Nathaniel Gorham
Rufus King

Connecticut
William Samuel Johnson
Roger Sherman

New York
Alexander Hamilton

New Jersey
William Livingston
David Brearley
William Paterson
Jonathan Dayton

Pennsylvania
Benjamin Franklin
Thomas Mifflin
Robert Morris
George Clymer
Thomas FitzSimons
Jared Ingersoll
James Wilson
Gouverneur Morris

Delaware
George Read
Gunning Bedford, Jr.
John Dickinson
Richard Bassett
Jacob Broom

Maryland
James McHenry
Daniel of St. Thomas Jenifer
Daniel Carroll

Virginia
John Blair
James Madison, Jr.

North Carolina
William Blount
Richard Dobbs Spaight
Hugh Williamson

South Carolina
John Rutledge
Charles Cotesworth Pinckney
Charles Pinckney
Pierce Butler

Georgia
William Few
Abraham Baldwin

Attest: *William Jackson,*
Secretary

Amendment I

Congress shall make no law respecting an establishment of religion, or prohibiting the free exercise thereof; or abridging the freedom of speech, or of the press; or the right of the people peaceably to assemble, and to petition the Government for a redress of grievances.

Amendment II

A well regulated Militia, being necessary to the security of a free State, the right of the people to keep and bear Arms, shall not be infringed.

Amendment III

No Soldier shall, in time of peace be quartered in any house, without the consent of the Owner, nor in time of war, but in a manner to be prescribed by law.

Amendment IV

The right of the people to be secure in their persons, houses, papers, and effects, against unreasonable searches and seizures, shall not be violated, and no Warrants shall issue, but upon probable cause, supported by Oath or affirmation, and particularly describing the place to be searched, and the persons or things to be seized.

Amendment V

No person shall be held to answer for a capital, or otherwise infamous crime, unless on a presentment or indictment of a Grand Jury, except in cases arising in the land or naval forces, or in the Militia, when in actual service in time of War or public danger; nor shall any person be subject for the same offence to be twice put in jeopardy of life or limb; nor shall be compelled in any criminal case to be a witness against himself, nor be deprived of life, liberty, or property, without due process of law; nor shall private property be taken for public use without just compensation.

Amendment VI

In all criminal prosecutions, the accused shall enjoy the right to a speedy and public trial, by an impartial jury of the State and district wherein the crime shall have been committed, which district shall have been previously ascertained by law, and to be informed of the nature and cause of the accusation; to be confronted with the witnesses against him; to have compulsory process for obtaining Witnesses in his favor, and to have the assistance of counsel for his defence.

Amendment VII

In Suits at common law, where the value in controversy shall exceed twenty dollars, the right of trial by jury shall be preserved, and no fact tried by a jury, shall be otherwise reexamined in any Court of the United States, than according to the rules of common law.

Amendment VIII

Excessive bail shall not be required, nor excessive fines imposed, nor cruel and unusual punishments inflicted.

Amendment IX

The enumeration in the Constitution, of certain rights, shall not be construed to deny or disparage others retained by the people.

What It Means
Powers of the People This amendment prevents government from claiming that the only rights people have are those listed in the Bill of Rights.

Amendment X

The powers not delegated to the United States by the Constitution, nor prohibited by it to the States, are reserved to the States respectively, or to the people.

What It Means
Powers of the States The final amendment of the Bill of Rights protects the states and the people from an all-powerful federal government. It establishes that powers not given to the national government—or denied to the states—by the Constitution belong to the states or to the people.

Amendment XI

The Judicial power of the United States shall not be construed to extend to any suit in law or equity, commenced or prosecuted against one of the United States by Citizens of another State, or by Citizens or Subjects of any Foreign State.

What It Means
Suits Against States The Eleventh Amendment (1795) limits the jurisdiction of the federal courts. The Supreme Court had ruled that a federal court could try a lawsuit brought by citizens of South Carolina against a citizen of Georgia. This case, *Chisholm* v. *Georgia*, decided in 1793, raised a storm of protest, leading to passage of the Eleventh Amendment.

Amendment XII

The electors shall meet in their respective states and vote by ballot for President and Vice-President, one of whom, at least, shall not be an inhabitant of the same state with themselves; they shall name in their ballots the person voted for as President, and in distinct ballots the person voted for as Vice-President, and they shall make distinct lists of all persons voted for as President, and of all persons voted for as Vice-President, and of the number of votes for each, which lists they shall sign and certify, and transmit sealed to the seat of the government of the United States, directed to the President of the Senate;—The President of the Senate shall, in the presence of the Senate and House of Representatives, open all the certificates and the votes shall then be counted;—The person having the greatest number of votes for President, shall be the President, if such number be a majority of the whole number of Electors appointed; and if no person have such

Vocabulary

quarter: *to provide living accommodations*
probable cause: *police must have a reasonable basis to believe a person is linked to a crime*
warrant: *document that gives police particular rights or powers*
common law: *law established by previous court decisions*
bail: *money that an accused person provides to the court as a guarantee that he or she will be present for a trial*

What It Means

Elections The Twelfth Amendment (1804) corrects a problem that had arisen in the method of electing the president and vice president. This amendment provides for the Electoral College to use separate ballots in voting for president and vice president. *If no candidate receives a majority of the electoral votes, who elects the president?*

What It Means

Abolition of Slavery Amendments Thirteen (1865), Fourteen (1868), and Fifteen (1870) often are called the Civil War amendments because they grew out of that great conflict. The Thirteenth Amendment outlaws slavery.

What It Means

Rights of Citizens The Fourteenth Amendment (1868) originally was intended to protect the legal rights of the freed slaves. Today it protects the rights of citizenship in general by prohibiting a state from depriving any person of life, liberty, or property without "due process of law." In addition, it states that all citizens have the right to equal protection of the law in all states.

Vocabulary

majority: *more than half*
devolve: *to pass on*
abridge: *to reduce*
insurrection: *rebellion against the government*
emancipation: *freedom from slavery*

majority, then from the persons having the highest numbers not exceeding three on the list of those voted for as President, the House of Representatives shall choose immediately, by ballot, the President. But in choosing the President, the votes shall be taken by states, the representation from each state having one vote; a quorum for this purpose shall consist of a member or members from two-thirds of the states, and a majority of all the states shall be necessary to a choice. And if the House of Representatives shall not choose a President whenever the right of choice shall devolve upon them, before the fourth day of March next following, then the Vice-President shall act as President, as in the case of the death or other constitutional disability of the President. The person having the greatest number of votes as Vice-President, shall be the Vice-President, if such number be a majority of the whole number of Electors appointed, and if no person have a majority, then from the two highest numbers on the list, the Senate shall choose the Vice-President; a quorum for the purpose shall consist of two-thirds of the whole number of Senators, and a majority of the whole number shall be necessary to a choice. But no person constitutionally ineligible to the office of President shall be eligible to that of Vice-President of the United States.

Amendment XIII

Section 1

Neither slavery nor involuntary servitude, except as a punishment for crime whereof the party shall have been duly convicted, shall exist within the United States, or any place subject to their jurisdiction.

Section 2

Congress shall have power to enforce this article by appropriate legislation.

Amendment XIV

Section 1

All persons born or naturalized in the United States, and subject to the jurisdiction thereof, are citizens of the United States and of the State wherein they reside. No State shall make or enforce any law which shall abridge the privileges or immunities of citizens of the United States; nor shall any State deprive any person of life, liberty, or property, without due process of law; nor deny to any person within its jurisdiction the equal protection of the laws.

Section 2

Representatives shall be apportioned among the several States according to their respective numbers, counting the whole number of persons in each State, excluding Indians not taxed. But when the right to vote at any election for the choice of electors for President and Vice President of the United States, Representatives in Congress, the Executive and Judicial officers of a State, or the members of the Legislature thereof, is denied to any of the male inhabitants of such State, being twenty-one years of age, and citizens of the United States, or in any way abridged, except for participation in rebellion, or other crime, the basis of representation therein shall be reduced in the proportion which the number of such male citizens shall bear to the whole number of male citizens twenty-one years of age in such State.

Section 3

No person shall be a Senator or Representative in Congress, or elector of President and Vice President, or hold any office, civil or military, under the United States, or under any State, who, having previously taken an oath, as a member of Congress, or as an officer of the United States, or as a member of any State legislature, or as an executive or judicial officer of any State, to support the Constitution of the United States, shall have engaged in insurrection or rebellion against the same, or given aid or comfort to the enemies thereof. But Congress may by a vote of two-thirds of each House, remove such disability.

Section 4

The validity of the public debt of the United States, authorized by law, including debts incurred for payment of pensions and bounties for service in suppressing insurrection or rebellion, shall not be questioned. But neither the United States nor any State shall assume or pay any debt or obligation incurred in aid of insurrection or rebellion against the United States, or any claim for the loss or emancipation of any slave; but all such debts, obligations and claims shall be held illegal and void.

Section 5

The Congress shall have power to enforce, by appropriate legislation, the provisions of this article.

Amendment XV
Section 1

The right of citizens of the United States to vote shall not be denied or abridged by the United States or by any

What It Means

Representation in Congress This section reduced the number of members a state had in the House of Representatives if it denied its citizens the right to vote. Later civil rights laws and the Twenty-fourth Amendment guaranteed the vote to African Americans.

What It Means

Penalty The leaders of the Confederacy were barred from state or federal offices unless Congress agreed to remove this ban. By the end of Reconstruction all but a few Confederate leaders were allowed to return to public life.

What It Means

Public Debt The public debt acquired by the federal government during the Civil War was valid and could not be questioned by the South. However, the debts of the Confederacy were declared to be illegal. *Could former slaveholders collect payment for the loss of their slaves?*

What It Means

Right to Vote The Fifteenth Amendment (1870) prohibits the government from denying a person's right to vote on the basis of race. Despite the law, many states denied African Americans the right to vote by such means as poll taxes, literacy tests, and white primaries. During the 1950s and 1960s, Congress passed successively stronger laws to end racial discrimination in voting rights.

Internal Revenue Service

State on account of race, color, or previous condition of servitude.

Section 2
The Congress shall have power to enforce this article by appropriate legislation.

Amendment XVI
The Congress shall have power to lay and collect taxes on incomes, from whatever source derived, without apportionment among the several States and without regard to any census or enumeration.

Amendment XVII
Section 1
The Senate of the United States shall be composed of two Senators from each State, elected by the people thereof, for six years; and each Senator shall have one vote. The electors in each State shall have the qualifications requisite for electors of the most numerous branch of the State legislatures.

Section 2
When vacancies happen in the representation of any State in the Senate, the executive authority of such State shall issue writs of election to fill such vacancies: *Provided*, That the legislature of any State may empower the executive thereof to make temporary appointments until the people fill the vacancies by election as the legislature may direct.

Section 3
This amendment shall not be so construed as to affect the election or term of any Senator chosen before it becomes valid as part of the Constitution.

Amendment XVIII
Section 1
After one year from ratification of this article, the manufacture, sale, or transportation of intoxicating liquors within, the importation thereof into, or the exportation thereof from the United States and all territory subject to the jurisdiction thereof for beverage purposes is hereby prohibited.

Section 2
The Congress and the several States shall have concurrent power to enforce this article by appropriate legislation.

What It Means
Election of Senators The Seventeenth Amendment (1913) states that the people, instead of state legislatures, elect United States senators. *How many years are in a Senate term?*

What It Means
Prohibition The Eighteenth Amendment (1919) prohibited the production, sale, or transportation of alcoholic beverages in the United States. Prohibition proved to be difficult to enforce. This amendment was later repealed by the Twenty-first Amendment.

Vocabulary
apportionment: *distribution of seats in House based on population*
vacancy: *an office or position that is unfilled or unoccupied*

Section 3

This article shall be inoperative unless it shall have been ratified as an amendment to the Constitution by the legislatures of the several States, as provided in the Constitution, within seven years from the date of the submission hereof to the States by the Congress.

Amendment XIX

Section 1

The right of citizens of the United States to vote shall not be denied or abridged by the United States or by any State on account of sex.

Section 2

Congress shall have power by appropriate legislation to enforce the provisions of this article.

> **What It Means**
> **Woman Suffrage** The Nineteenth Amendment (1920) guaranteed women the right to vote. By then women had already won the right to vote in many state elections, but the amendment put their right to vote in all state and national elections on a constitutional basis.

Amendment XX

Section 1

The terms of the President and Vice President shall end at noon on the 20th day of January, and the terms of the Senators and Representatives at noon on the 3d day of January, of the years in which such terms would have ended if this article had not been ratified; and the terms of their successors shall then begin.

Section 2

The Congress shall assemble at least once in every year, and such meeting shall begin at noon on the 3d day of January, unless they shall by law appoint a different day.

Section 3

If, at the time fixed for the beginning of the term of the President, the President elect shall have died, the Vice President elect shall become President. If a President shall not have been chosen before the time fixed for the beginning of his term, or if the President elect shall have failed to qualify, then the Vice President elect shall act as President until a President shall have qualified; and the Congress may by law provide for the case wherein neither a President elect nor a Vice President elect shall have qualified, declaring who shall then act as President, or the manner in which one who is to act shall be selected, and such person shall act accordingly until a President or Vice President shall have qualified.

> **What It Means**
> **"Lame-Duck" Amendments** The Twentieth Amendment (1933) sets new dates for Congress to begin its term and for the inauguration of the president and vice president. Under the original Constitution, elected officials who retired or who had been defeated remained in office for several months. For the outgoing president, this period ran from November until March. Such outgoing officials had little influence and accomplished little, and they were called lame ducks because they were so inactive. *What date was fixed as Inauguration Day?*

> **What It Means**
> **Succession** This section provides that if the president-elect dies before taking office, the vice president-elect becomes president.

John Tyler was the first vice president to become president when a chief executive died.

Section 4

The Congress may by law provide for the case of the death of any of the persons from whom the House of Representatives may choose a President whenever the right of choice shall have devolved upon them, and for the case of the death of any of the persons from whom the Senate may choose a Vice President whenever the right of choice shall have devolved upon them.

Section 5

Sections 1 and 2 shall take effect on the 15th day of October following the ratification of this article.

Section 6

This article shall be inoperative unless it shall have been ratified as an amendment to the Constitution by the legislatures of three-fourths of the several States within seven years from the date of its submission.

What It Means
Repeal of Prohibition The Twenty-first Amendment (1933) repeals the Eighteenth Amendment. It is the only amendment ever passed to overturn an earlier amendment. It is also the only amendment ratified by special state conventions instead of state legislatures.

Amendment XXI

Section 1

The eighteenth article of amendment to the Constitution of the United States is hereby repealed.

Section 2

The transportation or importation into any State, Territory, or possession of the United States for delivery or use therein of intoxicating liquors, in violation of the laws thereof, is hereby prohibited.

Section 3

This article shall be inoperative unless it shall have been ratified as an amendment to the Constitution by conventions in the several States, as provided in the Constitution, within seven years from the date of the submission hereof to the States by the Congress.

What It Means
Term Limit The Twenty-second Amendment (1951) limits presidents to a maximum of two elected terms. It was passed largely as a reaction to Franklin D. Roosevelt's election to four terms between 1933 and 1945.

Amendment XXII

Section 1

No person shall be elected to the office of the President more than twice, and no person who had held the office of President, or acted as President, for more than two years of a term to which some other person was elected President shall be elected to the office of the President more than once. But this Article shall not apply to any person holding the office of President when this Article was proposed by the Congress, and shall not prevent any person who may be holding the office of President, or acting as President,

Vocabulary

president-elect: *individual who is elected president but has not yet begun serving his or her term*
District of Columbia: *site of nation's capital, occupying an area between Maryland and Virginia*

during the term within which this Article becomes operative from holding the office of President or acting as President during the remainder of such term.

Presidential campaign buttons

Section 2

This article shall be inoperative unless it shall have been ratified as an amendment to the Constitution by the legislatures of three-fourths of the several States within seven years from the date of its submission to the States by the Congress.

Amendment XXIII

Section 1

The District constituting the seat of Government of the United States shall appoint in such manner as the Congress may direct:

A number of electors of President and Vice President equal to the whole number of Senators and Representatives in Congress to which the District would be entitled if it were a State, but in no event more than the least populous State; they shall be in addition to those appointed by the States, but they shall be considered, for the purposes of the election of President and Vice President, to be electors appointed by a State; and they shall meet in the District and perform such duties as provided by the twelfth article of amendment.

Section 2

The Congress shall have power to enforce this article by appropriate legislation.

What It Means

Electors for the District of Columbia The Twenty-third Amendment (1961) allows citizens living in Washington, D.C., to vote for president and vice president, a right previously denied residents of the nation's capital. The District of Columbia now has three presidential electors, the number to which it would be entitled if it were a state.

Amendment XXIV

Section 1

The right of citizens of the United States to vote in any primary or other election for President or Vice President, for electors for President or Vice President, or for Senator or Representative in Congress, shall not be denied or abridged by the United States or any State by reason of failure to pay any poll tax or other tax.

Section 2

The Congress shall have power to enforce this article by appropriate legislation.

What It Means

Abolition of Poll Tax The Twenty-fourth Amendment (1964) prohibits poll taxes in federal elections. Prior to the passage of this amendment, some states had used such taxes to keep low-income African Americans from voting. In 1966 the Supreme Court banned poll taxes in state elections as well.

President Gerald Ford

Amendment XXV

Section 1

In case of the removal of the President from office or his death or resignation, the Vice President shall become President.

Section 2

Whenever there is a vacancy in the office of the Vice President, the President shall nominate a Vice President who shall take the office upon confirmation by a majority vote of both Houses of Congress.

Section 3

Whenever the President transmits to the President pro tempore of the Senate and the Speaker of the House of Representatives his written declaration that he is unable to discharge the powers and duties of his office, and until he transmits to them a written declaration to the contrary, such powers and duties shall be discharged by the Vice President as Acting President.

Section 4

Whenever the Vice President and a majority of either the principal officers of the executive departments or of such other body as Congress may by law provide, transmit to the President pro tempore of the Senate and the Speaker of the House of Representatives their written declaration that the President is unable to discharge the powers and duties of his office, the Vice President shall immediately assume the power and duties of the office of Acting President.

Thereafter, when the President transmits to the President pro tempore of the Senate and the Speaker of the House of Representatives his written declaration that no inability exists, he shall resume the powers and duties of his office unless the Vice President and a majority of either the principal officers of the executive department or of such other body as Congress may by law provide, transmit within four days to the President pro tempore of the Senate and the Speaker of the House of Representatives their written declaration that the President is unable to discharge the powers and duties of his office. Thereupon Congress shall decide the issue, assembling within forty-eight hours for that purpose if not in session. If the Congress, within twenty-one days after receipt of the latter written declaration, or, if Congress is not in session, within twenty-one days after Congress is required to assemble, determines by two-thirds vote of both Houses that the President is unable to discharge the powers and duties of his office, the Vice President shall continue to discharge the same as Acting

President; otherwise, the President shall resume the power and duties of his office.

Amendment XXVI

Section 1

The right of citizens of the United States, who are eighteen years of age or older, to vote shall not be denied or abridged by the United States or by any State on account of age.

Section 2

The Congress shall have power to enforce this article by appropriate legislation.

Amendment XXVII

No law, varying the compensation for the services of Senators and Representatives, shall take effect, until an election of representatives shall have intervened.

What It Means
Voting Age The Twenty-sixth Amendment (1971) lowered the voting age in both federal and state elections to 18.

What It Means
Congressional Pay Raises The Twenty-seventh Amendment (1992) makes congressional pay raises effective during the term following their passage. James Madison offered the amendment in 1789, but it was never adopted. In 1982 Gregory Watson, then a student at the University of Texas, discovered the forgotten amendment while doing research for a school paper. Watson made the amendment's passage his crusade.

Joint meeting of Congress

Throughout his remarkable career, Patrick Henry stood out as a supporter of the colonists and their rights. At the First Continental Congress in 1774, he energetically spoke for measures that assumed the unity of the colonies. At the same time, he was against a strong central government. Though selected to be a delegate, he refused to attend sessions in 1787 and 1788, while the Constitution was being drafted. Henry was perhaps the most famous Anti-Federalist to speak against ratification of the Constitution. With the addition of the Bill of Rights, however, Henry embraced the Constitution. As a Federalist, Henry won a seat in the Virginia legislature. He died before he could assume his post.

Patrick Henry

The Constitution and Its Parts

Men with strong but often opposing ideas about the role of government shaped the Constitution. When you read the Constitution, you discover how remarkable it is. In the words of Harry S. Truman, our thirty-third president, "It's a plan, but not a straitjacket, flexible and short." In very few pages, it manages to provide an adaptable framework for government that has held up for more than 200 years.

Although the main purpose of the Constitution is to provide a framework for the U.S. government, it does much more than that. It is the highest authority in the nation. It is the basic law of the United States. The powers of all the branches of government come from the Constitution. Like the American flag, the Constitution is a symbol of our nation. It represents our system of government and our basic beliefs and ideals, such as liberty and freedom.

The Constitution has three main parts. First is the **Preamble**, an *introduction that states the goals and purposes of the government.* Next are seven articles that describe the structure of the government. Third are 27 amendments, or additions and changes, to the Constitution.

The Preamble

The Preamble is the opening section of the Constitution, which tells why the Constitution was written. It consists of a single, concise sentence that begins and ends as follows:

> *"We the People of the United States . . . do ordain and establish this Constitution for the United States of America."*

These carefully chosen words make clear that the power of government comes from the people. The government depends on the people for its power and exists to serve them.

The middle part of the Preamble states six purposes of the government:

FIGURE 6–21.

Every American president takes an oath to "preserve, protect, and defend the Constitution of the United States." George Washington and George W. Bush were sworn in as the first and forty-third presidents.

- To form a more perfect Union"—to unite the states more effectively so they can operate as a single nation, for the good of all
- "To establish Justice"—to create a system of fair laws and courts and make certain that all citizens are treated equally
- "To insure domestic Tranquility"—to maintain peace and order, keeping citizens and their property safe from harm
- "To provide for the common defense"—to be ready militarily to protect the country and its citizens from outside attacks
- "To promote the general Welfare"—to help people live healthy, happy, and prosperous lives
- "To secure the Blessings of Liberty to ourselves and our Posterity"—to guarantee the freedom and basic rights of all Americans, including future generations (posterity)

The Articles

The seven articles that follow the Preamble explain how the government is to work. The first three articles describe the powers and responsibilities of each branch of government in turn. The remaining articles address more general matters.

Article I: The Legislative Branch

It is no accident that the first article deals with the legislative branch. The Framers of the Constitution intended the legislature to take the leading role in government.

Article I says that a Congress made of two houses—the Senate and the House of Representatives—will have all lawmaking authority. The article then describes how members of each house will be chosen and what rules they must follow in making laws. For example, a majority of both senators and representatives must vote for a bill before it can become a law.

Article I also lists specific powers that Congress does and does not have. For example, Congress may collect taxes, regulate foreign and interstate trade, coin money, and declare war. It may not tax exports, however, or favor one state over another.

Article II: The Executive Branch

Article II provides for an executive, or law-enforcing, branch of government headed by a president and vice president. Article II explains how these leaders are to be elected and how they can be removed from office. The article also describes some of the president's powers and duties. These include commanding the armed forces, dealing with the leaders of other countries, and appointing certain government officials.

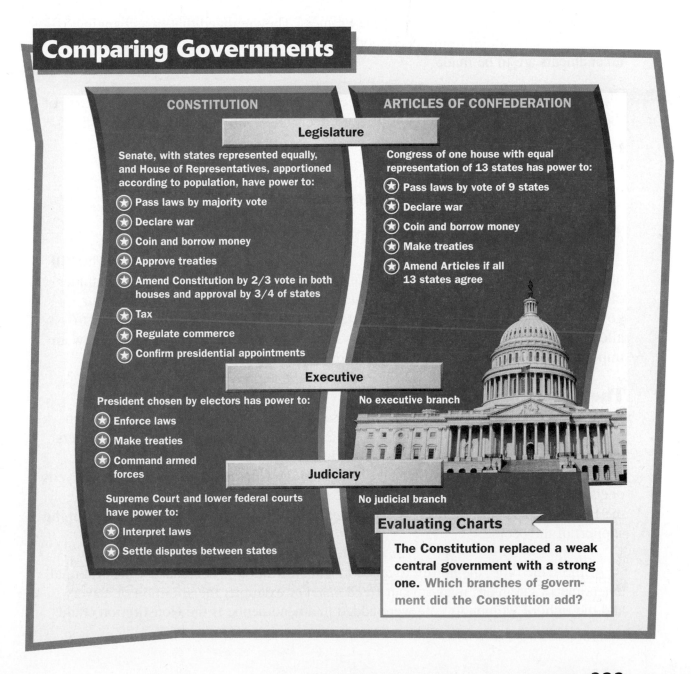

Comparing Governments

CONSTITUTION

Legislature

Senate, with states represented equally, and House of Representatives, apportioned according to population, have power to:

* Pass laws by majority vote
* Declare war
* Coin and borrow money
* Approve treaties
* Amend Constitution by 2/3 vote in both houses and approval by 3/4 of states
* Tax
* Regulate commerce
* Confirm presidential appointments

Executive

President chosen by electors has power to:

* Enforce laws
* Make treaties
* Command armed forces

Judiciary

Supreme Court and lower federal courts have power to:

* Interpret laws
* Settle disputes between states

ARTICLES OF CONFEDERATION

Legislature

Congress of one house with equal representation of 13 states has power to:

* Pass laws by vote of 9 states
* Declare war
* Coin and borrow money
* Make treaties
* Amend Articles if all 13 states agree

Executive

No executive branch

Judiciary

No judicial branch

Evaluating Charts

The Constitution replaced a weak central government with a strong one. Which branches of government did the Constitution add?

Article III: The Judicial Branch

The judicial branch is the part of government that interprets the laws and sees that they are fairly applied. Article III calls for "one Supreme Court" and such lower courts as Congress deems appropriate.

Article III then lists the powers of the federal courts and describes the kinds of cases they may hear. These include cases involving the Constitution, federal laws and treaties, and disputes between states.

Articles IV-VII

In Article IV of the Constitution, the Framers shifted their focus to the states. The article says that all states must respect each other's laws, court decisions, and records. Article IV also explains the process for creating new states, and it promises that the federal government will protect and defend the states.

Article V reveals the foresight of the Framers. They realized that in a changing world, the Constitution might need modification over time. Thus they specified how amendments are to be made.

Article VI contains a key statement declaring the Constitution the "supreme Law of the Land." It adds that if state laws or court decisions conflict with federal law, the federal law shall prevail.

In Article VII, the Framers dealt with practical matters. They wrote that the Constitution would take effect when nine states had ratified it.

Amending the Constitution

Since the Constitution was signed in 1787, it has been amended 27 times. The **Bill of Rights** consists of *the first 10 amendments,* which were added in 1791. A number of amendments address entirely different matters, such as improving the way our government works. For example, the Sixteenth Amendment was passed in 1913 to allow Congress to collect an **income tax**—*a tax on people's earnings.* This is now an important source of money for the government, helping it pay for services.

The Amendment Process

Would it surprise you to know that thousands of amendments to the Constitution have been considered over the years? Only 27 have become law because the Framers deliberately made the amendment process difficult. After months of debate and compromise, they knew how delicately balanced the Constitution was. Changing even one small detail could have dramatic effects throughout the government. Therefore, the Framers made sure the Constitution could not be altered without the overwhelming support of the people.

At the same time, the ability to amend the Constitution is necessary. Constitutional amendments safeguard many of our freedoms. For example, the abolition of slavery and the right of women to vote were added in amendments. If the Constitution could

Ammending the Constitution

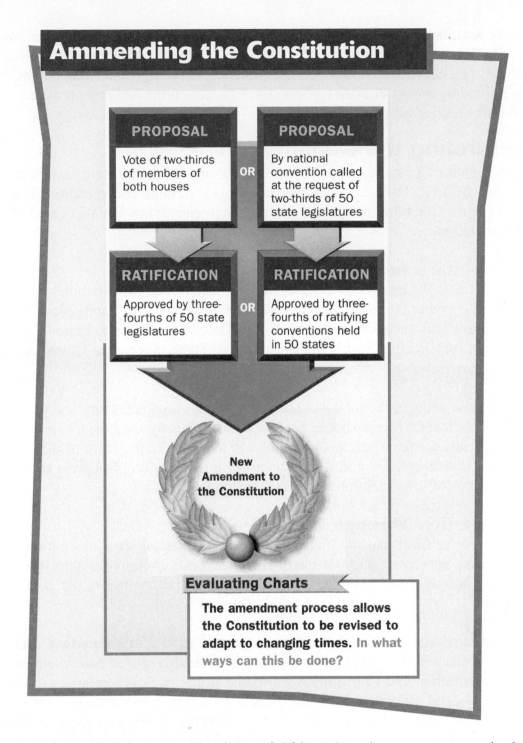

PROPOSAL

Vote of two-thirds of members of both houses

OR

PROPOSAL

By national convention called at the request of two-thirds of 50 state legislatures

RATIFICATION

Approved by three-fourths of 50 state legislatures

OR

RATIFICATION

Approved by three-fourths of ratifying conventions held in 50 states

New Amendment to the Constitution

Evaluating Charts

The amendment process allows the Constitution to be revised to adapt to changing times. In what ways can this be done?

not have been amended to protect the rights of African Americans, women, and other oppressed groups, it—and our government—might not have survived.

The process for making an amendment to the Constitution, as outlined in Article V, involves two steps: proposal and ratification. An amendment may be proposed in either of two ways. The first method—used for all amendments so far—is by congressional action. A vote of two-thirds of the members of both houses of Congress is required. The second method is by a national convention requested by two-thirds of the state legislatures.

Once a national amendment has been proposed, three-fourths of the states must ratify it. The states have two ways to do this: by a vote of either the state legislature or a special state convention. Only one amendment, the Twenty-first Amendment, has been ratified by means of state conventions. Congress proposed and the state legislatures ratified all others.

Interpreting the Constitution

Although the Constitution has been amended only 27 times, there have been many other changes to it. These changes have taken place through interpretation. The Framers of the Constitution wrote a general document, so many matters are left open to interpretation.

The Necessary and Proper Clause

Article I lists the powers of Congress. In this article, the Constitution gives Congress the power "to make all Laws which shall be necessary and proper" to carry out its duties. This necessary and proper clause allows Congress to exercise powers that are not specifically listed in the Constitution. These powers are known as "implied powers."

Americans, though, do not agree about which laws are "necessary and proper." Some people feel Congress should be allowed to make any laws the Constitution does not specifically forbid. These people believe in a loose interpretation of the Constitution. Others believe in a strict interpretation. They feel Congress should make only the kinds of laws mentioned by the Constitution.

Interpretation Through Court Decisions

The Supreme Court has the final authority on interpreting the Constitution. Over the years, the Supreme Court has interpreted the Constitution in different ways— sometimes strictly, sometimes loosely. With each new interpretation, our government changes.

Interpretation Through Congressional and Presidential Actions

Actions taken by Congress and the president have also caused new interpretations of the Constitution. The Constitution allows the House of Representatives to impeach, or accuse, federal officials, while the Senate determines the person's guilt or innocence. Congress has investigated more than 60 people on impeachment charges.

How has the president interpreted the Constitution? In 1841 William Henry Harrison became the first president to die in office. Vice President John Tyler assumed the powers of the president according to the Constitution. The Constitution, however, was unclear on this matter. Did Tyler automatically become president, or was he merely acting as president until the next election? Tyler went ahead and took the presidential oath. Not until 1967, when the Twenty-fifth Amendment was ratified, was Tyler's action officially part of the Constitution.

Presidents interpret the Constitution in other ways, too. Not only does the president make agreements with other countries without congressional approval, the president also requests legislation from Congress. The Constitution does not direct the president to take these actions.

Interpretation Through Custom

The interpretation of the Constitution has also changed through customs that have developed. For example, although the Constitution does not mention political parties, they are a very important part of today's political system. Today, parties help organize the government and conduct elections.

The government under the Constitution today is very different from the government set up by the Constitution in 1787. It will probably go through many more changes, too. However, the basic structure and principles of our government—a delicate balance between three branches—will no doubt remain.

CHECKPOINTS

Lesson 3 Review

1. Write a paragraph about the Constitution in which you use all of the following terms: *Preamble, amendment, Bill of Rights, income tax.*

2. What is the purpose of the Preamble to the U.S. Constitution?

3. In what two ways can an amendment to the U.S. Constitution be ratified? How are the states involved in these processes?

4. Which part of the Constitution do you think is the most important? Explain your answer.

5. Describe the features of Articles I, II, and III of the Constitution. Format your descriptions in a three-column table.

6. Review the chart that compares the Articles of Confederation to the U.S. Constitution. How did Congress differ under both forms of government?

Applying Citizenship Skills

7. Read a section of your state's constitution. Find one similarity to and one difference from the U.S. Constitution.

The Bill of Rights

The Bill of Rights—the first 10 amendments to the U.S. Constitution—guarantees certain basic rights to all Americans. Among the most important is freedom of speech. This right allows Americans to speak out on issues and make their feelings known.

First Amendment Freedoms

The Founders of the United States believed that protecting individual rights and providing for the safety and well being of citizens were important purposes of government. The Constitution might not have been ratified had the Bill of Rights not been promised. Added in 1791, the 10 amendments in the Bill of Rights place strict limits on how the national government can use its power over the people. The Bill of Rights protects our **civil liberties**—*the freedoms we have to think and act without government interference or fear of unfair treatment.*

The First Amendment to the Constitution protects five basic freedoms: freedom of religion, freedom of speech, freedom of the press, freedom of assembly, and freedom to petition the government.

These civil liberties are the cornerstone of our democracy. They ensure that each of us can develop our own beliefs, express ourselves freely, meet openly with others, and have our views on public matters heard by those who govern.

Freedom of Religion

Intolerance of different beliefs in their homelands forced many colonists to come to America in the first place. To safeguard religious freedom, the First Amendment prohibits Congress from establishing an official religion in the United States. It protects the freedom of Americans to practice their faith as they wish. The government may not favor one religion over another or treat people differently because of their personal beliefs.

Freedom of Speech

In some countries, people can be jailed for criticizing the government or voicing unpopular ideas, even if they do so only in

Quick Write

As American citizens, we have many rights. List some of the rights that are important to you.

LEARN ABOUT...

- the amendments in the Bill of Rights.
- protecting our rights and freedom as American citizens.
- key people who upheld American rights and freedom.

VOCABULARY

- civil liberties
- censorship
- petition
- slander
- libel
- search warrant
- indictment
- grand jury
- double jeopardy
- due process
- eminent domain

private conversations. In the United States, however, the First Amendment guarantees that we can say what is on our minds, in public or in private, without fear of punishment by the government.

Face-to-face discussions, telephone conversations, lectures, and radio and TV broadcasts are covered by the guarantee of free speech; so are other forms of expression besides the spoken word. As interpreted by the Supreme Court, "speech" can mean Internet communication, art, music, or even clothing.

In 1965, for example, 13-year-old Mary Beth Tinker and two other students wore black armbands to school to mourn those who died in the Vietnam War. School authorities suspended them for wearing the armbands, and the teens eventually took their case to the Supreme Court. In its landmark 1969 decision, the Court ruled that the armbands were a form of speech protected by the First Amendment.

VOCABULARY

- bail
- Federalists
- federalism
- suffrage
- poll taxes
- discrimination
- segregation
- civil rights
- affirmative action
- racial profiling

Freedom of the Press

The First Amendment allows Americans to express themselves in print as well as in speech. When the Bill of Rights was written, "the press" referred to printed publications such as books, newspapers, and magazines. Today the press includes many other sources of media, such as radio, television, and computer networks.

Freedom of the press ensures that the American people are exposed to a wide variety of viewpoints. The government cannot practice censorship. **Censorship** includes *banning printed materials or films just because they contain alarming or offensive ideas.* The government also cannot censor information before it is published or broadcast.

AMERICANS IN ACTION

Thomas Jefferson was an outspoken supporter of Americans' personal freedoms. In a letter to Colonel Edward Carrington, dated January 16, 1787, Jefferson wrote: " . . . [W]ere it left to me to decide whether we should have a government without newspapers, or newspapers without a government, I should not hesitate a moment to prefer the latter." In his lifetime, Jefferson took full advantage of the freedom of the press. He wrote and published dozens of articles and papers to express his views and to encourage his fellow citizens to think and act according to their beliefs.

Thomas Jefferson

The First Amendment

Freedom of Speech

Freedom of the Press

Freedom of Religion

Freedom of Assembly

Freedom to Petition the Government

Evaluating Charts

The First Amendment protects five basic freedoms of the American way of life. Which freedoms protect your right to demonstrate against a government policy?

Freedom of Assembly

The First Amendment protects our right to gather in groups for any reason, so long as the assemblies are peaceful. We have the right to attend meetings, parades, political rallies, and public celebrations. Governments may make rules about when and where such activities can be held, but they cannot ban them.

The Supreme Court has decided that freedom of assembly implies freedom of association. Thus the First Amendment also protects our right to form and join social clubs, political parties, labor unions, and other organizations. Even if we never assemble with fellow members, we have the right to belong to such groups.

Freedom to Petition

Finally, the First Amendment guarantees all Americans the right to petition the government. A **petition** is simply *a formal request*. Often we use the word to refer to a specific kind of document—a brief, written statement signed by hundreds or thousands of people. Even a simple letter or e-mail written by an individual, however, could be considered a petition.

The right to petition means the right to express one's ideas to the government. If you want to complain about overcrowded schools, for example, or suggest that a

FIGURE 6–22.
Many early colonists and immigrants throughout history came
to the United States so they could freely practice religion.

skating park be built in your community, you can write to your elected representatives.
If enough people express similar views, government leaders may take action.

Limits to First Amendment Freedoms

The Supreme Court has decided that compelling public interests—the safety and
security of Americans—may justify limitations on our First Amendment freedoms.
Freedom of speech, for example, does not include the right to endanger our
government or other Americans. You do not have freedom to provoke a riot or other
violent behavior. You are not free to speak or write in a way that immediately leads to
criminal activities or efforts to overthrow the government by force.

Citizens should use their civil liberties responsibly, which means they should not
interfere with the rights of others. For example, you are free to talk with your friends
in the street, but you must not block traffic. You may campaign for causes, but you
may not disturb your neighbors with blaring loudspeaker broadcasts. You may criticize
government officials, but you may not spread lies that harm a person's reputation.
Spreading such lies is a crime called **slander** *if the lies are spoken* and **libel** *if they are
printed.*

The First Amendment was never intended to allow Americans to do whatever they
please. Unlimited freedom is not possible in a society of many people. The rights of
one individual must be balanced against the rights of others and against the rights of
the community. When there is a conflict, the rights of the community often come first.
Otherwise, the society would break apart.

The Fourth Amendment is an important safeguard against "unreasonable searches and seizures." This amendment protects Americans from unlawful searches by the police. However, you, as a student, are not protected in the same way. In the case of *New Jersey v. T.L.O.*, the Supreme Court ruled that the Fourth Amendment's "warrant requirement . . . is unsuited to the school environment." The Constitution includes other amendments that protect the rights of Americans accused of crimes.

Are school lockers private?

Protecting the Rights of the Accused

The First Amendment freedoms you have just read about are among our most important civil liberties. Equally precious, however, is the right to fair legal treatment. This is the subject of several amendments in the Bill of Rights.

Suppose someone accuses you of committing a crime. In some countries, government agents might ransack your home, drag you off to jail, beat you, and hold a trial without even letting you respond to the charges. In the United States, the Fourth, Fifth, Sixth, and Eighth Amendments help prevent such a scenario from occurring.

The Fourth Amendment

The Fourth Amendment protects Americans "against unreasonable searches and seizures." No soldier, government agent, or police officer can search your home or take your property without good cause.

However, if law enforcement officers believe you have committed a crime, they can ask a judge to issue a search warrant. A **search warrant** is *a court order allowing law enforcement officers to search a suspect's home or business and take specific items as evidence.*

Judges do not give out search warrants readily. They must be convinced that a search will probably turn up evidence of criminal activity. If warrants were issued frivolously, the Fourth Amendment would give us little sense of security. Any time of the day or night, the police could invade our privacy and confiscate our possessions.

The Fifth Amendment

The Fifth Amendment protects the rights of people accused of crimes. It states that no one can be put on trial for a serious federal crime without an **indictment**—*a* *formal charge.* The charge is made by the **grand jury**, which is *a group of citizens who make the indictment and review the evidence against the accused.*

A person who is indicted is not necessarily guilty of a crime. An indictment simply indicates the grand jury's belief that an individual *may* have committed a crime. This provision protects people from being brought to trial hastily and perhaps needlessly.

The Fifth Amendment also protects people from **double jeopardy**. This means that *people who are accused of a crime and judged not guilty may not be put on trial again for the same crime.*

In addition, the Fifth Amendment protects an accused person's right to remain silent. Throughout history, innocent people have been threatened, tortured, or bullied into confessing to crimes they did not commit. To prevent this, the Fifth Amendment states that people cannot be forced to testify against themselves. This is called protection against self-incrimination.

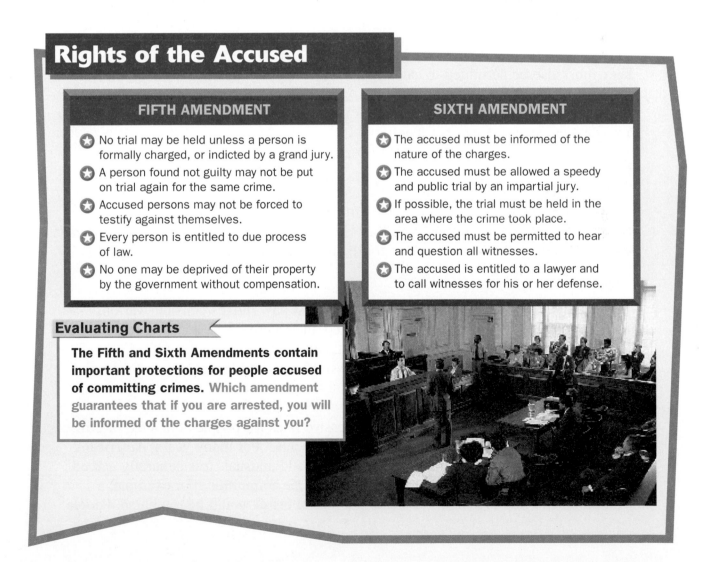

Rights of the Accused

FIFTH AMENDMENT

- ★ No trial may be held unless a person is formally charged, or indicted by a grand jury.
- ★ A person found not guilty may not be put on trial again for the same crime.
- ★ Accused persons may not be forced to testify against themselves.
- ★ Every person is entitled to due process of law.
- ★ No one may be deprived of their property by the government without compensation.

SIXTH AMENDMENT

- ★ The accused must be informed of the nature of the charges.
- ★ The accused must be allowed a speedy and public trial by an impartial jury.
- ★ If possible, the trial must be held in the area where the crime took place.
- ★ The accused must be permitted to hear and question all witnesses.
- ★ The accused is entitled to a lawyer and to call witnesses for his or her defense.

Evaluating Charts

The Fifth and Sixth Amendments contain important protections for people accused of committing crimes. Which amendment guarantees that if you are arrested, you will be informed of the charges against you?

The Fifth Amendment goes on to say that no one may be denied life, liberty, or property "without due process of law." **Due process** means *following established legal procedures.* It also includes the idea that the laws themselves must be reasonable.

Finally, the Fifth Amendment protects citizens' property rights by limiting the government's power of eminent domain. **Eminent domain** is *the right of the government to take private property—usually land—for public use.* For example, if your home lies in the path of a proposed highway, the government may legally take the land and destroy your house. Under the Fifth Amendment, however, the government must pay you a fair price for the property.

The Sixth Amendment

The Sixth Amendment gives additional due process rights to people accused of crimes. It requires that they be told the exact nature of the charges against them. It also guarantees them a trial by jury, although they may ask to be tried by only a judge instead.

If an accused person requests a jury trial, the trial must be speedy and public, and jurors must be impartial. If possible, the trial should be held in the same district where the crime took place.

Accused individuals have the right to hear and question all witnesses against them. They must also be permitted to call witnesses in their own defense. Finally, they are entitled to have a lawyer. Since the Sixth Amendment was written, the Supreme Court has ruled that if an accused person cannot afford a lawyer, the government must provide one and pay his or her fees.

The Eighth Amendment

Although the Sixth Amendment guarantees a speedy trial, sometimes months go by before a case can be heard. During that time, the accused may have two choices: stay in jail or remain free by paying bail. **Bail** is *a sum of money used as a security deposit.* If the accused person comes to court for the trial, the bail is returned. If the person fails to appear, the bail is forfeited.

The judge decides how much bail a person must pay. Judges consider various factors, including the type of crime committed, the record of the accused person, the likelihood that he or she will appear in court, and what he or she can afford. The Eighth Amendment, however, forbids "excessive" bail—that is, an amount that is much too high.

The Eighth Amendment also forbids excessive fines for people convicted of crimes. In addition, it forbids "cruel and unusual punishments." For many years, Americans have debated what kinds of punishment are cruel and unusual. It is generally agreed that punishment should be in proportion to the crime committed. For example, a sentence of life imprisonment for stealing a loaf of bread would be too harsh. People

JAMES MADISON (1751–1836)

Even in his day, James Madison, the nation's fourth president, was known as the "Father of the Constitution." Madison protested: "You give me credit to which I have no claim. . . . It ought to be regarded as the work of many heads and many hands."

However, when it came to creating a constitution, Madison had few equals. He not only played a leading role in shaping the Constitution, he wrote many of the Federalist papers defending it. Madison, though, at first opposed the addition of a bill of rights. He felt the Constitution gave the people the power to protect their own rights through the election of officials. The Constitution also limited the powers of government by such means as separation of powers and checks and balances. He feared that future governments might honor only those rights listed in the bill.

When some leaders threatened to call a second constitutional convention, Madison agreed to a list of rights. To make sure the amendments did not weaken the new government, he helped write them himself. Then, as the U.S. representative from Virginia, Madison pushed the amendments through Congress, fulfilling the Constitution's promise to create a "more perfect union."

disagree strongly, however, about whether the death penalty for very serious crimes is cruel and unusual punishment.

Protecting Other Rights

In addition to the First Amendment freedoms and due process guarantees, the Bill of Rights includes other protections for American citizens.

The Second Amendment

There is much debate over what exact rights are guaranteed by the Second Amendment. Some argue that it provides only for each state to maintain "a well regulated militia" by allowing the members of those militias to carry arms. When the Second Amendment was written, a militia was a small, local army made up of volunteer soldiers. These militias helped to win America's independence from Great Britain. Later, they helped defend the states and their communities.

Other people hold that the Second Amendment guarantees the right of all individual citizens to "keep and bear arms" without the interference of the government. The courts have generally ruled that the government can pass laws to control, but not prevent, the possession of weapons. For example, federal and state laws determine who can be licensed to own firearms.

Lawmakers continue to discuss the extent of our right to bear arms today. They also debate the kinds of gun regulations that may be necessary for public safety.

The Third Amendment

One cause of the American Revolution was the colonists' resentment of the law requiring them to house and feed British soldiers. The Third Amendment makes it unlikely that Americans will ever be forced to shelter the military again. The amendment says that, in peacetime, soldiers may not move into private homes without the consent of the homeowner. In times of war, Congress must authorize the practice.

The Seventh Amendment

The Fifth, Sixth, and Eighth Amendments deal with people's rights in criminal cases. The Seventh Amendment concerns civil cases—lawsuits that involve disagreements between people rather than crimes. If you were disputing a contract, for example, or claiming that a doctor had not treated you properly, you could initiate a civil suit.

FIGURE 6–23.

Federal District Judge Sonia Sotomayer of New York issued the ruling that ended the baseball players' strike in 1995. The Seventh Amendment states that the players could have settled their case by a jury trial.

The Seventh Amendment guarantees the right to a jury trial in civil cases if the amount of money involved is more than $20. The amendment does not, however, require a jury trial. Both sides may decide to have their dispute settled by a judge instead.

The Ninth Amendment

The people who wrote the Bill of Rights realized that they could not spell out every right of the American people. The Ninth Amendment makes it clear that citizens have other rights beyond those listed in the Constitution. These unwritten rights are just as valuable and may not be taken away.

The right to privacy, for example, is not mentioned in the Constitution. However, the Supreme Court has drawn on the First, Fourth, Fifth, and Ninth Amendments to uphold this right. We thus enjoy privacy in our homes, confidentiality in our medical and financial records, and freedom from government interference in our personal choices regarding friends, families, and careers.

The Tenth Amendment

The Constitution discusses certain powers of the national and state governments. Many other powers of government—such as the authority to set up schools and license lawyers—are not mentioned at all.

Tinker v. Des Moines Independent Community School District

Background of the Case

Division over the war in Vietnam racked the nation during the 1960s. Millions of Americans agreed with the war, while other millions disagreed. Protests occurred frequently. One night in December 1965, a group of public school students, led by high-school sophomores Christopher Eckhardt and John Tinker and eighth-grader Mary Beth Tinker, planned their own protest. They decided to wear black armbands to school as silent expressions of mourning for deaths on both sides in the war. As other students joined the armband protest, principals and members of the school board met the growing protest with a ban on armbands—to prevent "disturbing influences."

On December 16, 1965, Christopher, John, and Mary Beth were suspended for wearing their armbands to school. Their parents protested the suspensions in federal courts. They contended the students' First Amendment free speech rights had been violated.

The Decision

On February 24, 1969, the United States Supreme Court in a 7–2 decision declared the school suspensions unconstitutional. Justice Abe Fortas, who wrote the majority opinion, first established that the students' action was "akin to pure speech." Even though their protest involved no speaking, it deserved "protection under the First Amendment." Then he wrote:

The Tinkers show their armbands.

It can hardly be argued that either students or teachers shed their constitutional rights to freedom of speech or expression at the schoolhouse gate.

Why It Matters

Supporters saluted the decision. Critics predicted harmful consequences. Dissenter Justice Hugo Black suggested that the Court's decision was "the beginning of a new revolutionary era of permissiveness in this country fostered by the judiciary." He argued that no one has a complete right to freedom of speech and expression.

Analyzing the Court Decision

1. How did Justice Fortas's concept of "pure speech" extend First Amendment free speech rights?

2. What arguments might you use to support or oppose the viewpoints of Justice Fortas and Justice Black?

Under the Tenth Amendment, any powers the Constitution does not specifically give to the national government are reserved to the states or to the people. In this way, the Tenth Amendment prevents Congress and the president from becoming too strong. The government of the United States can have only the powers the people give it.

The *people who originally supported the Constitution* called themselves **Federalists**. They chose this name to emphasize that the Constitution would create a system of **federalism**, *a form of government in which power is divided between the federal, or national, government and the states.*

Protecting All Americans

The Bill of Rights was passed to safeguard individual liberties. However, the rights guaranteed to all Americans have not always been applied equally and fairly. The Bill of Rights was intended originally to restrain only the national government. For many years, local and state governments were not bound by its terms. As a result, states sometimes used their reserved powers to pass laws that violated civil liberties. In most parts of the country, for example, women and African Americans could not vote to elect representatives in government. Before 1865, many states had laws that sanctioned the enslavement of African Americans, who were treated as property and had almost no rights at all.

Gradually, however, the Bill of Rights came to cover all Americans equally and to limit government power at all levels. Additional amendments to the Constitution and court rulings both played a part in this process.

Three amendments were passed after the Civil War to extend civil liberties to African Americans. The promise of these Civil War amendments, as they are known, was not fulfilled, however, for almost 100 years. Many states were slow to change

AMERICANS IN ACTION

Even as a teenager, William Lloyd Garrison's dedication to the abolition of slavery was apparent. As a newspaper apprentice, and later as the owner of his own newspapers, ending slavery was nearly his sole concern. In the first edition of *The Liberator*, published in 1831, Garrison promised his readers, "I am in earnest—I will not equivocate—I will not excuse—I will not retreat a single inch—AND I WILL BE HEARD." Thirty-four years later came proof that Garrison's words had been heard when the Thirteenth Amendment was passed.

William Lloyd Garrison

their customs; some actively resisted. The federal government, including the Supreme Court, often seemed indifferent. Nonetheless, the Civil War amendments signaled a move toward greater equality.

The Thirteenth Amendment (1865)

The Thirteenth Amendment officially outlawed slavery in the United States and thus freed thousands of African Americans. It also outlawed any sort of forced labor, except as punishment for a crime.

The Fourteenth Amendment (1868)

Although the Thirteenth Amendment ensured the freedom of African Americans, it did not guarantee them full rights. After the Civil War, many Southern states passed "black codes" that kept African Americans from holding certain jobs, limited their property rights, and restricted them in other ways.

To remedy this situation, the Fourteenth Amendment was enacted in 1868. It defined a United States citizen as anyone "born or naturalized in the United States," a definition that included most African Americans. The amendment also required every state to grant its citizens "equal protection of the laws." This clause has been extremely important. In recent years, it has been used to benefit women, people with disabilities, and other groups whose rights have not always been protected fairly.

Another element of the Fourteenth Amendment forbids state governments from interfering with the "privileges or immunities of citizens of the United States." Further, state governments may not take an individual's "life, liberty, or property, without due process of law." The intent of these provisions was to make the Bill of Rights binding for state governments as well as the federal government. This is called the nationalization of the Bill of Rights.

For many years, however, the Supreme Court ignored this interpretation of the Fourteenth Amendment. Then, in 1925, in *Gitlow v. New York,* the Court ruled that the Fourteenth Amendment could safeguard free speech and a free press "from impairment by the states."

Since the *Gitlow* case, the Supreme Court has used the Fourteenth Amendment to apply other rights in the Bill of Rights to the states. This "incorporation" of the Bill of Rights by the Fourteenth Amendment's due process clause means that U.S. citizens in every part of the country have the same basic rights. A string of later cases further extended the reach of the Bill of Rights. By the end of the 1960s, most protections in the Bill of Rights were considered to apply at the state level.

The Fifteenth Amendment (1870)

The last of the Civil War amendments, the Fifteenth, says that no state may take away a person's voting rights on the basis of race, color, or previous enslavement. The amendment clearly aimed to guarantee **suffrage**—*the right to vote*—to African Americans. Still, many states found ways to keep African Americans away from the polls.

Constitutional Amendments 11–27

AMEND-MENTS	DATE	PURPOSE
11	1795	Removed cases in which a state was sued without its consent from the jurisdiction of the federal courts
12	1804	Required presidential electors to vote separately for president and vice president
13	1865	Abolished slavery and authorized Congress to pass legislation implementing its abolition
14	1868	Granted citizenship to all persons born or naturalized in the United States; banned states from denying any person life, liberty, or property without due process of law; and banned states from denying any person equal protection under the laws
15	1870	Guaranteed voting rights to African Americans by outlawing denial of the right to vote on the basis of race, color, or previous condition of servitude
16	1913	Empowered Congress to levy an income tax
17	1913	Provided for the election of U.S. senators by direct popular vote instead of by the state legislatures
18	1919	Authorized Congress to prohibit the manufacture, sale, and transportation of liquor
19	1920	Guaranteed the right to vote to women
20	1933	Shortened the time between a presidential election and inauguration by designating January 20 as Inauguration Day; set January 3 as the date for the opening of a new Congress
21	1933	Repealed the Eighteenth Amendment and empowered Congress to regulate the liquor industry
22	1951	Limited presidents to two full terms in office
23	1961	Granted voters in the District of Columbia the right to vote for president and vice president
24	1964	Forbade requiring the payment of a poll tax to vote in a federal election
25	1967	Provided for succession to the office of president in the event of death or incapacity and for filling vacancies in the office of the vice president
26	1971	Guaranteed the right to vote to 18-year-olds
27	1992	Banned Congress from increasing its members' salaries until after the next election

○ Amendments changing the powers of the national and state governments

● Amendments changing the government structure or function

◐ Amendments extending the suffrage and powers of voters

Evaluating Charts

One of the strengths of the Constitution is its ability to respond to changes in society. The amendment process contributes to that flexibility. Which amendment establishes the process by which the vice president takes over when the president is disabled?

The Fifteenth Amendment protected only men in practice. The various states had the power to decide whether women could vote. Women, regardless of their race, could not vote in most federal or state elections.

The Seventeenth Amendment (1913)

According to Article I of the Constitution, the people were to elect members of the House of Representatives, but the state legislatures were to choose members of the Senate. The Seventeenth Amendment was passed in order to allow voters to elect their senators directly. This change in the election process gave Americans a greater voice in their government.

The Nineteenth Amendment (1920)

Although the Constitution did not guarantee women the right to vote, it did not explicitly deny them suffrage. As a result, states made their own laws on the matter, using the powers reserved to them under the Tenth Amendment. The territory of Wyoming permitted women to vote in 1869, and several other territories and states did so as well in the years that followed.

However, national support for woman suffrage was slow in coming. Leaders like Susan B. Anthony and Elizabeth Cady Stanton had insisted as early as 1848 that women belonged at the polls. It was only in 1920, however, that the Nineteenth Amendment protected the right of women to vote in all national and state elections.

The Twenty-third Amendment (1961)

African Americans and women were not the only citizens who were denied voting rights for many years. Residents of our nation's capital, Washington, D.C., also fell into this group.

"D.C.," as you may know, stands for the District of Columbia, an area between Maryland and Virginia. Because the District is not a state, the people who lived there were not initially allowed to vote in national elections. The Twenty-third Amendment changed that in 1961. The amendment says that residents of the District of Columbia may vote for the president and vice president, just as other Americans do.

The Twenty-fourth Amendment (1964)

Although the Fifteenth Amendment gave African Americans the right to vote, many had trouble exercising this right. One reason was that several Southern states had **poll taxes**. In other words, they *required voters to pay a sum of money before casting a ballot*. Because many African Americans could not afford the tax, they could not vote. Poor whites were in the same situation.

In 1964, the Twenty-fourth Amendment made poll taxes illegal in national elections. Two years later, the Supreme Court ruled that poll taxes were illegal in state elections as well.

On August 23, 1963, more than 200,000 people marched in Washington D.C., for their rights. On that day, they heard Reverend Martin Luther King Jr., utter these words: "I have a dream that one day this nation will rise up and live out the true meaning of its creed: 'We hold these truths to be self-evident; that all men are created equal' . . . I have a dream that my four little children will one day live in a nation where they will not be judged by the color of their skin but by the content of their character. . . ."

Martin Luther King, Jr., leads a march in Mississippi.

The Twenty-sixth Amendment (1971)

Throughout our nation's history, people still in their teens have bravely fought for our country. By law, however, they were not old enough to vote for the leaders who sent them into battle. Although the Constitution did not specify a minimum age for voters, most states set the minimum at 21.

That standard finally changed in 1971, a year when many young Americans were fighting in the Vietnam War. The Twenty-sixth Amendment guaranteed the right to vote to citizens 18 and older for all national and state elections. As a result, millions more Americans could now exercise their right to vote.

The Civil Rights Struggle

Background of the Struggle

Despite the advances made after the Civil War, African Americans routinely faced **discrimination**, or *unfair treatment based on prejudice against a certain group.* Southern states, for example, passed so-called "Jim Crow" laws requiring African Americans and whites to be separated in most public places, such as schools. Later, African Americans had to ride in the back of buses and sit in separate sections of restaurants and theaters. They even had to use separate public restrooms. *The social separation of the races* was known as **segregation**. African Americans in the North fared better. They could vote freely, and segregation was less noticeable. Even so, prejudice restricted opportunities for many. It would take more than 100 years for African Americans to secure their **civil rights**—*the rights of full citizenship and equality under the law.*

From an early time, many Americans objected to the treatment of African Americans as "second-class citizens." In 1909 a group of African Americans and whites founded the National Association for the Advancement of Colored People (NAACP). The association worked mainly through the courts to challenge laws and customs that denied African Americans their constitutional rights.

In 1910 other concerned citizens formed the National Urban League. The Urban League aided the growing numbers of African Americans in cities, helping them find jobs and improve their opportunities to get ahead.

Gradually, these organizations and other groups and individuals built a civil rights movement supported by millions. An important gain came in 1948, when President Harry Truman ordered an end to segregation in the nation's armed forces. A bigger victory was the Supreme Court's decision *Brown v. Board of Education, Topeka Kansas* (1954). In the landmark case, NAACP lawyers successfully argued that racial segregation in the public schools was unconstitutional. Segregation violated the Fourteenth Amendment's principle of equal protection under the law.

In the 1950s, Dr. Martin Luther King, Jr., became one of the main leaders of the civil rights movement. A Baptist minister and stirring speaker, King believed in non-violent resistance—the peaceful protest of unfair laws. He helped organize marches, boycotts, and demonstrations that opened many people's eyes to the need for change.

African American students began staging "sit-ins" at lunch counters that served only whites. White and African American "Freedom Riders" traveled together on buses to protest segregation. In his 1963 "I Have a Dream" speech, King inspired thousands with his hopes for racial equality and harmony. As the civil rights movement gained strength, however, some whites opposed it with violence.

In response to the growing demand for government action, Congress passed the Civil Rights Act of 1964. This far-reaching law prohibited discrimination in public facilities, employment, education, and voter registration. It also banned discrimination not only by race and color, but also by gender, religion, and national origin.

Earlier that same year, the Twenty-fourth Amendment had outlawed poll taxes. The Voting Rights Act of 1965 took further steps to protect the free access of minorities to the polls.

Ongoing Challenges

The civil rights laws of the 1960s certainly opened more doors for minorities. African Americans, Hispanic Americans, and other minorities have made striking gains in educational achievement. They increasingly hold professional and managerial jobs and serve in government, yet whites still tend to have more opportunities.

In the 1970s, the federal government began affirmative action programs to try to make up for past discrimination. **Affirmative action** programs *encouraged the hiring and promoting of minorities and women in fields that were traditionally closed to them.* Colleges, too, practiced affirmative action to help minorities gain admission.

As planned, affirmative action was supposed to be a short-term policy to make up for past discrimination. From the start, affirmative action was controversial. Critics complained that giving preferential treatment to women and minorities amounted to discrimination against men and whites. Recent court decisions and state laws have curtailed many affirmative action programs.

The struggle for equal rights continues. Each year, the federal government receives more than 75,000 complaints of workplace discrimination. Many Americans and others are sometimes subject to **racial profiling** by law enforcement officers—*being singled out as suspects because of the way they look.* Some Americans even become the victims of hate crimes—acts of violence based on a person's race, color, national origin, gender, or disability.

Landmark Acts of the Civil Rights Movement

BROWN v. BOARD OF EDUCATION OF TOPEKA, KANSAS, 1954

⭐ Supreme Court rules segregated schools unconstitutional

CIVIL RIGHTS ACT OF 1957

⭐ Congress sets up commission on civil rights and creates a division of civil rights in Justice Department

EQUAL PAY ACT OF 1963

⭐ Bans wage discrimination based on race, gender, religion, or national origin

CIVIL RIGHTS ACT OF 1964

⭐ Strengthens Fourteenth Amendment protections; bans discrimination in employment, voting, and public accommodations

VOTING RIGHTS ACT OF 1965

⭐ Empowers federal government to intervene in voter registration discrimination

OPEN HOUSING ACT OF 1968

⭐ Prevents people selling or renting homes from using certain forms of discrimination

EQUAL EMPLOYMENT OPPORTUNITY ACT OF 1972

⭐ Provides that businesses receiving federal funds must have affirmative action programs to increase number of female and minority employees

AMERICANS WITH DISABILITIES ACT OF 1990

⭐ Bans discrimination in employment, transportation, public accommodations, and telecommunications against persons with physical or mental disabilities

Evaluating Charts

It was not until 1964 with the passage of the Civil Rights Act that racial segregation in public places became illegal. What legislation banned wage discrimination?

Lesson 4 Review

1. Define the following terms and use them in sentences related to the First Amendment: *civil liberties, censorship, petition, slander, libel.*

2. Besides the spoken word, "speech" refers to what other forms of expression?

3. What are the limits to First Amendment freedoms? Give an example of a limit to a First Amendment right.

4. Which First Amendment right do you think is the most important?

5. Use the following terms in sentences related to the Bill of Rights: *search warrant, indictment, grand jury, double jeopardy, due process, eminent domain, bail.*

6. When can law enforcement officers search a suspect's house?

7. What current controversial issue is tied to the Eighth Amendment's prohibition of cruel and unusual punishment?

8. Which of the first 10 amendments do you think is the most important? Why?

9. Define the following terms and use them in sentences related to voting rights: *suffrage, poll tax.*

10. How was the promise of the Civil War amendments fulfilled in the mid-twentieth century?

11. How did the Twenty-fourth Amendment expand voting rights?

12. Which of the voting rights amendments (17, 19, 23, 24, or 26) do you think was the most important? Why?

13. Explain the effects of poll taxes in the South.

14. Use the following terms in a paragraph that summarizes the civil rights movement: *discrimination, segregation, civil rights, affirmative action, racial profiling.*

15. List examples of the discrimination that African Americans faced after the Civil War.

16. What was the purpose of the Civil Rights Act of 1964?

17. Why was the civil rights movement started?

18. List Martin Luther King, Jr.'s tactics in the civil rights movement.

Applying Citizenship Skills

19. Read your local newspaper for a week. Note all the examples of people exercising First Amendment rights that you can find. Report your findings to the class.

20. Select an issue related to the amendments in this section, such as the death penalty or gun control. Write a letter to the editor of your local newspaper expressing your views on the issue.

21. Do you think that affirmative action laws are a fair way to change past discrimination? Write your opinion in a letter to the editor.

U.S. National Government

Congress: The Legislative Branch

Every year, inside the U.S. Capitol in Washington, D.C., 535 of our fellow citizens gather to make new laws and address countless issues facing our country. These are our elected representatives, the members of Congress.

The Framers of the U.S. Constitution intended to make the legislative branch of government more powerful than any other branch. In fact, Congress is described in the first part of the Constitution, Article I. As James Madison said, Congress is "the First Branch of this Government."

Terms of Congress

Each term of Congress starts on January 3 of odd-numbered years (unless a different day is appointed) and lasts for two years. Each "new" Congress is given a number to identify its two-year term. For example, the first Congress met in 1789, and the 109th Congress began meeting in 2005.

Each term of Congress is divided into two sessions, or meetings. A typical session of Congress today lasts from January until November or December. Congress may also meet in times of crisis during special sessions. A joint session occurs when the House and Senate meet together. This usually occurs when the Congress gathers to hear the president's State of the Union address.

A Bicameral Legislature

One of the major conflicts at the Constitutional Convention in 1787 concerned state representation in Congress. While delegates from the smaller states wanted equal representation, delegates from the larger states wanted representation to be based on population. The resulting Great Compromise established Congress as a bicameral body. **Bicameral** means *having two parts*. The two parts of Congress became the House of Representatives and the Senate.

The House of Representatives

The House of Representatives, the larger body of Congress, has 435 voting members. The voting members are allotted to the states according to population. According to the Constitution, each state is entitled to at least one seat in the House, no matter how small its population. After each 10-year **census**, or *population count* taken by the Census Bureau, Congress adjusts the number of representatives given to each state.

Each state is divided into one or more congressional districts, or areas, with one representative elected from each district. State legislatures must draw the boundaries so that the districts include roughly the same number of **constituents**, or *people represented*. Sometimes states abuse this process by gerrymandering.

In 1812 Governor Elbridge Gerry created a new voting district in Andover, Massachusetts. In response, artist Gilbert Stuart drew the outline of the district and added a head, claws, and wings. A newspaper editor named the fictional beast, which resembled a salamander, a "Gerrymander."

A **gerrymander** is *an oddly shaped district designed to increase the voting strength of a particular group.* For example, if most of a state's representatives are Republican, they might draw the lines so that as many districts as possible have more Republican than Democratic voters.

Representatives serve two-year terms and may not be well known outside their districts. They usually focus on concerns in their districts, rather than the concerns of the state as a whole. This is as the Framers of the Constitution intended. They designed Congress so that members of the House would be closer to the people than would members of the Senate.

The Senate

The Senate has 100 members—two from each of the 50 states. Each senator represents his or her entire state rather than a particular district.

Senators serve six-year terms, but elections are staggered so that no more than one-third of the senators are up for reelection at any one time. This ensures a certain amount of stability and continuity.

VOCABULARY

- bicameral
- census
- constituents
- gerrymander
- majority party
- minority party
- standing committees
- seniority
- joint resolutions
- special-interest groups
- riders
- filibuster
- cloture
- voice vote
- standing vote
- roll-call vote
- veto
- pocket veto
- Electoral College
- electors
- jurisdiction
- exclusive jurisdiction
- concurrent jurisdiction
- district courts
- original jurisdiction
- appeals courts
- appellate jurisdiction
- circuit
- remand
- opinion
- precedent

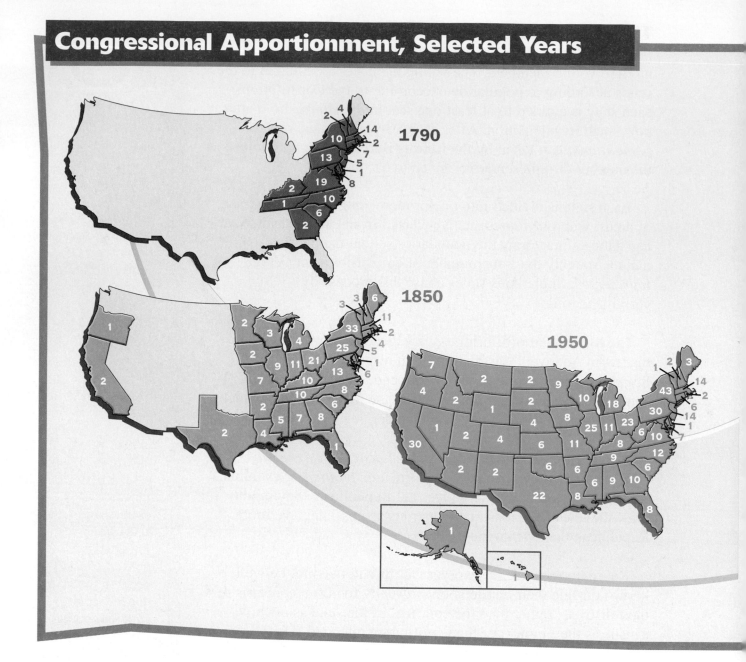

Congressional Leaders

In both the House and the Senate, the **majority party** is *the political party to which more than half the members belong.* The **minority party** is *the other party to which the rest of the members belong.* At the beginning of each term, the party members in each house choose leaders to direct their activities. The Constitution states that the House "shall choose their Speaker and other officers." Members of the majority party of the House choose the Speaker at a caucus, or closed meeting. The entire membership of the House then approves the choice of Speaker of the House.

The Speaker of the House is the most powerful leader within the House of Representatives. Always an experienced member of the majority party, the Speaker steers legislation through the House. The Speaker is also in charge of floor debates (those in which all representatives may participate) and influences most other House

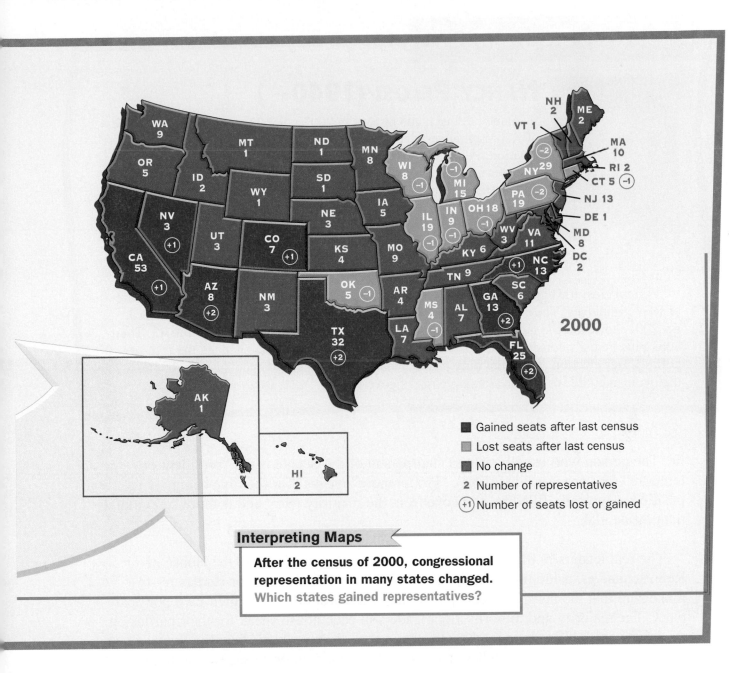

WA 9
OR 5
ID 2
MT 1
WY 1
ND 1
SD 1
NE 3
MN 8
IA 5
WI 8 (-1)
MI 15 (-1)
NY 29 (-2)
VT 1
NH 2
ME 2
MA 10
RI 2
CT 5 (-1)
NJ 13
DE 1
MD 8
DC 2
PA 19 (-2)
OH 18 (-1)
IN 9 (-1)
IL 19 (-1)
WV 3
VA 11
KY 6
NV 3 (+1)
UT 3
CO 7 (+1)
KS 4
MO 9
CA 53 (+1)
AZ 8 (+2)
NM 3
OK 5 (-1)
AR 4
TN 9
NC 13 (+1)
SC 6
GA 13 (+2)
MS 4 (-1)
AL 7
TX 32 (+2)
LA 7
FL 25 (+2)

2000

AK 1

HI 2

■ Gained seats after last census
■ Lost seats after last census
■ No change
2 Number of representatives
(+1) Number of seats lost or gained

Interpreting Maps

After the census of 2000, congressional representation in many states changed.
Which states gained representatives?

business. If anything happens to the president and vice president, the Speaker is next in line to become president, provided he or she is legally qualified.

Speakers today rely on their powers of persuasion as much as their formal powers to exercise influence. On a typical day, the Speaker may talk with dozens of members of Congress. Often the Speaker does this just to listen to requests for a favor. Former Speaker of the House Thomas P. "Tip" O'Neill once stated: "The world is full of little things you can do for people." The Speaker, though, expects something in return—the representatives' support on important issues.

The Senate has no leader with comparable power. The presiding officer is technically the vice president of the United States, called the president of the Senate. However, the vice president rarely attends Senate debates and votes only in case of a

NANCY PELOSI (1940–)

Nancy Pelosi made history in 2002 when Democrats in the House of Representatives elected her as minority leader. In winning the position, Pelosi claimed the highest post ever held by a woman in Congress.

Politics runs in Pelosi's family. Both her father and brother served as the mayor of Baltimore, Maryland. Her father, Thomas D'Alesandro, Jr., also represented the city for five terms in Congress. Pelosi, the mother of five children, carried the family tradition to California. In 1987 she waged a successful campaign to represent San Francisco in Congress.

When Pelosi traveled to Washington, D.C., only 12 Democratic women sat in the House of Representatives. They lacked the numbers and the seniority to make their voices heard. By 2001, however, the number of Democratic female representatives had grown to 42. Their vote, plus Pelosi's considerable experience on important committees, changed the face of politics. Her election meant not only that Democrats would hear women's issues, but also that women could win top leadership posts in government.

tie. The person who usually acts as chairperson of the Senate is the "president pro tempore" (or "pro tem," for short). "Pro tempore" means "for the time being." This position is typically filled by someone from the majority party and is more ceremonial than influential.

The real leaders in the Senate, and the most powerful players in the House of Representatives, aside from the Speaker, are the floor leaders. Floor leaders try to make sure that the laws Congress passes are in the best interest of their own political party. The majority and minority floor leaders in each house speak for their parties on the issues, push bills along, and try to sway votes. Party "whips" help the floor leaders. They keep track of where party members stand on proposed legislation and round up their colleagues for key votes.

Committees: Little Legislatures

The detailed work of lawmaking is done in committee rather than on the House or Senate floor. So many bills are introduced each year that few of them would be considered if the work were not divided among smaller groups of legislators.

Types of Committees

Each house of Congress has both well-established, ongoing committees and those set up for a specific short-term purpose. *The permanent committees that continue their work from session to session* are called **standing committees**. The Senate has 17 standing committees and the House has 19, covering areas such as education, veterans affairs, and commerce.

Standing Committees

HOUSE OF REPRESENTATIVES
Standing Committees

⭐ Agriculture
⭐ Appropriations
⭐ Armed Services
⭐ Budget
⭐ Education and the Workforce
⭐ Energy and Commerce
⭐ Financial Services
⭐ Government Reform
⭐ House Administration
⭐ International Relations

⭐ Judiciary
⭐ Resources
⭐ Rules
⭐ Science
⭐ Small Business
⭐ Standards of Official Conduct
⭐ Transportation and Infrastructure
⭐ Veterans Affairs
⭐ Ways and Means

Select and Special Committees

⭐ Intelligence
⭐ Aging
⭐ Ethics
⭐ Intelligence

Joint Committees

⭐ Economic
⭐ Printing
⭐ Taxation
⭐ Library

SENATE
Standing Committees

⭐ Agriculture, Nutrition, and Forestry
⭐ Appropriations
⭐ Armed Services
⭐ Banking, Housing, and Urban Affairs
⭐ Budget
⭐ Commerce, Science, and Transportation
⭐ Energy and Natural Resources
⭐ Environment and Public Works
⭐ Finance

⭐ Foreign Relations
⭐ Governmental Affairs
⭐ Health, Education, Labor, and Pensions
⭐ Indian Affairs
⭐ Judiciary
⭐ Rules and Administration
⭐ Small Business and Entrepreneurship
⭐ Veterans Affairs

⭐ House Committee
⭐ Senate Committee
⭐ Joint Committee

Evaluating Charts

Most of the legislative work of Congress is done in committees. Which Senate committee deals with appointments of judges to the federal courts?

Most standing committees are divided into smaller subcommittees that deal with more specialized issues. For example, the Senate Armed Services Committee has subcommittees on military readiness, personnel, and armament. Some subcommittees are very powerful. Others are not.

In addition to standing committees, both houses of Congress also have select committees that are created to do a special job for a limited period. In 1976, for example, the House formed the Select Committee on Assassinations to investigate the deaths of President John F. Kennedy and Dr. Martin Luther King, Jr. Like all select committees, the House Assassinations Committee disbanded when it finished its work.

The House and Senate have also formed four joint committees, which include members of both houses. The Joint Economic Committee reviews economic conditions and recommends improvements in economic policy. Other joint committees focus on federal tax policy, the Library of Congress, and the Government Printing Office.

A fourth type of committee is a temporary committee, the conference committee, which helps the House and Senate agree on the details of a proposed law.

Committee Assignments

When senators and representatives first come to Congress, they try to get assigned to important committees that affect the people who elected them. For example, members of Congress from farm areas might want to serve on agriculture committees. Those with many factories in their districts might be interested in serving on labor committees.

Leaders of the political parties make committee assignments. In doing so, they consider members' preferences, expertise, and loyalty to the party. Another key factor is **seniority**, or *years of service*. The senators and representatives who have been in Congress longest usually get the preferred committee spots. The longest-serving committee member from the majority party traditionally becomes chairperson. Chairpersons of standing committees are the most powerful members of Congress. These members decide when and if a committee will meet, what bills will be studied, and who will serve on which subcommittees.

Some people think the seniority system is a good idea. They say it prevents fights over committee jobs and ensures that chairpersons will have experience. Other people complain that talented people may be overlooked in favor of those who have simply been around for a while. There has been so much criticism of the seniority system

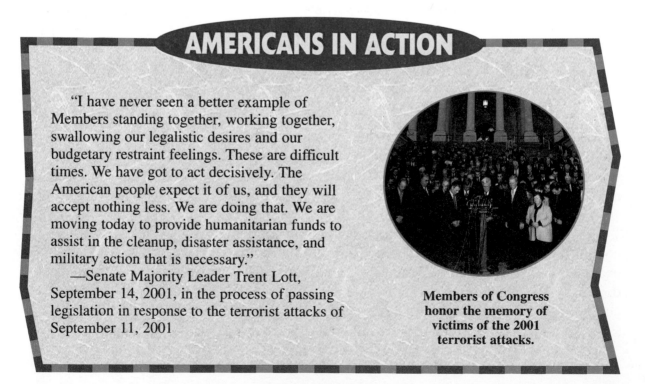

AMERICANS IN ACTION

"I have never seen a better example of Members standing together, working together, swallowing our legalistic desires and our budgetary restraint feelings. These are difficult times. We have got to act decisively. The American people expect it of us, and they will accept nothing less. We are doing that. We are moving today to provide humanitarian funds to assist in the cleanup, disaster assistance, and military action that is necessary."
—Senate Majority Leader Trent Lott, September 14, 2001, in the process of passing legislation in response to the terrorist attacks of September 11, 2001

Members of Congress honor the memory of victims of the 2001 terrorist attacks.

over the years that both political parties have moved slightly away from it. The senior majority party member on a committee still usually wins the role of chairperson, but it is no longer guaranteed.

Types of Bills

It is Congress's job to pass laws that the nation needs. However, have you heard people say there are two things you should never watch being made—sausages and laws? Strange elements may go into the final product, and the process requires patience. One scholar has compared lawmaking to running an obstacle course. More than 10,000 bills are often introduced during each term of Congress, yet only several hundred pass all the hurdles and become law.

Bills generally fall into two categories. Private bills concern individual people or places. They usually deal with people's claims against the government. Public bills apply to the entire nation and involve general matters like taxation, civil rights, or terrorism. They may be debated for months and get much media coverage.

Along with bills, Congress considers different kinds of resolutions, or formal statements expressing lawmakers' opinions or decisions. Many resolutions, such as those creating a new congressional committee or permitting a ceremony in the Capitol, do not have the force of law. **Joint resolutions**, however, which are *passed by both houses of Congress,* do become laws if signed by the president. Congress uses joint resolutions to propose constitutional amendments, to designate money for a special purpose, and to correct errors in bills already passed.

From Bill to Law

Every bill starts with an idea. Some of these ideas come from members of Congress or private citizens. Many more ideas begin in the White House. Other bills are suggested by **special-interest groups**, or *organizations made up of people with some common interest who try to influence government decisions.*

Whatever their source, only senators and representatives can introduce bills in Congress. Any bill that involves money must start in the House. Every bill is given a title and a number when it is submitted. For

FIGURE 6–24.

Senator Kent Conrad, a Democrat from North Dakota, speaks during a hearing on the president's 2002 budget before the Senate budget committee.

example, during the first session of Congress, the first bill introduced is called S.1 in the Senate and H.R.1 in the House. The bill is then sent to the standing committee that seems most qualified to handle it.

Committee Action

Committees receive far more bills than they can process. The chairperson is the main person to decide which bills get ignored and which get studied. Those that merit attention are often researched and reported on by a subcommittee. Public hearings may be held to allow experts and concerned citizens to voice their opinions. People may also submit written statements for or against the bill.

Standing committees have life-and-death power over bills. The committee can

1. pass the bill without changes.
2. mark up a bill with changes and suggest that it be passed.
3. replace the original bill with a new alternative.
4. ignore the bill and let it die (which is called "pigeonholing" the bill).
5. kill the bill outright by majority vote.

The full House or Senate can overrule the decisions of its committees, but this rarely happens. When a committee is against a bill, it almost never becomes a law.

Floor Debate

Bills approved in committee are ready for consideration by the full House or Senate. The bills are put on calendars, or schedules, in chronological order as they come out of committees. The Senate usually takes up bills in the order listed. The powerful Rules Committee, however, controls the House schedule. This "traffic cop" can give priority to the bills that are most important. It can also kill a bill by not letting it get to the floor.

When bills do reach the floor of the House or Senate, the members argue their pros and cons. They may also discuss amendments. The House accepts only amendments relevant to the bill. The Senate, however, allows **riders**—*completely unrelated amendments*—to be tacked onto the bill. Senators include riders to bills that are likely to pass. Sometimes they attach these riders to benefit their constituents.

In the House, the Rules Committee sets the terms for debate. It usually puts time limits on the discussion, for example, to speed up action. The Senate, because it is smaller, has fewer rules. Senators can speak as long as they wish, and they are not even required to address the topic at hand. Now and then they take advantage of this custom to **filibuster**, or *talk a bill "to death."* One member can hold the floor for hour after hour, delaying a vote until the bill's sponsor gives up and withdraws the measure.

The Senate can end a filibuster if three-fifths of the members vote for **cloture**. Under cloture, *no one may speak for more than one hour.* Senators rarely resort to

How a Bill Becomes Law

HOUSE

1. Representative hands bill to clerk or drops it in hopper.
2. Bill given *HR* number.

SENATE

1. Senator announces bill on the floor.
2. Bill given *S* number.

Committee Action

House:
1. Referred to House standing committee.
2. Referred to House subcommittee.
3. Reported by standing committee.
4. Rules Committee sets rules for debate and amendments.

Center:
Bill is placed on committee calendar.

Bill sent to subcommittee for hearings and revisions.

Standing committee may recommend passage or kill the bill.

Senate:
1. Referred to Senate standing committee.
2. Referred to Senate subcommittee.
3. Reported by standing committee.

Floor Action

House:
1. House debates, votes on passage.
2. Bill passes; goes to Senate for approval.
OR
A different version passes; goes to conference committee.

Senate:
1. Senate debates, votes on passage.
2. Bill passes; goes to House for approval.
OR
A different version passes; goes to conference committee.

Conference Action

★ Conference committee works out differences and sends identical compromise bill to both chambers for final approval.

★ House votes on compromise bill.   ★ Senate votes on compromise bill.

Passage

★ President signs bill or allows bill to become law without signing.*
OR
★ President vetoes bill.

★ Congress can override a veto by a 2/3 majority in both chambers. If either fails to override, the bill dies.

* President can keep bill for 10 days and bill becomes law. If Congress adjourns before the 10 days (Sundays excluded) then it does not become law.

Evaluating Charts

The process by which all bills become law is complex. Who can introduce bills in Congress?

Source: *Congress A to Z*, 2nd ed. (Washington D.C.: CQ Inc., 1993).

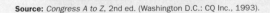

cloture, though. In 1964, during debate on the Civil Rights Act, the Senate waited out a 74-day filibuster by senators opposed to the legislation.

Voting on a Bill

When members of Congress are ready to vote on a proposed law, they may do so in several ways. In the House and Senate, the simplest is a **voice vote**, in which *those in favor say "Yea" and those against say "No."* In a **standing vote**, *those in favor of a bill stand to be counted, and then those against it stand to be counted.* Today the House uses a computerized voting system to produce a permanent record of each representative's vote. In the more tradition-bound Senate, *members voice their votes in turn as an official records them* in a **roll-call vote**.

A simple majority of all members that are present is needed to pass a bill. If a bill passes in one house, it is sent to the other. If either the Senate or the House rejects a bill, it dies.

The Constitution requires that the Senate and House pass a bill in identical form before it becomes law. If either house of Congress makes changes in a bill after receiving it from the other house, a conference committee is formed with members from both houses. They meet privately to work out differences between the two versions of the bill. Once they have a revised bill, the House and Senate must either accept it without amendments or completely reject it.

Presidential Action

After both houses of Congress approve a bill, it goes to the president. One of four things may then happen. The president may sign the bill and declare it a new law. The president may **veto**, or *refuse to sign,* the bill. The president may also do nothing for 10 days. At that point, if Congress is in session, the bill becomes law without the president's signature. *If Congress had adjourned, the bill dies,* which is called a **pocket veto**.

If the president vetoes a bill, Congress has one last chance to save it. As you read earlier, Congress can override the veto with a two-thirds vote of each house. This is not an easy task, though. In recent decades, Congress has managed to overturn only about one in five regular vetoes.

The President and the Executive Branch

Qualifications for President

The president heads the executive branch of the United States government. The presidency is the top political job in the country. Because of the power and global influence of the United States, the president is generally considered to hold the most important job in the world. Our country's first president was George Washington. Just as the nation has grown tremendously since that time, so has the office of the presidency.

"The presidency of the United States carries with it a responsibility so personal as to be without parallel. . . . No one can make decisions for him. . . . Even those closest to him . . . never know all the reasons why he does certain things and why he comes to certain conclusions. To be President of the United States is to be lonely, very lonely at times of great decisions."

—Harry S. Truman

President
Truman

The constitutional requirements for the presidency remain the same as they did when George Washington was president. The U.S. Constitution lists only three rules about who can become president of the United States. A person must be

1. at least 35 years old.

2. a native-born American citizen.

3. a resident of the United States for at least 14 years.

By law, anyone who meets these qualifications can become president. Of course, someone who hopes to become president must have many more qualifications than those three.

So far, every American president has been a white male. All but one have been Protestant Christians. Most have won elections before. Most have had a college education. Many have been lawyers. Most came from states with large populations.

Only in the past few decades has the presidency become a possibility for a wider group of Americans. John F. Kennedy became the first Catholic president in 1960. In 1984 the Democratic Party nominated Geraldine Ferraro as its first female vice-presidential candidate. Four years later Jesse Jackson, an African American, ran a close second in the race to become the Democratic candidate for president. In 2000 the Democrats nominated Connecticut senator Joseph Lieberman as the first Jewish candidate for vice president.

Electing a President

Presidential elections take place every four years in years evenly divisible by the number 4—for example, 1996, 2000, 2004, 2008. The Constitution does not provide for direct popular election of the president. Instead, it set up *an indirect method of election* called the **Electoral College**. The Constitution says that each state "shall appoint" **electors**, *who then vote for one of the major candidates.* Although the ballot will show the names of the presidential candidates, when you vote for a candidate, you are actually voting for a list of presidential electors pledged to that candidate.

Each state has as many electoral votes as the total of its U.S. senators and representatives. The Electoral College includes 538 electors. (Washington, D.C., has three electoral votes.) This means that the states with large populations have many more electoral votes than less populated states. In almost every state, the Electoral College is a "winner-take-all" system. Even if a candidate wins the popular vote by just a tiny majority, that candidate usually gets all of the state's electoral votes. Candidates thus pay much more attention to these states during election campaigns. Even so, the electoral votes of a few small states can decide the outcome of a close election.

FIGURE 6–25.
John F. Kennedy won the presidency in 1960.

To be elected president or vice president, a candidate must win at least 270 of the 538 electoral votes. The winner-take-all system makes it difficult for third-party candidates—candidates not from the two major parties—to win electoral votes.

Although the winning presidential candidate is usually announced on the same evening as the popular election, the formal election by the Electoral College doesn't take place until December, when the electors meet in each state capital to cast their ballots. Congress counts the electoral votes and declares the winner as the next president.

Term of Office

Presidents serve four-year terms. Originally, the Constitution placed no limits on how many terms a president could serve. The nation's first president, George Washington, served for eight years, then refused to run for a third term. Presidents followed Washington's example, and no president served more than two terms until 1940, when Franklin D. Roosevelt ran for and won a third term. In 1944 Roosevelt won a fourth term. The Twenty-second Amendment, ratified in 1951, limits each president to two elected terms in office, or a maximum of 10 years if the presidency began during another president's term.

Salary and Benefits

The president receives a salary of $400,000 per year, plus money for expenses and travel. The president lives and works in the White House, which contains a private movie theater, a small gym, a bowling alley, and a heated pool. A White House domestic staff of more than 80 people takes care of the president's family.

In addition, the president has the use of Camp David, a beautiful estate in the Catoctin Mountains of Maryland, about 60 miles north of Washington, D.C. It serves as a retreat and as a place to host foreign leaders. When presidents need to travel, they command a fleet of special cars, helicopters, and airplanes. For long trips, the president uses Air Force One, a specially equipped jet.

The Vice President

The vice president is elected with the president through the Electoral College system. The qualifications for the office are the same as those for the presidency. The Constitution gives little authority to the vice president. Article I states that the vice president shall preside over the Senate and vote in that body in case of a tie.

Vice presidents are usually not very visible to the public. Their activities rarely receive front-page newspaper coverage. Yet, if the president dies, is removed from office, becomes seriously ill, or resigns, the vice president becomes president. Nine vice presidents have become president due to the death or resignation of a president. John Adams, our nation's first vice president, described the situation well. He said, "I am Vice President. In this I am nothing, but I may become everything."

Presidential Succession

Eight presidents have died while in office. The original wording of the Constitution states that if the president dies or leaves office during his term, the vice president takes on the "powers and duties" of the presidency. Early government officials were not sure what that meant. Should the vice president become president, or should he remain vice president while doing the president's job?

In 1841 Vice President John Tyler settled the question when William Henry Harrison became the first president to die in office. Tyler declared himself president, took the oath of office, moved into the White House, and served out the remainder of Harrison's term.

In 1947 Congress passed the Presidential Succession Act, which indicates the line of succession after the vice president. According to this law, if both the president and vice president die or leave office, the Speaker of the House becomes president. Next in line is the president pro tempore of the Senate, then the secretary of state and other members of the cabinet.

Twenty-fifth Amendment

Twenty years later, remaining questions about presidential succession were answered with the adoption of a constitutional amendment. The Twenty-fifth Amendment says that if the president dies or leaves office, the vice president becomes president. The new president then chooses another vice president. Both the Senate and House of Representatives must approve the choice. This amendment also gives the vice president a role in determining whether a president is disabled and unable to do the job. Should that occur, the vice president would serve as acting president until the president is able to go back to work.

The Twenty-fifth Amendment has been used only three times. In 1973 Vice President Spiro Agnew resigned, and President Richard Nixon replaced him with Gerald Ford, a

Presidential Succession

- ⭐ Vice President
- ⭐ Speaker of the House
- ⭐ President Pro Tempore of the Senate
- ⭐ Secretary of State
- ⭐ Secretary of the Treasury
- ⭐ Secretary of Defense
- ⭐ Attorney General
- ⭐ Secretary of the Interior
- ⭐ Secretary of Agriculture
- ⭐ Secretary of Commerce
- ⭐ Secretary of Labor
- ⭐ Secretary of Health and Human Services
- ⭐ Secretary of Housing and Urban Development
- ⭐ Secretary of Transportation
- ⭐ Secretary of Energy
- ⭐ Secretary of Education
- ⭐ Secretary of Veterans Affairs

Evaluating Charts

In 1947 Congress passed a law on the order of succession to the presidency. Who follows the Speaker of the House in succession?

Source: Nelson, Ed. *The Presidency A to Z*, 2nd ed. (Washington, D.C.: CQ Inc., 1994).

representative from Michigan. When Nixon resigned from the presidency in 1974, Ford became the new president and chose Nelson A. Rockefeller to be his vice president. In 1985 President Ronald Reagan informed Congress that he would need to undergo surgery and be unable to carry out his presidential duties. As a result, Vice President George H.W. Bush served as acting president for about eight hours.

The Judicial Branch—Equal Justice for All

In the 1940s, the Supreme Court upheld an act of Congress that allowed the relocation of thousands of Japanese Americans to internment camps. The Supreme Court claimed such camps were constitutional. Later the United States government would acknowledge the injustice of the camps and apologize. Shortly after the Court made its decision in the *Ex parte Endo* case, many detained Japanese Americans were released and returned home.

Federal courts, like the Supreme Court, make up the third branch of the U.S. government. Courts use the law to settle civil disputes and to decide on the guilt or innocence of people accused of crimes.

In 1942 the government dismissed Mitsuye Endo from her civil service job in California and ordered her to a relocation center. Although Endo was a U.S. citizen with a brother serving in the U.S. Army, she and other Japanese Americans were forced into relocation camps during World War II because the government questioned their loyalty. Endo took the matter to the Supreme Court and won her case. The Court ruled that Endo "should be given her liberty." Justice William O. Douglas proclaimed that "loyalty is a matter of the heart and mind, not of race, creed or color. . . ."

Japanese Americans were locked up in internment camps during World War II.

Whether a civil dispute is between two private parties (people, companies, or organizations), between a private party and the government, or between the United States and a state or local government, both sides come before a court. Each side presents its position. The court then applies the law to the facts that have been presented and makes a decision in favor of one or the other. The courts also hold criminal trials in which witnesses present evidence and a jury or a judge delivers a verdict.

The United States Supreme Court is at the top of the federal court system. If you visit the Supreme Court, you will see the words "Equal Justice Under Law" on the face of its marble building. Our legal system is based on this important ideal. The goal of the legal system is to treat every person the same. Under the Constitution, every person accused of breaking the law has the right to have a public trial and a lawyer. If an accused person cannot afford a lawyer, the court will appoint and pay for one. Each person is considered innocent until proven guilty. Each person also has the right to ask for a review of his or her case if, in that person's view, the courts have made a mistake.

The ideal of equal justice is difficult to achieve. Judges and juries are not free from personal prejudices or the prejudices of their communities. Poor people do not have the money to spend on the best available legal help, unlike wealthy citizens and large companies. Nonetheless, American courts try to uphold the ideal of equal justice.

The Federal Court System

The Founders created the federal court system in Article III of the Constitution. This article established a national Supreme Court. It also gave Congress the power to establish lower federal courts.

Federal Judicial Circuits and Districts

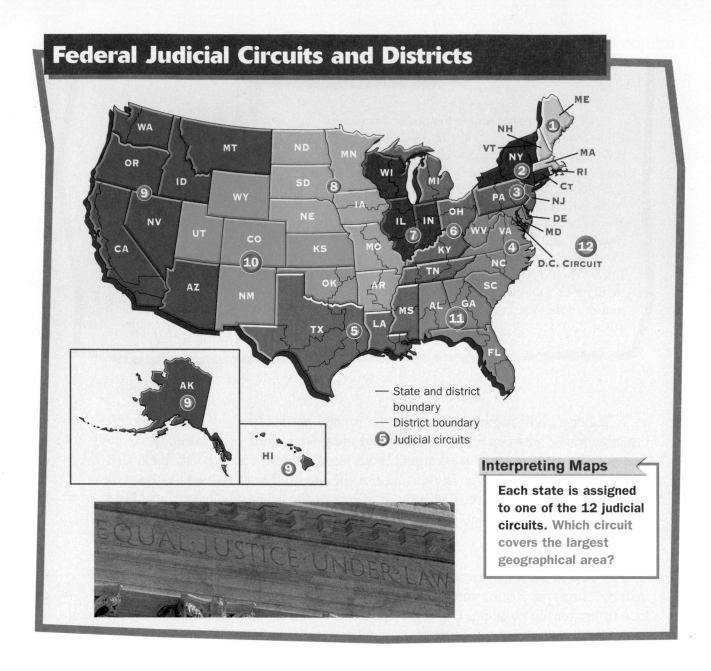

— State and district boundary

— District boundary

⑤ Judicial circuits

Interpreting Maps

Each state is assigned to one of the 12 judicial circuits. Which circuit covers the largest geographical area?

EQUAL JUSTICE UNDER LAW

Over the years, Congress has created two kinds of lower courts. In 1789 it passed the Judiciary Act, which established federal district courts and circuit courts of appeals. Much later, in 1891, Congress created a system of federal appeals courts. Thus, the federal court system has three levels—the district courts at the bottom, the appeals courts in the middle, and the Supreme Court at the top.

Our federal court system exists alongside 50 separate state court systems. Each state has its own laws and courts. The state courts get their powers from state constitutions and laws.

Cases Heard in Federal Courts

Jurisdiction: Jurisdiction is *a court's authority to hear and decide cases.* Article III of the Constitution gives the federal courts jurisdiction over eight kinds of cases.

Cases Involving the Constitution: If the law in question applies to the U.S. Constitution, the case must be heard in a federal court. For example, if a person believes a constitutional right, such as freedom of speech, has been violated, that person has a right to be heard in a federal court.

Violations of Federal Laws: If the government accuses a person of a federal crime—for example, kidnapping, tax evasion, or counterfeiting—a federal court has jurisdiction. Disputes regarding the issues over which the Constitution gives the federal government control, such as patent rights or bankruptcy, also go to a federal court.

Controversies between States: Disagreements between state governments are resolved in federal courts. If Colorado and California, for example, disagree over rights to water in the Colorado River, it is a federal case.

Disputes between Parties from Different States: Lawsuits between citizens of different states also come under the federal courts. For example, Ms. Jones of Maine may bring suit in a federal court against Mr. Smith of Iowa for not fulfilling his part of a business agreement.

FIGURE 6–26.

This U.S. Secret Service agent displays counterfeit Federal Reserve bonds. More than $2 trillion worth of fake bonds were seized in the Philippines in this incident in 2001.

Suits Involving the Federal Government: The U.S. government may sue someone. For example, the Defense Department might sue a company that contracted to build missile parts but did not complete the work on time. The suit would be heard in a federal court. Also, private parties can sue the government. For example, if a mail truck hit you, you could sue the U.S. Postal Service for damages; or if the Department of Agriculture failed to pay your company for equipment it ordered, you could sue for your money.

Cases Involving Foreign Governments and Treaties: Any dispute between a foreign government and either the U.S. government or an American private party is heard in a federal court. A treaty case might involve a dispute over the way the State Department interpreted a trade agreement.

Cases Based on Admiralty and Maritime Laws: These laws concern accidents or crimes on the high seas. One recent case involved a dispute over the rights to millions of dollars in sunken treasure recovered from a shipwreck 160 miles off the coast of South Carolina.

Cases Involving U.S. Diplomats: If, for example, an American diplomat working in the U.S. embassy in France is accused of breaking an American law, the case would go to a federal court.

Relation to State Courts

For most of the areas just described, federal courts have **exclusive jurisdiction**, which means that *only these courts may hear and decide such cases.* State courts have jurisdiction over all other matters. Most U.S. court cases involve state law and are tried in state courts.

In a few circumstances, however, a case can be heard in either a state or a federal court. In these instances, the state and federal courts have **concurrent jurisdiction**, meaning that *they share jurisdiction.* Either court may try crimes that violate both state and federal law. Concurrent jurisdiction also applies when citizens of different states are involved in a dispute concerning at least $50,000. In such a case, a person may sue in either a federal court or a state court. If the person being sued insists, however, the case must be tried in a federal court. Such appeals might eventually reach the United States Supreme Court.

U.S. District Courts

The federal court system can be illustrated as a pyramid. The Supreme Court sits alone above a number of appeals courts, and has a broad base of district courts.

Most federal cases are handled in the 94 U.S. district courts. **District courts** are *the federal courts where trials are held and lawsuits are begun.* Every state has at least one district court, and some states have two, three, or four. All federal cases must begin in a district court, because district courts have **original jurisdiction**, *the authority to hear cases for the first time.* District courts are responsible for

AMERICANS IN ACTION

The Ninth U.S. Circuit
Court of Appeals

Mary M. Schroeder used to be a judge for the Arizona Court of Appeals in Phoenix. Now she's the chief judge of the United States Court of Appeals for the Ninth Circuit. She is the first woman to serve in this post in the Ninth Circuit. This, the largest circuit, comprises the seven westernmost continental states, plus Alaska, Hawaii, and the islands of Guam and the Northern Marianas. Schroeder has come a long way from the days in the 1960s, when she was one of just six women in her law school class. Her role, and that of other female judges, says Schroeder, is "not to feminize the courts but to humanize them."

determining the facts of a case; they are the trial courts for both criminal and civil federal cases. Thus, in a criminal case, a district court will decide if a person is guilty or innocent based on the evidence presented. District courts are the only federal courts in which witnesses testify and juries hear cases and reach verdicts.

U.S. Courts of Appeals

A large percentage of people who lose their cases in a district court appeal to the next highest level—a U.S. court of appeals. These courts are also referred to as federal appeals courts, circuit courts of appeals, or appellate courts.

The job of the **appeals courts** is to *review decisions made in lower district courts.* This is referred to as **appellate jurisdiction**, or *the authority of a court to hear a case appealed from a lower court.* Lawyers usually appeal when they think the judge in their case applied the law incorrectly, used the wrong procedures, or if new evidence turns up. Appeals courts may also review federal regulatory agency rulings, if the people or groups involved believe the agency acted unfairly.

There are 12 United States courts of appeals. *Each one covers a particular geographic area called a* **circuit**. In addition, a thirteenth appeals court, the Court of Appeals for the Federal Circuit, has nationwide jurisdiction to hear special cases, such as those involving patent law or international trade.

Making a Decision

Appeals courts do not hold trials. Instead, these courts may decide an appeal in one of three ways: uphold the original decision, reverse that decision, or remand the case. To **remand** a case means to *send the case back to the lower court to be tried again.* A panel of three or more judges reviews the record of the case being appealed and listens to arguments from lawyers for each side. The judges then meet and make a decision by majority vote.

The judges do not decide the guilt or innocence of a defendant in a criminal case or which side should win in a civil lawsuit. They rule only on whether the defendant's rights have been protected and on whether he or she received a fair trial. In the majority of cases, the decision of the appeals court is final. In some cases, however, lawyers may appeal the decision to the U.S. Supreme Court.

Announcing the Decision

When an appeals court makes a decision, one judge writes an opinion for the court. The **opinion** offers *a detailed explanation of the legal thinking behind the court's decision.* The opinion sets a precedent for all courts and agencies within the district. A **precedent** gives guidance to other judges by offering *a model upon which to base their own decisions on similar cases.* A precedent does not have the force of law, but it is a very powerful argument to use in court. Judges and courts follow precedents in nearly all cases.

Federal Judges

The chief decision makers in the judicial branch are the federal judges. There are more than 550 judges who preside over the district courts. Each district court has at least two judges. Some district courts in high-population areas have more judges because there are more cases to hear. Each appeals court has from 6 to 27 judges. The Supreme Court has 9 justices.

Selection and Tenure of Judges

According to the U.S. Constitution, the president appoints judges, with the approval of the Senate. The Constitution sets forth no particular qualifications for federal judges. Presidents want to appoint judges who share their ideas about politics and justice. Thus, they usually choose people who belong to their political party. Because judges are appointed for life, presidents view their judicial appointments as an opportunity to affect the country after they have left the White House.

When naming judges, presidents usually follow a practice called senatorial courtesy. Under this system, a president submits the name of a candidate for judicial

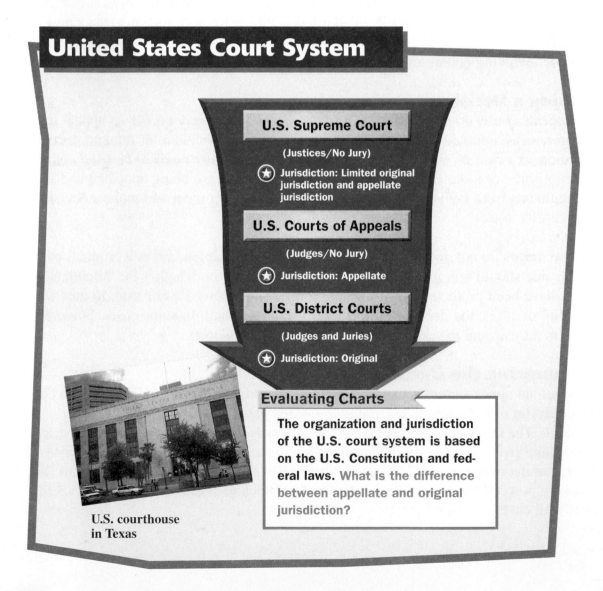

United States Court System

U.S. Supreme Court

(Justices/No Jury)

★ Jurisdiction: Limited original jurisdiction and appellate jurisdiction

U.S. Courts of Appeals

(Judges/No Jury)

★ Jurisdiction: Appellate

U.S. District Courts

(Judges and Juries)

★ Jurisdiction: Original

U.S. courthouse in Texas

Evaluating Charts

The organization and jurisdiction of the U.S. court system is based on the U.S. Constitution and federal laws. What is the difference between appellate and original jurisdiction?

appointment to the senators from the candidate's state before formally submitting it to the entire Senate for approval. If either or both senators object to the candidate, the president will usually withdraw the name and nominate another candidate. The practice of senatorial courtesy usually applies only to the selection of judges to the district courts and other trial courts, not to the selection of judges to courts of appeals or the Supreme Court.

Once appointed, federal judges may have their jobs for life. A judge can be removed from office only through the process of impeachment. The writers of the Constitution gave federal judges this sort of job security because they wanted judges to be able to decide cases free from public or political pressures. Federal judges know that their jobs are safe even if they make unpopular decisions.

Other Court Officials

Judges do not work alone. They have help from clerks, secretaries, court reporters, probation officers, and other workers.

Each district court has magistrate judges. These officials take care of much of a judge's routine work. They issue court orders, like search and arrest warrants in federal cases. They hear preliminary evidence in a case to determine whether the case should be brought to trial. They also decide whether people who have been arrested should be held in jail or released on bail. Magistrates may also hear minor cases.

Every federal judicial district also has a United States attorney and one or more deputies. The U.S. attorneys are government lawyers who prosecute people accused of breaking federal laws. They look into complaints of crime, prepare formal charges, and then present evidence in court. It is the U.S. attorney's job to represent the United States in civil cases in which the government is involved. U.S. attorneys are appointed

AMERICANS IN ACTION

Stephen G. Breyer received President Bill Clinton's Supreme Court nomination on May 14, 1994. The Senate confirmed Breyer with an 87–9 vote. Breyer has summarized his view of the Court's role in the following way: "It is important that the public, trying to cope with the problems of the nation, state, and local community, understand that the Constitution does not resolve, and was not intended to resolve, society's problems. Rather, the Constitution provides a framework for the creation of democratically determined solutions, which protect each individual's basic liberties . . . while securing a democratic form of government. We judges cannot insist that Americans participate in that government, but we can make clear that our Constitution depends upon it."

Justice Breyer

to four-year terms by the president, with consent of the Senate. They report to the attorney general of the United States, who is the head of the Justice Department.

Each federal judicial district also has a United States marshal. Marshals and their staffs make arrests, collect fines, and take convicted persons to prison. They protect jurors, keep order in federal courts, and serve legal papers, including subpoenas. A subpoena is a court order requiring someone to appear in court. Marshals work for the Department of Justice. The president appoints U.S. marshals with Senate approval.

The Supreme Court Justices

The Supreme Court exerts its influence all across the United States. The Court stands above all other courts. Its main job is to decide whether laws are allowable under the U.S. Constitution.

The Supreme Court has original jurisdiction in only two instances. It can preside over trials in cases that involve diplomats from foreign countries and in cases in which a state is involved. In all other instances, the Supreme Court hears cases that have come on appeal from lower district courts or from federal regulatory agencies. The Supreme Court is not required to hear all the cases presented to it. It carefully chooses the cases it hears. It has final authority in any case involving the Constitution, acts of Congress, and treaties with other nations. The decisions of the Court are binding on all lower courts. When the Court refuses to review a case, the decision of the lower court remains unchanged.

The Supreme Court is made of eight associate justices led by a chief justice. Congress sets this number and has the power to change it. The justices are important political decision makers.

FIGURE 6–27.

Since 1869 there have been nine justices on the Supreme Court.

Their rulings often affect citizens as much as do presidential or congressional decisions.

The main duty of justices is to hear and rule on cases. They choose which cases to hear from among the thousands appealed to the Court each year, then decide the case itself and issue a written explanation for the decision, called the Court's opinion. The chief justice has additional duties, such as presiding over sessions and conferences at which cases are discussed.

Selection of Justices

The president appoints Supreme Court justices, with the consent of the Senate. Presidents are careful to choose nominees who are likely to be approved by the Senate. When selecting nominees, the president often gets help from the attorney general and other Justice Department officials. The president's decision may also be influenced by the American Bar Association, the largest national organization of attorneys; interest groups, such as labor and civil rights groups; and other Supreme Court justices, who may recommend or support certain candidates. Senators have usually felt that the president should have a fairly free hand in appointing new justices. Throughout history, though, the Senate has rejected many presidential nominees to the Supreme Court because of doubts about the qualifications or the legal philosophy of the persons nominated.

Background of the Justices

Supreme Court justices are always lawyers. They have had successful careers practicing or teaching law, serving as judges in lower courts, or holding other public positions prior to appointment.

Political support and agreement with the president's ideas are important factors in who gets appointed. Of course, once appointed, a justice may make rulings that the president does not like.

The first African American justice, Thurgood Marshall, joined the Court in 1967. The first female justice, Sandra Day O'Connor, was appointed in 1981.

CHECKPOINTS

Lesson 5 Review

1. Write sentences or short paragraphs in which you use the following terms: *bicameral, census, constituent, gerrymander, majority party, minority party, standing committee, seniority.*

2. How many members does the Senate have? How does the U.S. Constitution provide for stability and continuity in the Senate?

3. Why is so much of the business of Congress conducted in committees? How are senators and representatives assigned to committees?

4. Do you think that the seniority system in Congress is an effective way to select leaders and assign committee members? Why or why not?

5. Use the following terms in sentences that relate to the lawmaking process: *joint resolution, special-interest group, rider, filibuster, cloture, voice vote, roll-call vote, veto, pocket veto.*

6. What is the difference between public and private bills? What are resolutions?

7. Describe what can happen to a bill once it passes Congress and reaches the president's desk.

8. Why do you think members of the House of Representatives consider assignment to the Rules Committee an important appointment?

9. Write complete sentences about the United States presidency using each of the following terms: *Electoral College, elector.*

10. What three qualifications for the U.S. presidency are listed in the Constitution of the United States?

11. What are the constitutional duties of the vice president of the United States?

12. What did John Adams mean by saying, "I may become everything"?

13. Define *jurisdiction.* Then explain the difference between *exclusive* and *concurrent jurisdiction.*

14. Name the three levels of federal courts. What is the relationship between the federal district court system and the state court system?

15. Define what is meant by the words that are inscribed on the United States Supreme Court building: "Equal Justice Under Law."

16. Why do you think Congress established federal appeals courts in 1891?

17. Use the following terms in sentences: *district courts, original jurisdiction, appeals courts, appellate jurisdiction.*

18. What takes place in federal district courts that does not happen in federal appeals courts or in the Supreme Court?

19. Explain the three rulings that are possible in a U.S. court of appeals case.

20. Do you agree with the practice of appointing federal judges for life? Explain your answer.

Applying Citizenship Skills

21. Choose a representative from your state. Check the House or Senate Web site (www.house.gov or www.senate.gov) to find out on what committees that person serves. Write a letter to that person about an issue related to that committee.

22. Review what you have learned about the characteristics of the two houses of Congress. Create a chart that compares and contrasts the basic characteristics of each body.

Comparing Systems of Government

Like snowflakes, no two governments are exactly alike. Each country is unique, shaped by its history, culture, political interests, and economic needs. Yet, for thousands of years, people have been studying and classifying governments.

Aristotle, for example, was a scholar who lived in ancient Greece. He identified three types of government: rule by a single person; rule by a small, elite group; and rule by the people. Many scholars prefer to describe governments by using two broad categories on a spectrum: those that are democratic (on one end of the spectrum) and those that are authoritarian (on the other end of the spectrum). In democratic regimes, as you know, the people rule. In **authoritarian** regimes, *power is held by an individual or group not accountable to the people.*

Winston Churchill, Great Britain's leader during World War II, said that "no one pretends that democracy is perfect or all-wise." Yet most people who live in democratic countries—and many who don't—would agree that democracy beats the alternatives.

Authoritarian Governments

Non-democratic (authoritarian) governments take various forms. What they all have in common is that only a few people wield power, giving ordinary citizens little voice in government.

Absolute Monarchy

The word *monarchy* describes a government with a hereditary ruler—a king or queen (or czar, empress, sultan, or other royal figure) who inherits this position of power. Until about the 1600s, such rulers were mostly **absolute monarchs**. That is, *they had unlimited authority to rule as they wished.*

Many countries still have monarchs, but absolute monarchy is almost nonexistent. In the Middle East, however, the king of Saudi

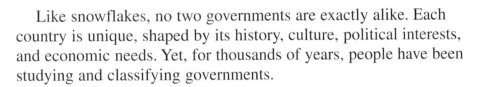

Quick Write

List some facts you know about the governments of the United States and China. Why do you think there are different forms of government?

LEARN ABOUT...

- authoritarian governments, including monarchies, dictatorships, and totalitarianism.
- the People's Republic of China.
- communism in Cuba.
- the Islamic Republic of Iran.
- the Republic of Iraq.
- the Democratic People's Republic of Korea.
- Russia and the collapse of Soviet communism.
- democratic governments and the presidential versus parliamentary systems.

Arabia and the emir of Qatar might still be considered "absolute." Their power is technically unrestricted, although they do consult with advisers and are constrained by Islamic law.

VOCABULARY

- authoritarian
- absolute monarch
- dictator
- totalitarian
- cadre
- shah
- faqih
- gross national product
- state farms
- collective farm
- coup
- constitutional monarchy
- parliamentary system
- prime minister

Dictatorships

Dictators, like absolute monarchs, *exercise complete control over the state.* They usually take power by force, although sometimes, when a crisis situation demands a strong leader, authorities may place them in charge. To stay in power, most dictators rely on the police and military. They often tamper with elections or refuse to hold them. They also limit freedom of speech, assembly, and the press.

Scores of dictators have ruled throughout history. Those who only seek personal gain are often overthrown quickly. The ruler of Uganda, Idi Amin, was deposed (removed from power) in 1979. His brutal regime led to hundreds of thousands of deaths and plunged the country into chaos and poverty. With the help of the United States, the dictator of Panama, Manuel Noriega, was deposed in 1989.

Others endure for decades. Fidel Castro has been in power in Cuba since 1959. Libya's leader, Muammar al-Qaddhafi, has governed as a military dictator since 1969.

Totalitarianism

Many dictators impose totalitarian rule on their people. In a **totalitarian** state, *the government's control extends to almost all aspects of people's lives.* Totalitarian

AMERICANS IN ACTION

As a teenager in World War II in Italy, Ginetta Sagan joined the underground resistance movement. During the war, the young girl helped publish an underground paper and carried information to the Allies in Switzerland. She escorted hundreds of fugitives—Jews, antifascists, soldiers who deserted, and many others—across a barbed wire fence that separated Italy from Switzerland. Ginetta immigrated to the United States in 1951 and over time helped found Amnesty International USA. Ginetta also worked to abolish torture practices in foreign prisons. For her efforts on behalf of the oppressed, she received the Presidential Medal of Freedom, the nation's highest civilian award.

Ginetta Sagan, proponent of amnesty and prisoners' rights

leaders typically have a master plan for the economy and society. They ban political opposition. They regulate what industries and farms produce. They suppress individual freedom, dictating what people should believe and with whom they may associate. To enforce their ideology, totalitarian leaders control the media and use propaganda, scare tactics, and violence.

Three of the most notorious totalitarian regimes arose in the 1920s and 1930s. They were: Nazi Germany under Adolf Hitler; Fascist Italy under Benito Mussolini; and the Soviet Union under Joseph Stalin. Today, China, Cuba, and North Korea are usually considered totalitarian states.

The People's Republic of China

In a speech delivered to the Russian parliament, Boris Yeltsin said that the socialist experiment had left the people of the former Soviet Union at the "tail end of world civilization." Even as Russian leaders acknowledged the triumph of market economies and political democracy, Chinese Communists held fast to their control of China's government. However, they did initiate some economic reforms that opened certain areas of the rigidly controlled economy to free enterprise. In 1989 the Chinese Communist leadership suppressed a growing pro-democracy movement, but continued the current economic reforms.

China's Political Background

After China became a republic in 1912, rival factions divided the country. In 1927 the Nationalist Party, under the leadership of Chiang Kaishek, defeated the Communists and gained partial control of the nation. When Japan invaded China in the 1930s, the Nationalists and Communists came together to defend their country. After Japan's defeat in World War II, a civil war broke out between the two rival parties.

In 1949 Communist revolutionaries led by Mao Zedong seized power in the China, the world's most heavily populated nation. The Nationalists fled to safety on the offshore island of Taiwan, where they remain today.

As a guide to establishing a Communist economy and government, the People's Republic of China turned to the Soviet Union:

> We must learn . . . from the advanced experience of the Soviet Union. The Soviet Union has been building socialism for forty years, and its experience is very valuable to us. . . . Now there are two different attitudes towards learning from others. One is the dogmatic attitude of transplanting everything, whether or not it is suited to our conditions. . . . The other attitude is to use our heads and learn those things which suit our conditions, that is to absorb whatever experience is useful to us. That is the attitude we should adopt.
>
> —Mao Zedong, 1957

Following the Soviet Union's example, the Chinese leaders proceeded to establish a totalitarian government strictly controlled by the Chinese Communist Party (CCP), in much the same way that the Soviet Communist Party once controlled the Soviet Union.

Communist Party Government

Despite upheavals in Eastern Europe and the former Soviet Union, in the People's Republic of China the CCP and its leaders remain firmly in control of the government. Although the CCP is not an official organ of the government, it determines governmental policies and ensures that the government carries out the party's policies and decisions. At every level, officials referred to as cadre hold key posts. A **cadre** is *a core group of trained people who can take control when necessary and train others*. Most of these officials are party members, even though only about 4 percent of the Chinese people belong to the Communist Party.

In 1982, China adopted two new constitutions, one for the party and another for the national government. Under its new constitution, theoretically at least, the Communist Party's highest governing body is the National Party Congress, composed of between 1,500 and 2,000 delegates. Members of party organizations across the nation select these delegates. In practice, however, the National Party Congress merely serves as a rubber stamp for policies of the party's leaders.

The National Party Congress does, however, elect the party's Central Committee, which serves in place of the Congress when it is not in session. The number of members of the Central Committee runs between 200 and 300 full and alternate members. Its major responsibility is to elect the members of the party's Political Bureau—the Politburo. The Politburo usually is composed of about 20 top party leaders.

FIGURE 6–28.

Red Guards, or young radical Communists, honored Mao Zedong in the 1960s.

The Politburo's Standing Committee, which functions when the full Politburo is not meeting, is even more elitist and is composed of the top six CCP leaders. The Politburo's Standing Committee appoints members of the Secretariat. The Secretariat then implements party policies by supervising the daily activities of the party. In addition, the CCP has various other organizations that carry out special functions under the direction of the Secretariat.

At the top of the CCP, and probably the most powerful party leader, is the General Secretary, who may or may not be a prominent government official as well. Many members of the Politburo hold top government posts. Politburo member Jiang Zemin, for example, also serves as China's president. From the late 1970s to the 1990s, however, the unquestioned leader of China was Deng Xiaoping, who held no official government or party position. Leadership in China often may rest upon background rather than upon position.

China's National Government

The People's Republic of China operates under a constitution adopted in 1982. The new constitution is designed to enable China to achieve a stable and relatively advanced industrialized nation by the end of the century. The 1982 constitution calls the Chinese Communist Party the "core of the leadership of the whole Chinese people," while it describes the nation as "led by the Communist Party." It adds, "The Chinese people will continue to uphold the people's democratic dictatorship and socialist road."

Established by the constitution, the National People's Congress (NPC) is identified as "the highest organ of state power." In theory, legislative power in China rests with the NPC and its Standing Committee that serves when the NPC is not in formal session. The Chinese NPC and its Standing Committee, however, have little independent legislative power. A large number of the leaders of the Standing Committee do hold important leadership posts in the Communist Party, which actually decides on the government's actions and policies. The NPC serves as a symbol of citizen participation in the nation's government when it selects the country's ceremonial president and vice president and the premier who actually presides over the body called the State Council.

In China the State Council carries out the same functions that a cabinet or council of ministers carries out in other nations. Although the State Council is supposed to be responsible to the National People's Congress and its Standing Committee, it answers in fact to the CCP's Politburo. Most of the leaders in the State Council also hold high posts in the CCP.

The State Council, which meets about once a month, operates as the executive branch of the government. It makes decisions, prepares legislation for the National People's Congress, determines the nation's budget, and ensures the Communist Party's policies are followed. The State Council's Standing Committee, headed by the premier, carries out most of these functions, however.

Political Parties

Although the Chinese Communist Party dominates the government in China, it permits eight minority parties to exist. These are largely made up of intellectuals or people from China's middle class—a term that often also includes students. These parties are expected to work under the leadership of the CCP. An opposition party—

the Federation for a Democratic China (FDC)—was formed in Paris following the Chinese government's massacre of protesters at Tiananmen Square in Beijing, China, in 1989.

Tiananmen Square

Historically, the Chinese Communist Party has tolerated little opposition. In April 1989 resentment against low pay for professional workers, restrictions on students studying abroad, and growing inflation brought thousands of demonstrators to Tiananmen Square. One student said the demonstrations were "for democracy, for freedom." Soon, protesters began a hunger strike in the square. Coming at the time of Soviet leader Mikhail Gorbachev's visit to China, the protest embarrassed China's leaders.

On May 20 Premier Li Peng sent unarmed troops to clear the square. When that failed, armed troops moved in. On June 3, 1989, they began firing on demonstrators. On the following day news of the Tiananmen Square massacre shocked the world. Government and civilian estimates of death differ, with nationally published sources citing that the number of casualties may have been several hundred to thousands. An eyewitness, upon visiting one hospital, described the tragedy:

> *The doctors were crying, and took me to the morgue. They didn't have enough drawers for the bodies, so they had to stack them. All of the victims were young men, all of them were bare-chested, and none of them had any shoes. Many had writing on their chests and were wearing headbands. They were just piled up in there, halfway to the ceiling.*
>
> *—Margaret Herbst, 1989*

Since the massacre at Tiananmen Square, the Chinese government has imposed strict controls on the nation's younger generation.

Communism in Cuba

Fidel Castro led Cubans in a revolt that ousted dictator Fulgencio Batista in January 1959. When Castro promised democratic reforms, he did not mean holding elections. He did begin a program to redistribute ownership of land and nationalize industries. This angered Americans who lost property they owned in Cuba. When the United States cut off sugar imports from Cuba, Castro turned to the Soviet Union for help.

Communist Dictatorship

Under Fidel Castro Cuba became a Communist dictatorship. He supported revolutionary movements in Latin America and Africa while maintaining strict control over Cuba's political and economic institutions. Tensions and disagreement between Cuba and the United States led to two crises. In 1961 anti-Castro exiles, trained by the United States, invaded Cuba at the Bay of Pigs. The failed invasion left Castro in power and embarrassed the United States. One year later the United States discovered that Soviet missiles were being installed in Cuba. Tense negotiations with the Soviet

Appeals for Democracy

Present Demonstrators carry a banner depicting the Goddess of Democracy during a march through a Hong Kong street in 1997. The demonstrators were honoring those killed in the massacre at Tiananmen Square.

Past A student leader on a hunger strike borrows a phrase from the American Revolution as he addresses his comrades in Tiananmen Square.

The Power of Protest *What message about popular protest did the Chinese government send its citizens in 1989?*

Union brought the crisis to an end, but U.S.-Cuban relations were strictly limited after this event that had nearly brought the world to the brink of nuclear war.

Economic Crisis

The end of the Cold War left Cuba isolated in the early 1990s. The loss of Soviet aid and low prices for sugar exports caused a deep economic crisis. The United States maintained its trade embargo against Cuba, hoping that Fidel Castro would agree to a greater respect for human rights and move to a democratic system in exchange for better relations and economic aid. To put pressure on Castro, the United States Congress passed and President Clinton signed the Cuban Democracy Act in 1992. However, the administration believed that this law failed to move Castro toward democratic reforms.

Cuba's Future

In 1993 Cuba held its first popular elections to the National Assembly. There was only one candidate for each seat, however. Fidel Castro has been remarkably capable of controlling his people for four decades. Will democracy ever come to Cuba?

Islamic Republic of Iran

The Middle Eastern nation of Iran built a capitalistic economy based on oil revenues in the 1960s and 1970s. A major military power, Iran was controlled by a **shah**, or *king,* Mohammed Reza Pahlavi, who strengthened economic ties to Western nations. Muslim religious leaders resented the shah's Western values and sought a return to Muslim traditions. However, the shah's secret police helped silence all dissent for many years.

Islamic Revolt

Muslims who opposed the shah rallied around Ayatollah Ruhollah Khomeini, a Shiite Muslim leader living in exile in France. In early 1979 massive demonstrations forced the shah to flee to the United States. Khomeini returned from France to form a government according to Islamic principles. Iran soon demanded that the United States return the shah to stand trial. When the United States refused and the shah took refuge in Egypt, anti-American sentiment heightened in Iran. In November 1979 Iranians stormed the U.S. Embassy, took American diplomats hostage, and held them for more than a year.

Institutions of Government

The establishment of the Islamic Republic of Iran began a process of increasing state power. Khomeini and his Islamic followers established a regime in which Iran's religious leaders had the veto power over the actions of political leaders. The state used perceived and real threats from Iraq and America's trade embargo to consolidate power. Since the death of Khomeini in 1989, the government has centralized functions in the **faqih** *(the top religious-political leader),* the presidency, and the judiciary. The office of prime minister was eliminated, and its power was transferred to the president.

Republic of Iraq

Beginning with its emergence as a national state in 1921, Iraq has been ruled by strong military leaders. The most powerful dictator was Saddam Hussein, who ruled the country from 1979 to 2003. He ruled through shrewd politics and the ruthless destruction of any opposition.

In 1980 Hussein kept Shiite Muslims from gaining influence in Iraq by invading Iran. The eight-year war killed about 1 million people in the two countries. Hussein invaded neighboring Kuwait in 1990. He did this to try to boost oil reserves and shift the blame for Iraq's deteriorating economy. When Iraqi troops headed toward the border of Saudi Arabia, the Saudis asked the United States for protection. The Persian Gulf War broke out between Iraq and coalition forces from seven nations in January 1991. After his forces set fire to several oil fields, Hussein quickly withdrew them from Kuwait. Defeated in war, he focused on crushing opposition within Iraq and rebuilding his military strength.

After the Persian Gulf War, the United Nations (UN) required Iraq to disclose and destroy all of its chemical and biological weapons. The UN also imposed economic sanctions on Iraq to force compliance. The sanctions placed severe economic hardships on Iraq and threatened to weaken Hussein's hold on the country. Hussein tried to break the sanctions by capitalizing on the differences among UN Security Council members. In 1997, Iraq refused to allow UN teams that included Americans to inspect its weapons plants. Under intense international pressure, the Iraqis backed down, but doubts remained about Hussein's willingness to cooperate with the UN.

U.S. troops invaded Iraq in March 2003 to help free the country from Hussein's dictatorship. Saddam Hussein was overthrown and later captured. The Iraqi government went through a transitional phase, then held democratic elections. On April 7, 2005, Shiite Arab Ibrahim al-Jaafari was sworn in as interim prime minister, the country's most powerful position. Kurdish leader Jalal Talabani was also sworn in as Iraq's new interim president. This gave Iraq its first freely elected government in 50 years. The new government's first task was to draft a permanent constitution for Iraq to help pave the way for permanent elections in the future.

Democratic People's Republic of Korea

After the end of World War II, the Korean peninsula was divided into two zones, with the 38th parallel marking the separation between the zones. North Korea was controlled by the Soviets, while South Korea was in the U.S. charge. The Democratic People's Republic of Korea (North Korea) was established on May 1, 1948.

The government of North Korea is Communist, with a one-man dictatorship. It was headed by Kim Il Sung until his death in 1994. His son, Kim Jong Il, inherited his position as head of the government after his father's death. He was officially named General Secretary of the Korean Workers' Party in October 1997. After the death of Kim Il Sung, the title of President was abolished in honor of his leadership. At that time, the position of Chairman of the National Defense Commission (NDC) became the "highest official of state." Kim Jong Il was appointed chairman of the NDC in 1998.

During his rule, the country's economy has declined, and a widespread famine took place in the late 1990s. The country remains one of the most isolated places in the world, with restrictions on travel to and from the country and no free press.

In the 1990s, concern about North Korea's nuclear weapons program began to arise. In January 2002, President Bush described North Korea as part of an "axis of evil," grouping it with Iraq and Iran.

In December 2003, North Korea expelled United Nations weapons inspectors from the country. In February 2005, North Korea admitted that it possessed nuclear weapons, but said it would not engage in further disarmament talks.

Russia and the Collapse of Soviet Communism

Beginning in 1922, the Soviet Union built the world's leading communist economic system, calling itself a socialist economy. The Soviet Union saw its socialism as an intermediate stage in the transformation from capitalism to pure communism.

A major difference between noncommunist socialist systems and the Soviet economy was that an authoritarian political party—the Communist Party—closely controlled the Soviet economy. In the Soviet Union the government, meaning in actual practice the Communist Party, made nearly all of the economic decisions. With few exceptions, all enterprises were state owned and operated. The Soviet government also controlled labor unions, wages, and prices.

Soviet Economic Problems

The Soviet Union built one of the world's largest economies and came to rival the United States as a superpower. Its defense industries were strong, yet the rest of the Soviet economy faced very serious problems.

Beginning in the mid-1980s, the Soviet **gross national product** (GNP), *the sum of all the nation's goods and services,* grew by only 2 or 3 percent a year. Development of heavy industry slowed. Soviet products could not compete in world markets. The huge, oppressive state bureaucracy that managed every detail of Soviet production bred economic stagnation.

COVER STORY

Russian Economy Stumbles

MOSCOW, RUSSIA, JULY 14, 2001

Adjustment from a government-controlled economy to a combination of socialism and capitalism has left many Russians in various stages of economic desperation. Over 80 percent of the population makes less than $70 a month. In buying power, the Russian ruble has lost about 18 percent since 1999. Even when they have the money, the average Russian often finds consumer products, including daily necessities, unavailable.

Signs of progress, however, are beginning to show. Industrial output has grown almost 8 percent in the last two years, unemployment has fallen by 11 percent, and inflation is down by almost 57 percent.

Workers face hardships

Soviet central planning created five main problems. First, it encouraged producers to meet targets with goods that were easy to produce rather than with goods that were the most needed. Second, the system failed to produce badly needed consumer goods and services. Third, the quality of goods suffered. Fourth, the system discouraged new ideas. Finally, farming became unproductive.

Few Consumer Goods and Services

Central planning directed most Soviet resources into heavy industry and military hardware. In an era that stressed consumer goods, the Soviet economy was not able to deliver the goods and services consumers needed. Items such as potatoes, onions, toothpaste, well-made clothing, coffee, and sugar were hard to find in state stores. People had money, but there was little or nothing to buy.

To meet their production targets, factory managers often turned out those goods that were easiest to produce. For example, a factory that made nails was told to produce 100 tons of nails. The factory manager produced large nails because fewer such nails were needed to reach the 100-ton target. Builders and carpenters in another part of the economy, however, really needed small nails.

Little Concern for Quality

Economic planners made few provisions for quality. Instead, they focused on quantity. As a result, the quality of goods produced suffered because the Soviets had, in effect, created a system that valued the production of 100 clunking, low-quality tractors more highly than the production of 10 smoothly running ones. Consumer goods in the Soviet Union acquired a reputation for shoddiness.

Resistance to New Ideas

Hard-pressed Soviet plant managers trying to meet production targets often resisted efforts to install new machines or new methods. The managers believed interruption would slow down production and cause them to miss their production quotas.

Unproductive Agriculture

About 98 percent of all Soviet farmland was under government control. As a result, farming, like industry, had to follow government production plans. About two-thirds of Soviet farmland consisted of state farms. **State farms** were *owned by the government and run like factories,* with the farm workers being paid wages. The remaining one-third of Soviet farmland consisted of collective farms. On a **collective farm**, *the government owned the land but rented it to families.*

Farm workers had little incentive to work hard on vast state-run farms. Inefficiency was widespread. For example, 20 percent of the grain and fruit harvest and 50 percent of the potato crop were wasted each year because of either late harvesting or inadequate storage facilities.

The Breakup of the Soviet Union

The last communist leader of the Soviet Union, Mikhail Gorbachev, came to power in 1985. He tried to reform the communist state by persuading Soviet officials to adopt hundreds of new economic policies aimed at stimulating the faltering Soviet economy. These measures were called *perestroika,* or economic restructuring. Despite restructuring, over the next six years the Soviet economy continued to decline. In 1991 a group of Communist hard-liners attempted to overthrow the government. *Such a planned but sudden grab for power* is called a **coup**. Although the coup failed, unrest continued, and Gorbachev resigned as Communist Party leader but remained Soviet president.

Several Soviet republics declared their independence. They formed a loose confederation called the Commonwealth of Independent States, effectively ending the Soviet Union. Each republic, including Russia, would now have to carve out its own economic and political future.

FIGURE 6–29.

The small quantity of eggs for sale shrank as many Soviet citizens lined up to buy them. Under central planning, Soviets had money, but nothing to buy. More recently, Russians produced consumer goods, but inflation soared to incredible heights.

Transforming Russia

Do capitalism and democracy have a future in Russia? Will Russia be able to build a free enterprise system that can compete effectively in the global economy? Some progress has been made. Russians are freer to travel and have more access to information than in the past. The West applauded when Russia held democratic elections in 1996, re-electing Boris Yeltsin as President.

In 2000, Russia elected Vladimir Putin to succeed Yeltsin. President Putin and other Russian leaders, however, have been unable to push through the basic political and economic reforms needed to correct the major problems that plagued the country under Communism. Even with periodic reforms, the country is being run much as it was during the communist years—and by many of the same people. President Putin, for example, is a former lieutenant colonel in the old KGB, the Soviet secret police. After a year, Putin prescribed the "strengthening of the state" as the cure for many of Russia's economic ills. Several factors help to explain the slow pace of change in Russia.

One has been the strong resistance to reform by a group of powerful bureaucrats who have come to be known as the oligarchs, from the Greek word *oligarchy,* meaning rule of the few. In the mid-1990s, these officials used inside knowledge of policy changes to buy state properties, such as newspapers, banks, and oil and gas companies, at bargain rates. As a result, they become rich businessmen, controlling many of Russia's resources. Through bribes, mutual favors, and other strategies, entrenched powers have found a way to protect their newly acquired wealth and power.

Another factor may be the lack of social consensus among Russian citizens on democratic values and the main characteristics of capitalism. Economist Robert Samuelson explains the importance of such shared beliefs:

> *Market capitalism is not just an economic system. It is also a set of cultural values that emphasizes the virtues of competition, the legitimacy of profit and the value of freedom.*

> —Newsweek, *September, 1998*

Throughout their history, Russians have been most familiar with order imposed from above. Recent public opinion polls have shown that the vast majority of Russians, 79 percent in one poll, consistently express regret for the breakup of the Soviet Union and respect for leaders such as Vladimir Lenin. One member of the Russian Parliament noted that ten years of trying to develop a free-enterprise democracy in Russia could not be expected to easily overcome 70 years of communist party authority and centuries of czarist autocracy before that: "The totalitarian mind-set is still an organic part of public consciousness." Only time will tell whether such attitudes reflect simple nostalgia or deeply held beliefs that an authoritarian state with leaders who decide what is best for the people is more important than economic and political freedom.

FIGURE 6–30.
Russian President Vladimir Putin

Russia's attempt to transform its economy illustrates the close relationship between capitalism, democracy, and the rule of law. Although not every capitalist country is governed democratically, every democratic country has some type of market economy. Nobel prize-winning economist Milton Friedman states:

> *Economic freedom is an essential requisite for political freedom. By enabling people to cooperate with one another without coercion or central direction, it reduces the area over which political power is exercised. . . . I know of no example . . . of a society that has been marked by a large measure of political freedom, and has not also used something comparable to a free market to organize the bulk of economic activity.*

> —*Milton Friedman, 1982*

SHIRLEY TEMPLE BLACK (1928–)

At the height of the Depression, President Franklin D. Roosevelt once remarked, "As long as our country has Shirley Temple, we will be all right." The child film star sang and danced her way through more than 40 movies before turning age 12. To a troubled world, Temple was America's best-loved "ambassador of goodwill."

At age 21, Temple retired, but only from films. After marrying Charles Black, she devoted her life to public service. She served as a delegate to the United Nations, the first female Chief of White House Protocol, teacher at the State Department, and ambassador to two countries—Ghana and Czechoslovakia.

Black arrived in Czechoslovakia as communism crumbled and the nation split into the Czech and Slovak republics. "My main job was human rights," Black later said, "trying to keep people like future [Czech] president Vaclav Havel out of jail."

In 1998, Black received a lifetime achievement medal at the Kennedy Center. She is a charter member and former vice president of the American Academy of Diplomacy in Washington, D.C.

Democratic Governments

Until the late 1600s, absolute monarchy was the dominant form of government. As early as the 1200s, however, the English began to place restrictions on their king. In most countries with monarchs, absolute monarchy has now given way to **constitutional monarchy**, in which *the country's constitution and laws limit the power of the hereditary ruler.*

Modern constitutional monarchies generally follow democratic practices. As you learned earlier, the characteristics of a democracy include individual liberty, majority rule with minority rights, and free elections with secret ballots.

The people participate in governing, and elected officials make laws and policies. The monarchs are heads of state only, presiding at ceremonies and serving as symbols of unity and continuity. The queen of Great Britain, the emperor of Japan, and the prince of Monaco are a few examples.

Another type of democracy is the republic—a representative government in which no leaders inherit office. The voters hold sovereign power in a republic. The people elect representatives and give them the responsibility and power to make laws and conduct government. For most Americans today, the terms *representative democracy, republic,* and *constitutional republic* mean the same thing: a system of limited government in which the people are the ultimate source of governmental power. The United States, of course, was the first such democracy. From Argentina to Zimbabwe, there are now many more.

The Expansion of Democracy

The number of democratic states grew considerably in the mid-1900s, after World War II. Since the mid-1970s, a new wave of democratization has swept Latin America and parts of Europe, Asia, and Africa. Dozens of countries that were once authoritarian are now giving citizens more rights, letting opposition parties organize, holding fair elections, unshackling the press, and making other political reforms.

Democracy is more widespread today than ever before. Of the more than 190 countries in the world, nearly two-thirds have democratic governments elected by the people. Democracy, of course, can be extensive or limited, stable or fragile. Democratic governments can also take different forms. For example, no country today has a direct democracy, in which all citizens participate in governing firsthand. Instead, representative democracy is the norm, with citizens electing leaders to act for them. Individual countries, however, have various ways of choosing their representatives and organizing the government.

Presidential versus Parliamentary Systems

The United States, Mexico, and the Philippines are among the handful of democracies with a presidential system of government. Most democratic countries in the world today, following the model of Great Britain, use the parliamentary system of government instead. A **parliamentary system** of government has *a cabinet composed of members of the legislature, who share the real executive power.*

Two Forms of Democracy

	Relationship Among Branches of Government	Method of Choosing Top Official	Role of Top Official
PRESIDENTIAL SYSTEM	Powers of executive, legislative, and judicial branches are separated	President is elected directly by popular vote	President acts as head of government *and* head of state
PARLIAMENTARY SYSTEM	Executive and legislative functions are united; judiciary operates independently	Prime minister is chosen by members of Parliament	Prime minister usually acts as head of government only (monarch or president is head of state)

Evaluating Charts

The branches of government have different responsibilities under the various forms of democratic government. How does the method of choosing the top official differ?

Such countries usually call their legislature a parliament, and their **prime minister** is *the head of government.* The terminology can vary, though. Japan's parliament, for example, is known as the Diet. Israel's is the Knesset. The German prime minister has the title of chancellor.

A major feature of a parliamentary system is that the top government officials perform both executive and legislative functions. The prime minister is not only the chief executive, responsible for carrying out the laws, but also a member of parliament, the arm of government responsible for making the laws.

Likewise, the cabinet ministers—the advisers who help the prime minister with executive work—also serve in the parliament. In a presidential system, by contrast, the executive and legislative branches of government operate independently.

Another important difference involves the method of choosing the head of government. In a presidential system, the voters of the nation elect the president directly. In a parliamentary system of government, the prime minister is elected or approved by members of the parliament.

The top office in each system can differ in another way, too. In presidential systems, the president acts not only as head of government (the country's political leader) but also as head of state (the country's ceremonial leader). In parliamentary systems, someone other than the prime minister may be the official head of state. In parliamentary monarchies like Great Britain, Spain, and Sweden, the head of state is the king or queen. In parliamentary republics like the Czech Republic, India, and Italy, the head of state is a president, chosen in most cases by the parliament.

Pros and Cons of the Parliamentary System

With a parliamentary system of government, as we have said, power is not strictly separated between the legislative and executive branches. This means there are fewer checks and balances on government leaders—a potential drawback. However, the unity among the legislative and executive branches does help the government run smoothly and act quickly.

Consider what happens in the United States when different political parties control the presidency and Congress. Disagreements along party lines often lead to "gridlock" that stalls political action. If Congress repeatedly rejects the president's budget proposals, for example, and the president frequently vetoes laws passed by Congress, little gets accomplished. Under a parliamentary system of government, however, the chief executive is typically from the majority party in the legislature. As a result, serious conflicts rarely erupt over laws, policies, or political appointees.

Changing with the Times

More than half of the countries in the world today didn't even exist in 1950. Many young countries, such as the republics that broke away from the Soviet Union in 1991, are still making the transition to democracy. However, even in well-established nations, systems of government evolve as times change and people with new agendas come to power.

CHECKPOINTS

Lesson 6 Review

1. Use each of the following words in a sentence: *authoritarian, absolute monarch, dictator, totalitarian.*

2. What totalitarian rulers took control in Germany and Italy in the 1920s and 1930s?

3. Define the following words: *cadre, shah, faqih, coup.*

4. Identify the following names: Tiananmen Square, Ayatollah Ruhollah Khomeini, Saddam Hussein.

5. Why is China not a democratic nation?

6. Why did Mao Zedong believe China should study the Soviet Union's experience?

7. What events in 1979 returned Iran to Muslim control?

8. Identify Mikhail Gorbachev, Boris Yeltsin, Vladimir Putin.

9. List four main causes of Soviet economic problems.

10. What events in 1991 led to the collapse of the Soviet Union?

11. How did perestroika help reshape the Soviet economy?

12. Name a country that has a constitutional monarchy.

Applying Citizenship Skills

13. Write a one-page paper describing how you think your life would have been different if you had been reared in a country under authoritarian rule.

14. Choose a country discussed in this lesson. Research recent political developments in this country. Imagine that you are traveling to the country that you chose. Write a letter to a friend describing the country, its government, and the extent to which the government affects people's lives.

Glossary

A

abdominal thrusts—quick, upward pulls into the diaphragm to force out an obstruction blocking the airway. (p. 176)

absolute monarch—a person who has unlimited authority to rule as he or she wishes. (p. 371)

active listening—hearing, thinking about, and responding to the other person's message. (p. 122)

addiction—a physical or psychological need for a drug. (p. 219 & 235)

addictive—capable of causing a user to develop intense cravings for it. (p. 232)

adrenaline—the "emergency hormone" that prepares the body to respond to a stressor; secreted by the adrenal glands. (p. 94)

aerobic exercise—rhythmic, nonstop, moderate to vigorous activity that requires large amounts of oxygen and works the heart. (p. 185)

affirmative action—encouraging the hiring and promoting of minorities and women in fields that were traditionally closed to them. (p. 343)

alcohol—a drug that is produced by a chemical reaction in fruits, vegetables, and grains. (p. 243)

alcoholism—a progressive, chronic disease involving a mental and physical need for alcohol. (p. 247)

aliens—people who are not citizens. (p. 285)

allegiance—loyalty or the obligation of loyalty, as to a person, nation, sovereign, or cause. (p. 35)

alternatives—other ways of thinking or acting. (p. 252)

amino acids—small units that make up protein. (p. 158)

amphetamine—a drug that stimulates the central nervous system. (p. 220)

anabolic steroids—drugs that cause muscle tissue to develop at an abnormally fast rate. (p. 199)

anaerobic exercise—intense physical activity that requires little oxygen but uses short bursts of energy. (p. 185)

anorexia nervosa—an eating disorder characterized by self-starvation leading to extreme weight loss. (p. 207)

antibiotics—medicines that reduce or kill harmful bacteria in the body. (p. 215)

antibodies—proteins that attack and kill or disable specific germs that cause disease. (p. 215)

anxiety disorder—a condition in which intense anxiety or fear keeps a person from functioning normally. (p. 131)

anxiety—an overwhelming feeling of dread, much like fear. (p. 128)

appeals courts—review decisions made in lower district courts. (p. 365)

appellate jurisdiction—the authority of a court to hear a case appealed from a lower court. (p. 365)

appetite—the psychological desire for food. (p. 156)

appropriate weight—the weight that is best for your body. (p. 202)

assertive—behaving with confidence and clearly stating your intentions. (p. 124)

attitude—a state of mind; affects the success or failure of most of your activities. (p. 48)

authenticate—to establish or prove as real or true. (p. 273)

authoritarian—power is held by an individual or group not accountable to the people. (p. 371)

B

bail—a sum of money used as a security deposit to get a person out of jail. (p. 334)

bicameral—having two parts. (p. 346)

Bill of Rights—the first 10 amendments to the Constitution of the United States. (p. 324)

binge drinking—the consumption of several alcoholic drinks in a very short period of time. (p. 245)

binge eating disorder—compulsive overeating. (p. 208)

blood alcohol concentration (BAC)—the amount of alcohol in a person's bloodstream. (p. 244)

body composition—the ratio of body fat to lean body tissue, such as bone, muscle, and fluid. (p. 190)

body image—the way you see yourself. (p. 202)

body language—a form of nonverbal communication. (p. 121)

Body Mass Index (BMI)—a measurement that allows you to assess your body size, taking your height and weight into account. (p. 202)

budget—a plan for collecting and spending money. (p. 280)

bulimia—a condition in which a person eats large amounts of food and then tries to purge. (p. 208)

bulk—the distance that the hair projects from the scalp when groomed. (p. 24)

bunting—a lightweight, loosely woven fabric used mainly for flags and festive decorations. (p. 265)

bureaucracies—complex systems with many departments, many rules, and many people in the chain of command. (p. 292)

C

cadre—a core group of trained people who can take control when necessary and train others. (p. 374)

calories—units of heat that measure the energy used by the body and the energy that foods supply to the body. (p. 155)

carbohydrates—the sugars and starches that provide your body with most of its energy. (p. 157)

carbon monoxide—a colorless, odorless, poisonous gas that is produced when tobacco burns. (p. 233)

censorship—banning printed materials or films just because they contain alarming or offensive ideas. (p. 329)

census—a population count. (p. 347)

cholesterol—a waxy substance used by the body to build cells and hormones and to protect nerve fibers. (p. 161)

cilia—tiny, hair-like structures that protect the lungs. (p. 233)

circuit—a particular geographic area covered by a United States court of appeals. (p. 365)

cirrhosis—scarring and destruction of the liver. (p. 244)

citizens—community members who owe loyalty to the government and are entitled to protection from it. (p. 277)

civics—the study of the rights and duties of citizens. (p. 277)

civil liberties—the freedoms we have to think and act without government interference or fear of unfair treatment. (p. 328)

civil rights—the rights of full citizenship and equality under the law. (p. 342)

clinical depression—a mood disorder in which people lose interest in life and can no longer find enjoyment in anything. (p. 132)

cloture—in the Senate, when no one may speak for more than one hour. (p. 354)

cold turkey—stopping an addictive substance all at once. (p. 240)

collective farm—type of farm in the Soviet Union in which the government owned the land but rented it to families. (p. 381)

community—a group of people who share the same interests and concerns. (p. 292)

comradeship—companionship. (p. 44)

concurrent jurisdiction—when state and federal courts share jurisdiction. (p. 364)

conscience—the awareness of a desire to act properly and the awareness of guilt when improper acts are committed or intended. (p. 66)

constituents—people represented. (p. 347)

constitutional monarchy—when a country's constitution and laws limit the power of the hereditary ruler. (p. 384)

cool-down—a period of low to moderate exercise to prepare your body to end a workout session. (p. 195)

coup—a planned but sudden grab for power. (p. 381)

court martial—a military or naval court of officers and occasionally enlisted personnel appointed by a commander to try offenders under military law. (p. 43)

CPR—cardio-pulmonary resuscitation; a first aid procedure that combines rescue breaths with chest compressions to restore breathing and circulation. (p. 179)

cross-training—switching between different types of exercises. (p. 188)

custom—a common tradition or usage so long established that it has the force or validity of law; a practice followed as a matter of course among a people; or the habit or practice of an individual. (p. 34)

D

decision making—the process of making a choice or finding a solution. (p. 117)

dehydration—excessive water loss from the body. (p. 198)

democracy—a government in which the people rule. (p. 281)

deport—to send people back to their own country. (p. 287)

depressants—substances that slow down the body's functions and reactions. (p. 221)

detoxification—the physical process of freeing the body of an addictive substance. (p. 227 & 248)

dictator—a person who exercises complete control over the state. (p. 372)

dictatorship—a government controlled by one person or a small group of people. (p. 281)

Dietary Guidelines for Americans—recommendations about food choices for all healthy Americans age 2 and over. (p. 163)

dignitary—a person of importance or someone who holds a high office. (p. 76)

dining-in—a formal dinner for members of the military only. (p. 43)

dining-out—a formal dinner to which non-military guests are invited. (p. 43)

direct democracy—all the citizens met to debate government matters and vote firsthand. (p. 281)

discipline—the mental attitude and state of training that renders innate obedience and proper conduct under all conditions. (p. 51)

discrimination—unfair treatment based on prejudice against a certain group. (p. 342)

distress—negative stress. (p. 92)

district courts—the federal courts where trials are held and lawsuits are begun. (p. 364)

double jeopardy— being accused of a crime and judged not guilty, and then being put on trial again for the same crime; the Fifth Amendment protects people from this. (p. 333)

draft—to select for military service. (p. 289)

drugs—substances other than food that change the structure or function of the body or mind. (p. 214)

due process—following established legal procedures. (p. 334)

duties—things that we must do. (p. 288)

E

eating disorders—extreme and damaging eating behaviors that can lead to sickness and even death. (p. 207)

Electoral College—an indirect method of election. (p. 357)

electors—people who vote for one of the major candidates in a presidential election. (p. 357)

eminent domain—the right of the government to take private property—usually land—for public use. (p. 334)

emotional needs—needs that affect your feelings and sense of well-being. (p. 129)

emotions—your feelings created in response to thoughts, remarks, and events. (p. 127)

empathy—the ability to understand and share another person's feelings. (p. 128)

endorphin—a tranquilizing chemical, which is released in the brain during exercise. (p. 100)

ensign—a national flag displayed on ships and aircraft, often with the special insignia of a branch or unit of the armed forces. (p. 259)

esprit de corps—a common spirit of enthusiasm and devotion to a cause among the members of a group. (p. 35)

ethics—the rules of conduct that people should follow. (p. 54)

etiquette—a code of behavior or courtesy based on rules of a polite society. (p. 74)

eustress—positive stress. (p. 92)

evaluate—to determine the value of something. (p. 118)

exclusive jurisdiction—when only federal courts may hear and decide certain types of cases. (p. 364)

executive or military department—any agency listed under sections 101 and 102 of title 5, United States Code. (p. 265)

exercise—a specifically planned and organized session of physical activity that you do to improve or maintain your physical fitness. (p. 184)

eye contact—direct visual contact with another person's eyes. (p. 122)

F

family therapy—counseling that seeks to improve troubled family relationships. (p. 136)

faqih—the top religious-political leader in Iran. (p. 378)

fatigue—when exposure to stress is prolonged and the body loses its ability to adapt to the situation; a tired feeling that lowers your level of activity. (p. 94)

federalism—a form of government in which power is divided between the federal, or national, government and the states. (p. 338)

Federalists—people who originally supported the Constitution. (p. 338)

feedback—a response by the listener to what the speaker has said. (p. 123)

fetal alcohol spectrum disorders (FASD)—a range (spectrum) of alcohol-related birth defects that include both physical and mental problems. (p. 245)

fiber—the part of fruits, vegetables, grains, and beans that your body cannot digest. (p. 161)

fight-or-flight response—prepares the body to either defend itself or flee from a threat; part of the alarm stage of stress. (p. 93)

filibuster—talk a bill "to death" in the Senate. (p. 354)

first aid—the immediate temporary care given to an injured or ill person until he or she can get professional help. (p. 169)

flexibility—the ability of your body's joints to move easily through a full range of motion. (p. 190)

flight—two or more elements. (p. 6)

foodborne illness—a sickness that results from eating food that is not safe to eat. (p. 166)

fracture—a break in a bone. (p. 172)

G

gang—a group of people who associate with one another to take part in criminal activity. (p. 139)

gerrymander—an oddly shaped district designed to increase the voting strength of a particular group. (p. 347)

goal setting—the process of working toward something you want to accomplish. (p. 118)

government—the ruling authority for a community. (p. 278)

grand jury—a group of citizens who make the indictment and review the evidence against the accused. (p. 333)

gross national product—the sum of all a nation's goods and services. (p. 380)

group—two or more squadrons. (p. 6)

H

half-staff—the position of the flag when it is one-half the distance between the top and bottom of the staff. (p. 264)

hallucinogens—drugs that distort moods, thoughts, and senses. (p. 222)

halyard—a rope for hoisting and lowering things. (p. 263)

health care system—all the medical care available to a nation's people, the way they receive the care, and the way the care is paid for. (p. 148)

health insurance—a plan in which private companies or government programs pay for part of a person's medical costs. (p. 150)

health maintenance organization (HMO)—an organization that provides health care for a fixed price. (p. 150)

heart and lung endurance—how effectively your heart and lungs work when you exercise and how quickly they return to normal when you stop. (p. 187)

heat cramps—painful, involuntary muscle spasms that usually occur during heavy exercise in hot weather. (p. 175)

heat exhaustion—a condition characterized by faintness, nausea, rapid heartbeat, and hot, red, dry, or sweaty skin. (p. 175)

heatstroke—the most serious form of heat illness. (p. 175)

homicide—the killing of one human being by another. (p. 139)

hunger—the physical need for food. (p. 156)

I

immigrants—people who move permanently to a new country. (p. 285)

income tax—a tax on people's earnings. (p. 324)

indictment—a formal charge. (p. 332)

individual sports—physical activities that you can do on your own or with a friend. (p. 196)

inhalant—any substance whose fumes are sniffed and inhaled to produce mind-altering sensations. (p. 223)

insignia—a badge or mark of an office or honor. (p. 24)

integrity—a firm adherence to a code of especially moral or artistic values. (p. 53)

interpersonal communication—the exchange of thoughts, feelings, and beliefs between two or more people. (p. 120)

intoxicated—physically and mentally impaired by the use of alcohol. (p. 245)

J

joint resolutions—passed by both houses of Congress. (p. 353)

jurisdiction—a court's authority to hear and decide cases. (p. 362)

L

libel—spreading lies that harm a person's reputation (printed form). (p. 331)

M

mainstream smoke—smoke that a smoker inhales and then exhales. (p. 237)

majority party—in the House and the Senate, the political party to which more than half the members belong. (p. 348)

majority rule—when differences of opinion arise, we will abide by what most people want. (p. 282)

malnutrition—a condition in which the body doesn't get the nutrients it needs to grow and function properly. (p. 208)

manners—socially correct ways of acting as shown in widespread customs. (p. 74)

Medicaid—a joint federal and state program that helps pay medical costs for people who qualify, due to limited income or limited financial resources. (p. 151)

Medicare—health coverage for people age 65 and over and some people younger than 65 who have medical disabilities or other specific conditions. (p. 151)

medicines—drugs that are used to treat or prevent diseases and other conditions. (p. 214)

member of Congress—a senator, a representative, a delegate, or the resident commissioner from Puerto Rico. (p. 265)

metabolism—the process by which your body gets energy from food. (p. 185)

methamphetamine—a stimulant similar to amphetamine. (p. 220)

minerals—elements needed in small quantities for forming healthy bones and teeth, and for regulating certain body processes. (p. 159)

minority party—in the House and the Senate, the political party to which those who are not in the majority party belong. (p. 348)

mixed message—when your words say one thing but your body language says another. (p. 121)

monopolize—to take exclusive ownership or control. (p. 83)

mood disorder—a disorder in which a person undergoes changes in mood that seem inappropriate or extreme. (p. 132)

muscle endurance—the ability of a muscle to repeatedly exert a force over a prolonged period of time. (p. 188)

muscle strength—the most weight you can lift or the most force you can exert at one time. (p. 188)

N

narcotics—specific drugs that are obtainable only by prescription and are used to relieve pain. (p. 219)

naturalization—the legal process by which foreigners can choose to become American citizens. (p. 283)

nicotine—an addictive drug found in tobacco leaves and in all tobacco products. (p. 232)

nicotine patch—a medication that allows tobacco users to give up tobacco right away while gradually cutting down on nicotine. (p. 240)

nutrient deficiency—a shortage of a nutrient. (p. 156)

nutrients—substances in food that your body needs. (p. 155)

nutrition—the process of using food and its substances to help your body have energy, grow, develop, and work properly. (p. 155)

O

obverse—the front of an official seal or insignia. (p. 273)

opinion—a detailed explanation of the legal thinking behind a court's decision. (p. 365)

original jurisdiction—the authority to hear court cases for the first time. (p. 364)

over-the-counter (OTC) medicines—medicines that are safe enough to be taken without a written order from a physician. (p. 215)

overweight—more than the appropriate weight for gender, height, age, body frame, and growth pattern. (p. 202)

P

panic—a feeling of sudden, intense fear. (p. 128)

parliamentary system—a cabinet composed of members of the legislature who share the real executive power. (p. 385)

Percent Daily Value—the percent of the recommended daily amount of a nutrient provided in a serving of food. (p. 166)

personality disorder—a variety of psychological conditions that affect a person's ability to get along with others. (p. 131)

petition—a formal request. (p. 330)

phobia—intense and exaggerated fear of a specific situation or object. (p. 131)

physical activity—any kind of movement that uses up energy. (p. 184)

physical dependence—a type of addiction in which the body itself feels a direct need for a drug. (p. 223 & 235)

physical fitness—the ability to handle the physical demands of everyday life without becoming overly tired. (p. 184)

place card—a name card for a formal dinner. (p. 82)

pocket veto—when Congress adjourns and a bill "dies." (p. 356)

point of service plan (POS)—a health plan that allows members to choose providers inside or outside the plan. (p. 150)

political party—a group of individuals with broad, common interests who organize to support candidates for office and determine public policy. (p. 282)

poll taxes—sum of money voters were required to pay before casting a ballot. (p. 341)

Preamble—(of the Constitution of the United States) an introduction that states the goals and purposes of the government. (p. 321)

precedent—a model upon which judges can base their decisions on similar cases. (p. 365)

preferred provider organization (PPO)—a type of insurance in which medical providers agree to charge less for members of the plan. (p. 150)

prejudice—an unfair opinion or judgment of a particular group of people. (p. 125)

prescription medicines—medicines that can be sold only with a written order from a physician. (p. 214)

preventive care—keeping disease or injury from happening or getting worse. (p. 148)

primary care physician—the medical doctors who provide physical checkups and general care. (p. 148)

prime minister—the head of government in most parliamentary systems. (p. 386)

proteins—nutrients your body uses to build, repair, and maintain cells and tissues. (p. 158)

protocol—a code of precedence in rank and status and of correct procedure in ceremonies; a form of etiquette observed in ceremonies; a combination of good manners and common sense that facilitates effective communication. (p. 43)

psychiatrist—a medical doctor who treats mental health problems. (p. 138)

psychological dependence—an addiction in which the mind sends the body a message that it needs more of a drug. (p. 223 & 235)

psychologist—a mental health professional who is trained and licensed by the state to counsel. (p. 138)

public health—the protection and promotion of health at the community level. (p. 150)

public policy—a course of government action to achieve community goals. (p. 280)

R

RHIP—rank has its privileges. (p. 40)

R.S.V.P.—comes from the French expression "Repondez s'il vous plait," which means "please reply." When on an invitation, you must reply to the hosts to let them know if you can or cannot attend the function to which you've been invited. (p. 84)

racial profiling—singling out people as suspects because of the way they look. (p. 344)

rape—any kind of sexual intercourse against a person's will. (p. 142)

ratification—an approval or sanction. (p. 273)

receiving line—a group of people, including the host and honored guests, who stand in line and individually welcome guests attending a function. (p. 75)

recovery—the process of learning to live an alcohol-free life. (p. 247)

refusal skills—communication strategies that help you say no effectively. (p. 123)

remand—send the case back to the lower court to be tried again. (p. 365)

representative democracy—the citizens choose a smaller group to represent them, make laws, and govern on their behalf, but the people remain the source of the government's authority. (p. 281)

resilience—the ability to adapt to and recover from disappointment, difficulty, or crisis. (p. 128)

responsibilities—things we should do; obligations that we fulfill voluntarily. (p. 288)

retreat—signals the end of the official duty day and also serves as a ceremony for paying respect to the flag. (p. 266)

reveille—the signal for the start of the official duty day. (p. 266)

riders—completely unrelated amendments. (p. 354)

roll-call vote—members voice their votes in turn as an official records them. (p. 356)

S

saturated fats—fats that are solid at room temperature. (p. 158)

schizophrenia—a severe mental disorder in which people lose contact with reality. (p. 131)

search warrant—a court order allowing law enforcement officers to search a suspect's home or business and take specific items as evidence. (p. 332)

secondhand smoke—air that has been contaminated by tobacco smoke. (p. 237)

segregation—the social separation of different races. (p. 342)

Senior Aerospace Science Instructor (SASI)—officer who is responsible for the overall function and management of the Air Force Junior ROTC unit. (p. 6)

seniority—years of service. (p. 352)

shah—a king in Iran. (p. 378)

shock—a life-threatening condition in which the circulatory system fails to deliver enough blood to vital tissues and organs. (p. 177)

side effect—any effect of a medicine other than the one intended. (p. 217)

sidestream smoke—smoke given off by the burning end of a cigarette, cigar, or pipe. (p. 237)

slander—spreading lies that harm a person's reputation (verbal form). (p. 331)

sobriety—living without alcohol. (p. 248)

special-interest groups—organizations made up of people with some common interest who try to influence government decisions. (p. 353)

specialist—doctor trained to handle particular kinds of patients or medical conditions. (p. 148)

sports conditioning—regular physical activity or exercise to strengthen and condition muscles for a particular sport. (p. 197)

sprain—a condition in which the ligaments that hold the joints in position are stretched or torn. (p. 172)

squadron—two or more flights. (p. 6)

standing committees—the permanent committees in each house of Congress that continue their work from session to session. (p. 350)

standing vote—those in favor of a bill stand to be counted, and then those against it stand to be counted. (p. 356)

state farms—farms that are owned by the government in the Soviet Union and run like factories. (p. 381)

stilted—stiffly or artificially dignified or formal, pompous, or lofty. (p. 87)

stimulants—substances that speed up the body's functions. (p. 219)

stress—your body's response to change; a normal part of life. (p. 92)

stress management skills—ways to deal with and overcome problems. (p. 97)

stressor—anything that causes stress. (p. 92)

suffrage—the right to vote. (p. 339)

suicide—intentionally killing oneself. (p. 133)

T

taboo—a prohibition excluding something from use, approach, or mention. (p. 42)

tar—a dark, thick, sticky liquid that forms when tobacco burns. (p. 233)

team sports—organized physical activities with specific rules, in which groups of people play together against other groups. (p. 197)

therapy—treatment. (p. 135)

time management—using your time wisely. (p. 102)

tolerance—a condition in which a person's body becomes used to the effect of a medicine and needs greater and greater amounts of it in order for it to be effective. (p. 217)

tolerance—respecting and accepting others, regardless of their beliefs, practices, or differences. (p. 125 & 291)

totalitarian—the government's control extends to almost all aspects of people's lives. (p. 372)

trans fatty acids—artificial fats made when hydrogen gas reacts with oil. (p. 161)

triglycerides—the chemical form in which most fat exists in food and the chief form of fat storage in the body. (p. 159)

U

underweight—less than the appropriate weight for gender, height, age, body frame, and growth pattern. (p. 202)

uniform—a distinctive mode of dress. (p. 17)

union—the upper left corner of the flag. (p. 258)

universal norms—the normal beliefs of people in most cultures. (p. 61)

universal precautions—actions taken to prevent the spread of disease by treating all blood as if it were contaminated. (p. 169)

unsaturated fats—fats that remain liquid at room temperature. (p. 159)

V

vaccine—a preparation of dead or weakened germs that causes the immune system to produce antibodies. (p. 215)

value system—our set of ideals, beliefs, interests, likes and dislikes that we use every day to make decisions. (p. 56)

values—the beliefs and ideals that guide the way a person lives. (p. 118)

veto—refuse to sign. (p. 356)

violence—any act that causes physical or psychological harm to a person or damage to property. (p. 139)

vitamins—substances needed in small quantities to help regulate body functions. (p. 159)

voice vote—those in favor say "Yea" and those against say "No." (p. 356)

volunteerism—the practice of offering your time and services to others without payment. (p. 293)

W

warm-up—a period of low to moderate exercise to prepare your body for more vigorous activity. (p. 194)

welfare—health, prosperity, and happiness. (p. 293)

withdrawal—the physical and psychological symptoms that occur when someone stops using an addictive substance. (p. 226 & 237)

Z

zero tolerance policy—a policy that makes no exceptions for anybody for any reason. (p. 140)

Index